TO THE WALLS OF
DERNE

TO THE WALLS OF
DERNE

WILLIAM EATON, THE TRIPOLI COUP
AND THE END OF THE FIRST BARBARY WAR

 CHIPP REID

NAVAL INSTITUTE PRESS

Annapolis, Maryland

This book has been brought to publication with the
generous assistance of Marguerite and Gerry Lenfest.

Naval Institute Press
291 Wood Road
Annapolis, MD 21402

Library of Congress Cataloging-in-Publication Data
Names: Reid, Chipp, author.
Title: To the walls of Derne : William Eaton, the Tripoli Coup, and the end
    of the First Barbary War / Chipp Reid.
Description: Annapolis, Maryland : Naval Institute Press, 2017. | Includes
    bibliographical references and index.
Identifiers: LCCN 2017025946 | ISBN 9781612518138 (alk. paper) |
    ISBN 9781612518145 (epdf) | ISBN 9781612518145 (mobi)
Subjects: LCSH: United States—History—Tripolitan War, 1801–1805—
    Biography. | United States—History—Tripolitan War, 1801–1805—
    Campaigns. | Eaton, William, 1764-1811. | Yusuf Basha
    al-Qaramanli, Ruler of Tripoli, –1838. | Darnah (Libya)—History,
    Military—19th century.
Classification: LCC E335 .R453 2017 | DDC 973.4/7—dc23 LC
    record available at https://lccn.loc.gov/2017025946

25 24 23 22 21 20 19 18 17   9 8 7 6 5 4 3 2 1
First printing

Maps were created by Chris Robinson.

To my Uncles
Carmine Braccia *and* Nicholas Braccia

I have no words but thank you.

CONTENTS

PREFACE

THIS BOOK PICKS UP where *Intrepid Sailors: The Legacy of Preble's Boys and the Tripoli Campaign* left off in the story of America's first overseas conflict, the war with Tripoli and the Barbary pirates. Although it might seem to be the first chapter in the current war against terrorism and Islamic extremism, it isn't. *Walls of Derne* and *Intrepid Sailors* relate the history of a young, up-and-coming country, the United States—a nation imbued with a strong, simple sense of right and wrong. The Barbary pirates were menaces not because of their religion but because of how they treated U.S. merchant vessels. The four Barbary States demanded nations pay for the right to enter the Mediterranean; for many Americans, this was extortion, little better than the taxes Britain had levied on the colonies. Just as patriots took up arms to fight British tyranny, the new United States built a navy and marine corps to combat the tyranny the Barbary States imposed on trade.

Unlike so many current chroniclers of events surrounding William Eaton, Hamet and Yusuf Karamanli, Presley O'Bannon, and the others who took part in the campaign of 1804–05, I do not try to recast their deeds to reflect current events. In other words, readers will find nothing about modern-day terrorism or radical Islam in these pages. The war with Tripoli predated those phenomena by two hundred years, and despite the best efforts of some to prove otherwise, the First Barbary War had very little to do with religion. I do, however, make a concerted effort to detail what this long-forgotten and often misunderstood war meant to the U.S. Marine Corps, which emerged as the real winner of the conflict.

The First Barbary War solved nothing. Despite Thomas Jefferson's fervent dislike of buying off the North African corsairs, he ultimately did just that, to end what was becoming a protracted and costly war. The war also did nothing to end the practice of paying tribute. Throughout the four-year conflict, the United States continued to deliver tribute and "gifts" to Algiers, Morocco, and Tunis, and it did so until the War of 1812.

Another area in which I veer away from previous accounts of William Eaton's epic campaign is in my depiction of his archenemy, Yusuf Karamanli. Most Western historians have depicted Yusuf as little more than a mindless brute who used piracy to force Western nations to pay his petty kingdom to leave their ships alone. Yusuf did indeed exact tribute, but he was anything but mindless. He was, and is, a fascinating character who was arguably the first true Arab nationalist. In that connection I must thank Jason Pack, of the United Kingdom–based Libya Analysis, who pointed me toward sources few if any other Western historians have used and who, prior to a dramatic increase in instability in Libya, helped me contact the Libyan National Library, which in turn provided electronic copies of two books specifically about the Karamanli family. I also need to thank my friend Omar Abd El Hamid for his help in translations.

Hollywood could not come up with a better story than the attempt to overthrow Yusuf Karamanli and replace him with his brother Hamet to end the scourge of Barbary piracy, all against the backdrop of political double-dealing, both in Washington, D.C., and in the theater of operations. It is also a story that keeps repeating. Just as I firmly believe the stories of Edward Preble, Stephen Decatur Jr., and Richard Somers have much to teach Americans about what it means to be American, so too do I believe that the story of William Eaton, Presley O'Bannon, Tobias Lear, and the Karamanli family has a great deal to teach us about how honor and patriotism still apply in our high-tech, instant-gratification world.

As with any book, there are numerous people to thank. First, there is my new editor, Glenn Griffith, who did a great job setting up peer reviews. I am neither infallible nor all-knowing; peer review is an excellent reminder of this and prevents mistakes, both silly and serious.

I would also like to thank Adam Nettina, my former editor at the Naval Institute Press, who recently moved to other projects; my old friend Wayne Travers for copyediting help; and my friends and colleagues at my job, who suffered with me while I tried to balance writing this book and another one at roughly the same time.

Thanks also to Master Chief Petty Officer Jon Port, Force Master Chief at Pensacola, Florida, who wrote the preface to *Intrepid Sailors.* When I hit a stone wall writing-wise and simply could not get anything down on paper, he gave me the pep talk of all pep talks, reminding me of the sacrifice so many sailors and Marines have made for our nation. If they could sacrifice all, I could "man up" and write!

There are many others that deserve thanks: Dr. Olga Tsapina, at the Huntington Library, in San Marino, California; everyone at the Marine Corps Archives and Library at Quantico, Virginia; the wonderful staff at the Beineke and Sterling Libraries at Yale University, in New Haven, Connecticut; the staff at Mystic Seaport, in Connecticut, which remains one of the best and yet least-used maritime history repositories in the country; and, as always, my family, who also served as sounding boards and inspirations.

I hope that this book will resonate with people the way *Intrepid Sailors* has. It is our history, and I have attempted to make it fun and interesting for the reader while also teaching a few lessons—among them that the price of freedom is always high and that love of country is still an admirable trait.

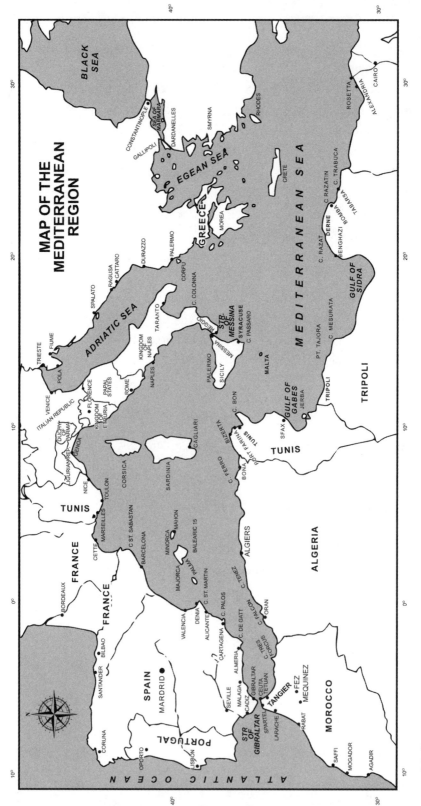

Mediterranean region

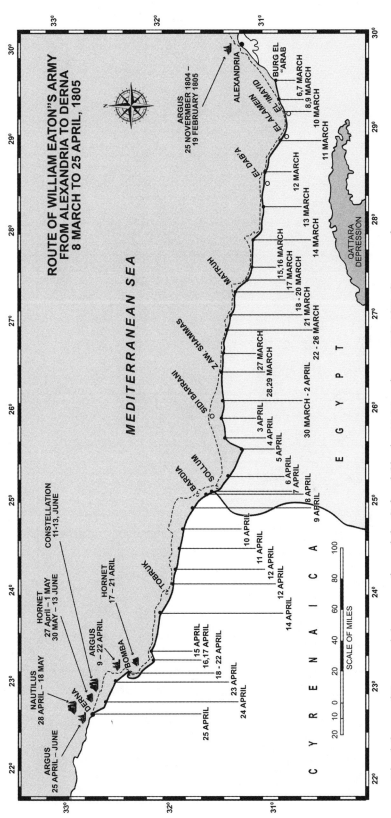

The defenses of Derne and the route of assault by Colonel Charles H. Waterhouse, USMCR. Courtesy of Art Collection, National Museum of the Marine Corps, Triangle, Virginia.

TO THE WALLS OF
DERNE

1

SHORES OF TRIPOLI

IN APRIL 1805, the war with Tripoli was in its fourth year and showed no real sign of coming to a close. The war President Thomas Jefferson wanted to fight was fast becoming the war he wanted to end. In 1786, well before he became president, Jefferson envisioned a "coalition of the willing," nations that would band together to end the scourge of piracy along the North African coast. It was both an economic and a moral cause. That four nations could extort thousands of dollars in protection money, or "tribute," from the United States and other Christian nations just so their vessels could enter or leave the Mediterranean was anathema to Jefferson. So too was the notion the United States had to pay those four petty kingdoms—Morocco, Algiers, Tunis, and Tripoli—for peace treaties that allowed the free passage of ships on the high seas.[1]

Jefferson got his wish when the smallest of the four "Barbary powers," Tripoli, declared war on the United States in May 1801 when the president refused demands for increased tribute. The war pitted Jefferson's ideals against the leader, or bashaw, of Tripoli, Yusuf Karamanli, who had entirely different views as to his nation's actions.[2] Tripoli was not actually a nation but a province of the Ottoman Empire. The practice of levying tribute from Western countries and demanding annual payments for peace allowed Karamanli and the other leaders of the Barbary States to retain their autonomy.[3] This was especially important to Karamanli, who was the only non-Turkish ruler of the Ottoman sultan's North African holdings. (Morocco was an independent nation.) Karamanli needed tribute and peace payments to maintain his authority over Tripoli and to placate the sultan in Constantinople so he could remain in power.[4]

Three years after the war started, neither Jefferson nor Karamanli was any closer to a resolution. The first two naval expeditions Jefferson dispatched had accomplished very little. The third, in 1804, under Commodore Edward Preble, had very nearly battered Karamanli into submission. Preble enforced a stringent blockade that caused widespread starvation in Karamanli's province, and his seaborne attacks smashed the bashaw's fleet. Preble, however, lacked the strength to press his advantage, and his attempts to open negotiations failed. While Preble was starving and bombarding Tripoli, Jefferson was fretting. One of the two frigates in Preble's squadron, the *Philadelphia*, had run aground, fallen into Tripolitan hands, and required a daring night mission to destroy her. The capture of the frigate handed Karamanli 302 American captives, a massive bargaining chip.[5]

Jefferson's reaction was to order a fourth squadron to the Mediterranean. Although he would later come to regret relieving Preble of command, the slowness of communication from the region led him to believe Preble had failed even more than his previous two commanders. While ordering a new squadron to assemble, Jefferson received a visit from a soldier turned diplomat turned would-be adventurer, William Eaton. The former Army captain presented Jefferson with a wild-sounding plan to replace Yusuf with his older brother—and the legitimate ruler of Tripoli— Hamet Karamanli, who would then conclude a no-fee, no-tribute treaty with the United States and release all American prisoners without ransom. Eaton was in earnest, and he convinced Jefferson to back Hamet, who had even promised to repay all U.S. expenses for restoring him to his throne.[6]

As unorthodox (for 1805) as Eaton's plan sounded, it handed Jefferson another way to defeat Yusuf. The president now had three routes to victory. Commodore Samuel Barron sailed that summer with a force of four frigates, which, when combined with Preble's squadron, would give

Barron a massive military force with which to subdue Tripoli. If Barron failed to batter Yusuf to his knees, the president had Eaton and Hamet, a combination that at the very least might frighten Yusuf enough to open peace talks and agree to a settlement favorable to the United States. A year earlier, in 1803, Jefferson had dispatched a personal friend, Tobias Lear, to Algiers as consul general; at the same time he was meeting with Eaton and issuing orders to Barron, he sent instructions to Lear to open talks with Yusuf. One way or another, Jefferson was going to end the war.

The three-pronged approach would bring an end to the war, despite Jefferson's failure to establish a chain of command or timetable between the Rodgers, Lear and Eaton. Lear believed he had authority to open talks at any time Yusuf appeared amenable, no matter what might be happening elsewhere. Eaton set off on his quest to oust Yusuf believing he had the full backing of the president and that his campaign would take priority. Barron left Hampton Roads, Virginia, believing he had authority over both Eaton and Lear. It was a system that was doomed to disappoint at least two of three principal American players.

The moment Jefferson endorsed Eaton's project, the character of the war changed, at least for Yusuf Karamanli. Although he had usurped the throne from his brother, Yusuf had the official backing of the sultan of the Ottoman Empire and was the recognized ruler of Tripoli. By backing Hamet's coup Jefferson committed the United States to regime change, and Yusuf had no intention of going quietly. The war morphed from one of free passage of merchant vessels to one that would decide who would rule Tripoli, and pulled Hamet Karamanli into the conflict. Hamet had never expected to rule and in many ways did not want to. Had Yusuf treated his older brother with some semblance of family loyalty, Hamet probably never would have considered trying to oust him. Yusuf, however, was determined not only to rule Tripoli but to gain the respect of tributary nations and the other leaders of Ottoman holdings. He might even have harbored thoughts of complete independence for his nation.[7]

That Jefferson backed Eaton's scheme to oust Yusuf was a surprise given Eaton's reputation. Eaton was an outspoken Federalist and an ardent patriot. The ideals of the young republic resonated so much for Eaton that he could not understand others for whom patriotism was not their first thought. He was also a glory seeker, and wanted to achieve that glory on the field of battle. Eaton's patriotism and ego, however, had led him to make a series of poor decisions while he was consul in Tunis, and when he arrived at the executive mansion to discuss his plan with Jefferson, his reputation was just short of seedy.[8] Eaton and Lear detested one another yet were very much alike. Lear too yearned for glory—or recognition— and like Eaton, he saw it elude him just when it was in his grasp. Lear too was ardent in his politics and was a committed Jeffersonian Democratic-Republican. Lear, in his personal quest for financial glory, had made poor decisions of his own while he was secretary to George Washington, becoming involved in a land development deal that had cost investors thousands when it collapsed. For both men, success in Tripoli meant redemption.

Commodore Samuel Barron did not need redemption. Barron had clear orders and multiple options. The Eaton expedition was to begin at his discretion, as were any talks. He would command the largest American naval force then in operation, and he expected to win. Barron was lukewarm, at best, to Eaton's plan and did not appear to be in a hurry to open talks with Yusuf. As commodore, Barron wanted to reap the glory of subduing Tripoli with military force, but became ill and incapacitated before he could launch an attack.

Amid all the political and strategic wrangling in the Mediterranean, another battle for survival was taking shape in Washington, this one revolving around the U.S. Marine Corps. The Marine Corps was still new in 1805 and had yet to prove its usefulness. As the cost of the Tripoli war escalated, many Democratic-Republican members of Congress began to view it as an expensive luxury, one the country could do without. During the war Democrats made two concerted efforts to abolish the Corps or the Office of the Commandant or both, failing only by slim margins. By 1805, Commandant Franklin Wharton worried a renewed effort might succeed. Wharton needed a victory, something that would capture the public imagination, much in the way Stephen Decatur had when he burned the *Philadelphia* in 1804. He found his answer in a twenty-five-year-old first lieutenant from Virginia. Presley Neville O'Bannon commanded a squad of Marines in Eaton's army that crossed the desert in support of Hamet. O'Bannon would plant the Stars and Stripes on the parapets of Derne, marking the first time the American flag had ever flown over conquered territory. The descriptions of O'Bannon's charge and his Marines' bravery in combat would provide Wharton the public relations victory he needed.

O'Bannon would set off on his quest in March 1805 amid a backdrop of diplomacy, competing authorities, petty jealousies, and service rivalries. At times it seemed only his will held together the polyglot army he assembled and led on a five-hundred-mile trek from Egypt to Derne. The epic march and subsequent attack on the second city of Yusuf's kingdom would come to inspire generations of Americans and became part of American lore. It gave rise to the second line of the Marines' Hymn—". . . to the shores of Tripoli . . ."—the Corps' homage to O'Bannon's role in the campaign.[9]

Finally war with Tripoli was *not* a war between Christianity and Islam, nor was it a battle against radicals seeking to conquer territory and gain converts. Although there have been many attempts to cast the Tripoli war as a first battle against radical Islam, it was in fact an economic, not religious, conflict. There is no evidence in any primary source that Jefferson, Yusuf or Hamet Karamanli, Lear, Eaton, Preble, Barron, O'Bannon, or any other principal in the campaign viewed the war as anything other than an effort to, on one hand, end the practices of piracy and tribute or, on the other, retain control of Tripoli. Radical Islam, as espoused and practiced in the twenty-first century, simply didn't exist in 1805. Although the Barbary corsairs used "terror" as a weapon to frighten tributary nations and then squeeze every dime out of them they could, they did so for economic reasons, not religious. Certainly the corsairs picked their targets on religious grounds, targeting Christian nations, but even a cursory look at a map of the late eighteenth and early nineteenth centuries provides a quick and easy explanation. The bulk of the Mediterranean Muslim world, like the Barbary States except for Morocco, was in the Ottoman Empire. That didn't prevent attacks on Ottoman shipping, but it made them rare.[10]

The real legacy of the Tripoli war has nothing to do with modern-day terrorism. It has to do with the American spirit. The fact the more "cultured" nations of Europe were willing to buy off the Barbary pirates did not mean the Americans had to follow suit. The idea of a small nation such as Tripoli extorting funds from the United States to allow its merchantmen free access to trade was simply too much for the liberty-fueled, independent-minded Americans. It was, in many ways, the first time the United States fought a war for an ideal, as opposed to conquering new territory. In that respect, the Tripoli war does indeed resonate to this day.

2

THE GENERAL

ALMOST FROM THE DAY he was born, William Eaton dreamed of being a military hero. The would-be Alexander was born February 23, 1764, in Woodstock, Connecticut. His father, Nathan, was a farmer, while his mother, Sarah, minded an ever-growing family. William was the couple's second son and one of thirteen children. He grew up in Mansfield, Connecticut, after his father purchased a farm there and became headmaster of a local school.[1] As a boy, William showed little disposition toward being a farmer, later saying he had "early in life discovered intellectual vigor and eccentricity." His father encouraged William to read, and the boy did so voraciously. Eaton later claimed to have memorized the poem *Paradise Lost* when he was just six years old and that he always had a book in his pocket while working in the fields of the family farm, snatching time from his chores to escape in it. Thanks to his schoolmaster father, he studied Shakespeare, Greek, Latin, and mathematics. He also learned to shoot at an early age, a skill he honed throughout his life, and showed an ability to learn languages easily and quickly.[2] His father also instilled in Eaton a desire to serve in the military. Nathan Eaton was a captain in the Connecticut militia during the French and Indian War and had served on the frontier, where he fought Algonquin and Ottawa tribes. His stories of combat enthralled young William and further stoked in the boy what was apparently an innate appetite for adventure.[3]

By 1780 Eaton was six feet tall, with the muscular build of a field laborer. That July he abruptly left home, lied about his age, and enlisted in the 1st Connecticut militia regiment.[4] Despite his robust size, Eaton found himself detailed to duty as an orderly, serving for six months in New Haven, where he contracted influenza and was discharged.[5] Oddly, Eaton himself claimed, as have several biographers, that he was with the 1st Connecticut for up to a year, but the regimental records show he served for just five months and three days.[6] By the spring of 1781 Eaton had recovered his health and again enlisted, serving on Long Island and in Connecticut under the command of Brigadier General David Waterbury. He claimed he mustered out of service in April 1783 as a sergeant.[7] Company records, however, indicate no such promotion and that Eaton served out his time as a private.[8] He enrolled at Dartmouth University in Hanover, New Hampshire, in 1785, but he was unable to pay for school. He found work as a teacher and spent two years trying to earn enough money to return to Dartmouth, finally doing so in 1787. He paid his way through Dartmouth by tutoring other students and then opened his own school, in Windsor, Vermont.[9]

Eaton was an intelligent, though somewhat arrogant, individual. His two-plus years in the militia had fired his martial passions, and by the time he reached Dartmouth, Eaton was determined to pursue a military career, in spite of the fact the entire armed forces of the newly independent United States consisted of just a handful of full-time soldiers. His studies only deepened his admiration of Alexander the Great, and he memorized Xenophon's epic *Retreat of the Ten Thousand Greeks*. A classmate remembered Eaton and another student getting into a heated argument over Alexander after the other student called Eaton's hero a murderer. "A murderer though you think him to have been, had you the opportunity, you would not hesitate to tread in his steps," Eaton snapped back.[10]

It was at Dartmouth that Eaton's eccentric though charismatic personality developed. Eaton, said a classmate, was simply different from most others: "His general deportment distinguished him from all the other members of the college, and it was his good fortune, eccentric as he was, to secure the good will of all. . . . All liked him in the literal sense of the word, for something in his character, and yet that something was undefinable."[11]

"The best way to describe his personality," said another classmate, was "odd. He was . . . precise in his language—full of decision—sometimes a little morose. . . . He was subject to fits of melancholy which . . . rendered him apparently miserable." Those bouts of melancholy (today called depression), however, failed to diminish Eaton's popularity among his fellow students.[12] Part of that popularity rested on his reputation for bravery; he exhibited courage that bordered on recklessness. While an undergraduate, Eaton saw a local constable chase a robbery suspect to a shed. The officer called for help in apprehending the man, who was armed with a knife and two pistols. Eaton bravely stepped forward, and before the constable could assist, attacked the thief, wresting the knife from his hands before knocking him sprawling with a punch.[13]

A renowned athlete, Eaton could outrun anyone and was a crack shot. According to a classmate, he once gave a particularly fast runner a head start in a race. Eaton not only easily caught up to the other runner but leapfrogged over him before crossing the finish line well ahead of his competitor.[14] His classmates also remembered Eaton as having something of a dry sense of humor, one that would help him to garner attention. He once took a job transporting a bell across town from the manufacturer to the Dartmouth campus. Eaton slung the bell under a wagon and slowly made his way across Hanover, the bell clanging all the time. Eaton told an "acquaintance" he met on the way that he liked the clamor—and the attention it drew—as "he was resolved not to go through the world without making a noise in it."[15]

Eaton graduated from Dartmouth on August 25, 1790, and returned to Windsor, where he reopened his school. He taught for a year before securing an appointment as clerk of the Vermont House of Delegates. Eaton most likely owed his appointment to Stephen R. Bradley, an influential politician who, with Governor Thomas Crittenden, spent ample time in Windsor, where they probably met Eaton.[16] Vermont in 1791 was just the place for the twenty-five-year-old Eaton to gain an introduction to politics. The newest state in the Union still had a frontier feel to it, and its politics were nearly as wild as its passage to statehood had been.[17] It was the perfect place for an aggressive self-promoter such as Eaton to make his case for an appointment to the fledgling U.S. Army, which was then undergoing a massive reorganization.

In 1792, in answer to a pair of defeats inflicted by Indians on a handful of federal soldiers and state militia, President George Washington convinced a skeptical, penny-pinching Congress to authorize the expansion of the Army into the "Legion of the United States." The legion had an authorized strength of eight heavy infantry battalions, four rifle battalions, four dragoon companies, and four artillery companies, elements that were to operate as combined-arms "sublegions."[18] On March 25, 1792, Bradley, now a U.S. senator, secured Eaton an appointment as a captain in the 4th Sublegion.[19]

Before reporting for duty, Eaton visited his brother, Calvin, in Brimfield, Massachusetts. While there he renewed his "acquaintance" with twenty-five-year-old Eliza Danielson, the widow of Brigadier General Timothy Danielson, who had been a wealthy landowner and friend of his brother. Eaton must have struck a dashing figure on his visit. With his new blue uniform, his athletic, muscular build, and piercing blue eyes, he made a strong impression on the young widow, and the two decided to marry following a whirlwind romance.[20]

Eaton reported for duty at Legionville, Pennsylvania, a depot Major General Anthony Wayne had established outside Pittsburgh to train the Legion of the United States. Wayne was the perfect general to command what was an experimental force. During the Revolutionary War, after a couple of missteps, including a horrendous defeat in 1777 at Paoli, Pennsylvania, he had developed into one of George Washington's best battlefield commanders. He catapulted to fame when he captured the British fort at Stony Point, New York, and commanded a division of Washington's army at Yorktown. In 1782 he served under Nathaniel Greene in the south, helping to drive the British out of Savannah. After the war he returned to Pennsylvania, where he served in the state assembly and was a member of the Constitutional Convention. In 1792 Washington turned to Wayne to check Chief Little Turtle of the Miami, who since 1790 had, with British backing, led an Indian confederation in the Northwest Territory. Little

THE GENERAL ⮾ 11

Turtle had conducted raids along the Ohio River and all but wiped out the forces of first General Josiah Hamar and then Arthur St. Clair that Washington sent against him.

It was in Legionville that another of Eaton's quirks came out—his belief that he was always right. On March 17, 1793, during a review before General Wayne, Eaton was leading his company on a maneuver when the regimental adjutant, Captain Edward Butler, issued a series of frantic orders countermanding those of Eaton. Butler, like Eaton a political appointee, believed Eaton's company was about to collide with another unit. Eaton promptly ordered his men to maintain their order of march, which enraged Butler. The adjutant, who was on horseback, confronted Eaton, who was on foot. "I was positively right," Eaton recalled, "and was confident that I was bringing the column in the position which he himself wished."[21]

Instead, Butler berated Eaton "and in the presence of the General taxed me with having disobeyed a positive general order. I told him I positively had not, but was right." The two began to shout at one another. Butler "threatened to make me repent my conduct—I challenged him to do so," Eaton recalled. Butler, brandishing his sword, spurred his horse toward Eaton, who held his ground and lowered his spontoon, a long, halberd-like weapon officers carried to identify themselves to their men in combat. Wayne intervened just as the two men were about to come to blows. He ordered both to return to their posts, ending the altercation but not the ill will.

That night Eaton sent a curt note to Butler, calling him out. Butler replied that before fighting a duel, he wanted a panel of fellow officers to judge both men's conduct. Eaton agreed.[22] The two officers met with their fellows on March 18, and the "court" quickly came to the conclusion both men were wrong and suggested they both apologize. "To this opinion Capt. B[utler] conceded, and offered me his hand," Eaton recalled. "I observed that I would ever sacrifice my own to the opinion of my friends and accepted it."[23]

Eaton took quickly to army life. Although raised on a farm and an outstanding athlete, the young captain realized there was more to being a good officer than a uniform. He came to idolize Wayne: "He is firm in constitution as in resolution—industrious, indefatigable, determined and persevering—fixed in opinion, and unbiased in judgment—not over accessible; but studious to reward merit." Wayne's toughness especially impressed Eaton, who noted the general "endures fatigue and hardship with a fortitude uncommon to men of his years. . . . When in danger, he is in his element; and never shows to so good advantage, as when leading a charge. His name is better in an action, or in an enemy's country, than a brigade of undisciplined levies"[24]

Eaton fought in several skirmishes and small battles as Wayne led his forces into Indian-held territory. Eaton went on leave in February 1794 and returned home to Brimfield for the first time since he joined the Army. He missed the end of Wayne's campaign, in which the general handed the Indians a crushing defeat at Fallen Timbers, but managed to cultivate a friendship with Secretary of War Timothy Pickering, whom he met while traveling home to Massachusetts. Pickering was another of George Washington's close confidants to hold high office in the first president's administration, and the two Federalists apparently hit it off right away.

Pickering assigned Eaton to recruiting service, and the captain was able to spend nearly seven months at home. In October, Eaton received orders to bring his recruits to Georgia to join the federal force President Washington had organized to fight the Creek and Choctaw Indians. Eaton took his men first to Philadelphia, arriving in Savannah on December 26, 1795. They marched four days to Colerain, on the St. Mary's River, where they met Lieutenant Colonel Henry Gaither, the commander of the federal troops in Georgia. Gaither ordered Eaton to construct a fort and trading post along the river in a spot Eaton said was ill suited to the purpose; Gaither had chosen a mosquito-infested floodplain. Eaton protested, but Gaither was adamant. Eaton dutifully built his fort, which he named Fort Pickering, "not however that I might satirize a good man by erecting his measurement in mud."[25]

Southwestern Georgia was wide open. Sparsely settled Spanish-, French-, and Indian-controlled lands beckoned to all takers, on a first-come, first-claim basis. American settlement particularly incensed the Creek and Choctaw, who, with Spanish backing, resisted American expansion into their lands. A group of peace commissioners arrived in May 1796 to work out a treaty with the Creek, finally reaching an agreement a month later. The treaty, however, did nothing to end the rampant land speculation that gripped the region.

Relations between Eaton and Gaither, poor from the start, deteriorated while Eaton was at Fort Pickering. "I found myself placed between his animosity and my own duty," he told "Liza" in a letter.[26] According to Eaton, Gaither and many other officers participated in shady land deals that involved either falsified or fictitious deeds. Throughout the summer, Eaton sent a series of reports to Pickering detailing the alleged illegal activity. Gaither ordered Eaton to stop his reports, but Eaton refused. Gaither then offered Eaton 500,000 acres of land for just $35,000, but Eaton turned him down. On August 7, Gaither court-martialed Eaton on charges ranging from selling his soldiers' uniforms and withholding their bounties to disobeying orders.[27]

Eaton vehemently denied the charges. During the trial, a group of landowners sent a petition to the War Department asking for Eaton's reinstatement to command at Fort Pickering. Eaton, they said, "had given great satisfaction to the neighborhood, by restraining his soldiers from plunder." Since his arrest however, discipline had dissolved and they complained loudly about "the atrocious conduct of the soldiery, and the acquiescence of the officers." It made little difference. A tribunal of officers Gaither hand-selected found him guilty and suspended him from command for two months. Eaton immediately dashed off a letter to the secretary of war: "The perverted construction which has been put on all my measures, and repeated inattention to my repeated request of a more humane, yet as proper mode of investigating the facts, prove the vindictive temper of this prosecution, and a prepence intention to assassinate my reputation."[28]

The suspension was not enough for Gaither. He confined Eaton while he sent the findings of the court to the secretary of war. A month later, Gaither sent Eaton to Philadelphia to face Pickering, who not only tossed out the findings of the court but reinstated Eaton to his rank. Nevertheless, his days in the Army were over.[29]

Eaton returned to Brimfield, where he split his time between his family and executing special details for Pickering. When Eaton and Eliza married, it surprised many, as few knew of Eaton's passion for his wife. Eliza had three children from her previous marriage when she married Eaton, sons Timothy and Eli and daughter Sarah. She would bear three more for William—daughters Eliza, Charlotte, and Almira. Eaton doted on his children, who were, he told Eliza, "the little pledges of our mutual pleasures."[30] He asked his stepchildren to call him "Pa" and asked them to take the middle initial E. in their names as a sign of the family bond.[31] Most of all, William adored his wife. He wrote Eliza numerous passionate letters during his travels, many of them tinged with regret at having to leave her behind. "I love you and long to see you," he once wrote to his wife, saying it was "this invincible pride which has forced me from the bosom of a companion whose bosom is heaven."[32]

Pickering sent for Eaton in July 1797 to serve on a special detail. Now secretary of state under the new president, John Adams, Pickering had uncovered a plot that would allow the British to wrest control of Spanish Louisiana and the Floridas. The leader of the plot, Tennessee Senator William Blount, was Pickering's enemy. Pickering gave Eaton the mission of helping to arrest Blount and his co-conspirators. He ordered Eaton to Philadelphia to arrest Nicholas Romayne, a Philadelphia surgeon who was part of the plot. Romayne, however, was in New York, and on July 10 Eaton went to that city, where the next day he found and arrested Romayne, who was carrying papers detailing the cabal. Eaton returned to Philadelphia with his prisoner on July 12.[33]

The rapid apprehension impressed Pickering, who soon appointed Eaton as consul to Tunis. It was a plum assignment but also an unusual one. Eaton—blunt, direct, acerbic—had never been a diplomat, and the post at Tunis required an extremely deft touch. The United States had, through a French businessman, Joseph Etienne Famin, negotiated a new treaty with Tunis that called for "peace payments." The Senate, however, wanted to change a clause regarding taxes on trade goods. Eaton's job would be to conduct those negotiations and deliver his country's payments to the bey (governor) of Tunis. Pickering selected Eaton knowing he could count on the former Army officer's patriotism and sense of honor in representing his country.[34]

Eaton set off for his new post on December 22, 1799, sailing with fellow diplomats James Leander Cathcart, consul for Tripoli, and Richard O'Brien, consul general in Algiers. Cathcart and Eaton were kindred spirits and it was from Cathcart that Eaton learned firsthand of the barbarities the North African leaders could practice. Cathcart had spent ten years as a hostage after Algerian corsairs seized his ship and held the crew for ransom. Although Cathcart's education had spared him from manual labor (the dey, or prince, appointed him as one of his secretaries) he still had had a close look at the cruel manner in which the Barbary pirates treated their captives. The experience engendered in him a lifelong hatred of the Barbary States.[35]

Eaton and Cathcart reported to O'Brien in Algiers. Like Cathcart, O'Brien had spent ten years as a hostage in Algiers, but O'Brien's time in bondage had not made him overtly hostile toward the Barbary leaders. It had made him lonely, however, and when he saw Cathcart's maid, Betsey Robeson, he immediately fell in love. According to Eaton, Robeson had been the target of Cathcart's attentions as well, during the journey to Algiers, even though the new consul for Tripoli was traveling with his wife. When O'Brien began courting Betsey, a nasty rift emerged between the two diplomats, who refused to speak to one another. O'Brien married Robeson six weeks after meeting her, cementing the bad blood between the two senior American diplomats in the region.[36]

Algiers was the strongest of three Turkish-controlled "Barbary States" and the most bellicose. The United States, somewhat mistakenly, treated Algiers as though it held sway over Tunis and Tripoli and accordingly lavished gifts upon its leader. Eaton attempted to correct this policy, explaining to Pickering that "Algiers exerts all her means to maintain a commanding influence in the affairs of Tunis; and how ever reluctant the latter may be in yielding to this policy, imperious circumstances compel it. . . . It is nevertheless dangerous for Christian nations to employ the mediation of

Algiers in negotiation with Tunis: for these two powers generally play so understanding into each other's hands, that when the former has fleeced his client of the fee, the management of the cause becomes a matter of indifference."[37]

The dey of Algiers, Mustapha VI ben Ibrahim, had a reputation as a rapacious and cunning leader, one who, although an official of the Ottoman Turks, held the loyalty of his subjects. His attitude toward the United States was little better than outright contempt. Eaton learned that American actions had done little to warrant a change in the dey's demeanor. Upon arrival in Algiers, the three American diplomats paid their respects to Mustapha, whom Eaton described as "a huge, shaggy beast, sitting on his rump, upon a low bench, covered with a cushion of embroidered velvet, with his hind legs gathered up like a taylor [i.e., tailor], or a bear." The dey commanded the Americans to kiss his hand, which they dutifully did. "The animal seemed at that moment to be in a harmless mode: he grinned several times; but made very little noise," Eaton reported. The three diplomats remained in the dey's chamber in silence before receiving permission to leave, having suffered no "other injury than the humility of being obliged, in this involuntary manner, to violate the second commandment of God, and offend common decency." This first exposure to a Barbary potentate made an indelible impression on Eaton, who despairingly noted in his journal, "Can any man believe that this elevated brute has seven kings of Europe, two republics, and a continent, tributary to him, when his whole naval force is not equal to two line of battle ships? It is so."[38]

When Eaton arrived in Algiers, three warships built under contract for Algiers were already in the harbor—the twenty-two-gun brig *Hassan Bashaw,* the twenty-gun schooner *Skjoldebrand,* and the eighteen-gun schooner *Lelah Eisha.* Mustapha paid $98,000 for the three vessels, a price O'Brien said was a bargain. The other Barbary leaders had no idea Algiers bought the ships. Mustapha kept the contract to himself, a fact that became a point of contention in both Tunis and Tripoli as he allowed the others to believe the ships were gifts. Eaton went on by sea to Tunis and took up his post as consul on March 12. Two days later he learned for himself of the envy the North African leaders had for one another. Eaton met

Bey Hamouda ibn Ali on March 14, and after brief formalities, the bey launched into a tirade: Why, he demanded to know, hadn't Eaton asked for a gun salute from the port as, Hamouda said, was customary? Eaton cagily avoided a direct answer, telling the bey he did not know it was the Tunisian custom. Eaton, well aware of a clause in the treaty stipulating the United States had to provide a barrel of powder for each Tunisian gun used in a salute, confided to his journal, "We did not choose to demand a salute that would cost the United States eight hundred dollars."[39]

Hamouda let the matter drop for the moment and demanded to know why America gave Algiers three cruisers and none to Tunis. The question confused Eaton, who replied America had not given any warships to Mustapha, that Algiers had signed a contract and paid cash for the three ships. Hamouda pressed the diplomat, "You may inform me that the Dey of Algiers paid you cash for your vessels. I am at liberty to believe otherwise." Eaton did his best to explain the contract between Algiers and the United States for the ships, but Hamouda would not listen. Instead, he put his belief in what Joseph Famin had told him. Famin, a French businessman and acting U.S. chargé d'affaires in Tunis, claimed the U.S. government had ratified the treaty with Tunis, which it had not, and his misinformation was the source of the idea of "gift" to Algiers.

Hamouda dismissed Eaton peremptorily, telling him to return in two days, when they would begin discussing the articles of the peace treaty the U.S. Senate wanted changed. Two clauses in particular outraged the lawmakers: the demand that Eaton had avoided, powder in exchange for salutes; and the duties merchants would pay for trade goods. The treaty Famin had negotiated stipulated in its fourteenth article that Tunisian merchants would pay a duty of 3 percent in American ports, while American merchants would pay 10 percent in Tunisian markets. Before Hamouda would discuss any changes to the treaty, however, he again brought up the subject of tribute. The United States was overdue on its payments, Hamouda told Eaton, and yet it sent gifts to Algiers and Tripoli. Cathcart, who was with Eaton, explained that his government had dispatched a ship loaded with naval stores and other gifts but it was overdue, possibly because of the war with France. (In fact, the tribute ship, the *Hero*, had run into storms that not only damaged the vessel but ruined her cargo of lumber and other raw materials destined for Tunis. The *Hero* put into New York for repairs while State Department agents frantically tried to replace the cargo. She would not arrive in Tunis until April 12, 1800, nearly a year after Eaton took up his post.)[40]

Throughout that long year, Eaton did everything he could to stall, stymie, and placate the bey. At first he took his cues from Cathcart, who remained in Tunis until April 2. Both men took a very hard line in their negotiations with Hamouda and his officials. When the bey pressed Eaton to accept a clause by which the United States would either supply a set amount of powder to Tunis or pay for any salutes in powder, Eaton (and Cathcart) flatly refused: "We told him the concession was so degrading that our nation would not yield to it: both justice and honor forbade."[41]

The two American diplomats won Hamouda's grudging respect by their defiant defense of their country's interests. After one exchange, in which Eaton and Cathcart refused to accede to demands for trade concessions, the bey turned to the Sapitapa, his chief advisor, and said, "These people are Cheribeenas; they are so hard there is no dealing with them." Cheribeenas, Eaton explained, "are merchants from Persia. Mr. Cathcart translated this to me so loud that the Sapitapa heard him, and grasping [Cathcart's] hand, said the same thing in Italian."[42]

The seemingly interminable wait for the *Hero* left Eaton little choice but to dicker over any and every request the bey made. More often than not, demands for "gifts" accompanied "suggested" changes to the treaty. The Sapitapa was the usual originator of these "requests," but soon other officials came looking for jewels, gold, and anything else they thought they could extort from the Americans. When the chief magistrate of the harbor demanded Eaton give him a "double-barrel gun and a gold chain for a watch," Eaton finally had enough. "I told him plainly the United States would find it cheaper and better policy to send a force into these seas to defend their commerce than to yield to these accumulated demands."[43]

As the talks dragged on during the summer and into the fall of 1799, the bey grew more and more suspicious of American intentions. The continued failure of the *Hero* to arrive with her consignment of naval stores for Tunis only reinforced the bey's belief the Americans had much less regard for his city than for the other Barbary powers. He also continued to believe the United States gave Algiers the three warships and demanded from the Americans at least an eighteen-gun "cruiser" in addition to the stores Eaton assured him were en route. Hamouda then demanded jewels worth at least as much as a warship for his patience in waiting for the *Hero*. Eaton told the bey his country would never approve, but he duly reported the demands to Pickering.[44]

Eaton's disdain for Arabs in general and Tunisians in particular grew with each day. The soldier turned diplomat utterly detested the bey and all his subjects. The Tunisians, he said, were "deplorably wretched, because they have no property in the soil to inspire an ambition to cultivate it. They are abject slaves to the despotism of their government."[45] As for the bey and his court, "they are under no restraints of honor nor honesty. There is not a scoundrel among them, from the prince to the muleteer, who will not beg and steal."[46] What galled Eaton most, however, was the arrogant manner in which the bey and his officials spoke of the United States, an attitude Eaton blamed on his own countrymen. "To the United States, they believe they can dictate terms. Why should they not? Or why should they believe it will ever be otherwise? They have seen nothing in America to controvert this opinion. And all our talk of resistance, and reprisal, they view as the swaggering of a braggadocio."[47]

3

BROTHERLY LOVE

THE THREE BOYS galloped madly across the sand, their steeds' hooves kicking up a dust storm. A troop of mounted soldiers followed, riding with the same abandon. At a signal, the entire group wheeled, fired on a target, and then continued on, executing each maneuver with precision as their father watched with pride. The boys boasted as to who was the best and who impressed their father most. For the older two, Hassan and Ahmed, the boasts were simply the bravado of youth. For the youngest, Yusuf, they were deadly serious. Although just twelve years old, Yusuf Karamanli would grow to be highly intelligent, ambitious, and ruthless. He was already eyeing the throne his father occupied that, by right, his oldest brother, Hassan, would inherit.[1]

The Karamanli family had come to Tripolitania from central Anatolia in the mid-1500s, when the Ottoman Empire conquered the region. Among the Turkish soldiers, sailors, and officials that arrived in Tripoli was Mustafa Karamanli.[2] Many of the Turks intermarried with the Arab population, creating a new class, or tribe, within the local society—the Karaghla. The Karamanli family was among the elite of this new class.

Nevertheless, it was the Janissaries who ruled, in the sultan's name.[3] Often called slaves, the Janissaries were in fact an elite class of warrior/ social servants. Turkish officials selected young boys from among the captive populations of the empire—Greeks, Albanians, and Georgians were the favorites—and removed them from their families, sometimes forcibly, and trained them. Although technically slaves, the Janissaries were the backbone of the Ottoman Empire, striking fear into opponents from Vienna to Mecca while serving as the sultan's shock troops. After their military service, Janissaries ran the provinces and newly conquered lands.[4] Tripolitania was no different. A series of Italian, French, Greek, and Albanian Janissaries ruled over Tripoli, at first efficiently but as time passed with increasing arrogance, corruption, and negligence. As the Janissaries demanded increased taxation and otherwise oppressed the population, the Karaghla grew in power and popularity. In 1711, Ahmed Karamanli decided to seize the throne.[5]

Karamanli saw his opportunity when the ruler of Tripoli, Bashaw Mahmud Ummais, was in Constantinople, delivering the annual tribute to the sultan. Ummais had left Karamanli in charge, literally giving him the keys to the kingdom.[6] Karamanli had to eliminate the Janissaries still in Tripoli if he was to supplant Ummais, so he decided to lure them to their death. Announcing a great feast in honor of the Janissaries, he invited three hundred of them to his home outside Tripoli's walls. Anyone entering the house had to walk down a long, dark corridor, or "skiffer," so narrow that only one man at a time could fit.[7] As each Janissary entered, an unseen assassin slipped from hiding and silently strangled the man, disposing of the body before the next Janissary could witness his compatriot's fate. Karamanli's assassins killed all three hundred invitees. Meanwhile, troops loyal to the Karaghla fanned out in Tripoli and slaughtered the sultan's remaining soldiers. In a single night, Karamanli had seized control of Tripoli.[8] He then set about keeping it.

Ahmed first had to deal with Ummais, who returned from Constantinople to find his province in open rebellion. The Albanian-born Janissary attempted a half-hearted attack, but having few Turkish soldiers and fewer loyal subjects, he failed. Ummais dispatched a second force under a Janissary named Mohammed Pasha, but Karamanli defeated it. Before Sultan Ahmed III in Constantinople could send a third force, Karamanli sent a lavish amount of tribute to the Ottoman ruler. The largesse so completely overwhelmed Ahmed that he issued a *firman* (a royal decree) confirming Karamanli as ruler of Tripolitania and naming him a bashaw, a title the Ottomans usually reserved for ethnic Turks.[9]

Firmly in charge, Karamanli expanded his power, first conquering Cyrenaica, which became his nation's breadbasket. Next, he imposed order among the restive Arab and Berber tribes of the Fezzan (the southwest of modern Libya) and made that southern province tributary to Tripoli. He revived the trans-Sahara trade, bolstering Tripoli's coffers, and cemented his family's position as head of state, naming his son Mohammed as his successor. The sultan, in another firman, confirmed this line of succession.[10]

Ahmed made a concerted effort to revive his country's economy, introducing limited manufacturing and encouraging entrepreneurship. He invited many Turks from the empire's lands bordering the eastern Mediterranean to Tripolitania. The new agricultural techniques and crops, such as barley, they brought greatly increased Tripoli's exports and industries and boosted its economy, internally and externally. Ahmed reigned for thirty-four years, during which Tripoli enjoyed something of a golden age, leading the populace to refer to him as "the Great." Ahmed's sight began to fail as he entered the thirtieth year of his reign. Local legend claimed a Moorish holy man cursed Ahmed when the bashaw attempted to marry the Moor's youngest daughter and the unfortunate girl committed suicide rather than "succumb to the bashaw's passions."[11] Whatever the reason for the failure of his health, by 1741 Ahmed's grasp on power was slipping, and he began to plan the passage of power to his son, Mohammed. In 1745 Ahmed the Great, now completely blind, committed suicide rather than attempt to hang on to power.

Mohammed Karamanli lacked Ahmed's intellect and charisma, caring more for the trappings of power than for governance. Under Mohammed the conquered provinces of Fezzan and Cyrenaica began rumbling for more autonomy, and various Arab and Berber tribes revolted against Tripoli.[12] Mohammed died in 1753, leaving his eldest son, Ali, to take the throne. Mohammed's brother, Mustafa, however, rejected Ali as bashaw and attempted to organize a coup. Ali, to forestall a revolution, offered to make Mustafa the bey, or successor to the throne, and sent him to rule Derne, Tripolitania's second-largest city. The position failed to appease

Mustafa and by 1755 the situation had deteriorated into open war. Ali sent a force to Derne with orders to kill Mustafa and oust his loyalists. Mustafa heard about the move and fled to Tunis, from which he launched a series of attacks into Tripolitania. The result was nearly a decade of low-level warfare along the border of the two nominally Turkish provinces.[13]

Like his father, Ali paid little attention to running his kingdom, allowing his council, or *divan*, to conduct day-to-day business while he lived as a pampered overlord. The economic infrastructure his grandfather Ahmed had built had largely disintegrated by the time Ali took power. Ahmed had encouraged not only Levantine Turks to settle in Tripolitania but the descendants of Spanish Moors as well. This influx of artisans, traders, farmers, and merchants had broadened Tripoli's economic base and even stimulated small manufacturing. Ahmed's successors failed to sustain this practice and imposed increasingly heavy taxes on the burgeoning merchant class. The Turkish and Moorish immigrants left Tripoli for Egypt, Tunis, and other parts of the Ottoman Empire.[14]

In the 1770s and 1780s, a series of devastating droughts all but destroyed much of Tripoli's grain harvest, forcing Ali to depend on shipments from Tunis and Egypt. Locust infestation of Egyptian crops caused Ali to grow ever more dependent on Tunis, where his uncle continued to plot against him. In addition, plague struck several times during this period, forcing Ali and his retinue either to flee the capital or shut themselves in the castle. Sensing weakness, tribes in Fezzan rose in revolt. The rebels cut off the shipments from the Fezzan gold mines on which Ali depended to pay his own troops and make the occasional token payment to the sultan in Constantinople. Needing more and more resources to battle the insurrection, Ali levied more taxes.[15] The cost of war, in fact, kept Ali from sending his taxes (and gifts) to the sultan, who sent several reminders of his obligations to Constantinople and threats to depose him. Mustafa continued to launch cross-border raids from Tunis, further eroding Ali's hold on power.[16]

Despite these pressures, Ali devoted himself almost entirely to his personal affairs. In 1760, his wife gave birth to Hassan. Three years later, Hamet was born, followed by Yusuf in 1766. Almost from the start, Ali doted on Yusuf, who was an active, intelligent youth. At a very early age,

Yusuf was covetous of his father's power and his oldest brother's position as heir apparent. His jealousy only grew as he realized Hassan was the citizens' favorite—"a fine majestic figure, much beloved, being extremely mild and just to his people."[17]

The three boys shared an uncomfortable and increasingly strident relationship for nearly twenty years. By 1785, Yusuf was openly hostile toward Hassan and working hard to get Hamet under his control. Hamet, as the second son, would inherit the throne if anything happened to Hassan, and Yusuf wanted no interference from that quarter.[18] Hamet, although certainly aware of his brother's ambitions, was much more his father's dutiful son. Nothing about Hamet made him stand out, and he showed little ambition for the throne, appearing content with whatever subordinate responsibilities his father gave him. His mild nature allowed Yusuf to manipulate him, confident the second son of the bashaw posed no real threat to his plans.

⋖ ⋗

The brothers first came to blows in July 1786, when Hassan sparred with Hamet. Miss Tully, the sister-in-law of the British consul in Tripoli, claims Mahmoud, the son of Ali's sister, Lilla Udacia, had set his eyes upon Hamet's new wife. At first, she refused to tell her husband about Mahmoud's advances, fearing Lilla's power and influence over the bashaw. When she finally told Hamet about Mahmoud, Hamet immediately vowed to kill the boy, grabbing his sword, arming his servants, and beginning to search for him. However, a slave warned Mahmoud, and the would-be Romeo fled from his mother's apartments and ran through the castle looking for a place to hide. He finally found a spot in his Uncle Ali's harem, where the ladies hid him in a large box for a day. Donning a disguise, he escaped over the castle wall to his mother's country house.

Islamic law forbad Hamet from entering the harem but upon learning of Mahmoud's hiding place, he threatened to storm it unless Mahmoud surrendered. This enraged Hassan, as his younger brother had no right to make threats against the women. Though he did not know the full story, the bey vowed to protect Mahmoud. Even when he learned what had caused Hamet's anger, Hassan refused to rescind his declaration. Now livid,

Hamet swore vengeance. The feud simmered for several weeks, when the princes' mother, Lilla Halluma, attempted to mediate the dispute. She refused to allow her nephew to kiss her hand until he made peace with Hamet. Hassan assented and sent word to Hamet that he would meet Hamet's wife and allow her to kiss his hand. The message arrived when Hamet and family were at a dinner for Ramadan at which they broke a day-long fast. Hamet, furious at the idea of his wife kissing Hassan's hand, ordered his servants to return a "hotly worded reply." Hamet's wife attempted to soften the message's language, but a servant told Hassan Hamet's exact words. Hassan stormed out of his mother's apartment and returned to his own dwelling, where he learned his youngest brother, Yusuf, had involved himself in the dispute.

Unknown to Hassan, Yusuf had decided to "punish" one of his oldest brother's favorite servants, whipping the soles of the man's feet so badly he was left crippled. This reignited Hassan's rage, and the following day, when the three brothers appeared in court before their father, the bey warned his younger siblings against "putting his prudence any further to the trial." Speaking to their father and the entire court, Hassan told Hamet and Yusuf if they refused to show him the proper respect as the heir apparent, he would meet them both in duels, where they would "feel his power."[19] It was a tense moment. Bashaw Ali lacked the will to rein in his sons, and the retainers of the three sons squared off against one another.[20] Hands moved toward sword hilts, no one speaking a word. Finally, Hassan bade good night to his father and left. The rift that had begun over a woman would soon engulf the kingdom.[21]

Neither Hassan nor Yusuf made any effort to pretend they could stand the sight of one another. The one man who could have ordered an end to their feud, their father, was under Yusuf's spell. "No one else gives credit to Sidi [prince] Yusuf's professions; but the Bashaw places implicit confidence in all he says," reported the wife of the British consul. Yusuf spent the next four years plotting alternately with Hamet against Hassan and against both his brothers. Yusuf knew Hamet had no wish to be bashaw, in fact few ambitions at all, beyond taking care of his family and living a life of relative ease. Hamet knew of Yusuf's ambitions to become bashaw and that he stood in his younger brother's path to power but never seemed to grasp just how precarious that made his own position. Hamet seemed incapable of understanding his younger brother's thirst for power and never acted like a man who was ready to rule or to fight to protect his position.[22]

The uneasy truce between the brothers lasted until the summer of 1790, when Hamet and Yusuf nearly came to blows. Yusuf had one of Hamet's favorite servants whipped nearly to death, an act that forced Hamet to see his brother at his most ruthless. While Hamet never fully reconciled with his older brother, he never trusted his younger brother again.[23] Hassan, meanwhile, had continued to grow in stature. While Yusuf plotted, Hassan led his father's army against rebellions, the most serious in Fezzan during late 1789. Each time he returned from the field, his popularity grew. Miss Tully, in a letter dated September 18, 1789, reported, "The Bey is returned from the camp, and to the great satisfaction of the people of Tripoli, he is so well received by his father, that they yesterday went round the town in state together to the different mosques, to return thanks at the altar of the prophet."[24]

Hassan stabilized the kingdom by April 1790, and Yusuf decided he could wait no longer to make his move. He started by attempting to convince his older brother of his allegiance and even offered to swear an oath to Hassan in a mosque. Although Hassan never fully believed his younger brother, he began to relax his warlike stance against Yusuf. It was the opportunity Yusuf needed. On June 2, after Yusuf had spent the day riding with his brother, an assassin narrowly missed killing Hassan with a pistol shot. Hassan immediately blamed Yusuf but found his pleas of innocence convincing and declared his brother guiltless in the plot.[25] On June 12 Yusuf left the city to gather tribute from several Arab tribes. On his return in July, he continued to "act amicably" toward the royal family, so much so that many of those who suspected Yusuf of plotting treachery began to rethink their opinions of the bashaw's youngest son.[26]

∽⊙∽

On July 20, 1790, a servant arrived at Hassan Karamanli's apartment in Tripoli Castle, asking the bey to visit his mother, Lilla Halluma. His mother wanted Hassan to meet with Yusuf, who, she said, was finally ready to end their feud and swear allegiance. Hassan at first refused. The thirty-year-old bey did not believe that Yusuf was ready to meet, unarmed, and make an oath of fealty. Grabbing his pistols and saber, he made ready to hack his brother to pieces, but his wife, Lilla Aisher, reminded him that carrying weapons into his mother's abode was an unpardonable sin. Hassan briefly reflected, then handed his wife his pistols, but as he was about to remove his saber, Lilla Aisher fell at his feet and begged her husband not to go completely unarmed. He left for his mother's apartment, saber at his side.

Yusuf Karamanli arrived at his mother's apartment the morning of July 20 determined to depose Hassan. The only way he could do so was to kill him, and Yusuf had developed an elaborate plot, with his mother an unwitting accomplice. Yusuf arrived at Lilla Halluma's apartment unarmed. He begged his mother to set up a meeting so Yusuf could end the internal family fighting. Jumping at the chance to broker peace between her sons, she immediately sent word to Hassan that he was in her apartment, unarmed and ready to reconcile. What the princes' mother did not know was Yusuf, though unarmed, had his weapons nearby. Before he entered his mother's apartment, Yusuf gave four of his loyal African slaves a pair of pistols and a sword each to hide for when he would need the weapons, and instructed them to remain outside the apartment, hidden in one of the dark hallways of the castle.

Hassan arrived at the apartment several minutes after the summons. Seeing her oldest son's saber, she begged Hassan to remove it and place it on a windowsill. Hassan, observing Yusuf sitting on a sofa next to their mother, obliged. Lilla Halluma reached out to Hassan, pulled him to the sofa on her other side and clasped Hassan's and Yusuf's hands in her own. Hassan, who had several daughters but no sons, immediately declared his willingness to name Hamet and Yusuf his heirs. (His wife, Lilla Aisher, was pregnant, but the child's sex was unknown.) Yusuf swore he wished reconciliation "with all my heart" and offered to swear allegiance to his older brother on the Koran. At his mother's urging, Hassan agreed and visibly relaxed. It was the opportunity for which Yusuf had waited. In a prearranged signal, he called loudly for a Koran but when his slaves entered the room, they brought the pistols instead of a holy book. Yusuf grabbed the weapons, aimed the first pistol at his brother, and pulled the trigger. But the gun burst, sending shards into Hassan's side and mangling his mother's hands as she tried to protect Hassan. Yusuf pointed the second pistol and got off a clean shot, sending a ball through his brother's heart. Despite his wounds, Hassan was able to grab his saber and attempt to fight back, but he soon fell dead.

Yusuf, standing over his brother's body, told his slaves to drag away the body and "finish him." The slaves fired their own pistols into the bey's body, then hacked it apart with swords. Lilla Halluma attempted to prevent further desecration by draping her own body over her son's as Yusuf and his slaves fled. Hassan's wife rushed to the apartment to see her husband cut into pieces. She threatened to poison herself and her daughters unless Bashaw Ali gave her permission to leave the castle, declaring she "would not live to look on the walls of it, nor to walk over the stones that could no longer be seen for the Bey's blood, with which they were now covered."

As Yusuf fled the castle he murdered Bey Abdallah, the great *chiah*, or advisor, to his father, the last son of the last Turkish ruler of Tripoli and a man very popular with the people. Abdallah saw Yusuf covered in blood and asked him what had happened. Yusuf gave no reply and simply stabbed the old man in the heart. Bashaw Ali, meanwhile, tried to come to grips with his youngest son's action. He ordered everyone off the streets of Tripoli, but as word of the assassination spread, an armed group gathered outside the castle, demanding justice for the popular Hassan. Their numbers grew until Ali became afraid and ordered his own troops to clear the streets. The crowds only increased, calling for vengeance. Large numbers of armed men stationed themselves at the castle gates, expecting Yusuf to arrive at any moment at the head of an insurgent army. They remained throughout the night as a tense silence settled over the city.

⌒⌒

Hamet Karamanli was not in Tripoli the night of the assassination, returning the day after to find the city on edge. He ordered three hundred Arab soldiers to guard the castle while he visited his father and learned of his brother's treachery. It must have come as a shock to Ali's second son.

Hamet was intelligent—he could read, write, and speak Turkish, Italian, and French in addition to Arabic—and was a competent if somewhat colorless combat leader. What many perceived as laziness was in fact acceptance of what he thought his role in Tripoli would be—that of a loyal deputy to his older brother, carrying out whatever duties Hassan might choose to give him.[27] His father knew Hamet's qualities quite well but at first demurred from naming his second son as his heir.

Soon after Hamet arrived in Tripoli, Bashaw Ali sent for Yusuf, promising no harm would come to him. Yusuf, however, had established a blockade outside the castle and refused. As far as Ali knew, a filial feud was behind Hassan's murder, not Yusuf's desire for the throne, a false assumption Yusuf had propagated. Yusuf asked to meet with Hamet who was by right the next bey, but Ali insisted that Hamet have Yusuf's consent before assuming office. Hamet and Yusuf met outside the castle. Yusuf spurned the chance to become bey, telling Hamet he had no political ambitions. He insisted he killed Hassan only because of a personal dispute, one in which Hamet himself had a stake. Hamet reported back to the bashaw, who immediately proclaimed him the new bey. Yusuf, however, continued his blockade, gathering more and more troops.[28]

As Yusuf strengthened his hold on the area outside of Tripoli, he attempted to hatch a two-way plot to unseat his father as bashaw. He approached Hamet first for help in overthrowing their father. Once he was bashaw, Hamet was to make Yusuf the bey until Hamet's own son was old enough to assume those duties. Hamet refused, more from self-preservation than from paternal loyalty. He put little faith in Yusuf's assurances of good will and had no desire to see Yusuf that close to the throne. The rift between the two brothers widened.

Yusuf spent the remainder of 1790 and the first half of 1791 organizing forces and seeking a way to kill his father and older brother. He lacked the military strength to attack and seize the throne. Instead, he resorted to diplomacy, espionage, and the occasional skirmish to keep Ali and Hamet at bay and unsure of his real intentions. In May 1791, he made an attempt on Hamet's life, using tactics similar to those in Hassan's assassination. He sent his personal *iman,* or *marabout* Fataisi, to the bashaw with a request to meet Hamet, saying he, Yusuf, wanted to end the fighting. Fataisi had gained fame as a charismatic holy man, and the bashaw believed him when Fataisi said Yusuf would arrive with just twenty unarmed followers. He ordered Hamet to meet his brother, but neither Hamet nor those around him trusted Yusuf. Information reached Hamet that Yusuf was waiting with several hundred men near the gate. Hamet seized the marabout and dragged him before his father, detailing his brother's treachery. Hamet declared that were not Fataisi a holy man, he would already be dead at the bashaw's feet. He ordered Fataisi to return to Yusuf and tell him never again to enter the city, on pain of death.[29]

Yusuf, his plot foiled, launched a direct attack, but still lacked the forces to make a final push to take the city. His followers advanced to the castle gardens, but Hamet pushed the rebels back to the main city gate. With that attack, Bashaw Ali finally accepted what most of his subjects already knew and declared Yusuf a rebel.[30] Ali also, inexplicably, turned on Hamet, demanding he come to the palace with only two or three unarmed men. Hamet had been nothing but faithful to his father; it was apparently a younger sister, Fatima, who was aligned with Yusuf, who had poisoned Ali against the bey. Despite this latest family rift, Hamet continued to serve his father and took overall command of the defenses of Tripoli.[31] The civil war continued for another two years, with neither side able to gain an advantage until Yusuf won the backing of Bey Hamouda of Tunis, who provided cash and weapons. Yusuf brought up artillery and cut the city off from the rest of the country. For those in Tripoli, it appeared the youngest son of the bashaw was on the verge of winning, "as the town cannot hold out much longer for want of provisions."[32] On July 28, 1793, Yusuf launched what many in Tripoli thought would be his final assault. Ineptitude saved them. When Yusuf opened his cannonade, city residents soon realized the safest places were wherever Yusuf's gunners aimed. "If he had anybody about him as clever as himself, he must have been in the town long ago; but his engineers are so unskillful, that they hit every object but the one they aim at," reported the wife of the British consul.

The attack lasted throughout the day, but the bashaw's youngest son failed to break into the city. Yusuf organized another attack on July 29 but never launched it. At 5 p.m. on July 29, 1793, lookouts spotted a fleet of Turkish warships entering Tripoli Harbor. The Ottoman Empire was set to end not only the civil war but Tripoli's independence.

∽✧∾

Sultan Selim III and his court—the Sublime Porte of the Ottoman Empire—were growing weary of Tripolitania and the Karamanli family. When Ahmed the Great wrested the province from Ottoman control, successive sultans were content to allow the Karamanlis to rule, provided they sent the right amount of taxes and tribute. However, Mohammed, Yusuf's grandfather, began missing payments, while Bashaw Ali stopped making them altogether. When Selim III ascended to the throne in 1789, he warned Ali, to make his payments or face replacement.[33] Selim actually sent a force to oust Ali but at the last minute diverted it to Egypt.[34] The sultan put up with the incessant squabbling in Tripoli for another two years, but when the family infighting descended into civil war, he had no choice but to end it.

The family feud wasn't the only reason for action. Selim had very real fears that France or another European power might intervene in Tripoli and take the province away from Constantinople. The French already had a good deal of influence with the Karamanli family and were a chief supplier of arms to Ali. Selim feared the ongoing civil war could give the French a pretext to enter the city, which would almost inevitably force other European countries to intervene. Selim could conceivably lose all of North Africa if the Great Powers turned it into a battlefield. He ordered a fleet of eight warships and about 450 mercenary troops to Tripoli to restore order and the sultan's rule.[35]

To command the expedition, Selim chose Georgian-born Janissary Ali Borghul. Once a high-ranking official under the dey of Algiers, Mustafa V, Borghul had outlived his usefulness to the dey, who sent him to Constantinople, where he found work in the court of Selim and gradually rose in favor with the sultan. Borghul's knowledge of the North African provinces made him an easy choice to command the expedition. He set sail with not only soldiers but a firman from the sultan officially deposing the Karamanli family and restoring direct rule from Constantinople.

Landing at Tripoli, Borghul deployed his troops in strategic positions around the harbor. The Tripolitan defenders were unsure what to do, as were Bashaw Ali and Bey Hamet. The Karamanlis did not have the strength to fight both Yusuf and Borghul, and late in the night they decided to ask Yusuf to enter the city to fight the Turks. Yusuf's soldiers were unwilling to take on the Imperial soldiers, and in any case, by then it was too late. At midnight, Borghul arrived at the castle with the sultan's firman. Ali, Hamet, and their immediate families left the castle and, in a remarkable turnaround, found refuge with Yusuf, who almost overnight went from usurper to savior. At Yusuf's urging, Ali and Hamet went to Tunis to enlist help from Hamouda.

For the next year, Yusuf maintained a siege of sorts against Tripoli, while Borghul consolidated his position. Thanks to the sultan's firman, he was able to convince several important Arab tribes to join his forces and recruited another five hundred mercenaries from the Levant, mostly Syrians and Armenians. With these new troops, Borghul extended his control over Tripoli. He expanded his navy, demanded tribute payments from European nations in amounts equal to what they paid Algiers, and ruthlessly stamped out dissent, imprisoning many relatives of the Karamanli family.[36] Borghul, wishing to make Tripoli the strongest of the sultan's North African holdings, decided to expand at the expense of Tunis. He inflicted a heavy defeat on Yusuf on August 29, 1794, when his reinforced army broke through Yusuf's lines and lifted the siege. Despite the defeat, Yusuf kept most of his army together, as more and more Arabs grew dissatisfied with Borghul and his near-constant demands for newer and higher taxes.[37]

After defeating Yusuf, Borghul organized an expedition to push Tripoli's western boundary into Tunisian territory. It was all Yusuf needed finally to rally Bey Hamouda to the Karamanli cause. The bey, although Turkish, enjoyed the same autonomy the Karamanlis once enjoyed and had no desire to be wedged between Algiers and a suddenly powerful and land-hungry Tripoli. In November 1794, Hamouda committed 20,000 soldiers to oust Borghul. The Tunisian troops joined with Yusuf's army and slowly pushed Borghul's forces back toward Tripoli. On January 17, 1795, the combined army appeared before the gates of the city. For Borghul, it was time to leave. The Janissary stuffed everything of value he could find into several chests, murdered his political prisoners, and fled. As dawn broke on January 18, the Tripolitans celebrated as Borghul sailed away.[38]

Despite the victory, the city gates remained locked to Yusuf, as the Tripolitans feared the Tunisians would demand control. The Tunisians were eager for plunder and anxiously awaited their opportunity to loot Tripoli. The city's inhabitants pleaded with Yusuf to prevent his allies from ravaging the city. Yusuf managed to convince the Tunisian commander, Mustafa Khoja, to accept a payment levied among all the citizens as compensation for the Tunisians' help. The people of Tripoli then opened the gates and welcomed the return of Karamanli rule.

Bashaw Ali Karamanli, however, never returned to the throne. Already ill when he fled to Tunis, Ali now lay sick in bed, unable to leave Tunis when Yusuf and Hamet liberated Tripoli. Ali's incapacity made Hamet successor to the throne, and despite his own misgivings, on January 25, 1795, Hamet Karamanli became bashaw of Tripoli. Yusuf became bey. Ali Karamanli died in Tunis on July 23, 1796.[39]

Hamet took power at a time when Tripoli needed a strong leader, one capable of uniting the various factions that had fought for and against the Karamanlis and who could restore the country's tattered economy. As the second son, he had never really seriously thought about becoming bashaw and lacked the training his older brother, Hassan, had received.[40] He didn't trust Yusuf and expected him to take up residence in Derne. Instead, Yusuf remained in Tripoli, basking in the admiration of those who saw him as the city's deliverer. As the economic situation worsened, so too did Hamet's state of mind. He struggled mightily but was simply not up to the task of restoring his family's rule in Tripoli. British diplomat Simon Lucas reported to Foreign Secretary William Grenville that "Hamet has no feel nor enjoyment for governing," while "his brother, Yusuf, is the complete opposite."[41] As Hamet sank under the harsh realities of ruling, Yusuf rose in stature. On June 11, 1795, while Hamet was out riding with some of his retainers, Yusuf and his followers closed the city gates. Yusuf then proclaimed himself bashaw, "to the great joy of his loving subjects," finally achieving his life's goal.[42]

Now in power, Yusuf moved quickly to cement his position and remove any possibility of his brother Hamet returning to the throne. Yusuf confirmed his own son, Mehmed, as bey almost as soon as he took power. Mehmed, however, was still an infant, and Yusuf decided to make Hamet the bey of Tripoli's eastern provinces and "invited" Hamet's wife, Lilla Howisha, and their three children to stay at the castle with Yusuf while Hamet took charge of Benghazi. Hamet's family would remain with Yusuf until Hamet had settled into his new position, the timing of which Yusuf would determine. Hamet fully understood what Yusuf meant—his brother planned to hold his family hostage to ensure his loyalty.[43]

For all of Hamet's deficiencies as a ruler, he was a loyal family man and had a strong sense of right and wrong. Soon after his older brother's assassination and his own ascension to the status of bey, Hamet had refused a direct order from his father to crush an uprising among a local tribe of Arabs. Hamet believed it was Yusuf who had caused the rebellion by subjecting the tribe to abuse and insults. When his father renewed his orders to attack the rebels, Hamet again refused: "He would not lead [his followers] to be sacrificed in an unjust cause." The rebels offered to fight for Hamet against his brother and father and make him bashaw, but Hamet refused their offer. "Treachery is certainly not a part of Sidy [sic] Hamet's character," commented a British observer who knew him. "He has not yet shewn it in any one instance."[44] It was this same Hamet who two years later faced the choice between turning on his brother and endangering his family or complying with the new bashaw's demand. Hamet went east and set himself up in Derne, where he believed he would find more support than in Benghazi.[45]

As the only real threat to his position, Hamet was never far from Yusuf's mind, if only because Hamet's wife and children were hostages in Tripoli castle. He spent far more time consolidating his hold on power and legitimizing his seizure in the eyes of the Ottoman sultan. To do so, the new bashaw knew he had to attend to Tripoli's shattered economy and Yusuf turned to an old Barbary Coast custom—piracy. For more than two centuries, the North African coast had been alive with corsairs, who preyed on European and sometimes Turkish shipping. The Barbary leaders either extorted "peace payments" from European leaders or seized their ships, selling off the cargoes and holding the crews for ransom. To bolster Tripoli's economy, Karamanli decided to do both. Many countries had stopped making treaty payments during the Tripolitan civil war, and Yusuf, almost from the moment he took power, began demanding resumption. The first to respond was Spain, which gave Karamanli $20,000 in 1795 and loaned him eighteen shipwrights, carpenters, and sailmakers, worth much more than currency to the bashaw. He put his Spanish experts to work repairing three aging warships Borghul had left behind and building what would grow into a fleet of nineteen gunboats. Venetian merchants paid the bashaw more than $16,000 for free passage; the established naval superpowers, England and France, sent "gifts" of naval stores, lumber, sails, and rope worth $15,000.[46]

Not every country, however, was ready either to acknowledge Karamanli as bashaw or resume payments to Tripoli. The British consul, Simon Lucas, reported the Danes, Swedes, Dutch, governments of several German states, and Neapolitans had all balked when Karamanli demanded they pay for safe passage. In response, the bashaw unleashed his newly refurbished corsairs to terrorize the Mediterranean. They extorted $96,000 in ransoms and other payments in 1796–97. The attacks forced Denmark and Sweden to renew their treaties with Tripoli, at a combined price of $100,000. The Scandinavians also agreed to pay $5,000 a year to maintain peace with Tripoli. Sardinia followed suit in 1798, paying $40,000 for a treaty, while the Republic of Ragusa, a protectorate of the Ottoman Empire, agreed to pay $30,000.[47]

Another country Karamanli targeted was the United States. Diplomat Joel Barlow negotiated a treaty with Yusuf soon after he came to power, paying $16,000 for peace and pledging consular presents and a fee when America appointed a consul to Karamanli's court. The treaty revealed an American misconception about Tripoli. Barlow had negotiated it through the bey of Algiers, whom the Americans named as the arbitrator of any disputes. In American eyes, this made Karamanli somehow subservient to the bey. The United States considered Algiers to be the most dangerous of the Barbary States, viewing Tripoli as an also-ran. That did not sit well with Karamanli. In many ways, Yusuf was the first true Arab nationalist, aspiring to make his country the equal of any in Europe or the Near East, and he took as an insult any action that might impede that ambition. The United States delayed appointing a consul to Tripoli—in Yusuf's eyes, an unforgiveable affront. When finally in 1798 James Leander Cathcart arrived in Tripoli to take up the post as U.S. consul, the British consul met him with the news that "the Bashaw had ordered him to inform me that he would not receive me as consul for the United States of America, as I had not brought the stores and brig promised . . . two years ago, when our peace was concluded here." Yusuf was incensed "that the Americans had not fulfilled their promises to him, and [held] that consequently, he was under no obligations to fulfill his promises to them." Most of all, the wanted the Americans to realize "the Bashaw of Tripoli was an independent Prince, and would be respected as such in spite of Algiers, Tunis, or even the Grand Signore [the sultan]."[48]

Cathcart eventually took up his post, but Yusuf remained adamant, demanding from the United States $28,000 in naval stores and cash to atone for the country's tardy payments. The amount increased as talks dragged on. Cathcart, for his part, negotiated in good faith, but his constant referrals to Dey Hassan II of Algiers only made Karamanli more intractable. Cathcart, in a letter to the U.S. consul general in Algiers, Richard O'Brien, reported there was little point in further talks, "as no confidence whatever ought to be placed in the promises of the said Bashaw, he being destitute of honor and integrity and every other good qualification that dignifies the human heart."[49] For his part, Karamanli viewed the Americans as double-dealing and weak, writing O'Brien, "I am at a loss to know why the American nation has neglected Tripoli for so long."[50] In a letter to President John Adams he wrote, "Your negligence with regard to us . . . offended us." Karamanli now demanded the United States pay Tripoli $225,000 for a new peace treaty and $20,000 a year to maintain the peace, demands he likely knew the Americans would reject. He gave the new president, Thomas Jefferson, six months to decide, probably knowing the answering would be no.[51]

To the Americans, the exorbitant demand was typical of a leader they viewed as little better than a barbarian, one whom they needed to answer with guns, not gold. For Karamanli, whether the Americans paid him or fought him mattered little. "Tripoli is very different from what it was some years ago," Karamanli told Cathcart in one meeting, and to prove it, he would go to war.[52]

4

"TO CHASTISE THE BASHAW"

THE UNITED STATES officially went to war with Tripoli on May 14, 1801, when Bashaw Yusuf Karamanli entered the grounds of the American consulate and chopped down the flagpole. It was an act of great symbolism. Wood for flagpoles was scarce in Tripoli. By cutting down the American flagpole, Karamanli was in effect telling the United States that it was not an equal of either Tripoli or the other nations whose flags remained aloft.[1] This sentiment was at the heart of the problem between the United States and Tripoli and the rest of what the West called the "Barbary States."

The Romans, when they conquered North Africa, believed the inhabitants of the region were uneducated brutes whose language sounded like the bleating of sheep. The Romans slapped the term they used for all non-Latin people—"barbarian"—on those of North Africa, and the term stuck. Romans, and later Europeans, as well as Arabs who invaded the region in the 700s, branded the native peoples "Berbers," a derivative of "barbarian," while the region itself became known as Barbary, encompassing four nations: Morocco, Algiers, Tunis, and Tripoli.[2]

The Barbary States occupied a strategic part of the world. Stretching from the mouth of the Mediterranean to Egypt, the Barbary States could, and often did, dictate access to the Mediterranean by sending their corsairs to prey on unsuspecting merchant vessels. Of the four "states," Morocco was the only true nation. Situated on both the Atlantic Ocean and the Mediterranean, Morocco was the most powerful of the Barbary States and the only one not under the control of the Ottoman Empire. Moroccan emperor Muhammed III was the first foreign leader to recognize the United States as a nation and the first to enter into a treaty of friendship with the new country. His grandson, Muley Suleyman, was far more ambivalent toward the United States, often threatening war when it suited him or when he wanted something more from America.[3]

Algiers, Tunis, and Tripoli were all ostensibly provinces of the Ottoman Empire and subject to the will of the sultan in Constantinople. The reality was all three were, to varying degrees, semi- or completely autonomous city-states. Algiers was the most aggressive of the three and had the largest military. The Turkish rulers of the principality had fought at various times wars with Spain, Portugal, Naples, Venice, England, France, and even the Hapsburg Empire. Algiers was the first of the Barbary States to begin seizing U.S.-flagged vessels, taking its first American prize in 1785. It was Algeria's demands for higher protection payments and its threat of war in 1793 that prompted the creation of the U.S. Navy.[4] Next was Tunis. The smallest of the Barbary States, Tunis was arguably the most Turkish of the four. Descendants of Janissaries held firm sway over Tunis, and Tunisian corsairs plied the Mediterranean, extorting protection money from small and large nations alike. Finally there was Tripoli. The Karamanli family ruled over the province, formally called "Tripolitania." It was the most independent of the three Barbary States under Ottoman control. Tripoli was also the poorest of them, and although the United States began paying protection money in 1796, it was never enough.[5]

The common thread that bound the Barbary States and, in American and European eyes, earned them their name of "Barbary" was piracy. All four nations relied upon either the outright seizure of foreign ships plying the Mediterranean and parts of the Atlantics or the threat of seizure. Nearly every nation in Europe paid protection money, often called "tribute," to the Barbary States to ensure access to the Mediterranean. These payments, as well as the ransoms nations paid for crews and booty from captured ships, became the backbone of the economies of all four states, especially Tripoli.[6]

The relationship between Tripoli and the United States was strained almost from the start. Yusuf Karamanli expected the same sort of tribute payments from the new nation he knew the rulers in Algiers and Tunis received. Karamanli incessantly demanded more and more, and when payments were late, as they were in 1801, he grew more and more strident in his demands.[7] In January 1801 a frustrated Karamanli sent a new list of demands to an exasperated Jefferson. Karamanli's demand was simple: either the United States increased its protection payments or Tripoli would declare war. Jefferson refused, and Karamanli hacked down the American flag.[8] Jefferson, expecting trouble with the bashaw, had already dispatched the first squadron of American ships to the Mediterranean.

Commodore Richard Dale commanded the first squadron. A hero of the Continental Navy during the Revolutionary War, Dale had been the first lieutenant on the *Bon Homme Richard* when John Paul Jones captured the British frigate *Serapis* in 1779. By 1801 he was forty-seven, in somewhat poor health, and lacked the fire he had when he served under Jones.[9] Jefferson gave Dale orders to "chastise their insolence by sinking, burning or destroying their ships and vessels wherever you find them."[10] The commodore, however, did little to trouble the corsairs. Only a victory by the schooner *Enterprise* over the Tripolitan brig *Tripoli* prevented Dale's expedition from being a complete farce.[11] Dale returned to the United States in September with his reputation in tatters. His handling of the blockade had been laughable, and the very countries the young officers of the Navy and Marine Corps wanted to impress, namely England and France, did a lot of the laughing.

Jefferson next chose Richard V. Morris, another Revolutionary War veteran, to replace Dale as commander in the Mediterranean. Morris used the thirty-six-gun *Chesapeake* as his flagship. He brought his wife along for the campaign and seemingly allowed her to set the squadron's agenda. Morris spent most of his time ostensibly convoying American merchant vessels, at least those bound for the places Mrs. Morris wanted to visit. The situation frustrated many of the young officers, who itched for combat. Midshipman Henry Wadsworth, who served on the *Chesapeake*, dubbed

Mrs. Morris "the commodoress, neither beautiful nor even handsome, but she looks very well in a veil."[12]

Jefferson recalled Morris on April 26, 1803.[13] Two weeks later, he appointed Captain Edward Preble as the new commander of the Mediterranean squadron.[14] There was nothing timid about Preble. He was the first Navy commander to operate in the Indian Ocean, near the Dutch colonies of Java and Batavia (in present-day Indonesia). A stern disciplinarian, Preble refused to tolerate some of his young officers' excesses. He didn't care whether they understood the reason for an order as long as they obeyed it. As Midshipman Charles Morris put it, "A very violent temper and easily excited temper was one of the prominent characteristics of Commodore Preble, from the undue expression of which, when he was greatly excited, no officer could escape. Irresolution, no less than contradiction, was an offense in his eyes, and decision of action as well as obedience of orders was necessary to preserve his favorable opinion."[15] Preble's style didn't endear him to his officers, not that Preble cared. In a letter to his wife Preble raged he had "nothing but a pack of boys" to command. "A great disproportion of them are boys lightly deserving of any attention," Preble wrote. "They do not know discipline and do not understand it."[16]

A run-in with an English warship ended the distrust and galvanized the men behind their new squadron commander. When the captain of the English vessel, claiming to be an eighty-four-gun ship of the line, insulted Preble, the American commodore ordered the crew of his ship, forty-four-gun Constitution, to prepare to fire. The English captain, who actually commanded a thirty-two-gun frigate, immediately apologized, but the effect on the squadron was electric. Preble was ready to fight a ship he thought twice the size of Constitution, and if he was quick to anger, he was just as quick with praise. Here was a commander who wanted action as much as American officers and crews did.[17] Almost as important as Preble's aggressiveness was his eye for ability. He knew a good officer when he saw one and found ways to allow a young man either to prove himself or suffer the shame of failure. It was this trait, more than anything else, that allowed the officers under Preble's command to blossom, creating a seasoned cadre of leaders for this and subsequent conflicts.

Soon after arriving on station with the *Constitution*, Preble took the squadron into Gibraltar. Captain William Bainbridge had the thirty-eight-gun *Philadelphia*, and there were four new vessels: the sixteen-gun brigs *Argus* and *Syren* and two fourteen-gun schooners, the *Vixen* and *Nautilus*. The squadron workhorse, the twelve-gun schooner *Enterprise*, was also on station. Bainbridge was thirty, a veteran of the Quasi-War with France and Preble's oldest captain. The remaining ship commanders were all under twenty-five years old, except for Isaac Hull, who commanded the *Enterprise* at twenty-nine. The three lions among Preble's officers were Lieutenants Charles Stewart, twenty-five; Stephen Decatur Jr., twenty-four; and Richard Somers, twenty-four. The three men were bosom friends—especially Decatur and Somers—and had grown up together. Stewart commanded the *Syren*, Decatur (at least temporarily) the *Argus*, and Somers the *Nautilus*. Lieutenant John Smith commanded the *Vixen*.[18]

Preble had a simple plan. He intended to use his heavy, deep-draft frigates to close off Tripoli Harbor while his lighter, shallow-draft brigs and schooners worked the littorals, destroying the Tripolitan navy. He also planned to do what previous American commanders had failed to do—mount the blockade year-round, including the winter, when the weather could be fickle and the Mediterranean deadly. He decided he needed at least one ship to keep an eye on the remaining Barbary States and chose Hull for the job, putting him in command of the *Argus* while shifting Decatur to the *Enterprise*.[19] The new commodore's plan unraveled almost as soon as he arrived. Preble ordered Bainbridge and the *Philadelphia* and Lieutenant Smith in the *Vixen* to sail to Tripoli and begin the blockade. He gave Bainbridge explicit orders to keep the *Vixen* within eyesight at all times. Under no circumstances, Preble said, was Bainbridge to take the *Philadelphia* into the harbor, where reefs and uncharted shoals could easily sink the frigate.[20] Arriving off Tripoli, Bainbridge promptly tossed his orders overboard. He sent the *Vixen* east to interdict Tripolitan shipping while the *Philadelphia* operated on her own until October 31, 1803, when Bainbridge gave chase to a ship trying to slip into Tripoli. Bainbridge pushed the *Philadelphia* hard, raising all sail to chase down the blockade runner. He had his prey just within cannon range when the *Philadelphia* ran aground on Kaliusa Reef. After trying unsuccessfully to lighten the ship to get her off, Bainbridge hauled down his flag, handing Karamanli 302 American prisoners. The next day a storm refloated the *Philadelphia*, and the corsairs happily towed the frigate into the harbor.

The loss of the *Philadelphia* changed all of Preble's plans. He no longer had the force to attack Tripoli directly, and now he had to contend with the fact Karamanli had a warship that could match the *Constitution*. In early December, he led the *Constitution* and the *Enterprise* on a reconnaissance of the bashaw's defenses during which he snared a small ketch trying to sneak out of the harbor. Her name was the *Mastico*. After an admiralty court validated the capture, Preble took the sixty-eight-foot ketch into U.S. service as the *Intrepid*.[21]

In January, both Decatur and Stewart approached Preble with the idea of sneaking into Tripoli Harbor and either snatching the *Philadelphia* and sailing her out of the harbor or destroying her at her moorings. Stewart suggested disguising the *Syren* as a known blockade runner, the British brig *Transfer*, to carry out the mission. Decatur suggested the *Enterprise* was the ship for the job.[22] The *Enterprise*, however, was in need of a refit. Preble had in fact already been thinking about a mission to destroy the *Philadelphia*, but instead of possibly sacrificing one of the squadron's ships, he would use the *Intrepid*.

On January 30, 1804, Preble summoned Stewart and Decatur to the *Constitution*.[23] In the privacy of his cabin, the commodore detailed his plan. Stewart was to take the *Syren* and the *Intrepid* to a point off Tripoli, from which Decatur was to sail the *Intrepid*, which the corsairs believed was still one of their own vessels, into the harbor, tie up alongside the *Philadelphia*, then board and destroy her. Decatur selected sixty-two volunteers from the *Enterprise*, and Preble sent him extra officers from the *Constitution* and *Syren*. Among the selectees were the seven Marines assigned to the schooner, under the command of Sergeant Solomon Wren.[24]

On February 14, after an agonizingly long passage owing to severe weather, the two American ships arrived off Tripoli. Decatur wanted to go in right away. Stewart, however, overruled him and ordered the attack for the night of the sixteenth to give the men who had to board the *Intrepid* a day to shake off the effects of the recent weather.

Decatur set off the next morning, with the *Syren* trailing about three miles astern. The *Intrepid* slowly pulled away from the brig, entering the harbor alone. The little ketch needed all day to reach the anchorage, gliding in after dark to where the corsairs had anchored the *Philadelphia*. The locals all knew the *Intrepid*—as the *Mastico*—and at first paid little attention to the battered ketch. As *Intrepid* sailed closer to the *Philadelphia*, a guard on the frigate actually passed the Americans a line so they could tie up. When the ketch was within a few feet however, Decatur's cover story that *Intrepid* had lost her anchor in the storm fell apart. One of the guards screamed *"Americani,"* and after a pause Decatur led his boarding party onto the *Philadelphia*. Within minutes the bluejackets had overwhelmed the corsairs, either killing those who stood to fight or driving them overboard.

Once they had the frigate under their control, the Americans placed combustibles and set her on fire. As the shore batteries of the now-alerted Tripolitans opened fire, Decatur ordered his men back to the *Intrepid* to make good their escape. Despite the hand-to-hand combat on the *Philadelphia* and the fire of 115 cannon, the Americans suffered just one man slightly wounded.[25] The elated crews of the *Intrepid* and *Syren* set a course for Syracuse, on the island of Sicily, arriving there on February 19. The two ships were a welcome sight for Preble, who had no idea what had happened to either Stewart or Decatur. The same storms that lashed the brig and ketch off Tripoli had pounded Sicily and the commodore rightly worried for the safety of both crews, especially those on the *Intrepid*. The appearance of the *Syren* and *Intrepid* alleviated those fears, and soon the entire squadron was cheering as news spread of Decatur's exploit.[26]

The *Philadelphia* now destroyed, Preble set about the task of strangling Tripoli and forcing the bashaw to come to terms. He ordered Stewart with the *Syren* to take command of the blockade off Tripoli while Preble, after stops in Tunis, Algiers, and Tangier to check on the other Barbary leaders, went to Naples to borrow several gunboats and two mortar boats. Stewart pursued the blockade with a vigor that soon had the bashaw reeling. He stopped just about all major shipping from entering the port and bottled up the Tripolitan cruisers. One of his first prizes was the blockade runner *Transfer*. The English-built brig quickly became part of the American squadron, under the name of the *Scourge*. By summer Stewart had Tripoli on the verge of starvation, and Preble had obtained the loan of six gunboats and two mortar vessels from the king of Naples. The *Argus* too rejoined the squadron, as Preble saw no need to have one of his best ships and ablest captains guarding against an attack the commodore now knew would not come.[27]

The reinforced squadron arrived off Tripoli at the end of July. After a failed attempt at negotiation, Preble launched his first direct assault on the bashaw on August 3, 1804. He put Somers in charge of a division of three gunboats and Decatur in charge of the other three. To man the boats, Preble stripped crew members from his flagship as well as the smaller vessels. The gunboats moved out on the morning of August 3 and immediately found a force of nineteen Tripolitan gunboats advancing to meet them. The Americans sent their gunboats through a narrow gap in the rocks that marked the entrance to the harbor. Preble had the *Argus*, *Syren*, and *Vixen* deployed to cover the gunboats, while the two mortar boats took up a position about a mile from the city itself.[28]

The winds that helped propel the two Yankee divisions picked up as the gunboats came within range of the Tripolitans and separated Somers' three boats. Two of them, including a gunboat under the command of Lieutenant James Decatur, joined with James' brother Stephen, giving the elder Decatur a division of five gunboats. Somers continued his attack alone, engaging five enemy vessels while preventing a second group from flanking the American attack. Decatur's division drove right at the heart of the Tripolitan battle line, engaging nine more Tripolitan gunboats. The corsairs had a reputation for bravery and brutality in hand-to-hand combat, but it mattered little to the bluejackets. The Americans bore in on their opponents and met them, gun to gun, sword to sword, in a savage encounter that swept across the decks of the Tripolitan gunboats, capturing three of the corsair vessels. Although lighter than their opponents', the Americans' losses were bitter. James Decatur lay dead, the victim of the Tripolitan trick of fake surrender. Lieutenant Jonathon Trippe suffered a dozen wounds capturing one corsair gunboat; Stephen Decatur captured a pair of them.[29]

Somers and Decatur earned the bulk of the praise from both Preble and the squadron. The two young officers had once more proven their bravery, and if the victory was not quite as crippling to the Tripolitans as the commodore wanted, it was, in American eyes, a crushing blow. "Never was there a more complete victory," said Purser Noadiah Morris of the *Constitution*. "To recount every instance of personal bravery would be to name almost every officer in the squadron. The Turks were driven from their batteries in the greatest terror and confusion and I think I may say with propriety that since Charles the V of Austria never have any of the Barbary States met with so severe a check."[30]

The victory taught the bluejackets several important lessons, the biggest of which was the simple fact they could match their opponents sword for sword. Close-quarters combat—hand-to-hand fighting—was supposed to be the pirates' domain. Decatur and Trippe and their bluejackets, however, had beaten the Tripolitans at their own game. It hadn't been easy. As Decatur put it, "I find hand to hand is not child's play. Tis kill or be killed." Despite the difficulty, the American victory on August 3 raised morale throughout the fleet. "I always thought we could lick them their own way and give to them two to one," Decatur said. "The first boat they were 36 to 20 and we carried her without much fuss. The second was 24 to 10 and they also went."[31]

Preble waited five days before he launched his second assault. Charles Stewart planned the attack, looking to use the gunboats to destroy shore fortifications that guarded the entrance to the harbor to pave the way for the larger American warships to launch a direct attack on the city. Preble also had his two mortar boats in action. Although neither had made an impact in the first attack diplomats still in Tripoli told Preble the mortars frightened the Tripolitans more than any other weapon in the American arsenal.[32] Stewart hoped to goad the bashaw's fleet from its anchorage with his attack on the shore batteries and by directing the mortars to bombard Tripoli Castle. Once the Tripolitans were in open water, Stewart could use the American brigs and schooners to engage them while the *Constitution* provided covering fire.[33]

The Americans opened the attack of August 7 with their force of nine gunboats. Preble crewed the captured Tripolitan gunboats with men from the *Syren*, *Argus*, and *Vixen*. The assault went well until a chance shot destroyed *Gunboat No. 9*, killing most of the crew. As the remaining gunboats pressed the attack on the shore batteries, Stewart saw a line of enemy vessels, among them several galleys and schooners, heading for the American vessels. He ordered the *Argus*, *Vixen*, and his own *Syren* into action. The quick American reaction frightened the Tripolitans, who reversed course for the safety of their fortifications. The American gunboats and mortar boats continued to engage the shore batteries, silencing several of them. The hoped-for wholesale Tripolitan sally, however, never came, and Preble ordered an end to the attack at 6 p.m.[34] As the schooners and brigs took the gunboats under tow and steered toward the *Constitution*, Hull on the *Argus* spotted a strange sail and gave chase. She turned out to be the frigate *John Adams* under Master Commandant Isaac Chauncey.[35]

Chauncey arrived with dispatches confirming what Preble already knew—Commodore Samuel Barron was on his way with four frigates to reinforce the Mediterranean squadron and to take command of the campaign against Tripoli. President Thomas Jefferson had decided to send Barron with reinforcements soon after he received news of the loss of the *Philadelphia* but before news of her destruction had reached America. Chauncey, when he reported to Preble on August 7, thought Barron would arrive any day. By the twenty-fourth, however, there was still no word of the reinforcements, and Preble decided to launch at least one more major attack before he was relieved of command. Although he never said it publicly, the delay gave Preble time to deal with his own frustration at losing the squadron.

Preble now planned to throw everything he had at the bashaw. He stripped his larger vessels of crew as much as he dared to man the gunboats and thanks to the arrival of replacement crew on the *John Adams*, he had enough men to fully man the flagship.[36] He launched his attack the night of the twenty-fourth with the mortar boats, which had continued to underperform. Their attack fizzled, as the mortar shells were mostly duds. Preble recalled the mortar boats and waited another four days before renewing the onslaught.[37]

At 5 a.m. on August 28, the Americans opened fire. Dr. Jonathan Cowdery, formerly the surgeon from the *Philadelphia* and now something of a personal doctor to the bashaw, woke to the sound of "heavy and incessant fire of cannon and the whistling and rattling of shot all around me." He climbed out of bed and ventured to the window of his apartment. "I found that our gunboats were close in, and were firing upon the town and batteries," he said. "Every gun in Tripoli that could be brought to bear was returning the fire. The Tripolitan gunboats were close under the castle for protection."[38]

Preble augmented his force of small boats by arming three cutters and manning them with officers and men from the *Scourge* and *John Adams*. These three small boats joined the attack on the city, blasting away with twelve-pound carronades. The eight gunboats, with their twenty-four- and twenty-eight-pounder main guns, ripped into the massed Tripolitan warships, smashing a pair of galleys, before they attacked two forts. The American fire drove the two forts' defenders from their guns several times before finally silencing one of them for good.[39] When the gunboats ran out of ammunition, Preble ordered the *Constitution* into action. "The commodore's ship when standing in and during the engagement was the most elegant sight I ever saw," wrote Purser John Darby of the *John Adams*. "She had the tompions out and matches lit and batteries lighted up [and] all hands at quarters standing right in under the fort and received a heavy cannonading from their battery. The commodore gave them several broadsides which did great injury to their battery and the houses on shore."[40]

Despite the damage to his city and fleet, Karamanli remained defiant. The day after the attack he sent word through French Consul Bonaventure Beaussier that he would be willing to conduct a prisoner exchange—Preble had forty-two Tripolitans on board his ships—and cut a peace deal. His asking price of $400,000 didn't change. Beaussier said the ferocity of the attack did not dent Karamanli's resolve as, "the bashaw seems to care little about the injury done to the houses by the shots. . . . Menaces have no other effect than to inflame the mind of the prince."[41] Despite his defiance, however, Karamanli suffered from the storm of shot of shell. The attack drove the bashaw from the city, and August 29 found him at his "summer residence in the country." Karamanli also remained in constant fear of the mortars "which he fears may burn and destroy his town." There was, Beaussier said, only one thing the commodore could do now: "Attack the town and particularly the castle without intermission," the Frenchman advised. "You must persevere until the pacha, harassed at all points, shall himself ask for a parley."[42]

Preble had every intention of keeping the pressure on Karamanli, and he turned to an old tactic—the fireship. The commodore ordered Somers, now a master commandant, to convert the Intrepid into an "infernal," packing the ketch with shot, shell, and other combustibles. Preble planned to launch one final all-out assault on the city before sending in his "infernal." Poor winds, however, thwarted attempts on August 30 and September 2, forcing the squadron and the Intrepid to turn back. The attempt on the second also cost Preble the element of surprise, as Tripoli's defenders spotted the Intrepid and fired on her. Any further attempts to use the fireship would come with the full foreknowledge of the corsairs.[43]

Preble launched what proved to be his final attack on September 3. Once more the gunboats concentrated their fire on the Tripolitan warships anchored near the castle, as well as one of the newer shore batteries. The two mortar boats had their best success of the campaign, dropping round after round into the city. "The two bomb ketches . . . did considerable damage to several houses and completely destroyed the house of the Spanish carpenter, the bashaw's naval contractor," Dr. Cowdery said. "I observed the utmost confusion and random firing among the Tripolitans. The men, women and children ran out of the town in the utmost terror and distraction."[44]

Then it was once more the turn of the flagship. In a full breeze, the Constitution moved between the bombards and the shore. The Tripolitans turned every gun they could bring to bear and sent shot after shot toward the American flagship. "We were exposed to the fire of more than 80 guns," wrote Nathaniel Haraden, the ship's sailing master. "The spray of the shot wet our courses nearly to the lower yards." Master Commandant Chauncey, at the helm of the *Constitution,* drove the big frigate in as close to the beach as he dared. The range to the Tripolitan batteries and castles was only a few hundred yards, and every pirate cannon sent shot toward Preble's flagship. Finally, *Constitution* answered: "We brought to within point-blank shot of all the batteries and gave 11 broadsides of round and doublehead from our larboard [port] batteries," Haraden said.[45]

The next day Somers went in with the fireship *Intrepid,* on what he knew could well be and in fact it proved to be, a one-way trip. The ketch exploded just before 10 p.m., well before anyone expected. Uncertainty reigned in the squadron as to what had happened until Eaton later met in Egypt a Turkish naval officer who told him that a pair of Tripolitan gunboats intercepted the *Intrepid* as she entered the harbor. The corsairs attempted to board the ketch and Somers blew up the ship rather than allow her to fall into enemy hands. Five days later, Commodore Samuel Barron arrived, and the 1804 campaign against Tripoli was essentially over. In 1805 the emphasis of the war would shift from the sea to the ground.

5

DUNGEONS
AND DIPLOMACY

CAPTAIN WILLIAM BAINBRIDGE, along with 298 surviving members of the crew of the *Philadelphia*, was entering his second year as a captive of the bashaw when Commodore Samuel Barron arrived to take command of the Mediterranean squadron. For Bainbridge, the past year had been a period of mental torment coupled with concern for his crew, as well as for his own reputation. The New Jersey native and his officers lived every day knowing the bashaw, in a fit of capriciousness, could order them tortured or executed for just about any infraction.

Bainbridge was born May 7, 1774, in Princeton, New Jersey, to a fairly well-to-do family. He enjoyed a better-than-average early education and by the time he was thirteen he expressed a desire to go to the sea. He took his first voyage at age fifteen, and by the time he turned eighteen, he was first mate on a merchant brig. In 1797 he was among the first officers appointed to the new U.S. Navy. He was tall for his time (six feet), had jet-black hair, and a pair of thick muttonchop sideburns that framed his face.[1] Bainbridge was something of an enigma to his fellow officers. His peers, almost to a man, liked Bainbridge, and yet there was something about him that seemed at odds with the man who made friends freely with others. Seamen who sailed under Bainbridge loathed him. John Rea, who served under Bainbridge on the frigate *George Washington*, called his former captain "a man destitute of reason and humanity," and claimed Bainbridge beat one crewman with his own hands so badly the man suffered a split skull.[2] Bainbridge also had a reputation as an unlucky commander. He was the only captain to surrender a ship to the French during the Quasi-War. He suffered the indignity of having to transport the dey of Algiers to Constantinople after imprudently sailing the *George Washington* into the harbor of Algiers while delivering America's tribute payment, and he was now at the mercy of Yusuf Karamanli, again because of his own mistake.

Throughout his first year in captivity, Bainbridge used his pen as a lifeline, writing to diplomats, Commodore Preble, and his wife as often as he could. Danish Consul Nicholas Nissen provided a bridge to the outside world; he looked after the Americans as much as possible and also played postman, delivering Bainbridge's correspondence at every opportunity. As much as he worried about his crew—and he was genuinely concerned for his sailors' welfare—Bainbridge in his letters again and again broached the subject of his reputation back in the States. In a letter to Preble he admitted:

> I severely feel the loss which my country has sustained [in the loss of the *Philadelphia*] but feel conscious that no impropriety in truth can be attached to me, and have not a doubt on investigation but it will appear so to my government. Still I am no stranger to the censures of an ungenerous world; and the premature opinions, which are too hastily formed on the misfortunes of the unfortunate: but I trust that an accident occasioned by circumstances which no prudence could foresee, or valor control, will not weigh against years of zealously serving my country.[3]

Preble's offensive against the city did little to improve Bainbridge's situation. Although Karamanli knew the value of the Americans as hostages, the bashaw valued his pride even more and kept Bainbridge and his crew under lock and key. With each attack Preble launched, he upped his demands for ransom. Bainbridge was all too aware of Karamanli's ransom demands and began, slowly at first but with increasing desperation, to hope for any diplomatic plan that would win his and his crew's release. Even before his capture Bainbridge had a melancholy disposition, calling himself a "child of adversity" and lamenting, "Misfortune has attended me throughout my naval career." His year in captivity pushed the captain nearly into a state of depression, and a hint of that desperation replaced the militant tone he had once struck in his letters. To George Davis in Tunis he admonished, "In making peace with these people we must not consider them as savages, but treat them as a nation with whom we wish peace." He admitted, "Not a word from America, or the Commodore do we hear—perfectly in the dark as to all movements, and harassed in mind with dreadful anxiety."[4]

The captivity also took a physical toll on the captain. On September 30, 1804, Consul Nissen wrote to Davis, "Poor Capt. Bainbridge has been indisposed; but is now better; several of the officers are unwell, but of no danger, it has been common here the fever they [are] sick of."[5] Midshipman James Renshaw, in a letter to John Rodgers, commented on how frail Bainbridge looked after a year in captivity, owing to "the disagreeable situation in which we are placed at present [in] our confinement."[6] He was not at his breaking point yet, but William Bainbridge was ready to embrace anything that would earn his freedom, even if it meant paying the bashaw.

∾✦∾

Yusuf Karamanli was probably tired of looking over his shoulder to see who might be next in line to attack. On one side, the leader of Tripoli had the U.S. Navy. For nearly a year, the American squadron had battered and blockaded his city. The bluejackets had given Karamanli's forces a bloody nose in several engagements late in the summer of 1804. They had embarrassed him by destroying the captured frigate *Philadelphia*. Each morning he could look out the window of his castle and see the masts of the American fleet outside the harbor, out of gun range but still extremely close. Most of all, he could feel the effects of the American blockade. The Yankees were starving his city. Despite all this, Karamanli remained defiant— toward the Americans, toward his fellow North African leaders, and toward his nominal overlord, Sultan Selim III of the Ottoman Empire. "The fanaticism and fury of these Africans would be difficult to curb in case of a total destruction," French diplomat Bonaventure Beaussier told Preble. The bashaw had vowed "to make use of every method to oppose your attacks, the result of which would be ordained by providence. These are his own expressions."[7]

The fury of the American attacks came as a shock, yet Karamanli saw weakness in the American attempts to negotiate after each assault. "It must be construed to your disadvantage and tend to raise the pretensions of this Regency," Beaussier warned.[8] Starvation, however, was another story for the thirty-eight-year-old bashaw. The American blockade choked off critical supplies of grain from Tunis, on which the bulk of Tripoli's population depended. Grain and other supplies continued to reach Tripoli from Derne and Benghazi, but unrest among the Arab tribes in the east made those routes, as well as supplies from Egypt, sporadic. There was another problem in the east—Hamet. Yusuf's older brother was somewhere in Egypt, supposedly agitating among the Mamelukes and Arab tribes, trying to raise an army against the bashaw. Hamet's activity didn't worry Yusuf as much as it annoyed him. Yusuf had little confidence that his older brother had the wherewithal actually to foment a rebellion, but neither could he completely discount the possibility.

A bigger problem for Yusuf was his inability to pay his annual tribute to the Sublime Porte. Selim III had confirmed the return of Karamanli rule and made him bashaw in a *firman* in 1797 sent after Yusuf, thanks to his corsairs, had provided a huge payment to Constantinople. Yusuf had no problems meeting his obligations to the sultan for the first four years of his reign. In 1801, however, the problems with America began. Now, the Yankees had his principal city under blockade, preventing his corsairs from taking prizes, depriving him of one of his main sources of income. He began levying higher taxes on his people, increasing the possibility already unhappy Arab tribes might revolt. As hunger set in, he knew he had to find a way both to inspire and placate his people. Standing up to the American bombardment gave him the opportunity he needed. Karamanli sent messages to Morocco, Algiers, and Tunis reminding them of their own problems with the United States, calling the Americans' lateness in making its treaty-required payments not a mistake but an insult. He pointed out his own resistance to the Yankees and reminded his fellow North African rulers of their mutual bonds of religion and history and asked for their help in his war. Algiers and Morocco responded by increasing their overland shipments of wheat, barley, and oil, while Tunis responded politically.[9]

For the moment Yusuf was safe on his throne, but had begun to have doubts about how long his rule might last. Thanks to the French, he had information that a new American squadron that had just arrived off his capital carried more than cannon. On board one of the ships was a blustering, loud American who planned to yank Yusuf's throne from under him, using Hamet as the main weapon.[10]

William Eaton was on the sidelines of his nation's first overseas war, and he hated every moment he was not involved in the action. After he arrived in Tunis and concluded the peace treaty with the bey, Eaton did his best to settle into his diplomatic post. It wasn't easy for the former Army captain to navigate the diplomatic labyrinth in which he found himself. He quickly learned that paying tribute to Tunis and the other Barbary States made the United States subject to any and every whim of the Barbary princes, who viewed those who paid tribute as little better than slaves. It was a situation that made Eaton apoplectic. "Can avarice and the grave be satisfied? Give! Give! is the eternal cry! Every breeze will waft it to America; and as often as it is not responded with accord will be brandished over our heads the ottagan [whim] of a contemptible pirate!"[11]

Complicating Eaton's position was the fact the United States was always late in its payments to both Algiers and Tunis. The *Hero* finally arrived with the promised regalia and stores in 1800, but America was still three years in arrears to the bey. Eaton did his best to refuse new or excessive exactions. On June 18, 1801, he wrote to the new secretary of state, John Marshall, of a massive fire at the bey's palace that destroyed "50,000 stand of arms." The bey demanded the United States send him ten thousand new muskets, a demand Eaton dismissed out of hand. This sparked a heated argument between Eaton and one of the bey's ministers. The minister said the bey demanded the weapons as part of a late-payment fee, to which Eaton retorted the United States had just made two massive payments with a third was on its way across the Atlantic, which would bring his nation current. The minister replied that whether America was current on its payments was irrelevant.

"Your contributions, as you think proper to call them," said the minister, "will never have an end. If this be the language you think of holding at this court, you may prepare yourself to leave the country, and that very soon." Eaton fired back, "If change of style, on my part . . . be the condition of residence here, I will leave the Bey's kingdom to-morrow morning." As Eaton left the meeting, he heard the minister vow, "By God, that man is mad! But we shall bring him to terms; never fear." The United States never sent the weapons, but the minister's threat hung over Eaton's head. Eaton naively ignored it.[12]

Eaton's post in Tunis gave him the perfect vantage point from which to watch developments in Tripoli as well as in Europe. Napoleon's success on the Continent, he believed, made America even more vulnerable to ever-increasing tribute demands from the Barbary States as former tributary nations fell under French control. He argued meeting those demands would make it impossible for the United States either to stop the payments or fight the pirates and said it was well past the time when his country should answer calls for tribute with force of arms. "We must either bribe their avarice or chastise their audacity," he wrote. "Giving only increases their avidity for more. We have the only alternative then to yield unconditional accord to their claims, or straighten ourselves up a little, and look them out of countenance."[13]

As for Tripoli and its demands, Eaton said he agreed with Cathcart that the United States should reject the latest set of demands from Karamanli, a position President Jefferson supported. When Karamanli told Cathcart it would take $225,000 just to strike a peace and $20,000 annually to maintain it, Jefferson was finally able to follow his own advice and use force to compel a "piratical state" to sign a peace treaty without tribute, gifts, or any other type of payment. It was a stance with which Eaton agreed wholeheartedly. Throughout 1801 he wrote letter after letter calling for an armed response to every Barbary demand, not just those of Tripoli. Still, Eaton was sure, Tripoli was the logical place to begin. To Secretary of State

Marshall he opined, "It is devoutly to be hoped that the United State may have the honor (very easily obtained) of setting the first example, among the tributaries, of chastising the insolence of their lords. If Tripoli persist, does not Tripoli invite the experiment; and is not the occasion a good one? Show him two or three of our strongest, best built frigates. Set life and death before him. Leave to him the choice. If he prefer the latter, give it him. There is nothing impracticable in the thing."[14]

His year in Tunis fostered in Eaton a belief the Barbary military was simply no match for that of the United States. He was steadfast in his opinion that even America's small navy could frighten, or if necessary beat, Tripoli and the other Barbary States into submission in relatively short order. "Is there a citizen in America who would not rather contribute something extraordinary for an effectual resistance to the pretentions of these Beys, than by an elusive calculation of gaining by withholding those contributions, take the yoke of a Barbary pirate?"[15] Eaton dismissed the possibility of defeat at the hands of a Barbary power, expressing contempt for the soldiers and sailors whom America would meet in combat. "The Turks are a contemptible military, and at sea, lubbers. The ignorance, superstitious tradition and civil and religious tyranny, which depress the human mind here, exclude improvement of every kind; consequently the same habits, customs and manners, which were observed in the east three thousand years ago, are still prevalent here. Everything is done to the greatest possible disadvantage."[16]

The inability of first Dale and then Morris to bring Bashaw Yusuf Karamanli to terms was an embarrassment, not only for Eaton but for the United States. Eaton, as the American consul in Tunis, heard the snickers of the European consuls in the city as well as from around the Mediterranean. It was intolerable to the patriotic Eaton, who viewed the lackadaisical blockade of Tripoli as a farce. "I never thought to find a corner of this slanderous world where baseness and American were wedded. But here we are the byword of derision; quoted as precedents of baseness, even by Danes!" he thundered in his journal.[17] Publicly, Eaton remained outspoken as ever, writing James Madison, who became secretary of state in May

1801, "Our operations of the last and present year produce nothing in effect but addi-tional enemies and national contempt. If the same system of operations continue, so will the same consequences!"[18]

The lack of action on the part of the first two squadrons put Eaton in a difficult position. He resolutely refused any new demands of the bey for more "presents," naval stores, weapons, or ships. He pointed out to him that the United States now had an armed force in the Mediterranean and would meet any warlike moves on the part of Tunis in kind. His words, however, carried little weight, because Dale and then, especially, Morris had failed to act aggressively enough to persuade any of the Barbary regencies that the United States was capable of fighting. "The obstinate posture and affected indifference to menace, which have hitherto been my talisman in lieu of solid argument here, no longer avail," he told Madison. "The Minister puffs a whistle in my face, and says, 'We see how you carry on the war with Tripoli!' I have never ceased to give the alarm in due season: to suggest such measures as seemed to me indispensable to parry serious mischief; and to point out what I believed would be the consequence of neglecting that advice. I have now the melancholy reflection that my apprehensions have been but too well founded, and my predictions but too accurate."[19]

The situation with the bey continued to deteriorate, at least for Eaton. Hamouda, in August 1802, demanded the United States give him a thirty-six-gun frigate to make up for continued late payments. Eaton refused. The bey demanded Eaton write to President Jefferson to ask for the frigate. Eaton refused. The bey demanded Eaton arrange safe conduct for his ships carrying wheat, barley, oil, and other supplies to Tripoli. Again, Eaton refused. By the fall, the American consul was at his wits' end. On October 22, 1802, Eaton wrote Madison in frustration, "The indignities I have suffered at this court latterly, are insupportable. . . . I cannot maintain the position I have taken here, a position which has hitherto received the approbation of every distinguished officer of the general government with whom I have had the honor to correspond. And, suffer me to add, if further concessions are to be made here, I desire I may not be the medium through whom they shall be presented."[20]

When he wasn't railing against the ineptness of his own countrymen in prosecuting the war against Tripoli, Eaton was embroiling himself in the politics of the region. On July 4, 1800, Tunis declared war on Denmark for that country's failure to meet its tribute obligations. The Tunisians promptly captured seven Danish vessels, selling the cargoes and holding the sailors for ransom. The Danes had asked Eaton to act as chargé d'affaires for them while their own consul was in Leghorn (Livorno), Italy. Eaton agreed, and when the captains of the Danish ships approached him to purchase their vessels, using a credit in Tunis the Danes promised to secure in Leghorn, Eaton again agreed.[21] The bey at first balked, as one of his sources of income came from the sale of captured ships. Eaton submitted a bid, which the bey rejected. The shadowy Frenchman Famin had submitted his own bid, which was higher, and Eaton, believing the matter closed, left Tunis to spend the weekend at Bizerte. He had barely arrived at the vacation spot when a message arrived saying the bey had accepted Eaton's bid. "I returned immediately—finished the bargain—and fixed on the mode of payment," Eaton told Pickering.[22] Eaton now owned seven Danish merchant ships but had no idea what to do with them. One of the vessels, the brig *Pearle*, Eaton intended to keep: "She is an excellent vessel of about 200 tons—and, I believe, worth more money than I am to give for the whole."[23] Eaton spent ten thousand dollars to purchase the Danish ships, a cost he passed on to the U.S. government, believing the State Department would approve.[24] He returned the ships to their Danish owners in September 1801, receiving the thanks of the Danish king for his services, but the debt would return to haunt him.

Eaton found another project in Tunis in which he immersed himself, one that would have lasting repercussions. While fretting over his debt, he met a forty-something supposed prince lamenting the loss of his kingdom and throne. The prince was Hamet Karamanli.

For nearly five years Hamet Karamanli had vacillated between working for and against his brother Yusuf. After Yusuf ousted him from the throne in his bloodless coup in 1795, Hamet dutifully went to Benghazi, where he was, on paper at least, to rule the eastern part of Tripolitania. How long he stayed there is something of mystery. Some accounts have Hamet going to Tunis in 1799, others have him splitting time between Benghazi and Malta, while still others make him out to be a wandering vagabond.[25] Whatever he did for the first five years of his exile, by 1800 he was in Tunis, which was becoming the favorite spot for deposed Karamanlis to find sympathy and succor. Bey Hamouda tolerated Hamet's presence and apparently even gave him a stipend, seeing him as a potential check to his, Hamet's, brother should Yusuf begin to covet Tunisian territory.[26]

Hamet must have presented a pitiable sight. He was poor, pined for his family, and feared for their safety.[27] His prospects looked dim until 1801, when U.S. Consul James Leander Cathcart took notice of him. As Yusuf dug in his heels and refused to bend in his demands, Cathcart mentioned the former bashaw to Eaton, suggesting Hamet "might be used as an instrument in the hands of the United States, to chastise the temerity of the usurper, reestablish himself, and effect a cheap, honorable, and permanent peace to our country."[28] It was an option Eaton could not ignore.

Although Hamet arrived in Tunis broke and friendless. Cathcart claimed "the subjects of [Tripolitania] were very much attached" to Hamet;[29] a rather odd assertion, since it was the people who demanded Yusuf dethrone his brother in 1795. However, since that time, and especially since the start of the American blockade, Yusuf had grown more and more tyrannical. The American blockade failed to encompass the whole of his country and ships could still enter and leave Derne as they pleased, but the Yankees had his main fleet bottled up. His corsairs idling in port, his demands for taxes from his subjects grew ever more strident. Cathcart made a point to Eaton of the unrest Yusuf's policies were causing among many Arab tribes, especially those in the eastern and southern regions, information Eaton dutifully reported to James Madison. Hamet, Eaton believed, offered just the weapon the United States needed to defeat Tripoli. "The idea of dethroning our enemy, and placing a rightful Sovereign in his seat, makes a deeper impression on account of the lasting peace it will produce with that Regency, and the lesson of caution it will teach the other Barbary States," he told Madison. "These are objects which, to me seem so clearly in our power that they ought to command exertions."[30]

Hamet and Tripoli came to dominate Eaton's thoughts. He seemingly spent as much time planning for how he could support—and use—Hamet as he did in discharging his duties as consul. Suggesting tactics to fight Tripoli was nothing new for Eaton. Soon after the war broke out, Eaton concocted a scheme to kidnap Murad Rais, a renegade Scot who commanded Yusuf's fleet: "This would be an event so fatal to the Bashaw of Tripoli that it would at once put an end to the war." He said Dale could use Rais, who real name was Peter Lisle, as bait to lure Yusuf himself on board a ship, where the bluejackets could take him into custody.[31] Working with Hamet was different, however, as Eaton could actually sit down with the "rightful bashaw," as he called Hamet, and hammer out concrete plans. The two men met and planned secretly throughout 1801. Eaton's main task was to bolster Hamet's spirits, which waned as the year pressed on. Hamet's biggest complaint was Eaton's inability to answer the basic question of when would the Americans stop talking and start acting. Hamet needed money, weapons, and above all, confidence that America would support him. For Eaton, it was yet another situation that required a deft touch. He had no authority to enter into a compact with Hamet, little money, and no instructions from the State Department on how to proceed. "The friendly bashaw grew despondent," Eaton reported. "He had received satisfactory assurance that his subjects would revolt to receive him if he should be so offered to them, and I renewed to him some encouragements."[32]

The exertions took a toll on the usually energetic New Englander, and by the beginning of 1802 his health was starting to fail. A doctor suggested Eaton take a sea voyage, and the consul embarked on the *George Washington*, then in Tunis waiting to escort yet another tribute ship, for Leghorn. His sojourn lasted barely six weeks. Soon after arriving, Eaton received word the secret of his negotiations with Hamet was out. Yusuf apparently knew all about his brother's actions, and the cagey bashaw had decided the best way to deal with Hamet was to renew his offer to let Hamet rule Derne. Eaton immediately tried to return to Tunis, but there were no ships headed for the port. Instead, he decided to take his own ship, the brig *Pearle*—the lone Danish vessel he had kept of the seven he had ransomed. Eaton had renamed her the *Gloria* and armed her with fourteen twelve-pounder and six-pounder cannon. He hired American merchant captain Joseph Bounds to command the vessel, found thirty-seven "mostly American" sailors to man her, and set off for Tunis.[33] Upon his return, he found Hamet ready to leave in the company of forty "bodyguards" Yusuf had sent to "protect" him. Eaton advanced Hamet two thousand dollars and assured him of American aid. Hamet agreed to continue to work with Eaton, but he still had to leave Tunis.

Intrigue was never a forte of blunt, plain-spoken William Eaton, and just as he had found himself in a scandal as an Army officer in Georgia, he now found himself embroiled in Tunis. Bey Hamouda, most likely at the instigation of Yusuf Karamanli, had ordered Hamet to leave Tunis. Eaton frantically tried to convince Hamet to wait for an American warship to come to Tunis that would take him not to Derne but Leghorn or Naples. He also attempted to influence the bey by offering a bribe to Hamouda's favorite minister (and alleged gay lover), the Sapitapa. Eaton promised the Sapitapa ten thousand dollars if—and only if—he could persuade Hamouda to rescind his order to Hamet and restart the aid to the "rightful bashaw." The Sapitapa agreed, apparently hearing only "ten thousand dollars," nothing else. Next, Eaton sent the *Gloria* in search of Captain Daniel McNeill and the frigate *Boston*, which was supposed to be somewhere around Malta. Eaton desperately needed the approval of and aid from the U.S. Navy if his venture with Hamet was to work. Eaton, however, went a step farther and on his own accord placed the *Gloria* in U.S. service, making her a warship of the Navy, and sent her to report to McNeill for orders.[34] Bounds caught up with McNeill, who approved of using the *Gloria* as a messenger ship but little else. McNeill, who had a reputation for ignoring orders and acting independently, evidently saw the Hamet project as well beyond his purview and, while endorsing the idea, did not endorse the plan. Instead, he left messages for Richard Morris, who was on his way from the States to take command of the American squadron, asking him to make the decision about Hamet. The "rightful bashaw" left Tunis on March 23, 1802, and went to Malta.[35]

Eaton continued to plan as though the government in Washington and the Navy had endorsed his idea of using Hamet to unseat Yusuf. Those preparations took a nasty blow on May 6, 1802, when Captain Alexander Murray, commanding the frigate *Constellation,* fell in with the *Gloria* at Gibraltar. Murray was at that moment the senior American captain in the Mediterranean. He took one look at Eaton's dispatches and rejected the idea of helping Hamet.[36] In addition, Murray dismissed Bounds and the *Gloria* from government service, a move that would prevent Eaton from recouping any expense connected with the ship.

Murray's decision incensed Eaton. "Government may as well send out Quaker meeting-houses to float about this sea as frigates with Murray in command," he heatedly wrote to Madison. "The friendly salutes he may receive and return at Gibraltar produce nothing at Tripoli."[37] What made Eaton especially angry was that Morris and his squadron, which were supposedly blockading Tripoli Harbor, in fact were no-shows. The blockade had become, in Eaton's view, a complete joke. Morris had even allowed the Tripolitans to capture an American prize, the brig *Franklin,* an event that embarrassed Eaton and greatly amused the Barbary leaders.[38]

"I am aware that the expression found in my communication on the subject, *we are abandoned by our ships of war,* may have touched the feelings of gentlemen commanding them. I am not in fault for that. It is my duty, at least I consider it so, to report facts as they present themselves to me," he thundered in a letter to Madison. The frigate *Essex,* then under Bainbridge's command, had yet to take up station off Tripoli, Eaton claimed, while the *Constellation* had "shown herself off Tripoli just once and then for just six hours."[39] Eaton blamed two of Dale's commanders, Samuel Barron and Bainbridge, for "influencing" Murray despite having no information about the Hamet project. He told Madison that not only was the overthrow of Yusuf viable but the secretary of state should ignore the opinion of officers who, in Eaton's eyes, could not even close down one port. "This is a singularly economical mode of carrying on the war; and it is not extraordinary if gentlemen feelingly attached to it should take offense at a vigilance which should go to put an end to it."[40]

As he poured his energy into supporting Hamet, Eaton continued to find trouble in Tunis, involving himself in the case of a Sardinian family being held hostage there. Hamouda's corsairs had raided the island and carried off all of the residents of the town of San Pietro, including the Porcillo family, after the King of Sardinia failed to make his tribute payments. The Tunisians threatened to send all 928 people to the slave markets of Algiers unless the Sardinians made their tribute payment and paid ransom on each captive.[41]

A year went by before any money came from Sardinia, not nearly enough to ransom the inhabitants of San Pietro, who were now slaves of the leading families of Tunis. Some of the families sought help anywhere they could. When the French and British consuls refused to aid them, the Porcillos ended up at Eaton's door, begging the New Englander to save them from Barbary slavery. The Tunisians had set the ransom for the youngest of the Porcillo children, a seventeen-year-old beauty named Anna, at five thousand dollars; Eaton, receiving the weeping, terrified family on his doorstep guaranteed a loan to Anna's father for the ransom. Should the elder Porcillo not pay within six months, Eaton would be responsible for the debt. Despite numerous letters to Signore Porcillo, it became apparent the Sardinian would never be able to raise the money. The bey's minister, the Sapitapa, then called in the debt on Eaton. To raise that money, Eaton tried his hand at some speculative shipping schemes, but none of them made him a profit.[42]

The American consul was also responsible for costs involving the *Anna Maria*. A New York–based brig under the command of George Coffin, the *Anna Maria* arrived in Tunis in early 1801 with a shipment of naval stores for the bey. After he received the cargo, the bey seized the ship and demanded it pick up a shipment of oil and carry it to Marseilles, France. Eaton at first refused to issue a passport for the vessel, demanding Hamouda pay to use the brig, in accordance with the two nations' treaty. Hamouda at first refused but then agreed.[43] By then, however, a firman had arrived from Constantinople ordering Hamouda to rescind his peace treaty with France, which was still at war with the Ottoman Empire. Hamouda did so, which canceled his oil sale. This, in turn released the *Anna Maria*, or so Eaton thought, but Hamouda threatened to seize the ship outright and enslave the crew unless Eaton made good on the lost revenue from the abortive oil sale. Eaton at first refused, but the lack of any American war-ships near Tunis (or Tripoli, of which Hamouda constantly reminded Eaton) placed him in an essentially impossible position. He agreed to compen-sate the bey for the cargo, once more expecting the U.S. government to reimburse him.[44]

Eaton's situation in Tunis deteriorated throughout 1802. His refusal to grant passports for Tunisian vessels trying to enter Tripoli or accede to new demands for ships, arms, or "presents" had created bitterness between Hamouda and himself. The bey wanted to get rid of Eaton and replace him with someone more amenable to Tunisian demands. He turned to the Sapitapa to find a way to force Eaton to leave. Eaton's debts gave the Sapitapa the perfect opportunity to seek revenge on the American consul.

Eaton had a backlog of correspondence, including all of his accounts, sitting on his desk when he picked up quill and paper to write James Madi-son in early 1803. The reason the secretary of state had yet to receive any news from Tunis, Eaton explained, was "no ship of that squadron showed itself here for seven or eight months previously to leaving this sea." Inability to communicate with Washington had kept Eaton's creditors at bay, but when Commodore Richard Morris sent word at the end of February 1803 that he planned to come to Tunis, just to make sure the bey had no warlike intentions, the Sapitapa decided to act. Morris arrived on March 10, 1803, and after a brief meeting with Eaton, at which, the consul later claimed, he told Morris about his finances, the Sapitapa and Eaton's Tunisian credi-tor cornered Morris and demanded $22,000 to cover Eaton's debts—ten thousand dollars for the bribe Eaton offered the Sapitapa, five thousand dollars for the Porcillo girl, and seven thousand for the cargo of the *Anna Maria*.[45]

Eaton exploded, calling the Sapitapa a thief and a liar right to his face. He then turned on the bey and accused him of only wanting war with the United States. The outbursts shocked everyone. The Sapitapa announced that he would not allow Morris to leave Tunis until the commodore made good on Eaton's debt, which he claimed Eaton had promised the commodore would do. Eaton denied ever making such a promise, but Morris cut him off before the argument could begin anew. Eaton stalked off, leaving the bey and Morris alone for a moment. The bey asked the commodore to remove Eaton as consul, which Morris agreed to do. He also agreed to pay the $22,000 the Sapitapa claimed Eaton owed.

The entire episode left Morris in a rage. "I cannot forbear (in justice to myself, and the insult offered to my country) to attribute the cause to the duplicity of Mr. Eaton," he said in his official report. "Had he intimated to me his embarrassments, previous to my going on shore, and particularly, that he had bound the United States by placing their seal to the obligation given, I should not have put myself in the power of the Bey of Tunis."[46] Morris selected George Davis to act as chargé d'affairs for the United States until Washington could assign a new consul. He left Eaton to pack his things and prepare to leave Tunis, making sure everyone knew that "as a security for the money paid by me, I insisted on Mr. Eaton's assigning all his real and personal estate to the government."[47] Eaton boarded the frigate *Chesapeake* on March 10, 1803, his career and reputation in tatters. It might have destroyed a weaker man, but William Eaton was anything but weak.

6

GATHERING STORM

THE VOYAGE from Hampton Roads to Tripoli might have been the worst trip in the career of Captain Samuel Barron. The new commander of the U.S. Mediterranean squadron had qualms about his flagship, the forty-four-gun frigate *President;* concerns about at least one aspect of his mission; and most of all, worries about his health. Barron was not well, and the nearly two-month voyage from Hampton Roads to Tripoli had done little to ease the liver ailment from which he suffered. He could not walk well, could not sit without pain, and spent more and more time bedridden in his cabin.[1] The problems with the *President,* meanwhile, were many, Barron reported. The foremast was rotten and required replacing, the rigging was loose, and the ship needed a complete refit after sustaining damage in a gale.[2]

The weather on the voyage to the Mediterranean had done nothing to help. After a relatively quick dash across the Atlantic, the squadron ran into headwinds and squalls that made the final leg of the journey seem like an eternity.[3] It took the *President* twenty-two days to sail from Gibraltar to Tripoli, a passage that usually took about half that time. Barron's health steadily declined, and by the time he linked up with Preble off Tripoli, the commodore wanted not only the *President* to undergo repairs but to get himself on dry land, where he thought he could recover his health. "His physician, Doc. Cutbush, has been under serious apprehensions of alarm for him," William Eaton reported, "and, it seems, is not yet wholly relieved from them. It appears to me very improbable that he will be able to keep the sea this winter."[4] It must have a great disappointment to the thirty-nine-year-old Barron.

Samuel Barron was born on September 25, 1765, the oldest son of James Barron, a successful sea captain. His brother, James, who was now also a captain in the Navy and commanded the *Essex,* was born three years later. Samuel grew up in Hampton, Virginia, where his family owned a sprawling estate. When the Revolutionary War began, the state named his father commodore of the Virginia navy, one of the largest state navies to fight in the war. The Virginia navy was mostly a self-defense force, although several of the state's larger ships made transatlantic trips. Samuel spent the first years of the war studying at the College of William & Mary, in Williamsburg, Virginia. In 1780 his father secured him an appointment as a midshipman on the Virginia state cruiser *Dragon.* He served through the end of the war and then entered merchant service, spending fifteen years as a commercial mariner before applying for a commission in the fledgling U.S. Navy. The Quasi-War with France was then heating up, and the Navy was commissioning ships at a dizzying rate. President John Adams appointed Barron as a captain, due to his experience in the Revolutionary War.[5]

Barron first commanded the eighteen-gun sloop *Richmond,* patrolling the area around the Caribbean island of Guadeloupe as part of a squadron under Thomas Truxtun in 1799. He next commanded the twenty-two-gun sloop *Baltimore,* again under Truxtun. He took command of the *Constellation* in 1801 before transferring to the *Philadelphia,* part of Richard Dale's squadron in the Mediterranean. On his return, Barron became part of President Thomas Jefferson's project to build a gunboat fleet. He helped draw up designs for the small vessels and oversaw the construction of at least one gunboat at the Gosport Navy Yard in Norfolk before Jefferson put him in command of the most recent squadron to face Yusuf Karamanli. When his liver ailment began is unknown, but it is clear that by the time he reached Tripoli on September 10, 1804, his health was failing.

Doctor Jonathan Cowdery had a unique vantage point from which to observe Bashaw Yusuf Karamanli. Cowdery, who had been the surgeon on the now-destroyed frigate *Philadelphia*, had upon his capture become an unofficial doctor to Karamanli's family. Throughout Preble's campaign, Cowdery watched as the bashaw alternated between rage, fear, and depression as the American commodore battered Yusuf almost to his knees. In the wake of the failed mission of the fireship *Intrepid*, Yusuf declared an *eid*, or feast day, throughout the city. Everyone but the American captives had the day off from labor, although the famine that gripped Tripoli showed little sign of abating.[6]

Yusuf often consulted his marabout, who had accompanied him during his successful campaign against Ali Borgul in 1795. "It was said by the Turks that he foretold the stranding and capture of the *Philadelphia* and that he got offended with the bashaw and caused and foretold her being burnt," Cowdery said.[7] As Preble's campaign reached a crescendo, Yusuf again visited the holy man and invited Cowdery to go with him. The bashaw rode to the marabout's camp with his retainers but without his regalia of state—he wore no jewels and had on simple clothing. After Yusuf arrived, the marabout prepared for the ceremony: "For a length of time, in an act of devotion, turned round with such velocity that his features were not discernible, and continued to do so till he sunk on the ground through fatigue. At other times, he sang and played on the tambourine extremely well."[8] Sanctified, the marabout sat on the ground and began his prophecies. "He now said that the commodore's ship, the *Constitution*, would never return to America; that she would either be blown up, or run on shore; and that the Bashaw would have success in his warfare with America."[9]

It must have seemed to Yusuf that the marabout was correct about the *Constitution* when, on September 12, he saw a new pennant floating over the American squadron. Samuel Barron had officially taken command, and Preble had lowered his flag. He also could see that the U.S. squadron was smaller, although he had no information on which ships still patrolled off his city. The bashaw ordered the captives from the *Philadelphia* to erect new fortifications along the shoreline in front of the city walls. It was an odd location for the batteries. Yusuf had erected similar batteries in

August, but their exposed position left them vulnerable to American gunners. Karamanli's artillerymen too found the soft ground the worst possible for the batteries: "On being fired two or three times, they recoiled into the sand so deep that they could not be worked, and were abandoned."[10]

The bashaw undoubtedly knew about the drawback to the beach batteries. The construction effort was simply Yusuf's way of striking back at the only Americans he could hurt, surmised Marine Corps Private William Ray, one of the prisoners working on the forts. "We were taken out at intervals, to carry powder to the different forts, and treated worse than can be represented by words," Ray said. "They would place a barrel of powder on a man's back, and make him run every step, without resting, from the castle to the batteries, three quarters of a mile, with a driver behind him, dealing blows at every breath, amidst the pelting of stones from the soldiery, and every insult and indignity that could be offered or endured."[11]

Both Cowdery and Ray reported that random beatings, starvation, and daylong strenuous labor had become the routine for the men of the *Philadelphia*. "Our men suffer for the want of provisions. The bashaw does not allow them victuals or cash," Cowdery wrote. "They get but a small allowance of bread and that on the credit of their country. They are beat unmercifully and compelled to work hard every day. . . . [T]he bashaw [gave] orders . . . to treat the American prisoners with the utmost cruelty, in order to induce the United States the sooner to make peace. He was impatient for the money."[12]

The stress of fighting the Americans, quelling rebellions in the interior of his country, waging the battle against his brother Hamet, a struggle that had seesawed for nearly six months, and most of all feeding his people took a toll on the bashaw. The blockade was especially onerous, as it cut off his supplies of grain from Tunis and Egypt. Famine was quickly becoming a part of daily life, and Yusuf knew that historically, hungry people often rebelled. It all became too much. On November 9, 1804, Yusuf collapsed in his chamber, suffering from a seizure. His ministers called Cowdery to his side. "His people thought he was possessed by the devil," the doctor reported. "They performed many ceremonies to cast him out, which they said succeeded. The Turks said they saw many ghosts the night before and that a marabout drove the devil out of the Bashaw."[13]

Yusuf recovered from the seizure and continued to rule with an iron hand, no doubt finding new inspiration in the fact his nemesis, Edward Preble, was gone. "He [Preble] left a lasting impression on the bashaw— and all the barbarians of Tripoli—of American bravery," Ray wrote, repeating the whisperings of Tripolitan guards who watched the *Philadelphia* crew. "That a single frigate should dare venture under the batteries, in the manner that Preble did, they imputed to madness. . . . He was considered as a prodigy of valor and dreaded as the minister of destruction."[14] Preble's departure left Karamanli wondering what the new American commander would attempt. He already knew of talk that the Yankees might back Hamet in a new revolt, but as yet he had no solid information on whether the Americans and his brother were in contact, or even on his brother's exact whereabouts. The bashaw settled in to wait.

Commodore Edward Preble stood on the deck of the frigate *Constitution* on September 10, 1804, and ordered his sailors to lower the broad, blue pennant that had announced his status as the commander of the Mediterranean squadron. Although his men would forever refer to him as "commodore," Preble was again a captain in the Navy. The arrival of Commodore Samuel Barron with the frigates *President, Congress, Essex,* and *Constellation* gave the Americans for a brief time overwhelming firepower off Tripoli. Preble, however, apparently never thought of asking Barron to launch another assault on the city. Three days before Barron arrived, on September 7, Preble ordered the *John Adams, Enterprise, Syren,* and *Nautilus* to escort the borrowed Neapolitan gun- and mortar boats back to Sicily. The change of command ceremony was brief and without fanfare. Nathaniel Haraden noted in his ship's log, "4 p.m.—Commodore Preble hauled down his pennant and awaited Commodore Barron." That was it. After a year in command, a year in which he had groomed a generation of naval officers for command and did more to gain respect for the U.S. Navy than any predecessor, Edward Preble was headed home.

In May, when President Jefferson issued orders to replace Preble, he had no idea what the commodore had already accomplished or what he would accomplish in the coming summer months. Barron knew about Preble's accomplishments, however, and lamented the loss of Preble's aggressive nature and knowledge of their enemy. Jefferson and Secretary Smith gave Barron permission to try to convince Preble to remain in the Mediterranean, but Preble had already made up his mind to leave. The moment Barron arrived, Preble presented the new commodore with a letter: "I am honored with a letter from the Secretary of the Navy dated the 22d May, notifying me that you have been sent into these seas to supersede me in the command of the U.S. Squadron—I have therefore to request your permission to return to the United States in such ship as you may think proper to allow me for that purpose."

There was another reason why Preble had no intention of remaining on station—John Rodgers. The two had butted heads in October 1803, when Preble first arrived in the Mediterranean. Rodgers had taken command of the second squadron when Jefferson recalled Morris. Rodgers hoisted his own commodore's pennant and took it as an insult when Preble arrived flying his pennant. Rodgers was senior to Preble on the captain's list and believed that as long as he was in the Mediterranean he should have overall command. Preble was just as adamant that his orders gave *him* command of both squadrons. Rodgers at first refused to serve under Preble and appeared on the verge of challenging him to a duel when Preble suggested the two commodores "cooperate for the good of the service." Rodgers, who was due to return to the United States, agreed to accompany Preble to Algiers and Morocco in a show of force.

Now, Rodgers was again the second-ranking captain in the squadron, and if Preble stayed he would have no choice but to serve under the Marylander. "He shall never command me while I command myself," Preble had once vowed, and he kept to his word.[15] "Commodore Barron's arrival to supersede me in command of the fleet has determined me to return," Preble wrote his wife, Mary, "so it is not expected by our government that I shall serve on any station again excepting as commander in chief or with a separate squadron, having served so long a time in that capacity, and as they acknowledge, with reputation to myself and honor to my country."[16]

Before he left, though, Preble still had tasks to finish. First was the reassignment of many of the junior officers he had put in command of his flotilla of gunboats and mortar boats. Preble had stripped his larger ships of crewmen and officers to man the small boats, and now many of these officers held higher, though in some cases temporary, ranks. Several midshipmen, including Thomas Macdonough, Ralph Izard, and Charles Morris were acting lieutenants, while John Dent, James Lawrence, and John Smith were now lieutenants commandant. Preble's (and the squadron's) favorite officer, Stephen Decatur Jr., had jumped from lieutenant to full captain and as such rated a larger ship than the schooner *Enterprise,* which he had commanded through much of the 1803–4 campaign. Preble had to find appropriate slots for all of these officers. He also had numerous accounts to settle in Naples, Malta, and Syracuse and knew he should pay his respects to King Ferdinand of Naples and the king's British-born prime minister Sir John Acton to thank both for the loan of the gunboats. Further, his flagship, *Constitution,* was in dire need of an over-haul. He gave Barron a list of suggested assignments for some officers and issued direct orders to others, including Dent, who had commanded the prize brig *Scourge* during the summer campaign and would now command the *Nautilus,* replacing the slain Richard Somers.[17] He put Decatur in command of the *Constitution* and ordered him to go to Malta for refit. Barron agreed with all of Preble's actions and put the *John Adams* at his predecessor's disposal. Preble boarded the *John Adams* on September 15 and began his last trip as an active sea commander.[18]

Before he made his final farewell, however, Preble managed to get in a last shot at his own nemesis, Yusuf Karamanli. On September 12, 1804, lookouts on the *Constitution* and *Argus* spotted three vessels headed for Tripoli. Preble immediately gave chase and, with the *President,* Barron's flagship, captured two of three ships. They were Greek-flagged brigs laden with wheat, barley, and oil, all destined for Tripoli. The *Argus* chased the third ship, but the blockade runner managed to evade and disappeared.[19]

The captures pleased Barron, who told Preble, "From the confession of the masters of those vessels, they had a previous knowledge of the port being in a state of blockade and there is little doubt, in my mind, that they are good prizes. I submit entirely to your discretion the arrangement respecting the prizes."[20]

⮞⮜

John Rodgers loathed Edward Preble as much as Preble loathed him. Gruff, blunt, and extremely sensitive when it came to rank, Rodgers was one of the most aggressive captains in the U.S. Navy and had a reputation for preferring action to diplomacy. Rodgers was born in 1773 in Havre de Grace, Maryland, where his father was a prosperous merchant, tavern owner, and ferry operator. The businesses allowed Rodgers' father to cultivate ties with such political heavyweights as George Washington, James Madison, and Samuel Smith.[21]

John was the third of eight children—he had three brothers and four sisters—and early showed a predilection for hunting and fishing. He attended the local school, where he learned mathematics, reading, and writing and read his first books about the sea. The tales fired the young boy's dreams, and when he was thirteen his father apprenticed him to Benjamin Folger, a noted Baltimore merchant captain. The young Rodgers shipped out in 1786 on the 450-ton *Maryland*, a merchant vessel of which Samuel Smith was part owner. He made trips to the West Indies, Spain, Hamburg, and England, serving so well and learning so quickly that Folger highly recommended him to others. Rodgers obtained his first captaincy when he was nineteen, thanks in large part to a growing bond with Samuel Smith, who made him captain of Smith's three-hundred-ton merchantman *Jane*. Rodgers spent almost five years as captain of the *Jane*, sailing to ports in France, Holland, Prussia, Spain, and the port of Hamburg. Advertisements in contemporary local papers show that Rodgers carried loads of salt from Cadiz, wine and porcelain from Bordeaux, and earthenware, gloves, and salt from Hamburg.[22]

Rodgers earned a reputation as a taut, self-disciplined captain, and he expected the same from his crew. He was not afraid to use the lash to keep discipline among his sailors, although he also instinctively led by example.

During a voyage to Europe, a storm pushed the *Jane* well off course into the North Sea, where the freezing spray quickly iced the running rigging of the ship. Rodgers ordered his men aloft to ease the sails and reduce the strain on the frozen lines. The sailors refused. "Indignant at their pusillanimity, their young captain stripped off his jacket and shirt; and wearing only his trousers and shoes, he himself went aloft, telling his crew he would show them what a man could do. Ashamed of their weakness, they soon followed him, and never afterwards showed a disposition to question his orders. The *Jane* arrived safely in port."[23]

Even as a twenty-three-year-old merchant captain, Rodgers displayed the sort of aggressive patriotism that would later mark him as a naval officer. During a trip to England in 1796, he came across the political campaign of British general Banastre Tarleton, who was running for Parliament. Tarleton had earned a vile reputation as a cavalry commander during the Revolutionary War, and hatred of him continued to run high in America. Rodgers stumbled into a Tarleton rally that featured a large banner showing the British general trampling an American flag. Enraged, Rodgers dashed into the middle of the crowd, knocked down the flag bearer, and ran off with the banner. He then confronted Tarleton, who denied any knowledge of the banner, agreed it was offensive, and promised to destroy it. As the *Federal Gazette and Baltimore Daily Advertiser* put it, "Rodgers was carried to his lodgings in triumph by a party of Tarleton's supporters, who in this manner showed their admiration of the spirit and patriotism exhibited by the young American."[24]

Rodgers spent eleven years in the merchant service. In 1798, thanks to the help of Samuel Smith, he secured an appointment in the new U.S. Navy and an assignment to the *Constellation*, then fitting out in Baltimore. Her commander, Thomas Truxtun, was a Revolutionary War veteran, a successful merchant captain, and, like Rodgers, a believer in rigid discipline and the protocols (and perquisites) of rank. Truxtun had helped draft the "Articles of War" that governed the Navy and imposed those rules almost immediately on his crew.

Truxtun was the third-most-senior captain in the Navy, ranking behind John Barry and Samuel Nicholson. Richard Dale was fourth on the list and Silas Talbot, fifth, which both thought was insulting as they had more military experience. Truxtun, however, had made it clear that any effort to drop him on the list would result in his resignation. Secretary of the Navy Benjamin Stoddert asked President John Adams to issue a ruling on the seniority dispute, but Adams avoided the subject throughout his presidency. While Truxtun's prickly attitude toward rank had no immediate impact on Rodgers, it appeared to influence the young lieutenant in later years.[25]

Rodgers reported to the *Constellation* as the second lieutenant, but the resignation of Simon Gross, the first lieutenant, opened that slot, and Truxtun made Rodgers his second in command. Only twenty-four at the time, Rodgers was the youngest first lieutenant (executive officer) in the new navy. Truxtun expected Rodgers, despite his youth, to "carry all orders into execution without hesitation or demur. Such example will act as a stimulus to officers of an inferior grade, as well as others, and introduce that sort of subordination, which can only insure a happy and well governed ship."[26] It was one of many lessons Truxtun imparted to Rodgers that shaped the Marylander's career.

The 36-gun *Constellation* put to sea on June 10, 1798. Truxtun spent several months convoying merchant ships from the Florida coast to Havana, returning to the United States on October 23, 1798 after escorting sixty merchantmen through the Caribbean. Although it was a relatively uneventful cruise, Rodgers performed his duties well enough that Truxtun recommended him for a captaincy.[27] The *Constellation* returned to sea on December 31 as part of a squadron comprising the *Baltimore*, *Norfolk*, *Virginia*, and *Retaliation*. The squadron was one of four that were leaving the United States to tackle the French in the undeclared "Quasi-War" of 1798–1800. The cruise marked the first time that Rodgers worked with Captains Samuel Barron, commanding the *Norfolk*, and William Bainbridge, who commanded the *Retaliation*. The squadron arrived on station on January 9, 1799. Truxtun detailed part of his flotilla to escort duty while he took the *Constellation* on patrol.[28]

On February 9, while the *Constellation* was cruising between Nevis and St. Kitts, lookouts spotted a ship five miles away. Truxtun came up on the wind and gave chase. The unknown ship then ran up a French flag and fired a gun to windward—"the signal for an enemy," Truxtun wrote.[29] She was the thirty-six-gun *Insurgente*. The two ships maneuvered for the windward gauge, but a squall sprang up that drove them toward one another. The crew of the *Constellation* responded to the sudden change in the weather more rapidly than French, furling sails before the heavy wind could carry away spars or masts. Their slower response cost the French their main topgallant mast and sail, which came crashing down to the deck. Truxtun brought the *Constellation* up on the leeward side of *Insurgente* and opened fire.[30]

The two ships traded broadsides that failed to damage either vessel. Rodgers was on the gun deck, commanding the first division of five cannon. "The Commodore ordered myself with the other lieutenants commanding divisions, to fire directly into the hull, as soon as we could bring our guns to bear, and to load with two round shot principally during the action," Rodgers later reported, and the American gunners quickly found their marks.[31] The French captain attempted to break contact, but Truxtun maintained his hold. He crossed the stern and bow of the *Insurgente* several times, raking the Frenchman, causing heavy casualties on the enemy's quarterdeck and gun deck. The *Constellation*'s gunners riddled the *Insurgente*'s sails, destroying the mizzenmast and spanker. The duel continued for an hour and fifteen minutes when the French suddenly gave up. "At the time she struck we lay directly athwart her stern, and should certainly have sent her to the infernal regions had we fired whilst in that position," Rodgers reported.[32]

Truxtun's victory was complete. The *Constellation* had four men wounded and just one killed, while the French had suffered twenty-nine dead and forty-one wounded.[33] Truxtun sent Rodgers to accept the French surrender. The young officer was almost giddy from the excitement of his first combat. "Although I would not have you think me bloody minded," he wrote to Secretary Stoddert, "yet I must confess the most gratifying sight my eyes ever beheld was seventy French pirates (you know I have just cause to call them such) wallowing in their gore. . . . Though I am not in the habit of boasting yet I candidly tell you I should feel happy with the same officers, and same men on going along side of the best 50-gun ship the all-conquering French Republic have—at any hour."[34]

Rodgers' action earned him a promotion to full captain on June 13, 1799, and command of the newly built sloop of war *Maryland,* then fitting out in Baltimore. Rodgers, at twenty-six, was the youngest officer ever promoted to full captain until Stephen Decatur Jr. earned his captaincy in 1804 at the age of twenty-five.[35] Rodgers set sail on September 13 for Surinam, where he was to operate as part of a new squadron under Captain Daniel McNeill. Rodgers' standing orders for the *Maryland* show a clear Truxtun influence, covering every aspect of life on the *Maryland,* from when the crew should wash and dry clothes to how often the ship would exercise the cannons.[36]

Rodgers spent a year on station, returning to Baltimore on September 23, 1800.[37] After his ship refitted over the winter of 1800–1801, Rodgers received orders to sail to France carrying an amended treaty ending the unofficial war. The *Maryland* arrived on May 5 in Le Havre, where Rodgers cooled his heels until July 10 while Napoleon essentially ignored the treaty and American commissioner John Dawson. On August 28 the *Maryland* returned to Baltimore, where Rodgers found orders to pay off his crew and sell the ship. With the Quasi-War over and a new president in office, the winds of policy had shifted for the Navy.

The American fleet had grown to more than thirty ships during the Quasi-War, but in the wake of the election of Thomas Jefferson and Democrat-Republicans to Congress, there was a rush to reduce the size of the force. Naval commanders feared Jefferson planned to completely scrap the Navy; John Adams, in a last-minute action, signed the Peace Establishment Act into law. Under the act the Navy would keep thirteen ships, seven of them in ordinary ("mothballs") at any time. The act also greatly reduced the number of officers, shrinking the captain's list from thirty-one to nine (later thirteen).[38] Rodgers at first was one of the captains retained, ranking eighth on the list, one place ahead of Edward Preble. His mentor, Thomas Truxtun, was fourth. However, the new administration decided to keep only captains with Revolutionary War experience, which further reduced the list. On October 22, 1801, Rodgers received a courte-ous but pointed note from the new secretary of the Navy, Robert Smith, telling him he was out of the service.[39] Due to a quirk in the law, Rodgers retained his seniority on the captain's list, so while Preble continued to serve, Rodgers held his spot ahead of him.

Rodgers returned to merchant service, jumping into the burgeoning trade with Santo Domingo, which was then under Haitian control. He purchased the schooner *Nelly*, loaded her with goods, and on December 14, 1801, set out for Cape François (modern-day Cap Haitien), arriving there fifteen days later. While selling his goods and taking on cargo from the island, Rodgers met a young, Dartmouth-educated diplomat, Tobias Lear. The two men took an instant liking to each other, forming a lifelong friendship.[40] That friendship faced an immediate test when in late 1801 Napoleon decided to reassert French authority over both Haiti and Santo Domingo, dispatching a large expeditionary force to put down the slave revolt that had sent the French scurrying in 1800.

The French force arrived off Cape François on February 2, 1802, and demanded the surrender of the native troops. Rodgers and Lear were both ashore at the time and, seeing the likelihood of a major battle, began evac-uating Americans to thirty-five U.S. merchant ships waiting in the har-bor. On February 4, the French entered the harbor. The Haitian defenders set fire to the town and began to loot and pillage. Rodgers remained on shore throughout the day and well into the night, helping people flee. At one point he fell into the hands of the rioters but managed to escape. According to Lear, he "displayed that dauntless spirit which he is known to possess" and "by his good management and intrepidity secured the lives of many whom he got off from the flames, and was the means of saving several houses."[41]

Rodgers' time in the merchant service did not last long. War with Tripoli had erupted in 1801, and after the lackluster performance of the first squadron dispatched to the Mediterranean, a second flotilla was be-ing fitted out to execute a more vigorous campaign. Jefferson first selected Truxtun for the job, but when the president refused the added expense of a "flag captain" for Truxtun's flagship, Truxtun promptly resigned. Next in line was Richard Morris, who was to command a squadron composed of the *Chesapeake*, *Constellation*, *New York*, *Adams*, *John Adams*, and the ever-present schooner *Enterprise*.[42] As Richard Dale, with the *President*, *Philadelphia*, and *Essex*, was still in the Mediterranean and others on the list were too ill to serve, the Navy needed captains. On August 25, 1802, Rodgers received a letter from Secretary Smith returning him to active duty and putting him in command of the *John Adams*.[43]

Within a year of arriving on station, Rodgers was in command of the squadron. Morris did little more than escort American merchantmen and made only a halfhearted effort to blockade Tripoli. Rodgers himself led one of the few attempts under Morris to engage the Tripolitans, and when Jefferson recalled that commodore, command of the flotilla fell to Rodgers. Slightly less than a year later, Rodgers was once more in the Mediterranean as the second-ranking captain in the new squadron under Commodore Samuel Barron. Rodgers was well aware of the fragile state of Barron's health. He also knew about, and disapproved of, the plan to use Hamet Karamanli. Rodgers had accompanied Morris to Tunis when the former commodore had to remove William Eaton from the city, and his opinion of Eaton had not improved since. His return to the Mediterranean meant, however, that Rodgers would again be able to work with Tobias Lear, who was now the consul general in Algiers, empowered to negotiate a deal with Tripoli should the opportunity arrive. It was, for John Rodgers, a chance to increase the glory he had already won.

∞ ∞

Life on Malta was not what Hamet Karamanli had thought it would be. The "rightful bashaw" of Tripoli, after the bey of Tunis expelled him from that city, arrived on the British-controlled island in March 1803. The Tunisian ruler had also expelled his main benefactor, now former U.S. consul, William Eaton, who had returned to America. Hamet was alone, except for his nephew Ali, the oldest son of his sister. Hamet's brother Yusuf had banished Ali from Tripoli when he discovered the boy was involved in a plot against him.

Hamet took the title of "rightful bashaw" seriously, because it was true. He knew he, not his brother, should be the ruler of Tripoli, but Yusuf's bloodless coup in 1795 had left Hamet with few options. Now on Malta, nearly penniless, with only his nephew and forty bodyguards his brother had sent to "protect" him, Hamet seriously considered accepting Yusuf's offer to become governor or Derne. Hamet missed his family, which remained "guests" in Tripoli Castle, and had assurances from his brother he would come to no harm. Eaton, however, was adamant that Hamet should decline the invitation: "Remember that your brother thirsts for your blood. I have learned from a certain source that his project of getting you to Derne was to murder you," Eaton wrote to Hamet. "You cannot be safe therefore, in any part of your Regency, unless you enter it in your true character of sovereign."[44]

Eaton's support emboldened Hamet. When he arrived on Malta he surprised many who claimed to know him, especially in the American squadron, where the general consensus was Hamet was too weak to support.[45] First, Hamet dismissed the forty men his brother sent. How he did so is unknown, but he was able either to bribe or bully them into leaving. He then decided to go to Derne after all, but in the manner in which Eaton suggested. He sent a letter directly to President Jefferson asking for "20 quintals of powder, and 16,000 dollars in cash to assist his operations," while assuring the president he could raise an army of 30,000.[46] The Americans had never expected this show of will, but now Hamet managed to win grudging support even from Morris, who promised he would "consider how far, he would meet their proposals" and convey Hamet's letter to America.[47]

Hamet settled in to wait, but he apparently did not wait long. On November 15, 1803, Hamet's agent on Malta, Richard Farquhar, re-sent Hamet's letter to Jefferson, although the amount of money requested had ballooned from $16,000 to $40,000. Farquhar told Jefferson that Hamet was already back in Tripoli and had taken up power in Derne, where he was leading an insurrection.[48] "The Arabs had revolted immediately on Hamet's arrival in the territory of Tripoli," reported Said Ahmed Gurgi, Hamet's private secretary, "and having arrived into the territory of Tripoli was joined with a multitude of Arabs, both foot and cavalry."[49]

Hamet spent at least four months in Derne leading his revolt. It was an up-and-down fight for the "rightful bashaw." Short of money, arms, and equipment, Hamet was never able to gain the advantage over his brother's forces. He sent several messages to the Americans asking for money and weapons but most of all for an extension of the blockade to the eastern provinces of Tripoli. Yusuf was able to bottle up Hamet in Derne, thanks to his control of the sea. The "usurper," as Eaton called him, dispatched a ten-gun schooner and twelve-gun xebec (a small three-masted trading ship, often lateen rigged) to Derne, preventing Hamet from communicating with Malta, where he had agents.[50] Despite the blockade, one of Eaton's own agents, Salvatore Bufutil, managed to get messages out from Malta that found a sympathetic audience in Commodore Edward Preble, who took command in the Mediterranean in October 1803.

The idea of cooperation with Hamet intrigued Preble, who saw the merits of spending money to support Hamet rather than making peace or ransom payments. "I wish earlier notice had been taken of this man and his views," he told Secretary Robert Smith. "In fact, I am astonished that the first or second squadron did not oblige the Bashaw of Tripoli to sign any treaty they pleased."[51] Preble was unable to support Hamet, because of his own short resources. However, he remained in favor of working with the elder Karamanli brother and urged his replacement, Barron, to support Hamet's revolt.[52]

Preble's support, however, did not translate into any material gain for Hamet. By the late fall Yusuf had gained the upper hand in the fighting around Derne and had Hamet on the run. According to Farquhar, Yusuf had made peace with at least one tribe that had supported Hamet and sent reinforcements to the east, "but has lost many of his troops." Hamet, Farquhar said, "finding his brother's troops arrive daily from Tripoli and no help from America, thought proper to leave Derne for the present" and took refuge in Alexandria, Egypt, then in anarchy following the French invasion.[53] Joseph Pulis, the U.S. consul on Malta, confirmed Farquhar's story but was slightly less sanguine about Hamet: "He has been in Alexandria in Egypt dreading the loss of his head as his brother the Bashaw of Tripoli had dispatched some troops by land to seize him."[54]

Although his erstwhile American backers remained skeptical about him, Hamet, even in exile in Egypt, remained optimistic about returning to Tripoli. On January 4, 1804, Bufutil wrote to Preble asking the commodore for direct intervention. Bufutil had a copy of a letter Commodore Morris had written him just before Morris left the Mediterranean asking American ship captains to lend what aid they could to Hamet if they thought it expedient. Bufutil included a copy of that letter in his plea to Preble: "In the name of Sidi Ahmet Karamanli, the first born of the Dominion of Tripoli and late Bashaw, I ask the loan of two thousand dollars on purpose to purchase some more articles of War and to collect some of his friends to go with me to bring him to Derne with your assistance then we will take Benghazi and Tripoli."[55]

Preble was never able to help Hamet, but he did not forget about the "rightful bashaw." When he held his final meeting with Samuel Barron on September 15, 1804, he would have even more support in arguing for Hamet's cause, in the person of the naval agent for the Barbary Regencies, William Eaton.

7

PLANNING STAGE

WILLIAM EATON returned to the United States in what should have been disgrace: questionable finances, ignominious expulsion, failed diplomatic policies, a career seemingly in tatters. His detractors claimed he was, at the very least, guilty of a "misrepresentation of the facts" during his time in Tunis.[1] Eaton, however, believed he had forcefully and honorably defended the interests of the United States. Every time he denied a passport to a Tunisian ship looking to carry supplies to Tripoli, he believed he had materially helped the war effort. Every time he had refused another of the bey's extravagant demands, he believed he had saved his country from untold expenses, both in money and respect. "I do not arrogate to myself any peculiar merit in having rejected overtures and submitted sacrifices," he would later say. "My situation rendered it incumbent on me, but if any consideration be due to the principles of analogy or parity of reasoning, the inference will be natural here, that instead of abandoning the public interest to speculative views, I have sacrificed my own, as well as my personal tranquility, in a fixed adherence to my duties. . . . I ask nothing of my country except reciprocal support."[2]

Eaton arrived in Boston on June 2, 1803, and made his way back to Brimfield, where he reunited with his family, whom he had not seen for nearly five years. Just what he told his wife about his financial troubles is unknown. Eliza was wealthy, but not even her riches could cover the debts her husband had accrued in Tunis. William spent his time reacquainting himself with his children and stepchildren and preparing a detailed report on his expenses for Secretary of State James Madison. He fully expected the government to reimburse all of his expenses and endorse his idea of using Hamet Karamanli to unseat his brother. The plan to support Hamet's revolt remained firmly in Eaton's mind, although he knew it was no longer secret. "The [Sapitapa] had betrayed to the ruling bashaw the plot of his brother . . . to dethrone him. The alarm excited in the apprehensions of the usurper induced him to come forward with propositions of peace."[3] For Eaton, there could be no peace unless his nation achieved it with "honor," and that meant without ransom for the imprisoned crew of the *Philadelphia* and without other payment or tribute. Only that would suffice, and as Eaton saw it, the only way to reach that peace was to overthrow Yusuf Karamanli.[4]

First, though, were his family matters. His oldest stepson, Timothy, was bound for college. Fifteen-year-old Eli Danielson wanted to follow William and see the world, so his stepfather secured him an appointment as a midshipman. The girls, fourteen-year-old stepdaughter Sarah and his and Eliza's own Eliza, Charlotte, and Almira were either approaching or at school age, and William wanted them to get educations and attend boarding school. Eliza, however, wanted to keep her daughters close to home, especially if her husband was going to be absent for years at a time. The disagreement sparked a nasty argument, which Eaton noted in his diary, without saying how it ended.[5] There were also other issues with which he had to deal, mostly stemming from his long absence and his debts. He prepared a long report to Madison, detailing to the penny how much he had spent and why and requesting the State Department to reimburse him $22,000. Once he finished his report, Eaton apparently turned to more intimate matters. Eliza announced that summer that she was pregnant with their fourth child, who would turn out to be a boy, William Jr.

As the summer turned to fall, Eaton had another project on which to embark. An auditor at the State Department had determined that Eaton's actual debts from Tunis amounted to more than $40,000. A claim that high required authorization from the president, and the State Department duly sent all of Eaton's invoices to Jefferson—who held the key to Eaton's grand scheme of unseating Yusuf Karamanli and replacing him with Hamet. Plus there was the matter of Commodore Morris. Eaton knew that Morris had sent an extremely negative report about events in Tunis and the Hamet idea to Secretary of the Navy Smith. It was an affront Eaton could not let stand, and he decided to make the three-hundred-mile-plus journey to the nation's new capital city, Washington, to press his claims and plans. Jefferson had already met with Madison about Eaton's financial claims and denied all of them. Eaton decided to lobby Congress to overturn that decision.[6]

In a new report to Congress, Eaton vigorously defended himself, his actions, and his expenses. Every expense, he said, had arisen from his plan to help Hamet unseat his brother, a plan that if acted upon in 1802 or 1803 would have saved the United States thousands of dollars. The only reason why America was not pursuing the concept of using Hamet, Eaton believed, was that "one, and perhaps, two, individuals, who have *been* in the Mediterranean, who would be willing enough to see this termination of my affairs: Individuals who, with a view of shrouding positive delinquency in the imagery of malfeasance of office, on my part, have anonymously come forward and stamped my conduct before the public with the epithets of speculative and fraudulent!"[7] Those two men were Captains Alexander Murray and Richard V. Morris, and Eaton took every opportunity to disparage their actions while defending his own. Murray in particular earned Eaton's scorn: Murray "was entreated to send only one of his ships, with the agents to the friendly Bashaw in order to encourage his perseverance until he could bring the whole squadron to cooperate with him. This he refused on the pretext that the ships were on short rations. . . . This may have been the case; but, it is nevertheless true, that the whole squadron lay nine days after arriving at [Gibraltar] without taking in even a biscuit or a bucket of water."[8]

Eaton accused Morris of cowardice, without actually calling the former commodore a coward. "It is true that the first appearance of this Commodore before Tripoli was not till the 22d May, 1803. It is true that during this term of a year, from his first arrival on the station, he never burnt an ounce of powder. . . . And it is equally true, that, during the period of seventeen months he commanded the whole force of the United States in the Mediterranean, he was only nineteen days before the enemy's port."[9]

The reverses in the Mediterranean had made the Jefferson administration cautious to the point of inaction, due to the expense. America was not broke, but the 1803 Louisiana Purchase had severely drained the country's reserves of hard cash. Napoleon had stipulated an up-front payment of two million dollars in specie, as well as interest payments amounting to $800,000 a year in cash.[10] The short period of peace in Europe in 1802–1803 saw a decline in American import duties as continental nations did not need neutral U.S.-flagged merchant ships to carry cargoes.[11] The war with Tripoli, meanwhile, had already cost the country $3.6 million, with another $1.2 million expected for 1804.[12] The spiraling costs had dulled Jefferson's and Madison's enthusiasm for the war. Jefferson put his hopes in Edward Preble, that the aggressive New Englander could force a low-cost or even no-cost treaty on Yusuf. To Eaton, the hesitancy smacked of timidity, and he railed against it: "On my arrival at Washington, I remonstrated with Mr. Madison" about Hamet and he "evaded the subject," Eaton told a confidant in a letter.[13]

Next, Eaton met with Jefferson and Attorney General Levi Lincoln. He got nowhere.[14] He refused to give up. After several more meetings with Jefferson and Madison, Eaton finally made a breakthrough. Supporting Hamet, he argued, would actually make the United States money in the long run, as Hamet had promised to pay back any expenses once he was on the throne of Tripoli, as well as to sign a perpetual treaty of peace without tribute payments. Eaton estimated he would need $20,000 in hard currency, plus weapons, powder, supplies, and naval support to put Hamet on the throne. It would be, he said, money well spent: "It is presumed the project with Hamet is still feasible. Besides the impression to be made on the world by this species of chastisement, it would have a beneficial influence on the other Barbary Regencies. To them the precedent would be dreadful, for it would be no very difficult matter, in case of war, to start a rival in [Algiers or Tunis]."[15] The argument swayed Jefferson, who March 30, 1804, agreed to support Hamet.[16]

The decision did not last long. Days later, the president reversed himself when news began to arrive in Washington on the latest campaign to subdue Tripoli. First, word came of the loss of the *Philadelphia*. Jefferson's reaction was to order Barron to begin assembling a new squadron. At the same time, news arrived from Derne that Yusuf had forced Hamet to flee to Egypt, creating doubts that Hamet was worthy of American support. Eaton went back to the White House to attend an emergency meeting of the cabinet. He did not like what he heard. "On the first symptoms of a reverse . . . discouragement superceded resolution with our executive, and economy supplanted good faith and honesty," Eaton wrote to a confidant. "The President becomes reserved. The Secretary of War believes we had better pay tribute. He said this to me in his own office. [Treasury Secretary Albert] Gallatin, like a cowardly Jew, shrinks behind the counter. Madison leaves everything to the Secretary of the Navy."[17]

The Navy secretary, Robert Smith, was Eaton's lone ally. A proponent of a strong navy like his brother, powerful Maryland senator Samuel Smith, Robert Smith opposed Jefferson's plans to scale down the military and favored much more aggressive action against Tripoli. To what extent Smith supported Eaton's plan because Jefferson and Madison had misgivings about it is a question mark. Smith certainly endorsed the possibility of using Hamet to unseat his brother, one Preble, then commander in the Mediterranean, might have pursued but the loss of the *Philadelphia* and the many delays in negotiating the use of Neapolitan warships gave Preble no time for intrigue with the "rightful bashaw." Now, Eaton was presenting a new opportunity, one Smith believed was worth pursuing, especially since the funding was to come from the State Department, not the Navy. Smith also had Preble's strong endorsement of the plan, and Preble now wielded a good deal of political weight.[18]

In the end, though, it was the economic argument that won over Jefferson. The chance that Eaton could end the war with Tripoli for much less additional expense than it had already cost and extract a treaty at no cost at all was too much for Jefferson to ignore. The president still had his doubts about Hamet, and he also worried about the precedent the United States might set if Eaton succeeded. Madison shared those misgivings, but he too signed off on the plan, telling the president, "Although it does not accord with the general sentiments or views of the United States, to intermeddle in the domestic concerns of other countries, it cannot be unfair, in the prosecution of a just war, or the accomplishment of a reasonable peace, to turn to their advantage the enmity and pretensions of others against a common foe."[19]

Eaton now had official backing, but his actual plan remained somewhat ethereal. Hamet was no longer in Derne. Eaton would have to find him. He then had to get Hamet and his "army" first to Derne, then to Tripoli. He didn't have an exact plan for how he would do that, nor did he have any idea of the opposition he might face. All he knew—and he based that knowledge solely on belief, not hard evidence—was Hamet had promised the people of Tripolitania would rise up in revolt upon his return. This lack of intelligence had no effect on Eaton's determination or enthusiasm, and even though secrecy was long since gone, Smith handed Eaton a new "cover." The former consul was now the "naval agent for the Barbary Regencies," a title that carried with it no power or salary and no duties other than to find and aid Hamet Karamanli. "I am convinced that our captives cannot otherwise be released without ransom," Eaton confided to a friend, "and, as an individual, I would rather yield my person to the danger of war in almost any shape, than my pride to the humiliation of treating with a wretched pirate for the ransom of men who are the rightful heirs of freedom."[20]

So Eaton left Washington with a nebulous title, grudging support, and the weight of debt still on his mind. The State Department auditor had completely rejected Eaton's claim for reimbursement of the money given to the Sapitapa as a bribe, the money he borrowed to buy young Anna Porcillo out of bondage, and most of the expenses surrounding his ship, the *Gloria*. Congress appeared in no mood to reimburse him either. All told, Eaton was on the hook for nearly $23,000 ($373,059.29 in 2016 currency).[21] Eaton needed the Hamet expedition to succeed if only to bolster his claims before Congress and shore up his shaky personal finances.

After a quick visit to say his goodbyes to Eliza and the children, Eaton and his stepsons Timothy and Eli Danielson set out for New York. He was undoubtedly happy to be back in action, but his commission had changed since he left Washington. Eaton returned to Brimfield believing Jefferson had allotted $40,000, a thousand muskets, field artillery carriages, powder, shot, and other supplies to the expedition. When he received his actual commission from Smith on May 30, his orders said he was to "receive instructions from and obey the orders of Commodore Barron" and "render to our Squadron in the Mediterranean every assistance in your power."[22]

Just when and why Jefferson changed his mind is a mystery. The president had been lukewarm to Eaton's proposal from the start, but had still agreed to back the expedition to restore Hamet to power. Perhaps it was Eaton's fault for not having offered a concrete plan showing exactly how he would retrieve Hamet and get him to Tripoli. Whatever the reason, it was clear to Eaton there were no supplies, no cash, and no weapons for Hamet. He would have to convince Samuel Barron to provide everything he might need for his coup attempt. "I have no alternative but to place my breast in this breach of confidence and good faith," he wrote a friend. "This I am resolved to do, and, by exposing my temporal salvation, convince the ally and the world of a consistency and fidelity in my country which, I myself am convinced, does not exist with our administration any further than considerations purely individual render it convenient."[23]

The Mediterranean was alive with rumor and intrigue when Commodore Samuel Barron reached Gibraltar on August 12, 1804. Talk of an expanding war filled the diplomatic traffic between American consuls on Malta and Sicily and in Leghorn, France, Spain, Tunis, and Morocco. George Davis in Tunis and James Simpson in Tangiers both reported those regencies close to declaring war on America. The reason was Edward Preble's aggressive and complete blockade of Yusuf Karamanli's capital. Bey Hamouda of Tunis had loaded a ship full of wheat as a personal present to Karamanli, and Davis, because the ship sailed as a gift, duly issued the ship a passport. Preble, however, refused to honor the passport, stopped the vessel, and sent it into the nearest Tunisian port. The act enraged Hamouda, who demanded restitution in cash as well an apology and permission for his ship to sail into Tripoli. Preble ignored him, telling Davis to inform the bey that Preble, as the commodore of the U.S. squadron, had the final say as to which ships could pass through the blockade and what types of cargo they could convey to the city.[24]

The emperor of Morocco too bristled when Preble refused to grant a passport to a Moroccan vessel bound for Tripoli laden with wheat. Unlike Hamouda, who merely blustered, Emperor Suleyman readied three frigates for sea, and although he did not declare war, the implication was clear. "It is thought very probable" that Suleyman planned to "cruise against the U. States in the case of Consul Simpson refusing a passport," Captain John Rodgers reported to Secretary Smith.[25] Events in Europe were also having a profound impact in the Mediterranean; English, French, Spanish, Neapolitan, Ottoman, and Russian fleets were all said to be preparing for operations in the region. It was, as Davis described it, "an epoch more replete, with the destiny of Governments, than any period since the downfall of Rome. . . . The fate of the Northern Powers, the commercial existence of Great Britain, the Ottoman Empire, are all involved in such an event.[26]

Rodgers discovered events in Europe could also suddenly involve the United States. "It is believed here by the most knowing, that Spain intends to quarrel with us, and I think from a letter I saw from Mr. Pinckney to Consul Govino, that it is not improbable, as that government has refused to ratify the Louisiana Treaty."[27] Barron had no way to know what was rumor and what was fact. Word of possible new hostilities reached Washington before Barron's arrival at Gibraltar, and Smith dispatched an addendum to his original orders, which Barron found waiting for him. It advised the commodore it might be "prudent" to keep at least one frigate on patrol off Morocco.[28] Barron decided to leave two frigates behind—the *Congress*, under Rodgers, and the *Essex*, under his younger brother James—while he pushed on to Tripoli. Rodgers, as the senior captain, investigated the whereabouts of the Moroccan vessels and found them laid up in ordinary. Rodgers, on his own authority, ordered James Barron and the *Essex* to remain off the Moroccan and Tunisian coasts while Rodgers tried to reach Tripoli in time to play a role in any new attack.[29]

Barron arrived off Tripoli on September 10 knowing nothing of what Rodgers had found. As far as the new commodore was aware, he had already lost half of the combat power of his squadron, and now he found the strength of the remaining flotilla somewhat diminished. The *John Adams* had arrived with a new crew for the schooner *Enterprise,* but enlistments were now about to run out on the brigs *Argus* and *Syren,* as well as on the flagship, the *Constitution.* Barron and Preble both had orders to reenlist as many men as possible, and while they convinced many sailors to remain, it was a time-consuming effort, one that lasted well into the autumn.[30] Barron also had to approve of Preble's measures to dismantle his blockading force, which included the return of his borrowed Neapolitan warships and a reshuffling of officers and men from the gun- and mortar boats back to their original assignments. That, at least, was an easy task for the new commodore, who signed off on everything his predecessor did.[31]

Barron had one more decision to make upon his arrival in the Mediterranean. On board the *President* was the naval agent for the Barbary Regencies, William Eaton. On August 21, Eaton met with Barron to discuss supporting Hamet's revolt. The meeting did not go well. Barron already knew about Eaton's plan and was hesitant at best about supporting it. Barron had no orders mandating that he provide any aid to Hamet or Eaton. Instead, "with respect to the Ex-Bashaw of Tripoli, we have no objection to you availing yourself of his co-operation with you against Tripoli if you shall upon a full view of the subject after your arrival upon the Station, consider his co-operation expedient. The subject is committed entirely to your discretion."

The vagueness of Barron's orders must have been a huge disappointment to Eaton, who boarded the *President* back in June with the belief he had the full support of the government. He expected Barron to supply everything needed to help Hamet unseat his brother. Eaton spoke with "Commodore Barron concerning the apparent advantages of cooperating with Hamet Bashaw against Tripoli: and the probable disadvantages of acting without his cooperation."[32] He found Barron unimpressed. The commodore wanted to know exactly how Eaton planned to find Hamet, whose whereabouts were still unknown; how he planned to supply a force of thousands; how he planned to transport Hamet's army to Derne; and what would happen if Hamet succeeded in taking the city.

Eaton answered every challenge, pointing out that a land attack on Tripoli would cut off Yusuf from his supplies but hedging on just how Hamet would get to the city. As for supplying Hamet, the American squadron had recently captured three ships laden with wheat and sent them to Malta for adjudication. Those ships, Eaton said, carried "thirty-six thousand bushels," which Eaton called a "providential supply" that could either feed Hamet's army or buy off some of Yusuf's men, who Eaton claimed were starving due to the American blockade. Eaton also believed he could easily procure cannon, muskets, and other equipment either in Malta or Naples. He told Barron he believed he could overthrow Yusuf for $50,000.[33] Eaton also argued the presence of a rival army would prevent Yusuf from harming his American captives, for fear of retaliation. Finally, he said, whether Hamet was successful was not as important as honoring the U.S. commitment to the "rightful bashaw."

Barron remained noncommittal. "The only obstacles which seem to oppose the success of this measure are want of supplies to put it into operation. These are not in the fleet; and the Commodore is not decided whether any construction of the President's instructions extends to a discretion of procuring and furnishing them: he will probably express himself on this subject after having fixed on his plan of operations," Eaton reported.[34] The cloudy state of affairs baffled Eaton. In a report to Secretary Smith he blamed his old adversary, Alexander Murray, for his situation.

I cannot forbear, however, expressing, on this occasion, the extreme mortification I suffer on account of my actual situation; destitute of commission, rank, or command; and, I may say, consideration or credit. And even without instructions for the regulation of my conduct while ostensibly charged with the management of an enterprise on which, perhaps, depends the successful issue of this war. I am not ignorant that I ought to ascribe this mortifying situation, as a remote cause, to the indirect, undue influence of Captain Murray's insinuations. There is not one statement made by Murray, relative to Barbary affairs . . . but what has proved incorrect in matters of fact, if not maliciously false. . . . In the issue I have been materially wronged, both in my reputation and circumstances; so, indeed, has the public service.[35]

Barron continued to waffle until Eaton received two vital boosts. The first came on September 6, when news from Malta informed him that Hamet was waiting for him in Alexandria, Egypt, and needed only supplies to launch his campaign. It was the first positive news about Hamet in months. Then, on September 15, Eaton and Preble met with Barron, and at that conference Preble's unreserved endorsement of helping the elder Karamanli finally swayed Barron. He would push forward with the plan, although he had one pressing impediment left—his own health.

By the time Barron decided to back Eaton, the liver ailment that plagued him on the crossing had become debilitating. Barron needed to get on shore to seek treatment and decided to make for Syracuse. As the season was becoming too advanced for direct operations against Tripoli, Barron believed he could leave a small blockading force off Tripoli while the bulk of his squadron went to Sicily or Malta for repairs and refit and he sought medical attention.[36] His decision marked the end of operations for 1804. Preble, with the *Constitution* and the *Argus*, under Master Commandant Isaac Hull, headed for Malta, while Master Commandant Hugh Campbell in the *Constellation* and Master Commandant Charles Stewart in the *Syren* remained on blockade. Barron sailed the *President* to Syracuse where the commodore planned to seek treatment for his liver. Lieutenant John H. Dent took command of the *Nautilus* and with the *Vixen*, still under Master Commandant John Smith, set a course for Messina to return the Neapolitan gunboats and mortar boats. The *Enterprise*, now under the command of Lieutenant Commandant Thomas Robinson, was on her way to Venice for a complete overhaul. The schooner had been the busiest unit in the American squadron for nearly three years and required a bow-to-stern rebuild. She would play no part in the coming campaign. Nor would the *John Adams*, which was to return to the United States with Preble and the sailors from the squadron who had decided not to reenlist and there restock with supplies and sail once more for the Mediterranean.[37]

Continuing the blockade was only part of the planned direct-action operations against Tripoli. Barron already had a sizeable force, in three frigates (soon to be four, when Rodgers arrived), two brigs, and three schooners. He expected to receive even more firepower in the spring of 1805, when ten American-built gunboats and two mortar ketches were to arrive. Combined, it would be nearly double the strength Preble had over the summer and should be more than enough to blast Karamanli into submission. The second prong was Eaton, whose enterprise could act as a second front. The third prong was something about which Eaton hadn't been told and that he would have firmly opposed—a full-scale diplomatic effort that included, if necessary, paying off Yusuf. The call for a diplomatic solution had originated at the executive mansion, as Jefferson's eagerness to end a costly conflict led him to initiate an effort that would eventually undermine Eaton's effort. Jefferson put his friend Consul General Tobias Lear in charge of talks.

"Tobias Lear our Consul General at Algiers is invested by the President with full power and authority to negotiate a treaty of Peace with the Bashaw of Tripoli, and also to adjust such terms of conciliation as may be found necessary with any of the other Barbary Powers," Smith told Barron. "He is therefore to be conveyed by you to any of these Regencies as he may request of you, and you will cordially co-operate with him in all such measures as may be deemed the best calculated to effectuate a termination of The war with Tripoli and to ensure a continuance of the friendship and respect of the other Barbary Powers."[38]

The three prongs of Jefferson's strategy to defeat Tripoli were now in place.

8

WASHINGTON
INSIDER

EVEN TO THOSE who knew him well, Tobias Lear was something of an enigma. Highly intelligent, ambitious, well educated, and well connected politically, Lear should have been the model of success in the new republic. Instead, whenever he found himself thrust into the public spotlight, scandal and failure seemed to follow. Lear was also prone to long bouts of depression, during which he isolated himself, apparently wrestling with the reasons for failures. Unable to explain just why his potential never seemed to rise to the occasion, Lear once lamented, "My own affairs are now in that deranged state in which they occupy all my thoughts and all my time."[1]

Tobias Lear V was born in Portsmouth, New Hampshire, on September 19, 1762, the son of Tobias IV and Mary Stillson Lear. His father was a prosperous ship captain and merchant and later a farmer who owned a large estate. He sent Tobias to the prestigious Dummer Charity Academy in Portsmouth, a bustling seaport city, and on graduation Tobias V enrolled in Harvard in 1779. During his four years in Cambridge, Massachusetts, Lear rubbed shoulders with the sons of many of the most influential politicians in New England. He cultivated a long-standing friendship with the Lincoln family after he met Theodore Lincoln, the son of General Benjamin Lincoln, George Washington's close confidant and the first secretary of war.[2] Upon graduation, Lear went to Europe, both for family business and to finish his education by touring the Continent. He learned to speak fluent French and developed a dislike for English institutions.

He returned to Portsmouth in 1785 and began looking for a job. He wasn't particularly eager to become a teacher but saw few other options until he received a letter from a friend from Harvard. Theodore Lincoln told Lear that his father was hiring a private secretary for George Washington. Lear asked General Lincoln for a recommendation, and Washington's former second-in-command happily acquiesced. On May 29, 1786, Lear arrived at Mount Vernon, Washington's Virginia estate, to take up his post.[3]

Lear's first job was a difficult one, especially for a young man with no real experience. George Washington was the preeminent person in the country, and hundreds of people either wrote or came to see him. Lear had to schedule meetings for those whom Washington truly needed to see while dealing with those whose importance wasn't quite as high. Someone had to answer all the general's mail, and the burden usually fell on Lear. In addition, Lear was responsible for educating George Washington Parke Custis, Washington's stepson, as well as for any other duty the general might assign him.[4] Lear lived as part of Washington's family, sharing in holidays, birthdays, and most of all, serving as Washington's confidant. He was an observer at the Constitutional Convention, where he heard Washington express hesitancy and near shock at the realization that he would become president. He then helped the new president and his family find quarters, first in New York and then in Philadelphia.[5]

His position allowed Lear to cultivate personal contacts of his own. He rubbed shoulders with Thomas Jefferson, Alexander Hamilton, Timothy Pickering, James Madison, and James Monroe. He watched as the first two political parties emerged in the new United States: the Federalists, who rallied around Washington, and the Democrat-Republicans, who adhered to Jefferson's principles. The divide between the two parties had yet to split the country completely, and Lear, who was a mild adherent to Federalist views, found himself drifting more and more toward the Democrats. "I have a good opportunity of being acquainted with them [political subjects] from the principal characters in this and neighboring states who resort here," he told Theodore Lincoln in a letter.[6]

Soon after Washington hired him, Lear discovered one of the "perks" of working for the preeminent person in the country. Washington organized his staff along military lines, and Lear, as the private secretary, was Washington's top-ranking staffer—in effect, the chief of staff. During the Revolutionary War a colonel had run Washington's staff, and the first president, who saw no reason to change what worked before, obtained a colonel's commission for Lear.[7] Lear would use the title "Colonel" later in his career, as a point of pride, even though he had no actual military experience.[8]

"Colonel" Lear worked for Washington during both of the first president's administrations. His friendship with Thomas Jefferson, Washington's first secretary of state, deepened, as did his contacts with influential politicians and, increasingly, businessmen. Lear was beside the president when Washington laid the cornerstone of the U.S. Capitol in the new federal district on September 18, 1793. His thoughts turned to the newly planned city as a place not only of politics but of commerce.[9]

Seven years as Washington's private secretary gave Lear the type of an education that he had probably never dreamed of at Harvard. On the day Washington laid the cornerstone of the Capitol, Lear was just thirty-three years old and arguably among the most powerful people in the young republic as he controlled access to the president. His influence with Washington by then had become immense. When Washington expressed to him doubts about running for a second term, Lear used a trip home to Portsmouth as a fact-finding tour. On his return he reported to Washington that he had spoken with many people, all of whom said they wanted Washington to run again, that they believed the government had helped more than it hurt, that the government was still experimental, and that they wanted continuity.[10]

As his professional career burgeoned, however, tragedy marred his personal life. Lear had married his childhood sweetheart, Mary "Polly" Long, in 1790 and on July 11, 1791, welcomed a son, Benjamin Lincoln

Lear. George and Martha Washington were the boy's godparents, and the Lears lived with the first family both in Philadelphia and at Mount Vernon. The marriage was short-lived. Polly Lear contracted yellow fever during an outbreak in Philadelphia in 1793 and died that summer. Two years later, in 1795, Lear remarried, much to George and Martha Washington's delight. The new bride was Frances Bassett Washington—"Fanny"—who was the widow of George Augustine Washington and, according to reports, Martha's favorite niece. The first family lavished gifts on the newlyweds, especially the 360-acre Walnut Hill farm, adjacent to Mount Vernon, with more than a hundred slaves. Lear's newfound happiness was again short-lived. Fanny contracted tuberculosis in August 1795 and died on March 25, 1796. Lear despondently informed the Washingtons in a letter, "The partner of my life is no more!"[11]

The rapid losses of two loved ones, sent Lear into a depression. Although he continued to work for Washington, he spent more and more time at Walnut Farm, alone with his young son. His time away from Washington apparently deepened his affinity for Democrat-Republicanism. He met with Jefferson several times to discuss general government and told him he believed "the very men who called themselves 'anti-federalist' were the men who would save the government." How much Washington knew about his secretary's political views is uncertain. Lear describes numerous conversations about politics with the first president, but they appear to have been general in nature, focusing mostly on the continued British presence in American territories in the west.[12]

Whether from despondency or desperation, Lear began to see the new federal district, then under construction just upriver from Mount Vernon, as an opportunity to rebound from the loss of two wives and also to create some independence from the Washington family. Lear earned eight hundred dollars as Washington's secretary, and, increasingly, that income was not enough to cover the costs of running his new estate and providing for his son. As surveyors began laying out the grid pattern for the city, Lear cast his eyes upon plots along the Potomac where he could build warehouses and wharves or that he could reserve as manufacturing sites in what he was sure would become a rapidly growing city. He attempted to market the city and his own holdings by writing a book, *Observations of the River Potomack—the Country Adjacent and the City of Washington,* which George Washington helped edit. Although the idea the city would be named for him unnerved Washington, he nevertheless approved of Lear's real estate ventures.[13]

Lear was not alone in his belief the federal district would become a boomtown. Land speculation was rife in the district, and Lear seemed unable to spot real investors from those less trustworthy.[14] His own purchases involved him with James Greenleaf, a shady businessman who was buying up all the plots in Washington that he could. Greenleaf apparently had no lack of money—he had managed to persuade a Dutch lending house to advance him thousands of dollars—and his sales of plots were just strong enough to attract investors. Lear was one of them, as was Revolutionary War financier Robert Morris. For nearly two years the trio bought lots, with Greenleaf acting as point man. Neither Lear nor Morris had any idea that Greenleaf was using whatever money came in to finance an even bigger land purchase in the Appalachian Mountains. The land speculation turned into a classic "pyramid scheme," in which Greenleaf used new investment money to pay off previous investors. When new money began to dry up, he turned to his Dutch backers, who agreed to package mortgages on the lots Greenleaf had already bought and to sell those to Dutch investors.[15]

When war broke out in 1798 between France, England, and Holland, the Dutch lenders called in their loans, and Greenleaf could not pay. He promised his American backers that he would build houses on lots that he could either sell or rent to the workers, staff, and others who must certainly follow the government to the federal district, convincing Lear, Morris, and others to invest even more heavily. Greenleaf had also promised to pay the city commissioners $2,600 a month for his lots and to build at least five houses a month. When Greenleaf reneged on both promises, the commissioners moved to seize his properties, which caused Greenleaf's Appalachian investment to collapse and the entire scheme to unravel.[16]

The fallout was immense. Morris, who had helped America earn its independence, wound up in debtors' prison, his fortune gone. For Lear, the mounting debts were a personal crisis. Coming on the heels of his wives' deaths, the clamor of his creditors was simply too much and led Lear to make another bad and potentially career-ending decision. He began to divert rent money from Washington's accounts into his own to pay off his debt. Washington, who viewed Lear as family, was only vaguely aware of Lear's dire financial position. He certainly knew about Morris' troubles and Greenleaf's double-dealing, calling his contracts with the city commissioners "an unproductive and a disagreeable spectacle."[17] The depth of Lear's involvement and his fraud greatly upset the general when he learned of them, and he upbraided his secretary in unusually (for Washington) harsh terms: "I never had the most distant suspicion that every farthing you had received, or might receive, on my account would not be justly credited but this will not supply my wants, and it would be uncandid and inconsistent with the frankness of friendship, not to declare that I have not approved, nor cannot approve, of having my money received and applied to uses not my own, without my consent."[18]

Washington's reprimand was enough for Lear, who now worked for the general honestly and fastidiously. He still split his time between his own farm and Mount Vernon, and although his debts continued to hang over him, he never again diverted money that belonged to Washington. His close relationship with the general continued right up to Washington's death. Lear was at the first president's bedside on December 14, 1799, when Washington breathed his last, and he recorded Washington's last words.[19] Lear remained with the Washington family until February 1800, when, his services complete, he returned to Walnut Hill. He was unsure of his next move when yet another scandal erupted, this time involving his handling of Washington's personal letters.

Lear held onto Washington's personal papers for eight months after the general's death. During that time he and Washington's nephew, Bushrod Washington, had discussed writing a comprehensive biography of the first president. Lear's task was to arrange and organize Washington's papers, while Bushrod would write about Washington's last years. The two never formalized an agreement, and the project ended. When it did, Lear gave Martha Washington the collection of papers. George Washington had bequeathed in his will his papers—and Mount Vernon—to Bushrod, who began searching for a new partner for the biography project. He settled on John Marshall, chief justice of the U.S. Supreme Court. Marshall, when he began to read Washington's papers, questioned whether the collection was complete. Notably missing was a series of letters between Washington and Jefferson that had caused the two men never to speak again.

Jefferson, no fan of what had become the Federalist Party, just before the election of 1800 received a letter from Filippo Mazzei, a Tuscan who had helped procure weapons for Virginia state forces during the Revolution and had since become an ardent exponent of the ideals of the new American state, as well as Jefferson's Democratic-Republican philosophy. Mazzei had asked Jefferson about the current conditions in the United States. Jefferson, in his reply, blasted Federalists and Washington in particular for what he saw as their excesses: "The aspects of our politics has wonderfully changed since you left us; in place of that noble love of liberty and republican government which carried us triumphantly through the war, an Anglican, monarchial, aristocratical party has sprung up, whose avowed object is to draw over us the substance as they already have done, of the British government."[20]

Jefferson condemned Washington's use of many former military officers in Cabinet positions, as well as what he thought was John Adams' patrician approach to governing. Most of all, Jefferson railed against what he saw as both men's attempts to foist an English aristocratic system upon the American people: "It would give you a fever were I to name to you the apostates who have gone over to these heresies, men who were Samsons in the field and Solomons in the council, but who have had their heads shorn by the harlot England."[21]

When the letter leaked, it caused an incendiary exchange of letters with Washington. One of Jefferson's was so strongly worded that Washington reportedly was ready to challenge him to a duel. When Washington died, however, these letters, which would have made Jefferson look extraordinarily bad ahead of the election of 1800, disappeared.[22] As far as Bushrod and other young Washington relatives were concerned, the culprit was none other than Jefferson's confidant Tobias Lear.[23] The missing letters created a furor, and Marshall ordered an investigation. Former secretary of state and Federalist firebrand Timothy Pickering ratcheted up the attacks on Lear, publicly accusing him of purposely destroying documents that would make Jefferson look bad in order to gain leverage over him.[24] Lear denied the charges, but once more a cloud hung over his head.[25]

The latest scandal overwhelmed Lear. He cut himself off from the world and hid at Walnut Hill, which he had begun to sell off to pay his debts. He might have remained there for the rest of his life but for another strange turn in his fortunes. Thomas Jefferson, who won the election of 1800, appointed Lear as the commercial consul at Cape François (modern-day Cap Haitien) on the island of Hispaniola and capital of the newly independent nation of Haiti. The appointment renewed the cries that Lear had purposely destroyed documents and that Jefferson was simply repaying a crony.[26] If so, it wasn't much of a reward. The posting carried no salary and was on an island that had been in the throes of revolution for several years.[27] Still, as the principal commercial town in that region, Cape François was an important trading post, one where a savvy consul could make a small fortune with the right investments.

Lear arrived on July 7, 1800. He faced the difficult task of representing America to a new nation none of the major countries in the Caribbean wanted to exist. The United States, Britain, and France were still slave nations, but Toussaint Louverture, the leader of the Haitian revolution, had abolished slavery in his country. Diplomats and slave owners alike feared the slave revolt that had freed Haiti could spread to their own lands. The fledgling Haitian state, which at that time included all of Hispaniola, occupied a strategic place in the Caribbean and was a major trade stop, especially for American shipping. Lear, then, had somehow to balance his nation's fears with its needs. He would be able to do so, but only by devoting all of his time to his job, which left little time for investments. As he had to pay his own expenses, the consulship did little to alleviate Lear's financial burden; he complained several times to Secretary of State Madison about his lack of funds.[28]

Lear spent nearly two years in Cape François, watching as revolts convulsed the island and forces from Europe began to converge. A brief period of peace in 1801 led to rampant speculation that Napoleon planned to retake the island and was preparing an expeditionary force. Toussaint refused to believe the reports, but Lear was sure an invasion was imminent.[29] Americans began leaving the island, leading to accusations that Lear was spreading word of a coming attack. Lear denied the charge, telling Benjamin Lincoln in a letter, "So far from having engaged my passage, I have used all of my endeavors to persuade my countrymen from embarking, as I believed it would create an alarm which might be productive of much evil."[30]

The French did in fact plan to retake the island, and on February 3, 1802, a force of 20,000 veterans of Napoleon's army arrived off Cape François in a fleet of twenty-five ships. Panic gripped the town. For Lear, the outlook was bleak; anyone who could fled the island. He found at least one other person willing to remain, a young merchant captain from Maryland, named John Rodgers. The two men struck up an instant friendship, and when the French arrived Rodgers went with Lear to convince them not to attack. Lear wanted time for the American businessmen in Cape François to secure their homes and warehouses and evacuate their families. Toussaint, however, had vowed to burn the town rather than let the French take it. On February 4, Haitian troops fired on a French frigate reconnoitering the battery guarding the city. In the town, other Haitian soldiers began to set fires indiscriminately. The wanton destruction made for lurid tales back in America.

> Many massacres took place and the brutal rape of the negroes spared neither age nor their own color. . . . With one hand the black daemons were seen holding with one hand the wreathing infant and hacking off limbs with the sword with the other.
>
> On the morning of the 5th, of 2,000 houses, only 59 escaped the ravages of the flames, and their tenants, except for a wretched few on board American ships, were no where [sic] to be seen. All the plantations of the once flourishing plain around the Cape for many miles exhibited the same tremendous appearance.[31]

Lear and Rodgers spent the night on shore, trying to save as many people and as much property as possible. Their toils cemented their friendship; Lear commended Rodgers in his official report, and Rodgers never forgot that Lear was able to smooth his departure from the island with the French when every other American captain had to wait.[32] Lear returned to the United States on May 7, 1802, and after making his report to Secretary of State Madison went into seclusion at Walnut Hill.

Once again, depression gripped him. Martha Washington had died, severing just about all communication with the relatives of his former employer. His finances were a wreck, and it was a struggle for him to retain the small portion of Walnut Hill he had not sold. Lear, like William Eaton, turned to Congress for redress and submitted a bill for more than six thousand dollars in expenses.[33] As it would do with Eaton, the Senate deliberated without reaching a decision, deliberated again, and eventually denied Lear's claim.[34] The decision only deepened Lear's depression, and he remained secluded at Walnut Hill pondering his future. He was forty years old, still owed (and believed he was owed) thousands of dollars, and had no real prospects.

Despite the gloomy outlook, Lear had at least one visitor—Frances Dandridge Henley. Known as "Fanny," she was twenty-two, vivacious, and a niece of Martha Washington. Lear never recorded in his diary how many times his "dear Fanny" called at Walnut Hill, but the two of them fell in love. They married on June 10, 1803.[35] The marriage marked the start of yet another reversal of fortunes for Lear, this one for the better and one that Thomas Jefferson again helped to bolster. Jefferson had remained in contact with Lear throughout the latter's self-imposed isolation, from time to time asking him to play host to friends.[36] Jefferson clearly saw the potential in Lear, not just the pitfalls that had plagued him, and appointed him, despite his lack of diplomatic experience, the consul general for North Africa in Algiers.[37]

The new job and this show of confidence from the president immediately jolted Lear out of his funk. He restored his many ties to friends and family, and in a long, cleansing letter to his old mentor, General Benjamin

Lincoln, said he had intended his silence to prevent bothering his friends with his problems. He took the blame for his financial problems but also tore into the Washington family, accusing the younger relatives of being jealous of his former close and open relationship with the general and of resenting Lear for speaking his own mind.[38]

Lear spent the summer arranging for his son Benjamin's schooling while packing for the trip to Algiers. The war with Tripoli was then entering its third year, and the Lears were to sail to the Mediterranean on board the flagship of Commodore Edward Preble, who was to take command in the region. Jefferson's instructions, Lear told Preble, empowered him to negotiate an end to the war with Yusuf Karamanli if force alone could not bring him to negotiations. While on board the *Constitution,* Lear had the opportunity to discuss the war with Preble. They agreed the best possible solution was to force Karamanli to his knees militarily and extract a peace treaty with no fee or future payments. As to how much to pay for a peace if force alone failed, Preble and Lear differed greatly. The commodore was adamant there would be no talks.[39] Lear, however, pointed to his orders, which came directly from the president, and admonished the new commodore not to dismiss the idea of negotiations out of hand.[40]

Preble and Lear arrived in Algiers to find the dey making noise about joining the war on Tripoli's side. Preble's firm stance, which Lear backed, against the dey stifled Hamouda's saber rattling. Preble then set out to establish a base at Syracuse, only to learn of the loss of the *Philadelphia.*[41] That news forced him to change his plans against Tripoli and, sent ripples of shock across the Atlantic. For Lear, the capture of the American frigate and its 302-man crew meant he would now be at the center of any talks to liberate the officers and men, or so he thought. When Preble asked Lear how much the diplomat would and could pay to end the war, Lear was somewhat circumspect, but assumed potential responsibility for committing the United States to continue the practice of paying for peace: "As I have no *special* authority on this subject, I can only say, that I should not hesitate to take upon myself in behalf of the United States to pay at the rate of six hundred dollars for each [prisoner] (exclusive of what might be exchanged)."[42]

Throughout his summer campaign against Tripoli, Preble never asked Lear to open talks, instead trusting mostly to James Cathcart and the outgoing consul general, Richard O'Brien, for diplomatic advice. They were odd choices. Yusuf Karamanli detested Cathcart and would never negotiate with him. Preble certainly knew this and while he never officially sidelined Lear, having Cathcart around could justify the halfheartedness of his efforts to negotiate with the bashaw.[43] O'Brien, meanwhile, was much more like Lear and was willing to pay for a peace. Cathcart and O'Brien already disliked one another, and Cathcart took an immediate dislike to Lear, whom he saw as nothing more than a mouthpiece for Jeffersonian Democrats. He warned Preble not to trust Lear, O'Brien, or the administration: "Mr. O'Brien's being with you by Mr. Lear's appointment and Mr. Davis confirmed in Tunis by our government, does not alter my opinion of them, any more than it will tend to prove them honest men; I regret you have such iniquitous associates."[44]

Although Preble had essentially put Lear on the sidelines of the Tripoli War throughout 1804, the new consul general had more than enough to do in issuing instructions to George Davis in Tunis, James Simpson in Morocco, and other diplomats in the region. To all, Lear presented something of a dichotomy—part hawk and part dove, declaring to Captain William Bainbridge that "it is not for us to seek war. Peace is our object; but we will never have it on unjust terms. I think that all the Barbary Powers, if they know their own interest would cultivate our friendship; for we are a nation different from all others, we are now powerful, if we choose to exert our strength; and we are rising rapidly to a great pitch of importance while most other nations, which are known here, are at their full growth, or on the decline."[45]

The loss of the *Philadelphia* proved to be much more than a tactical loss for Preble's squadron. Newspapers barely had the time to publish the story before Jefferson decided to sack Preble and replace him with Samuel Barron. He issued new orders to Madison concerning talks with the bashaw, orders Madison passed on to Lear: "You are authorized in the last instance and in that only to the terms [of paying $20,000 for a treaty with annual tribute payments of no more than $10,000], with such modifications as may be convenient. . . . For the ransom of the Prisoners, if a ransom be unavoidable, you may stipulate [a] sum not exceeding five hundred dollars for each prisoner including officers.[46]

In those same orders, Madison told Lear about the plan to use Hamet Karamanli to unseat his brother. Far from the glowing endorsement of the scheme that Eaton had thought he had, Madison's instructions to Lear regarding Hamet were, at best, discretionary: "Of the co-operation Elder Brother of the Bashaw of Tripoli, we are still willing to avail ourselves . . . but the less reliance is placed upon his aid, as the force under the orders of the Commodore is deemed sufficient for any exercise of coercion which the obstinacy of the Bashaw may demand. The power of negotiation is confided to you."[47]

Even before Barron arrived in the Mediterranean, Lear sent to Gibraltar a message for the new commodore: "If a negotiation should be opened at Tripoli. I assure you, Sir, it will give me great satisfaction to co-operate with you in this business so interesting."[48] He then sent a self-serving note to Preble, lauding the commodore for his attempts to defeat Karamanli while tacitly knocking Preble for not availing himself of Lear's services: "I know to a mind of sensibility like yours how it must feel, in not having it in your power to accomplish so glorious an undertaking as you have commenced, while you may be in the Chief Command. I know also, my dear Sir, that your Patriotism will conquer your personal feelings. . . . I have received orders from home to repair to Tripoli whenever the comma[n]der shall inform me that there is a prospect of negotiation, and shall hold myself in readiness accordingly."[49]

9

BACKROOM
POLITICS

NEARLY TWO YEARS of nonstop combat operations had turned
Master Commandant Isaac Hull into a seasoned veteran. He arrived in the
Mediterranean in September 1802 as part of the squadron under Richard
Morris and took command of the schooner *Enterprise,* where he restored
morale to a crew that had suffered under the dictatorial Lieutenant Andrew
Sterrett.[1] When Preble took command, he put Hull in command of the
newly built sixteen-gun brig *Argus* and assigned him the diplomatically
sensitive task of preventing Morocco, Tunis, and Algiers from entering
the war. Hull spent four months patrolling off the North African coast,
reminding the other Barbary leaders that America's new navy was ready
should they decide to ally themselves with Tripoli. He returned to Tripoli
in the summer of 1804 and took part in the combat operations against the
city as Preble launched an all-out assault on Yusuf Karamanli. No matter
what he did, Hull excelled and earned the high praise of his commander.[2]

Nothing in the previous two years, however, had prepared him for
what Commodore Samuel Barron was about to tell him. Barron had summoned Hull on board the forty-four-gun *President* for a meeting on September 15, 1804, and Hull had dutifully reported, unaware of what Barron
wanted. He probably expected Barron to order him to bring the *Argus* into
Syracuse or even Malta for a refit as the brig needed a good overhaul and

his crew some time on land after many months at sea. However, in Barron's cabin he found Preble and a man he did not recognize sitting with the new commodore. As the senior officer, Barron would have made the introductions. Hull already knew Preble, and Barron introduced the other man as "Naval Agent for the Barbary Regencies William Eaton."

The orders Barron first handed Hull, dated September 13, were exactly what the thirty-year-old commander of the *Argus* had expected. Hull was to take the *brig* "with all practicable expedition to Malta or Syracuse, and there refit." Once the *Argus* was ready, Hull was to "take on board two months provisions and water and proceed for the Port of Alexandria and if at that port or Smyrna, you find any American vessels you will give them convoy as far as Malta, and immediately after join the squadron" off Tripoli.[3] Those orders, however, were simply a cover for the Connecticut native's real mission, which Barron revealed in a series of verbal instructions.[4]

The voyage to Malta or Syracuse, Barron said, was "intended to disguise the real object of your expedition which is to proceed with Mr. Eaton to Alexandria in search of Hamet Bashaw, the rival brother and legitimate sovereign of the reigning Bashaw of Tripoli."[5] It was a role Hull probably never thought he would play in the war. Hull was "to convey Hamet and his suite to Derne or such other place on the coast as may be determined the most proper for co-operating with the naval force under my command against the common enemy: or, if more agreeable to him, to bring him to me before Tripoli."[6]

Barron gave Hull the option that if he did not find Hamet at Alexandria, he could "proceed to any other place for him where the safety of your ship can be, in your opinion, relied upon." Once he found Hamet, Hull was to assure the elder Karamanli "of the support of [the U.S.] squadron at Benghazi or Derne; where you are at liberty to put in. . . . And you may assure him also that I will take the most effectual measures with the forces under my command for co-operating with him against the usurper, his brother; and *for re-establishing him in the regency of Tripoli.* Arrangements to this effect with him are confided to the discretion with which Mr. Eaton is invested by the government."[7]

Hull never recorded what he thought about his new mission.[8] Most likely he was lukewarm at best at the idea of unseating Yusuf and support-ing Eaton, whose reputation had suffered while he was in Tunis. Certainly, later in the campaign Hull expressed doubts about the mission, about Eaton, and about Hamet, but on September 15, 1804, he accepted the ver-bal orders of his commander. Hull was as brave as any officer in the Navy and had earned a reputation for clear, thoughtful, level-headed decisions, a talent many of the younger officers in the Navy were only beginning to acquire. Now Hull had another politically charged mission. Few American warships had been to Alexandria, and one misstep there could embroil the United States in the internal conflicts then tearing Egypt apart, as well as anger the sultan in Constantinople. Barron knew how well Hull had con-ducted his one-ship deterrence patrol off Morocco, Algiers, and Tunis; he selected the Connecticut officer for the job of supporting Eaton because he wanted an officer who was deliberate and could, if necessary, counterbal-ance the rash-thinking Eaton.[9]

⤜ ⤐

The crew of the *Philadelphia* was dying, albeit slowly. The harsh living conditions, brutal treatment, and lack of food claimed its latest victim on September 7, 1804, when Seaman John McDonald finally succumbed. McDonald was the fifty-fifth man recruited to serve on the frigate in 1803 and the fourth to die in captivity.[10] He would not be the last. *Philadelphia* surgeon Jonathan Cowdery noted McDonald's death in his journal. So too did Marine Corps Private William Ray, who, in addition to noting the sea-man's death, caustically added that "Doctor Cowdery has been nowhere to be seen."[11]

Cowdery's position as Yusuf Karamanli's unofficial doctor assured him more comfort than the enlisted men and Marines enjoyed. He resided in relative ease in the castle while the bulk of the prisoners first lived in a converted warehouse, but the Tripolitans had moved them to a larger build-ing, closer to the water. Ray found the new accommodations an improve-ment in terms of personal space but also directly in the line of fire of the American squadron. Ray reported that several shells from Preble's bor-rowed mortar boats had landed (but failed to explode) near the building.[12]

The unexploded shells were about the only excitement for the prisoners, who lived a frustratingly monotonous life. "Our men were employed in repairing the damages done in the several attacks upon the forts and batteries laying new platforms, building new gun-carriages, hauling timber and stone to build boats and erect fortifications, and nothing, worthy of remark, transhaped our fortune for a considerable time," Ray reported.[13]

Worse, the American sailors were also facing starvation. Although Captain William Bainbridge had arranged a line of credit so the enlisted men could buy food at the local markets while they were on work detail, there was simply no food for them to buy. "No bread to be had," Ray reported. "The Turks told us, that in consequence of the blockade which our shipping had maintained, we now had to suffer, and advised us to petition to our Commodore in Syracuse, to make peace and take us away. The Bashaw issued an edict prohibiting the inhabitants from purchasing, and the venders of grain from selling to any but the castellany. Money would not command bread, and starvation was whetting her teeth to devour us."[14]

The Americans were not just dying. Three sailors had "turned Turk," converted to Islam, to curry favor with the guards and the bashaw. The most hated of them was a Swede named John Wilson, who in addition to converting had spun wild tales of hidden treasure on board the *Philadelphia* and plans for armed insurrection among the prisoners. Wilson told the guards the other Americans were planning an armed attack in concert with Preble's assaults on the city. In response, the Tripolitans thoroughly searched the prison quarters. Although they found nothing, the guards subjected the *Philadelphia* crew to the usual round of beatings and whippings. Wilson was wrong—the prisoners had no weapons, and while they have muttered about attacking their guards, they had no plans to seize weapons and revolt. They did, however, have an escape plan. The bashaw had put the skilled American seamen to work repairing his warships. The ships' presence gave rise to the idea among the Americans of overpowering their jailors one night, stealing the now usable ships, and sailing to freedom.[15]

Captain William Bainbridge too was thinking about freedom. September 15, 1804, was day number 319 in captivity. Everyone was busy, the crew with forced labor, the officers with a school they had established—everyone, that is, but Bainbridge. The captain had little to do but write letters, deploring his situation and asking for information and also, in some cases, absolution. One of his favorite correspondents was diplomat George Davis, the chargé d'affaires in Tunis. Bainbridge wrote Davis more than thirty times. One reason for the flow of letters was that Davis had established the line of credit on which Bainbridge drew to pay for food for his sailors. Another was that Davis was a sympathetic shoulder on which Bainbridge could lean. Fears that his fellow officers and people back home might not approve of his actions haunted him, and Davis was always careful in his letters to bolster Bainbridge's ego and soothe his fear. On September 9, Davis wrote to Bainbridge, ostensibly to tell him there was no news but in invisible ink (lime juice) informing the captain that "letters from two or three Public Officers, imagine the war will be of some duration; I know not on what basis, their opinions are founded."[16]

Bainbridge found another sympathetic soul in Tobias Lear, with whom he developed a very close bond. The two men came to discuss everything, even tactics, as they exchanged letters. Lear too worked hard to keep up Bainbridge's spirits and to assure the captain that he, Lear, as the chief diplomat in the region, would do whatever it took to win the freedom of the captives. As Preble's campaign reached its climax, Lear, anticipating intransigence on the part of the bashaw, sought to bolster Bainbridge against the prospect (and eventual reality) that Preble would be ultimately unsuccessful in either securing the release of the hostages or forcing the bashaw to terms. "I hope before this reaches you, that your situation will be alleviated; and I trust that His Excellency, the Bashaw of Tripoli, will be convinced that it will be for his interest to be at peace with our nation on honorable and permanent grounds." And, like Davis, Lear made sure to offer his support: "The misfortune of yourself and our citizens with you has excited the commiseration of our countrymen, and your fortitude will be a subject of their admiration, you will come out like gold tried in the fire, and I trust Providence will yet smile upon you and place you among the favorite sons of America."[17]

The officers too suffered from lack of food. Danish consul Nicholas Nissen told Davis that several of them had been sick with "a fever with pains in limbs, everybody has felt here as contagious; not above 3 or 4, days neither dangerous; but Lord knows from what." Bainbridge too was in ill health as short rations and the strain of captivity took their toll.[18]

September 15 was a busy day at the home of the consul general in Algiers. The thirty-six-gun frigate *Congress* had arrived to pick up Lear, who was hastily packing his and Fanny's belongings, to direct any negotiations with Tripoli. Lear told his secretary, Timothy Mountford, "I am about to leave Algiers for a short time, to endeavor to negotiate a peace with the bashaw of Tripoli."[19] Lear and his wife boarded the warship, where he received a warm greeting from his friend from Santo Domingo, Captain John Rodgers. The *Congress* arrived off Tripoli on September 24. By then, Eaton had already left, shifting to the *Argus*, which was to take him to Syracuse, then Malta, and finally Alexandria. Lear boarded the *President* but found Barron too ill to meet with him. He and his wife settled in for the passage to Syracuse, where Barron planned to go ashore.

For Bainbridge, these comings and goings meant nothing as precious little information flowed to him. He had once championed the use of military might to smash the bashaw and free his crew. His time in captivity had dulled his ardor: "I conceive our case will be precisely thus—to comply with the terms that can be got after battering his town, send an army, or abandon us entirely to the hard fate which serving our country plunged us into."[20] In a letter to Davis, he also bemoaned his lack of information. "Not a word from America, or the Commodore do we hear—perfectly in the dark as to all movements, and harassed in mind with dreadful anxiety. . . . Please to inform Col. Lear that [I] write him often, but have not heard from him these five months past."[21]

One news item did manage to reach Tripoli: Tobias Lear and not James Cathcart was to lead any new negotiations. It was a glimmer of hope for Bainbridge. "No doubt but an American would [be] permitted to come and remain several days to negotiate, and he might trust himself with safety for I do not believe that this government would break its faith in such instances," he wrote to Davis. "This opinion of mine is hastily written, however, from it you will be able to get my meaning and can state the same to Col. Lear, and our Government."[22]

∞≀∞

William Bainbridge wasn't the only person in Tripoli watching and waiting for some sign of deliverance. Bashaw Yusuf Karamanli had mounted a vigil, keenly watching for the day when American warships could choke off his supply of grain entirely. Tripoli was starving and no edicts, no amount of rationing, could change that condition. "His Excellency the Bey, is wholly occupied, with devising every possible means, to ward off the evils, which might have resulted from the scarcity of grain," Davis reported to James Madison. "Agents have been sent to the Levant and almost every part of the Mediterranean. . . . [E]xtreme misery prevails throughout the interior of the country; the people subsisting on roots, a little herbage, and those who can procure it, oats. God only knows what will be the results."[23]

It was not only the populace that suffered from lack of food. The scarcity of grain caused fractures within Yusuf's inner circle. According to Cowdery, Yusuf's brother-in-law, Peter Lisle, who went by "Murad Rais" and was head of the bashaw's navy, got drunk one night and went to a private market to buy barley. When the seller refused, Lisle became enraged and demanded the barley, saying he had the right as a member of Karamanli's family. Guards soon arrived, as did Yusuf, who was "highly affronted," either at Lisle's insistence on the grain or his drunkenness, a dreadful sin for a Muslim, or for both reasons. He "flew at him with his all might, struck him and ordered his mamelukes to disarm him and put him in prison." Although the bashaw soon relented, released his brother-in-law, and whipped a servant who had told Lisle he could buy the barley, the damage had been done. Neither man trusted the other after the incident.[24]

As his city and people starved, Karamanli increasingly turned to a spiritual solution. More and more, he sought the counsel of his shadowy holy man, the marabout. It was this same holy man who had predicted Preble would never return to the United States and the U.S. Navy would lose two frigates in its attacks. Now, the holy man made new predictions that bolstered Karamanli's defiance—that he would be successful in his war with the Americans. After hearing this, Karamanli appeared to be in much lighter spirits. He even boasted to Cowdery that "if he had three frigates, he would blockade America. The bashaw believed he could do it as easily as a frigate and schooner could blockade Tripoli."[25]

☙❧

Commodore Samuel Barron needed to get ashore. Pain had almost completely invalided him, and he needed medical attention. Barron also knew he could not argue with success; information coming from diplomats, including Nissen in Tripoli, about the dire lack of food in the city convinced him to maintain the blockade. With his two largest warships, the *President* and *Constitution,* in need of repairs, and the frigate *John Adams,* brig *Argus,* and schooner *Enterprise* either on special missions or en route for refits, the Americans had five ships available to maintain the blockade: the frigates *Congress* and *Constellation,* the brig *Syren,* and the schooners *Nautilus* and *Vixen.*

On September 23, 1804, Barron left Rodgers in tactical command of the blockade. Barron intended to head to either Syracuse or Malta "to make some arrangements, with respect to the future operations of the squadron." Barron told Rodgers he was to remain off Tripoli "with the *Congress* and *Constellation,* until you are reinforced with some smaller vessels two of which I expect momentarily from Syracuse; as soon as they arrive, you will proceed with one of the frigates, to Syracuse to water leaving one of them here, to cooperate with the smaller vessels, until relieved by another frigate." Rodgers was to continue rotating the ships off Tripoli until *Constitution* and *President* were ready to rejoin the squadron, which Barron expected to happen "sometime in the next month."[26]

The blockade set, Barron sailed for Syracuse, where Preble and Eaton already were. Rodgers, however, did not remain off Tripoli for long and would cross swords, though not literally, with Preble once more. On October 16, Rodgers received a letter from Lear, who had arrived on Malta, informing him, "The *Constitution* will be ready for sea in a week or ten days. She is most completely fitted, and is as fine a ship as swims on the Sea. You will be tempted to take command of her, notwithstanding your partiality for your excellent ship, the *Congress.* I feel a strong predilection for the *Constitution.*

I think, besides being good, she will be a most fortunate ship; and I am sometimes good in my predictions."[27]

Rodgers had no authority to take command of the *Constitution*, although Barron's orders of September 23 did allow him to go to either Malta or Syracuse for supplies. It was common knowledge in the squadron that Preble handed command of the forty-four-gun frigate to his favorite officer, Captain Stephen Decatur Jr. Preble sounded more like a proud father than a commander when he gave his protégé orders to take what had been the squadron flagship: "I am happy that my supercedure [supersession] in the command of the squadron, and consequent return to the United-States affords an opportunity of placing you immediately in the exercise of the duties attached to that commission which you have so gallantly earned, and your country thus generously bestowed. I feel a pleasure in leaving the *Constitution* under the command of an officer whose enterprising and manly conduct in battle, I have so often witnessed; and who [*sic*] merits so eminently entitle to so handsome a command."[28] Preble made sure to inform Barron, who, as the new squadron commander, appeared to approve of the appointment.[29]

On October 23, Captain Hugh Campbell arrived off Tripoli with the *Constellation*. Rodgers decided to leave for Malta for supplies, ostensibly in keeping with his orders to rotate the frigates off Tripoli. Lieutenant Commandant John Dent with the *Nautilus* remained with the *Constellation*.[30] Rodgers set sail for Malta on October 24, arriving the twenty-eighth. On that same day, Preble finally said farewell to the *Constitution*, noting in his diary, "Took up my quarters on shore and left Capt. Decatur in command of the *Constitution*. *Congress* arrived."[31] Sometime after Rodgers arrived, he met with Preble. It did not go well. Preble had stated his intention to have good relations with all of his fellow officers, but there was something about Rodgers that simply irritated him and brought out his irascible side. For his part, Rodgers had the singular ability never to forget a perceived insult. Apparently, the two captains now argued over the merits of their respective ships, Preble making what Rodgers took as disparaging comments about the *Congress*, her crew, and his ability to maintain the ship. Neither man recorded how the argument began, but within a week Rodgers had relieved Decatur in command of the *Constitution* and ordered him to take over the smaller *Congress*. It could well be that Rodgers tipped his hand about his intentions to claim for himself the larger vessel, as more suited to his seniority on the captain's list, a topic that remained a sore point with Preble. Whatever the reason, the argument became so heated that Rodgers was prepared to challenge Preble to a duel. He composed (but never sent) a note that he carefully preserved among his personal papers:

> Sir
>
> A respect I owe to my country prevented me yesterday from requiring of you to explain the cause of your observations on the comparative good order of the *Constitution* and *Congress* and other incoherent remarks, feeling sensible that any dispute between us (in the situation I am now placed) could not fail to be productive of injury to the service. When we meet in the United States you shall then be explicitly informed of my opinion of your conduct. I am, with consideration, your obedient servant.
>
> John Rodgers[32]

Preble left Malta on November 6 to pay his respects to the court of Naples. That same day, Rodgers informed Secretary of the Navy Robert Smith that he had "changed my pendant" to the *Constitution*. He could not help but take a swipe at both Preble and Decatur in his report to Smith, remarking the *Constitution*, "although a larger ship I do not think so fine a one (for her rate) as the *Congress*, which has every good quality to recommend her, and her crew far (now) from being ordinary."[33]

For Decatur, the twenty-five-year-old hero of the *Philadelphia* raid and now clearly the star of Preble's campaign, loss of the *Constitution* was the start of what appeared to be an effort by Barron and Rodgers to limit his involvement in the campaign. Whether Barron and Rodgers contrived to push Decatur out of the spotlight or were simply adhering strictly to the rules of seniority, the result was the same. Decatur would no longer play a central role in the campaign to subjugate Tripoli. The same was true for Preble's other favorite, Master Commandant Charles Stewart, who quietly remained in command of the *Syren*. Stewart had helped Preble plan his summer attacks on Tripoli and commanded the blockade, but there is no evidence Barron or Rodgers ever consulted him when formulating their own plans.

∞≫

William Eaton arrived at Syracuse on September 20 and immediately composed a long report to Secretary Smith. Barron's poor health worried Eaton, as did Barron's circumspect nature: "I cannot but repeat my earnest wish that something more explicit may be expressed in the Commodore's instructions, and correspondent provisions made, concerning the aids to be advanced [to] Hamet Bashaw, in case this chief can be used to our advantage," he wrote Smith. "He [Barron] is cautious in using a discretion on the subject—and I believe, determined in any situation of the Bashaw's affairs not to furnish any supplies without special instructions."[34]

A bigger concern to Eaton was how, once he had found Hamet, he would equip and supply what could be a force of 30,000 followers. "The only obstacles which seem to oppose the success of this measure are want of supplies to put it into operation. These are not in the fleet; and the commodore is not decided whether any construction of the President's instructions extends to a discretion of procuring and furnishing them."[35]

Eaton detailed to Smith the argument that finally persuaded Barron to support the operation. He disparaged the idea of negotiated payments, which he knew Lear favored and for which Lear had funding. Also, in typical Eaton fashion, he played to Barron's sense of honor and vanity: "With half the sum authorized, according to Colonel Lear, to be given for a precarious peace with the reigning Bashaw of Tripoli, applied to assist the legitimate sovereign, the usurper may be made prisoner; an honorable and permanent peace secured; and this expense saved to the United States by the re-imbursement of Hamet Bashaw. Mr. O'Brien is decidedly in the opinion that this plan may be easily effected."[36]

Barron supported his operation, but his health and obvious doubts worried Eaton, who wanted Preble to remain in command. "I cannot withhold from you an expression of my serious apprehensions that, however justly we may appreciate the valor and abilities of his successor, the service will suffer from his retiring," Eaton wrote to his friend Thomas Dwight. "The unbounded confidence the officers on the station have in his capacities as a commander, and the very marked regrets they manifest at his leaving it, render this apprehension natural without detaching anything from the merits due to the manly and amiable disposition of Commodore Barron."[37]

Eaton did have the support of at least one major presence in the Mediterranean, the British governor of Malta, Sir Alexander Ball. Preble, who was a close friend of Ball, had already briefed the governor about Eaton's project, and Ball approved of it, even offering to support Eaton with letters of introduction to British officials in Egypt. Ball told Preble that action, any kind of action, was preferable to buying off the corsairs. "If I were to offer my humble opinion it would be, that you have done well in not purchasing a peace with money. . . . A few brave men have been sacrificed; but they could not have fallen in a better cause: and I even conceive it better to risk more lives than to submit to terms which might encourage the Barbary States to add fresh demands [and] insults."[38]

While Preble worked to gain allies for Eaton, the naval agent for the Barbary Regencies found himself marooned in Syracuse. After landing on Sicily on September 20, Eaton had little to do but wait for the *Argus*. Before he met with Barron, Hull had orders from Preble to escort the borrowed Neapolitan gunboats back to Messina. It was more than just a quick transit along the Sicilian coast. The gunboats were notoriously poor sailers, and the weather in late September in the Mediterranean was fickle. The *Argus* would have to tow the six gunboats most of the way, which meant the brig would make very slow headway. It took Hull nine days just to get the gunboats in good enough shape to make the transit to Messina.

Eaton spent that time in Syracuse, mostly in the company of Preble, who decided to show Eaton some of the many historical sites on the island. After passing the night at the home of George Dyson, the naval agent for Syracuse, Eaton set out on September 29 for Messina with Preble, Decatur, Midshipman Charles Morris, and a Ryland Randolph. Their guide, Lorenzo Abbate, brought the party first to Lentina, a small village on a lake of the same name. A thriving metropolis under the Greeks and Romans, Lentina in 1804 was little more than an agricultural backwater. The Americans toured the town and lake, which Eaton described as having "a stagnant, sickly surface exhaling a fetid atmosphere, very similar to that between the ruins of Carthage and the city of Tunis: said to have been created by an earthquake: covered with fowl, and full of fish, both of a wretched quality."[39]

The Americans spent three days visiting the ruins and curiosities of Catania, a major agricultural hub and one of the most important cities of Roman Sicily. Amphitheaters, baths, and temples all sparked the interest of the travelers, as did nearby Mount Etna, which Morris climbed right to the crater.[40] Everyone enjoyed the trip, except for the ever-impatient Eaton, who noted in his journal only, "Visited the natural and artificial curiosities of Catania."[41]

The Americans left Catania on October 3 for Messina, arriving there on the sixth. Once a rich, fertile region, the area between Catania and Messina had long since shed its luster. "Our journey . . . was over a horrid road, and through an uncultivated rocky country," Preble told Barron. "It is well however that we brought our allowance with us, or we might have starved. You were fortunate that you did not accompany us, as nothing we met with, could have compensated for the fatigue of travelling with such wretched cattle, and the torments suffered from bugs and fleas."[42] The poor traveling conditions did little to alleviate Eaton's impatience, and he clearly found nothing about the trip worthwhile, noting in his journal, "Average dividend of expense from Syracuse to Messina, dollars 36,30. Gratifications—the society only of our own party; and there damped by a continued series of melancholy proofs how fatal to human happiness is the hypocrisy of religious bigotry in the hands of a privileged priesthood. Everything is stamped with wretchedness; which nothing short of an entire revolution or the resurrection can erase."[43]

Arrival in Messina did not accelerate his mission, just his impatience. Eaton spent a month shuttling from Messina to Malta to Syracuse, all the time growing more and more irate at the delays. Finally, on November 8, after yet another trip from Malta back to Syracuse, he found Hull and the *Argus* waiting at anchor. He moved his baggage onto the brig on November 9, and on the tenth William Eaton set out at long last to overthrow Yusuf Karamanli.[44]

10

PLANS IN MOTION

HAMET KARAMANLI was somewhere in Egypt, his exact location a mystery. His brother Yusuf had spread the rumor that Hamet was a prisoner of the Mamelukes, but the reality was that no one really knew.[1] Meanwhile, Hamet's agents were hard at work trying to goad weapons and supplies out of the new American commodore. Samuel Barron had tried to keep American support for Hamet a secret, but it was a futile effort. William Eaton was partially to blame, as he alerted to his new mission many of his former diplomatic colleagues, including James Leander Cathcart: "I am on board the squadron in character of Navy Agent of the United States for the several Barbary Regencies but for the special purpose of reviving and giving effect to the plan of operation formed by yourself and me in conjunction with Hamet Bashaw."[2]

Edward Preble, Alexander Ball, Bonaventure Beaussier, the French consul in Tripoli, and Danish Consul Nicholas Nissen all knew about the plan and talked about it openly. Tobias Lear knew about and opposed the scheme, as did William Bainbridge, who learned about it through diplomatic scuttlebutt. Hamet Karamanli not only knew about the plan but also knew, thanks to Preble and Alexander Ball, that Barron had arrived in the Mediterranean with at the very least orders to aid him against his brother. He most likely did not know—yet—that Eaton too was back. He must soon have found out, as two of his agents contacted Barron almost the instant the commodore landed at Syracuse. Richard Farquhar, a shady Englishman living on Malta, wrote Barron twice, requesting information on what exactly Barron planned to do. Farquhar was apparently connected to Joseph Pulis, a local merchant who had acted as American consul on Malta until Preble caught him holding U.S. mail hostage. (Pulis would let the mail stack up then ask for funds to help him organize it. Preble caught on and chased the man from office.)

Farquhar's first letter made it plain that Eaton's scheme was no secret: "I understand you are going to cooperate with Sidi Ahmet Karamanli," Farquhar wrote. "I have had some conversation with those who is [sic] well acquainted with the affair of Tripoli, they say the people is [sic] displeased with the Bashaw and as they are distressed for grain and will be more so that the taking of Derne and Benghazi would complete the bashaw's ruin, and those places can be taken very easily now."[3] Farquhar asked Barron to bring him "and the Bashaw's consul" to Syracuse, likely to aid in the planning of any operation to help Hamet.[4] Barron never replied, so Farquhar wrote the commodore again, on October 21, asking for orders and claiming he had arranged for the pilot Stephen Decatur used in the raid to burn the *Philadelphia*. Again, Barron did not reply.[5] On November 1, Farquhar sent a third note, this time enclosing a letter from a known Hamet official— Salvatore Bufutil, Hamet's consul on Malta and the official with whom Preble had held talks in 1804 when he considered aiding Hamet.[6]

According to Bufutil, Hamet was indeed in Egypt and, far from hiding from his brother's assassins, was "waiting for the promised assistance of the United States of America." Bufutil claimed Hamet had "a great number of troops engaged for the purpose of cooperating with the U.S." and that Hamet promised he would "repay all money advanced on his account and give up all vessels and their cargos which may be taken in Tripoli, Benghazi, and Derne, as prizes to the U.S. ships of war," to help pay the overall costs of the conflict. To get his army from Egypt to Derne, Hamet needed "ten thousand dollars," an amount, Bufutil said, the Americans would immediately recoup from the prizes then lying at Derne.[7] "This is the proper time to assist him as the Arabs is [sic] now much displeased with his brother the bashaw of Tripoli, and provisions is [sic] now very scarce." Bufutil wrote.

Moreover, "the winter season is the best time for the troops to march from Egypt, therefore [I] hope your Excellency will not lose this favorable opportunity, which will have such an effect on all the Barbary Powers as will prevent them from going to War with the United States of America."[8]

Bufutil's letter was the first positive news to come from Hamet since Hamet's letter to Thomas Jefferson. For Eaton, it was proof that he was backing the right man. For Barron, it was simply proof that Hamet was alive and that he could proceed with the next steps of the mission.[9]

⌖

The plan to support Hamet was straightforward, at least on paper. The Navy would meet Hamet and transport him and his most trusted advisors from Alexandria to Derne, whose residents would throw open the gates and welcome Hamet as a liberator. From Derne, Hamet would lead an ever-increasing army across country to Tripoli. The Navy would help him take the city and unseat his brother. Once in charge, Hamet would release the American prisoners and sign a perpetual peace treaty with the United States. Barron was to coordinate the naval aspect, while Eaton was to advise Hamet. As such, the plan incorporated two of the three fronts on which Jefferson wanted to attack Yusuf—sea and land. Eaton's plan, however, made no mention of the third front—the diplomatic—which Jefferson also wanted to use. When Barron decided to push ahead with the Hamet scheme, it caught Jefferson's main regional diplomat by surprise.

Based on his latest orders, which he received just before Barron arrived to take command, Tobias Lear believed he was to be the catalyst for a peaceful resolution of the conflict with Tripoli. Although he knew of Eaton's plan to use Hamet against Yusuf, he did not approve of the tactic and given his new orders, he "presume[d] the co-operation of the brother of the bashaw of Tripoli will not be attempted." He wrote to James Madison, "Our force is thought sufficient to compel him [Yusuf] to terms without this aid, and in any event it is very doubtful whether he [Hamet] has it in his power, with any reasonable pecuniary assistance we might give, to render us service." To Lear, there was good reason why the United States should avoid any involvement with Hamet. "He is now in Egypt, driven by his brother from Derne, where it is presumed he might have made a stand, had he been a man of any force or influence; which, from the best accounts I can collect, he is not," he told Madison. "Indeed I should place much more confidence in the continuance of a peace with the present bashaw, if he is well beaten into it, than I should have with the other, if he should be placed on the throne by our means."[10]

It must have caught Lear off guard then, when Barron informed him on November 13, "I have sent the *Argus* to Alexandria for the purpose of making enquiry relative to the ex-bashaw and if he is found and willing to come to this place—Captain Hull is instructed to bring him down." Madison had not taken Lear's advice, and now the United States was prepared to back Hamet. Barron, however, made sure Lear realized the commodore had his own ideas as to what shape that support would take, ideas that diverged from those of Eaton. Barron wanted Hamet to come first to Syracuse, where the commodore could take his measure. "I conceive that if no other use can be made of him there will be no difficulty in placing him in possession of Derne and Benghazi. It may have a good effect, on his Brother it cannot I think, have an ill one," Barron wrote. Also, he promised, "should we succeed in getting him here, I shall take no ultimate measures, without informing you of them."[11] It was clear that Barron would proceed only if Hamet proved worthy of U.S. support.

Lear had spent most of October and the first half of November making the diplomatic rounds, stopping in Algiers and Tunis; off Tripoli, where he got a look at the greatly reduced blockade; and finally Malta, where he expected to find Barron. News of Barron's illness had already reached him, and Lear thought the commodore would avail himself of the British facilities on Malta.[12] Instead, Barron had gone to Syracuse, where he thought Lear would now go too. Instead, the diplomat told the commodore he wanted to remain on Malta, which was closer to Tripoli than the Sicilian port; he wanted to be close to Tripoli should an opportunity for talks arise.[13] It would also allow him to keep an eye on any of Hamet's agents trying to reach Barron, although Lear never gave that as a reason.

On November 30, Rodgers arrived in the *Constitution*, flying his broad commodore's pennant from the mainmast. Rodgers went ashore, where he met with Lear, whom he told that Barron's liver ailment had become so bad that on the twelfth Barron had sent him a letter relinquishing, at least temporarily, command of the squadron: "As I shall not be able to attend to the business afloat for some time, I request you will hoist the broad pendant on board the *Constitution* and give such orders for the safety of the squadron, from time to time, as may be most proper."[14]

Now in command, Rodgers left the *Constellation* to continue the blockade and sent the *President* to bolster it. He also oversaw a shuffling of officers and men among the squadron's Marine detachments. In a quirk, when Preble was outfitting his squadron a percentage of the Marines who enlisted had done so only for one year instead of the three years that Marine Corps Commandant Major William Burrows wanted.[15] Also, several officers had been on station for two, going on three, years and wanted to return home. Plus, Burrows liked to rotate his small officer corps to give each man the chance at sea duty. Barron detailed Rodgers to oversee and approve the arrangements the senior Marine officer in the squadron, Captain John Hall made for the Marines. One of the new assignments Hall ordered sent First Lieutenant Presley Neville O'Bannon from the *Constitution* to the *Argus*.[16]

⮠⮠⮠

William Eaton as well wanted to make changes to the original plan to aid Hamet. First, he unilaterally decided the American base at Syracuse would also be Hamet's base of supply, telling Secretary of the Navy Smith, "The expedition against Benghazi is to start from this rendezvous [Syracuse], after the resources of Hamet Bashaw are better known."[17] It was the first time anyone had mentioned actually mounting Hamet's campaign from the American naval base on Sicily. It made sense, as Barron wanted Hamet to come to Syracuse before the commodore made any final commitment to the "rightful bashaw," while Eaton likely viewed it as the most logical place from which to supply Hamet's army. The force could move quickly from Derne to Benghazi if unencumbered with an equipment train. That equipment, he told Smith, "should come out from America, that we may not be subject to the caprice of a foreigner who may influence the king [Ferdinand] of the two Sicilies to withhold them." Eaton knew of problems Preble had with the powder and shot manufactured in Naples—the Neapolitans had likely sabotaged them when Napoleon had conquered the city briefly in 1799 and forced the Italians to provide supplies to the French—and he wanted no ammunition or weapons that might fail at a crucial moment. Instead, he told Smith, "brass field pieces, well mounted, and excellent French arms are ready at Springfield [Massachusetts]; and as this place is in the vicinity of Hartford [Connecticut], the best port in the United States, perhaps, for shipping salt beef, fourteen brass 4-pounders and 500 or a thousand stands of arms may be sent out from thence. Good musket powder, flints and balls; and suitable ammunition for the artillery will be necessary."[18]

None of these requests were surprises. Eaton's orders designated him as Hamet's expediter—he was to procure arms and equipment for the men Hamet promised would follow him. Merely acting as an arms supplier, however, was not enough for the ambitious former Army captain. Once Hamet set off to attack Yusuf, Eaton decided, he would "accompany the bashaw by land in the expedition against Tripoli next summer. This I shall cheerfully do on condition that he will give the inspection, field discipline, and disposition of attack and defense of his army to me."[19]

Eaton had never previously expressed a desire to actually command the land attack on Tripoli. His highest command in the U.S. Army had been of an understrength company that saw little action. Now, the captain from Connecticut wanted to lead an attack on a fortified city in command of an army whose language he didn't speak and whose loyalty to a Christian leader was likely to be nil. It was typical Eaton.

The *Argus* left Syracuse on November 14, bound for Malta, where she arrived the next day. British officials on the island kept the American brig in quarantine when she arrived, a practice that dated to the Black Death of the fifteenth century. Port officials prevented ships arriving from overseas from delivering cargo or landing crew until certain they did not carry disease. This was especially true for ships from Sicily and the Italian mainland, where outbreaks of the plague had occurred as late as 1753 and where outbreaks of yellow fever, which originated in the Caribbean had traveled to southern Europe in trade vessels, were becoming increasingly frequent and virulent.[20] Eaton was well aware of the quarantine rules, especially those at Malta, and he arrived at the port prepared. Instead of insisting on a meeting with Ball, the British governor, Eaton sent two letters ashore for him, one Eaton wrote and one from Preble. The second letter was the more important. The former commodore asked Ball to help Eaton get his expeditions started by providing the special naval agent with introductions he would need to navigate the labyrinth of Egyptian politics. Ball was only too happy to oblige and gave Eaton an introductions to Samuel Briggs, the British proconsul at Alexandria, and to Major Edward Missett, the consul general in Cairo.[21]

There were two officials whom Eaton wanted to pick up from Malta and take to Alexandria—Richard Farquhar and Salvatore Bufutil. Both men boarded the *Argus*, but Eaton decided to leave Bufutil behind. "I don't like him," he told Commodore Barron. "There is too much wood about his head and beef about his ankles either to advance or retreat handsomely. Mr. Farquhar goes forward with us."[22]

The *Argus* left Malta on November 17, bound for Alexandria, where she arrived on the twenty-fifth. The passage across the Mediterranean was uneventful, but the *Argus* had to wait days for a pilot to enter the harbor. The U.S. brig of war sailed into the ancient city of Alexander the Great on November 26, saluting a Turkish ship of the line with seventeen guns and receiving seventeen guns in return. Oddly, Spanish and French warships did not salute the American brig.[23] After anchoring, Eaton got down to the business of organizing his coup. His scheme, months in planning, alternately in favor and out of favor, was finally about to start.

∞ ∞

Plans were in motion all around the Mediterranean. The U.S. Navy squadron continued to blockade Tripoli. Barron had left the *President* on station with the *Constellation* and *Vixen* and the three warships kept Yusuf Karamanli's capital city on the verge of starvation. It was boring, tiring duty. Any time a lookout spotted a strange sail on the horizon, one of the ships would give chase. As the topmen above deck worked the sails, gunners and Marines below decks readied the cannon, manhandling the heavy pieces into place. It was slightly easier on the *Vixen*—the schooner carried eighteen-pounder carronades that weighed roughly 1,200 pounds each.

The *President,* in contrast, carried twenty-four-pounders that weighed nearly three tons. It took four men to work the tackle that moved the piece into firing position, two to prepare the cannon for firing, and two more to fire the gun. All moved in a carefully choreographed ballet. First, spongers extinguished any embers left in the barrel from the last discharge before two men placed the next round and a bundle of wadding into the muzzle. A rammer then pushed into the gun the charge (which weighed on average six pounds), then the eighteen- or twenty-four-pound iron ball, and then more wadding. The second gun captain then pushed a metal prong into the touchhole to pierce the bag that contained the charge, and he primed the cannon. The first gun captain then touched off the weapon. The crew repeated the entire exercise until the ship's commander ordered "Cease fire."

On the *Constellation,* Midshipman Charles Morris recalled chasing unknown ships nearly every day over a two-week period from November 1 to the sixteenth.[24] For the crew, it meant constantly going to quarters, standing down, and then returning to quarters, in a mind- and body-sapping routine. It was a brutal grind that could break a man. Private William Williams, a Marine on the *President,* fell asleep while on duty, an unforgiveable offense. Barron ordered him court-martialed. At his trial Williams told the panel of officers hearing his case that he had spent more than a day "port and starboard," two hours on duty and two hours off, which afforded him no time to sleep. It was the same with all the Marines.

Any time a lookout spotted a "chase," the Marines, like their Navy counterparts, rushed to their battle stations. Some, usually the best shots, went aloft, climbing the shrouds to the fighting tops, platforms from which they could sweep an enemy's deck with musket fire. Others picked up pistols, tomahawks, pikes, or cutlasses and prepared either to board the enemy ship or repel boarders. Still other Marines manned cannon on the quarterdeck. When Commodore Edward Preble launched his direct attacks on Tripoli, he mounted six spare twenty-four-pounders on the quarterdeck of the *Constitution* that his Marines manned. He singled out those crews for praise after the attacks of August: "The Conduct of the Marines of the squadron, have [*sic*]. . . on every occasion, merited the highest encomiums."[25]

In addition to combat duties, the Marines had to mount guard. Marine sentries guarded the captain's cabin and key positions on deck.[26] When in pursuit of an enemy, which could last hours, a Marine might only have an hour's sleep in a twenty-four-hour period. Williams' defense, then, had some merit, and while not completely convincing, it swayed the six officers, who set aside hanging and instead sentenced him to fifty lashes, a punishment later reduced to ten.[27]

Blockade duty went well beyond the actual pursuit of blockade runners. There were still the mundane, everyday tasks that went into running a warship. Water and rations required distribution, the ship itself required nearly constant care and cleaning, as did the crewmen and their clothing. The busy work had a serious reason. William Amory, a Marine lieutenant on the *Constitution,* ensured his men hung their clothes up every morning to air them out, along with their bedding, to keep disease from striking the crew.[28] Officers also had to keep a close watch on their men, as tempers could easily fray during the long, dull stretches when little occurred on the blockade and the monotony of shipboard life seemed overwhelming. Hezekiel Loomis, the steward on the schooner *Vixen,* had a run-in with the *Vixen*'s cooper (barrel maker) over a seemingly innocuous problem. Loomis planned to serve salt pork to the ship's company and duly had a small party of sailors hoist barrels of meat and flour to the deck, where Loomis could dole it out. On inspecting one of the barrels, Loomis found it wasn't pork but beef—someone in America had mislabeled it. "I told the cooper that he must get up a barrel of pork," Loomis confided to his journal. "He said he could not get at any and that it was my d——d carelessness not marking them right. I told him that I must have the business done at once as it was late. He complied after great disputing."[29]

⚬⚬⚬

Yusuf Karamanli was busy with plans of his own, mostly how to get grain into his capital and keep his restive populace from rising in revolt. He knew about the American scheme involving his brother and had his own plan to force Hamet to reconsider. First, he made his oldest son, Ali, marry Hamet's oldest daughter. It could not have been a happy affair. Hamet's entire family had remained hostage to Yusuf since Hamet fled Tripoli. The girl was just twelve years old, although "said to be very handsome."[30] The marriage, Yusuf likely hoped, would tie Hamet even more to himself. If Hamet attacked, he would be taking up arms against his own son-in-law, potentially making his daughter a widow. It is unknown whether there was any bond between Ali and Hamet's daughter, although she certainly knew her cousin.[31]

Next, Karamanli started his own propaganda campaign. The minute he learned about Barron's health issues, when John Rodgers and not Samuel Barron arrived off Tripoli with the *Constitution* on November 17 to relieve the *Constellation*, the bashaw spread the rumor that Barron was dead and the Americans were leaderless. What he hoped to accomplish with the rumor is another unknown. He likely aimed it as his own people, rather than his fellow Barbary leaders, thinking the populace might take heart if it believed the bashaw's chief adversary was dead. If so, it didn't work. Soon after, Karamanli sent Ali to recruit troops to guard against a feared American land invasion. Ali spent ten days scouring for soldiers but returned empty-handed. The people, fighting starvation, had no stomach for warfare.[32]

The Barron rumor wasn't Karamanli's only ruse. As word of the American plan to use Hamet went from rumor to reality—Yusuf's spies made sure he knew Eaton had left Malta for Egypt—he announced he would rather die fighting than surrender to his brother. He vented his frustration on his American prisoners, once more denying them rations other than bread bought with credits that Captain Bainbridge secured. At the same time, he ordered his chief guard, a brute named Sossey, to "treat the American prisoners with the utmost cruelty, in order to induce the United States the sooner to make peace."[33] Letters soon reached the American squadron about the increasingly harsh treatment. Midshipman James Renshaw, in a letter to John Rodgers, declared the "situation at present my dear sir is beyond conception."[34]

The enlisted men decided enough was enough. After nearly two weeks of beatings and near starvation, the crew of the *Philadelphia* staged a revolt of sorts. On December 10, "our keepers or drivers, as usual, unlocked the prison doors early in the morning, and ordered us *tota fora* (all out),"

Marine private William Ray reported. None of the Americans moved. The prisoners had built a barricade out of their cots, "making it difficult for the drivers to come at us," Ray reported. "We then all spoke, and told them, that were we resolved, if death should be the consequence, not to turn out another day without food. They threatened to call the soldiers, and fire in on us, but they found we could not be moved by threats or blows, they left us and informed the bashaw of our refractory conduct." The show of solidarity impressed Yusuf, who sent the guards back with word "that if we would peaceably and tacitly obey their orders, we should have bread at twelve o'clock—this was agreed to and the stipulation fulfilled."[35]

For Bainbridge and his crew, December 10 was day number 406 in captivity, and the once hawkish captain had all but given up on a military solution. Since his capture Bainbridge advocated and even tried to help plan the subjugation of Tripoli by force of arms. Months of solitary confinement, bouts of disease, and the failure of the whirlwind of Preble's assaults had combined to drive down Bainbridge's spirits. "If peace can't be effected this winter I am of an opinion that after our squadron makes their exertions next spring and summer it will be to the honor and interest of the U.S. to make peace on the best terms attainable," he wrote to Tobias Lear, "for a continuation of the war would be attended with considerable expense without reducing much the demand."[36]

Bainbridge also began to snipe at those who were working so hard to win his freedom. In a letter to Lear, Bainbridge criticized Preble for underestimating Karamanli's financial demands and overestimating the bashaw's willingness to engage in a prisoner exchange. Getting a peace for a bargain price that included a free prisoner exchange was a key aspect of Preble's offers to negotiate with Yusuf. Bainbridge, however, complained, "I have heard that [Yusuf] declared he would not give an orange a piece for his subjects, prisoners to the Americans. The Minister of Foreign Affairs, has told me several times that the Bashaw would not give, one of the American Sailors, for all the prisoners the Commodore has."[37]

In some ways, Bainbridge was the best messenger Yusuf Karamanli could want. As soon as news reached Bainbridge that the Navy would cooperate with Hamet, he wrote to Lear saying he could not "conceive the most distant hope of any utility to be derived to the U.S. from pecuniary or other aid given the poor effeminate fugitive brother of the Bashaw of Tripoli."[38] It was exactly the picture Yusuf wanted the Americans to see. He knew his brother was neither the leader that William Eaton needed nor completely vapid, as Bainbridge made him out. Hamet was somewhere in between but as long as he conveyed the message the bashaw wanted, Yusuf was happy to let Bainbridge play messenger. Bainbridge was only too happy to be an unknowing accomplice in Yusuf's slander campaign against Hamet. The American was quick to repeat Yusuf's version of his brother's exile from Tripoli: "He was placed by his brother in command at Derne the most favorable province for his attempting a counter revolution. The present Bashaw suspecting that he was not conducting himself properly, drove him from that situation, only by an *order* without sending troops against him." Hamet, Bainbridge said, had not shown "spirit enough to retain his situation when placed in it, or has had interest sufficient among his own religious sect (Mussulmen) to re-establish himself in what he conceives his right but has wandered an exile far from country, wife and children for more than 8 years without disturbing the Regency of Tripoli."[39] He ended by asking, "What can be expected from such a pusillanimous being?"[40]

It would not be the last time Bainbridge attempted to forestall or even reverse plans involving Hamet, nor was it the last time he would try to use Lear as his voice in councils with Samuel Barron.

11

INTO EGYPT

THE U.S. BRIG OF WAR *ARGUS* looked tiny compared to the other warships tied up in Alexandria harbor. There was a massive Turkish ship of the line, four Turkish frigates, a French frigate, and a Spanish frigate. The Turkish vessels had all rendered the correct honors to Master Commandant Isaac Hull when the *Argus* entered the harbor on November 26, although the French and Spanish ships had not. Hull didn't care. A pilot who worked for the British consul had helped guide the *Argus* through the tricky waters that led to the anchorage, and now Hull was waiting for word as to when he would see the officials whom Malta governor Alexander Ball had arranged for him and Eaton to meet.[1]

William Eaton keenly observed the *Argus'* crew at work. He noted in his journal the salutes the *Argus* rendered and received (he counted eighteen guns from the Turks, not seventeen as Hull reported) and also noted the slow going in the harbor.[2] What he didn't record were his thoughts as the American brig of war carried him closer to realizing his goal. Hull soon welcomed Samuel Briggs on board. Briggs was the British consul in Alexandria, and he offered to set up meetings with the Turkish officials in the city.

Briggs was a polite, upright merchant engaged in what was then a new venture, Egyptian cotton. When he read the letter of introduction from

Alexander Ball, Briggs was only too happy to aid the Americans. The consul, however, had no idea of Eaton's mission and sent Hull that evening a note suggesting that Eaton come ashore at Admiral's Wharf the next morning. He promised to do what he could to help: "I beg my compliments to Mr. Eaton, and renew my assurances to both, that it will give me much pleasure in my public, as well as private capacity to render you any service in my power."[3]

Briggs was at the wharf at 9:30 a.m. the next day. He met Eaton, who wore civilian clothes, and Hull, who was in full-dress uniform. He accompanied them to the home of the Turkish governor of the city, who was with the Turkish squadron commander, an admiral. The Turks treated the Americans to an elaborate and long ceremony, aimed mostly at Hull, who was the first American naval officer to pay an official visit to Alexandria. For Eaton, perpetually in a rush, the ceremony was a necessary evil. He noted in his diary merely that the Turks "most hospitably received" them.[4] The niceties over, Eaton quickly got down to business, steering the conversation to Hamet. He asked if anyone knew the whereabouts of the "deposed bashaw" of Tripoli. The Turks said nothing. Briggs told Eaton he had heard that Hamet was somewhere well south of Cairo, where he had allegedly joined a band of rebelling Mamelukes. Eaton thanked Briggs and the Turkish officials for their hospitality and began making plans to go to Cairo. He saw in Briggs an ally, and he wanted his country to benefit from the Englishman's abilities. Eaton and Hull asked Briggs to become the U.S. Navy agent in Alexandria. Briggs accepted, and Eaton duly notified Secretary Smith of the offer, urging him to accept Briggs into U.S. service.[5]

The gateway to Cairo was the small port of Rosetta, where the Nile emptied into the Mediterranean, and that was Eaton's next destination. He arranged with Hull to take with him several officers from the *Argus*—Lieutenant Joshua Blake, Midshipmen George Mann and Eli Danielson (Eaton's stepson), and First Lieutenant Presley O'Bannon, commander of the brig's Marines. Eaton also brought Richard Farquhar, a Janissary interpreter named Selim, a servant named Ali, and six bodyguards. They embarked for Rosetta on a small sloop on the twenty-eighth, but contrary winds kept them in Alexandria. The next day the weather cleared, and Eaton and his party set out. They stopped at Aboukir Bay at 4 p.m. The layover allowed Eaton and his party to go ashore to visit the sites where the French had fought two large land battles against the Turks and Mamelukes and a massive naval battle against Horatio Nelson's British fleet. Everywhere Eaton, O'Bannon, and the others walked, they found the ground "covered with human skeletons, ghastly monuments of the savage influence of avarice and ambition on the human mind."[6]

Eaton's party departed Aboukir the next day and arrived in Rosetta on December 1, 1804. They raised an American flag over their craft and waited. At two-thirty that afternoon, a barge appeared flying a large British flag. On board was the dragoman, or "fixer," for Major Edward Missett, the British resident in Cairo, who had lately taken refuge in Rosetta. Eaton and Blake boarded the British barge and went ashore, where Eaton was reunited with Dr. Francesco Mendrici, an old friend from Tunis who was now the personal physician to the Turkish pasha in Egypt. "The doctor was sent out of [Tunis] about a year before me . . . for possessing dispositions congenial to the interest of the Bey's wife," Eaton explained to Smith.[7] In Missett Eaton seemed to find a kindred soul and he took an instant liking to the Englishman.[8] "You will find in Major Missett all that can be comprised in the term a gentleman, with the frankness of an old soldier, we certainly are very happy in our introductions from Governor Ball."[9]

Missett conducted Eaton's party to his home, where he offered to help Eaton as much as he could. He warned the Americans that travel to Cairo might be perilous and offered to send his own secretary, a Captain Vincents, and four armed bodyguards with them. The offer was more than Eaton could have wished for, and in a typically rash moment he "unreservedly opened to him the object of my voyage."[10] Eaton had previously covered the real reason for his presence in Egypt by saying he and the officers were simply sightseeing, taking in the grandeur of the ancient country. Missett likely had advance warning of Eaton's real mission from Ball, but whatever he knew he kept to himself. As for his offers of aid, Eaton readily accepted. He wrote Hull, "I find my party increasing, and am very desirous of seeing you here, that I may have the benefit of your advice in some measures I am meditating, you will find the tour agreeable and I have no doubt useful."[11]

Missett had more information on Hamet than Briggs. Hamet was indeed with a Mameluke sheik somewhere south of Cairo. Hamet commanded a small band of Tripolitan and Arab troops fighting alongside the Mamelukes against the Turks, who were trying to restore their authority over the country. This was good and bad news for Eaton. The good news was he now had an idea of Hamet's location. The bad news was Hamet had been pulled into the Egyptian civil war. It put Hamet directly in conflict with Sultan Selim III, who would be Hamet's nominal overlord if he regained the throne in Tripoli. Eaton inquired about boats but found that a "religious chief" had "seized all" of them, so he settled in for another night at the home of the British consul. He took the time to prepare two identical copies of a carefully worded message to the "rightful bashaw," informing him that Eaton was in Egypt and ready to help him regain his throne. He also made it clear, however, he would not allow Hamet's current circumstances to draw the United States into the turmoil in Egypt and wanted to be "informed of the channel of communication with your Excellency in such a manner as not to embroil my government with any of the chiefs of this country."[12]

It was an important point, one Eaton knew he had to include if he wanted to continue to receive support from the U.S. Navy. The United States was already at war with a province of the Ottoman Empire, a conflict in which the Porte appeared content to let the Tripolitans essentially reap what they sowed. Egypt was a very different story. There the Turks were determined to restore their control. They wanted to reap the benefits of the rich trade routes Egypt commanded, as well as the grain it could provide to the rest of the empire. They were now somewhat at odds with the British, who supported a restoration of Mameluke rule.[13] With Hamet literally in the middle of the battle between the Ottomans and the Mamelukes, Eaton would have to be at his diplomatic best in Egypt.

⌐⚔⌐

Egypt in 1805 was a maelstrom of competing interests, warring powers, wandering bands of brigands, and an impoverished people. Once the jewel in the crown of the Roman and Byzantine empires, Egypt by the start of the nineteenth century had lost much of its luster. Eaton had already glimpsed

in Alexandria how far the land of the pharaohs had sunk. The city a traveler had once described as having "four thousand palaces, an equal number
of public baths, four hundred markets" was now one "with towers almost
ruins, filled with the wrecks of houses."[14] At its height, Alexandria had
nearly a million residents. In 1805 it had barely "five thousand inhabitants,
of all colors, of all nations, and of all sects, established upon a little tongue
of land running out into the sea, which has no other means of subsistence
than the feeble resources of a languishing commerce."[15] The city might
have remained in relative obscurity had it not been for the grandiose plans
of Napoleon Bonaparte. The "Little Corporal" had dreams of following in
the footsteps of Alexander the Great by creating an empire that spanned
from the Nile to the Indus River in India. Napoleon's troops waded ashore
at Aboukir Bay on July 1, 1798, instantly transforming the seaport into a
major supply base. The French campaign ended in disaster two years later,
creating a political vacuum in the country that continued in 1805.

The Turks had conquered Egypt in 1515 and sent their Janissaries to
run the country. There the Janissaries intermingled with the Mamelukes,
who had ruled Egypt since the Crusades. The Mamelukes, who had originated in Georgia and Circassia, were mercenary soldiers whom the former
ruling caliphs had brought to Egypt to solidify their power. When the Ottomans conquered Egypt, they used the Mamelukes as an underclass of civil
servants. The four regiments of Janissaries the Ottomans stationed in the
country soon recruited four full regiments of Mamelukes to help them,
and for more than two hundred years the two groups competed for power.
By the 1750s, the Mamelukes had reasserted their authority over Egypt,
making the country all but independent of Constantinople.[16] The Turks
returned in force in 1782 but were never able to suppress the Mamelukes,
and Egypt slipped into anarchy. By the time of the French invasion, Egypt
was a whirlpool of competing political elements. In 1801 the sultan sent
nine thousand soldiers, mostly Albanians, to bolster the Turkish force already
fighting alongside the English army to oust the last of the French troops
still in Egypt. By 1803 the Albanians, under the command of the remarkable Mohammed Ali, were instead fighting the Turkish troops and winning

control of the country. The center of most of the fighting was Cairo, but incessant warfare spread throughout the country.[17]

One of toughest tasks facing Eaton was navigating the labyrinth of competing forces. With Hamet involved with the Mamelukes, there might be no way to avoid entrapment. Spies were everywhere, and even his visits to the British could well land him in trouble, as the competing factions all looked for reasons to accuse one another of double-dealing and perfidy. The chaotic political situation, however, created the perfect environment in which to recruit the specialized soldiers Hamet would need to capture both Benghazi and Tripoli. Egypt abounded in bands of Turkish, Albanian, Arab, and Mameluke soldiers, as well as a few handfuls of French deserters who were content to fight for anyone with money. Hamet's Tripolitan forces would likely lack the engineers, farriers, drivers, and above all, artillerymen he would need to mount his campaign. Egypt could provide them all.[18]

⋖⋗

Commodore Edward Preble had a way of inspiring his young officers not only to follow orders and maintain discipline but to execute missions other navies thought too difficult. One of those tasks was maintaining a blockade throughout the notoriously capricious Mediterranean winter. Preble always kept at least two warships off Tripoli throughout his time in command, which included the winter of 1803–04. Samuel Barron had other ideas. He apparently decided the horrible weather that marked winter at sea off the North African shore was more than enough to prevent shipping from entering Tripoli. On November 27, he sent orders to Hugh Campbell and the *Constellation* to break off from blockade duty and check on the other Barbary States, especially Tunis, where a nasty spat over a seized American merchant vessel threatened to spark a war. Barron decided not to replace the *Constellation*, instead keeping the *President* in port where she awaited repairs after a collision with the *Constitution*. The *Syren* continued on duty off Morocco, Charles Stewart filling the role Isaac Hull had the previous year with the *Argus*. Only the schooner *Vixen*, under Master Commandant John Smith, remained on actual blockade duty. The *Vixen* kept an eye out for the *Constitution*, not knowing that Barron had changed his orders to Rodgers. On the twenty-seventh the commodore sent Rodgers to Lisbon to recruit sailors for the squadron. Enlistments of many of the sailors in the squadron had either run out or were about to expire. Rodgers was to "[s]hip as many good Men as you can procure, on the same terms that the rest of your crew." If he could not find enough men in Lisbon, he had Barron's permission to stop in as many ports as necessary. He was also to find the *Syren* and, if the situation with Morocco was stable, send the brig to Syracuse.[19]

In a lull in the weather and the blockade, the crew of the *Vixen,* alone on station, was sealing deck seams with tar when a sailor knocked over a bucket of the flammable liquid in the galley, where a fire burned twenty-four hours a day. When the tar hit the galley fire it burst into flames. Fire was arguably the most dangerous enemy of a wooden ship, and crews spent much time learning to fight it. The sailors responded immediately and "by spirited exertions with wet swab" extinguished the blaze "without damage." The fire was about the most excitement the crew of the *Vixen* had for several weeks, during which they busied themselves with "coating the anchors, worming the cables, overhauling old rigging etc. until sunset," at which time they received their grog. The blockade was a grind that went on day after day.[20]

The same was true ashore, where the now 298 officers and men of the frigate *Philadelphia* continued to endure imprisonment. The prisoners' chief concern continued to be hunger. The Americans "were obliged to sell the clothes which they had lately drawn, and for which they were suffering, to procure something to sustain life," reported Private Ray. "The cravings of hunger predominated over the calls of external wants, and our clothes were sacrificed for a mere trifle but trifles are of magnitude when they preserve life."[21] Hunger drove some of the prisoners to extremes. Ray recounted how one American, "impelled by imperious hunger," decided liquor was as good as food and targeted a small Jewish-run distillery near the prison. Somehow the man managed to scale a wall "twenty feet high, broke or unlocked three doors," and got into the shop, where he drank an amount of a local brew Ray called "aquadiente." He returned to the prison with a pitcher of alcohol, which "he distributed amongst his companions so profusely that he was suspected and subsequently convicted of the robbery."

The unnamed American avoided a harsh penalty, as "he greased the fists of his keepers, who, for a share, put him in irons and gave him a slight punishment."[22]

Other prisoners came up with a far more ingenious method of getting food. Somehow, the Americans learned how to produce counterfeit Tripolitan coins, which they used to buy whatever they could find at local markets. Their guards, however, soon discovered the prisoners' mint and turned the coins over to Yusuf Karamanli. The bashaw "laughed heartily and said that the Americans were all wizards and devils, and protested that if the person was detected, he could not punish, but reward his invention."[23]

⊂⊗́ ⊗⊃

William Eaton finally set out for Cairo on December 4, admittedly "without having obtained any certain intelligence concerning the subject in pursuit." It took Eaton two days to secure a pair of small boats to sail from Rosetta to Cairo. Each weighed about forty tons and was armed with small cannon and swivel guns. The boats were typical Egyptian river schooners, called "marches," that plied the Nile. In one, Eaton put himself, his stepson Eli Danielson, George Mann, Presley O'Bannon, Richard Farquhar, Selim the Janissary, Ali, and six servants, all of whom were armed with muskets, pistols, and swords. Captain Vincents and Dr. Francesco Mendrici, with another ten servants and bodyguards, boarded the second vessel. Eaton hoisted the American flag over his craft, while Vincents raised the Union Jack. The heavily armed party set sail, taking all "precautions necessary to resist the predatory attacks of the wild Arabs, who infest the river's banks, and, during this general suspense of justice, prey upon the defenseless; as well as the outrage of the Albanian Turkish soldiery, who, restrained by no discipline, ravage and murder indiscriminately everywhere."[24]

The party sailed leisurely down the Nile, passing camps of wandering Arabs and small villages that were defenseless against any armed band that wanted whatever scraps the villages still had. Eaton reported watching one band of Arabs fall upon a herd of camels, cattle, and buffalo outside one village. The herders made angry cries but did nothing to stop the Arabs. "The shrieks of the villagers demonstrated their consternation and anxiety, while they offered no resistance to these mounted marauders of the desert and these, on the other hand, appeared to aim no mischief towards the persons of their inactive brethren of the plain."[25]

The travelers encountered no problems as they ascended the river. Eaton said the party's frequent hunting trips and profligate use of their firearms kept the Arabs at bay, although even the redoubtable American doubted whether twenty or so armed men would be enough to fend off one of the larger bands of brigands roaming the area. Eaton said the day before the Arabs attacked the herd, "five hundred Albanians, who had deserted from the Vice Roy's army and taken their rout to Damietta," had sacked the village. "Fortunate for us, perhaps, that they had not stayed a day longer; for it is doubtful whether our appearance would have been formidable to their avarice; or our resistance to their force."[26]

On December 7, the party "landed near a village on the east side of the Nile," Eaton recorded in his journal. "Villagers fled at our approach. On giving tokens of friendship some of them advanced towards us; when told we were English they flocked around with demonstrations of joy; offered us their services, and raised loud ejaculations for our establishment in the country." Later that same day, the two boats landed at the town of Bulac, a suburb of Cairo. There they ran into their only problems on the trip up the Nile: "By the imprudent behavior of my young dragoman, Ali, and of my Maltese servant, Lewis, firing a musket, we narrowly escaped an assault from the Turks, who boarded us sword in hand; but who were appeased by explanations."[27]

Eaton reached Cairo the next day. The British consul sent horses for the entire party, and the Americans and British rode into Cairo, where they were the center of curiosity. "A vast concourse of people of all ages and sexes whom curiosity or want had collected about us; but at that respectful distance peculiar to the people of the east towards strangers of distinction. We passed as American Officers of the army and navy, whom curiosity had brought from Malta to Egypt during the winter's suspense of operations." The remainder of the day, Eaton reported, "was consumed in receiving and returning visits." The most important visit came from the court interpreter of Turkish khedive (or viceroy), Khoussref Pacha, who asked the Americans to come to the ruler's palace at 9 p.m. the next evening. The interpreter apologized for the unusual time for the meeting, explaining that it was the fast of Ramadan, and the viceroy could not offer his guests food or beverage until after sundown.[28]

While he waited for his interview with the khedive, Eaton had the chance to see some of Cairo. Unlike Alexandria, Cairo was a thriving city and was the seat of Turkish power in Egypt, in the person of the khedive. In addition, the Ottoman Janissaries had their base in Cairo. Ali Bey, a Moroccan traveler in Egypt at the time, marveled at the cleanliness of Cairo, exclaiming he had "seen few cities in Europe that are cleaner than Cairo." Bey said the city had a vibrancy that was unique and on a par with any city in the West. "Far from the streets of Cairo exhibiting a dull appearance, they present as gay and agreeable view of the large cities of Europe, on account of the number of shops and warehouses, and the immense multitude of people who parade them at every moment."[29]

Bey was in Cairo for Ramadan, and the feast marking the end of the month-long fast must have been an interesting spectacle for the Americans. As Bey described it, "The mosques, the houses, and the streets are fully illuminated. Hundreds and thousands of lights may be seen in the great saloons of the rich, which consist in general of plain crystal or colored lamps, suspended to iron circles of different diameters, and placed one above another like lusters. They produce a charming effect."[30] Eaton, however, had little desire to take in the sights and sounds. Soon after his arrival, Eaton encountered two of Hamet's officials, his former secretary of state and an ex-governor who had remained loyal to the elder Karamanli. Both men, Eaton said, were "destitute of everything but resentment; for even hope had abandoned them."[31]

From Hamet's men Eaton learned "their Sovereign, after a series of vicissitudes and disasters had been reduced to the alternative of joining the Mamelukes; and that he was actually with them in command of a few Tripolitans and the Arab auxiliaries, besieged with Elfi and the other Mamelukes Beys in the village of Miniet in Upper Egypt."[32] This was extremely bad news for Eaton. Elfie Bey was one of the leaders of the Mameluke revolt in Egypt and the man England wanted to see ruling in Egypt. After defeating the French invasion, the British backed Elfie with arms and money. He opened a war against the Turkish pacha and, when he arrived, Mohammed Ali and his Albanians. Elfie also faced an internal struggle against fellow Mameluke leader Osman Bey Bardissi, "who among all the Mameluke beys had the most bravery and influence" and was extremely unhappy about Elfie Bey's close relationship with the British. Bardissi tried several times to assassinate Elfie, but each attempt ended in failure. The rivalry between the two split the Mamelukes and sparked a civil war. With British aid, Elfie Bey assembled a force just large enough to keep his Mameluke foes at bay but not to take total control of the country.[33]

The Mameluke civil war and British intervention frightened Sultan Selim III, who was determined to keep Egypt in the Ottoman Empire. After Mohammed Ali and his Albanians deserted the Ottoman cause, Selim sent in a third force, this one of Syrians, creating a three-way battle for control of Egypt.[34] In the middle of this fractured conflict was Hamet, who now commanded a band of Tripolitan and Arab cavalry and was under siege by eight thousand Turkish troops 129 miles south of Cairo.

Hamet's predicament placed Eaton in an almost impossible situation. Hamet was in open rebellion against the Porte and viceroy, but Eaton needed the viceroy to grant Hamet a firman allowing him to leave Egypt and return to Tripoli. "Though glad to hear that the Bashaw was still active, and that the Arabs were still attached to his interest, the embarrassments which have hitherto accumulated to impede the execution of our plan were now heightened by the impossibility of personal access to him; the difficulty of communication; and the uncertainty of obtaining the viceroy's firman for his departure, in case of succeeding to detach him from the rebel army, as the Mamelukes are here styled." Eaton knew he had only one choice: "I resolved therefore to throw myself on the honor and hospitality of the Turkish sovereign of the country."[35]

The "Turkish sovereign," Khoussref Pacha, was a Georgian-born Janissary who was just as keen to meet the Americans as Eaton was to meet him. Khoussref sent ornately uniformed Turkish cavalry to escort Eaton and his party to the viceroy's palace, as well as horses for his guests to ride. Eaton, O'Bannon, Mann, and Danielson, as well as Captain Vincents and

Dr. Mendrici, rode slowly to the palace. Along the way, Cairo citizens came out to gawk at the officers from a new nation of which most had never heard. Upon arrival, the viceroy ushered the party into his private chambers, whose sumptuous appointments impressed even Eaton.

> The flights of stairs which lead to the grand saloon were flanked with young men superbly armed and in rich Turkish uniform. The hall was large and splendid; and the court, which attended the Vice Roy, surpassed in magnificence everything I have ever seen of the kind. His Highness, with a dignified air of affability, rose from a sofa of embroidered purple and damask cushions; and, taking me by the hand, seated me next himself and the gentlemen in company on the right and left. Coffee, pipes and sherbet, were served in oriental style.[36]

After the "customary salutations passed," the khedive began to ask Eaton about the United States: How big was the new nation? What was the date of American independence? With whom was the United States at peace and at war? What were the chief forms of commerce, manufacturing, and trade? Eaton answered all of Khoussref Pacha's questions, speaking more and more freely as he described the United States; when the subject of war came up, Eaton held nothing back. He detailed "our intercourse and relation, with Tripoli; negotiations of peace with Joseph Bashaw; violation of his faith; commencement of the war, and such events in its progress as honor did not dictate to conceal." The viceroy, Eaton reported, "listened with attention and evident gratification." Eaton then used religion to win over Khoussref, telling the viceroy about "the affinity of principle between the Islam and American religion . . . both enjoined the universal exercise of humanity; and both forbade unnecessary bloodshed. He acknowledged these to be maxims of his religion."[37]

Eaton's discourse sparked something in the khedive. He dismissed everyone in attendance except his interpreter, looked at Eaton, and told him he did not believe Eaton and his fellow officers were in Egypt simply to take in the sights. He asked Eaton to reveal his true purpose. Once more,

Eaton did not hesitate. "Finding the Vice Roy a man of much more frankness and liberality than generally falls to the character of a Turk, I unreservedly opened to him the object of my visit to his country," Eaton told Edward Preble in a letter.[38] He candidly revealed to Khoussref that he was in Egypt to find the "legitimate sovereign of Tripoli; who had been treacherously driven from his government and country; and that we were ready to seize any honorable mean to prevent the further effusions of blood; and more especially as we found that, in prosecuting the war against the faithless Joseph, the severity of our resentment fell rather upon the innocent, deluded victims of his avarice and hypocrisy than upon the aggressor himself.[39]

Despite the obvious bluster, Eaton managed to impress the viceroy with his passion for and obvious belief in his mission. Khoussref Pacha, far from being angry that Eaton wanted to overthrow a fellow ruler of an Ottoman province, offered to help.[40] The reasons were his own, although this could well have been a case of competing interests finding mutual ground— removal of a Mameluke ally could only help the viceroy.

Khoussref told the American that he knew Hamet and had even tried to help him. Now, and although it placed the khedive in something of an awkward position, since he would be helping a rebel, he agreed to grant Hamet permission to cross Turkish lines and come to Cairo; there he would join forces with Eaton and return to Tripoli. The decision made Eaton ecstatic. "The most difficult part of our plan [was] accomplished; for I have the fullest assurance and as full confidence that th[r]ough his influence, we may bring any number of men on the back of Tripoli which may be deemed requisite to its entire success—and this done, with our naval force in front, all supplies will be effectually cut off from the enemy."[41]

The khedive's permission to let Hamet come to Cairo, however, did not get him there. Eaton still had to figure out how to contact Hamet, extricate him and his followers from the Mamelukes without the Mamelukes killing Hamet as a traitor, and get them through Turkish lines, where the Janissaries or the Albanian troops might kill Hamet to spite the khedive. Still, although well aware of the obstacles he still faced, Eaton was ebullient. On December 17 he wrote Hamet, "God ordained that you should see trouble. We believe he hath ordained also that your troubles shall now have an end."[42]

He told Hamet that Khoussref had granted him, the "rightful bashaw," permission to "pass, unmolested, through any part of his country, and embark with me at any port you please." Eaton hinted that Hamet had to win his own release from Mameluke service and that when he did, he should head north. "If the generals with whom you are, moved by equal goodness, will consent that your Excellency may profit of this occasion once more to see your subjects and embrace your family," Hamet should "lose no time in repairing, with your suit[e], to Rosetta."[43] Eaton then composed a note to Hull, informing him of the khedive's decision and optimistically advising the naval officer to "expect therefore an addition to your crew of about three Hundred, passengers, all Bashaws and Bashees." He estimated he could be in Rosetta with Hamet and his followers in ten days.[44] Unfortunately for Eaton, it would take much, much longer.

12

·•◆•·———————·◆•·

WAITING GAME

"HURRY UP AND WAIT" was not a concept that sat well with either Captain John Rodgers or William Eaton. As 1804 turned to 1805, both men found themselves cooling their heels in places where they did not want to be. Rodgers was on board the frigate *Constitution,* waiting for permission to enter the port of Lisbon, Portugal, while Eaton was still in Cairo, waiting to hear from Hamet Karamanli. For Rodgers, the enforced wait at Lisbon was not just maddening, it was insulting.

The *Constitution* arrived off Lisbon on December 27, 1804. Rodgers had orders to recruit seamen for his frigate and, if possible, the rest of the squadron. William Jarvis, the U.S. consul in Lisbon, had assured the squadron's officers they could easily recruit seamen in neutral Portugal, where many merchant ships languished. War had broken out anew between England and Spain, stranding numerous sailors in Lisbon as merchant-ship owners canceled cruises for fear of losing their ships and cargoes.[1] Rodgers expected to be in and out of Lisbon in a matter of days. However, Portuguese officials placed the frigate in quarantine for twenty days, because yellow fever was then raging across the Mediterranean. The move angered Rodgers, who had reported his past movements and the absence of disease on the *Constitution* to the Portuguese. He saw the long quarantine as a direct insult to the United States and the U.S. Navy. On December 29, he sent Jarvis a note asking him to have the Portuguese release the *Constitution* from quarantine and waited for a reply.[2] And waited. And waited.

By January 1 Rodgers, always prickly when it came to rank and the treatment rank merited, had had enough. He sent a terse note to Jarvis: "I wrote you on my arrival here, which is five days since, mentioning in part the cause of the *Constitution*'s coming to this port, but as yet have received no answer from you: A circumstance unparalleled in the history of consular administration at least with those who know their duty and wish well to their country."

In fact, though Rodgers had yet to hear from Jarvis himself, apparently, Jarvis' vice consul had gone out to the *Constitution* on December 29 and had assured Rodgers that Jarvis would meet his needs. Nevertheless, the continued waiting was, to Rodgers, an insult to him, his ship, the Navy, and the United States, and he dropped any remaining niceties in dealing with the consul. He demanded Jarvis tell him "immediately" whether he had spoken with the Portuguese officials in the port about the quarantine, "which if not complied with, I shall feel myself bound to solicit the interest of some respectable merchant in procuring the aid and assistance which the United States Ship *Constitution* at this moment requires." He warned Jarvis he would report his "conduct to the government, as the only means left me to prove that I have not neglected my duty."[3]

Rodgers' letter elicited an immediate response from Jarvis, who acknowledged receiving the first letter, although he never explained the delay in replying. He flatly—though politely—refused to intercede with the Portuguese to free the *Constitution* from quarantine: "In consequence of the fears entertained here owing to the ravages which the yellow fever has made in Spain I am apprehensive that you will not be released from your present disagreeable situation under 15 or twenty days." In what had to be a faux pas on Jarvis' part, one that proved he had never read Rodgers' first letter, the diplomat asked the captain to jot down the particulars of his voyage—"date of your sailing, where touched, what [ships] spoke with, the number of your Crew, the number sick if any, and the day arrived"—so he could file proper petition to release the frigate with the harbor master.

He also backtracked on his optimistic pronouncement regarding the ease of recruiting seamen, telling Rodgers, "Two months since there was the greatest number of unemployed seamen here but the Spanish and English holding out the ideal prospect of much prize money has tempted them to enter voluntarily into the British service." Jarvis dismissively ended, "In a day or two I shall do myself the pleasure to see you."[4]

The tone of the letter and the clear evidence that Jarvis had never read Rodgers' first letter sent the naval officer to new heights of anger. He fired off a scathing reply to the consul, handing him an ultimatum and refusing to submit to anything Rodgers believed insulting: "I now must be permitted to tell you that your neglect of this ship is beyond any bounds, which can restrain me from informing you, that your delay has led me into errors of no little importance." He rejected Jarvis' request for information, having already provided it. The captain demanded Jarvis intercede with the Portuguese for release from quarantine and give Rodgers an immediate reply: "If you answer me in the negative I will quit the Port . . . and proceed to Gibraltar and encounter the Yellow Fever and every other inconvenience sooner than tamely subject the American flag to such disgrace."[5]

Jarvis replied two days later, on January 3, telling Rodgers in no uncertain terms he could stay or leave, it was of no consequence to the consul. "I hope my language will not be deemed too strong, when I say, your precipitate and unjustifiable warmth I think determination, is likely to deprive the service of the benefit that would probably have resulted from a more temperate line of conduct; and I shall leave it to yourself, to calculate the consequences that are likely to ensue from it."[6] The naval officer, Jarvis declared, had crossed a line. "Allow me to express my surprise at the liberty you have taken to write in such a style to an officer with whom you are totally unacquainted, bearing a commission under the same government, as respectable at least as the one you hold . . . an officer who has rendered as much service to his country in his station as he believes you have done in yours."[7] As for arranging the quarantine, Jarvis told Rodgers there was nothing the diplomat could (or would) do. "Quarantines being mere measures of precaution to prevent the introduction of dangerous disorders, I cannot perceive that vessels of war ought to be exempted from a scrutiny as strict as what merchantmen are subjected to; and I confess myself so blind as not to be aware that any 'disgrace' is attached to our national character or to our officers from submitting to such investigation when it is a general custom."

Still, the consul realized a disagreement between the diplomatic corps and the Navy served no one, and he attempted to placate Rodgers somewhat: "I do not think a dispute between two officers under the same Government in a foreign country adds to your consequence or redounds to their honor, I hope that it will terminate here, and what letters the service of our country requires should pass between us may at least be couched in terms of civility."[8]

Jarvis arranged for the *Constitution* to receive "beef and vegetables" while in quarantine and asked Rodgers for a detailed list of the materials he needed to repair the frigate. Jarvis' letter, although positive, oozed condescension, and far from mollifying Rodgers, it further enraged him. Rodgers' reply of January 6 was clearly tantamount to a challenge to a duel: "You shall not only be accountable to your government for your neglect of her interests, but to me individually for your ungentlemanly invective and every disrespectful epithet which you have applied to myself and the Service."[9] Rodgers was certainly not alone in believing his rank afforded him special treatment, but the lengths to which he went to defend his personal honor often placed him in perilous positions from which he or his rivals had to back down to prevent duels.[10]

Most officers in the still-new U.S. Navy would have understood and approved of Rodgers' actions. For nearly three years in the Mediterranean, the American navy had been the butt of jokes among the English, French, Spanish, North Africans, and even the Russians.[11] Edward Preble had silenced some of those critics, but there were still many, at home and abroad, who looked on the U.S. Navy as little more than a toddler's toy.[12] Rodgers was well aware that he, as a captain in that service, had to defend and increase its reputation. He would brook no insult, real or perceived, whether it was from a fellow American officer, a foreign officer, or a diplomat. He was also unwilling to accept any challenge to either his authority or that of the Navy. If the Navy had orders to defeat an enemy, it would be the Navy that fought and won the glory. The epistolary offensive Rodgers launched against Jarvis was nothing more than an extension of Rodgers' belief that he had a duty to defend the honor of the service.[13] It was a conviction of which Jarvis did not completely understand the depth until he received Rodgers' note of January 6.

The idea of fighting a duel over policies beyond his control was ridiculous to Jarvis. He quickly penned a note to Rodgers that set aside the sarcasm that had filled his first two letters. "I declare in the fullest manner that I had not the most distant idea of passing an indiscriminate nor any reflection on the service: so far from which I think the officers of our Navy have done great honor to themselves and as a whole, it has done much credit to our country." Although not quite an apology, it was enough for Rodgers, who also backed down.[14] The weeklong spat ended with the *Constitution* enduring quarantine but Jarvis diligently arranging everything she needed for repairs.[15]

⋙⋘

The American blockade of Tripoli was fast becoming little more than words on paper. Commodore Samuel Barron was bedridden in Syracuse, his second-in-command, Captain John Rodgers, was stuck in quarantine in Lisbon, and the remaining U.S. frigates were all immobilized for repairs. Only the schooner *Vixen* showed herself off the city with regularity. The gaps in the blockade allowed Yusuf Karamanli to bring in several shipments of grain that helped avert outright famine.[16]

There was little Samuel Barron could do. The liver ailment that had forced him ashore showed no signs of abating, and there seemed very little physicians could do for him other than prescribe painkillers. Master Commandant George Cox, the captain of Barron's flagship, the *President*, agreed to exchange ships with James Barron, taking over the *Essex* so James could be close to his brother. The *President* was at Messina undergoing a refit, Cox having found her masts and many of her spars rotted.[17] With James Barron nursing his brother and Stephen Decatur in the *Congress* also at Messina for repairs, Hugh Campbell and Cox commanded the remaining frigates. Barron ordered both to convoy American vessels in the Mediterranean. Hull and the *Argus* were off in support of Eaton, leaving just the *Syren, Vixen,* and *Nautilus* available for blockade duty. *Syren,* under Charles Stewart, was on her way to Syracuse, where Rodgers had sent her for repairs, while the *Nautilus,* the *Enterprise* being in Venice for a complete rebuild, had become the squadron's messenger ship. That left John Smith's *Vixen* the lone American warship able to show the Star and Stripes off Tripoli, and a small schooner did not quite have the impact of a frigate.

For the officers of the U.S. squadron, as well as the prisoners in Tripoli, the lack of an aggressive strategy seemed like a return to the inept days of Richard Dale and Richard Morris. There was a leadership vacuum in the squadron as Samuel Barron languished in bed and John Rodgers stewed in quarantine. That the squadron as a whole kept functioning was yet another testimony to what Commodore Edward Preble accomplished during his year in command. The twenty-four- and twenty-five-year-old junior officers all knew their business and worked well together. They had learned how to command leading their gunboats, schooners, and brigs into combat. Preble had instilled in them both professionalism and aggressiveness, and now they were idle, repairing their warships or sitting in port. The leadership void appalled the officers who had served under Preble. "The removal of Preble from his command, besides being unjust to him, and entirely uncalled for by any necessities of the service, was a piece of bad policy on the part of the government. Barron, apart from the state of his health, was in no way comparable to Preble as an officer," lamented Lieutenant Charles Morris.[18] Private William Ray, who on January 3, 1805, marked day 430 in captivity, remarked in his journal that Preble had been "no *barron* commodore."

The wait for a resolution to their captivity was wearing on the *Philadelphia* crew, who had only hunger and hard labor as companions, and sailors began to look for better ways not only to pass the time but to confound their captors. Some of the prisoners, with help from the ship's carpenter, William Godby, boatswain George Hodge, and sailmaker Joseph Douglass, hatched a plot to seize Tripoli Castle. The plan called for the prisoners to rush their guards when they were released for work, free their officers, and capture the armory. Once armed, they would take Yusuf Karamanli hostage and hold him in exchange for their freedom. The Americans also planned to plant cannon, loaded with grape and canister, at each entrance of the castle to hold off reinforcing Tripolitan troops. "Could such a plot have been carried into operation when our squadron was cruising off the harbor, it might have been terminated with success," Ray noted, "but under the then existing circumstances, before relief could have reached us destruction must have swallowed us up."[19]

Across the Mediterranean, the American campaign to end Barbary piracy appeared to be on hold. The situation was no different in Egypt, where William Eaton continued to wait in Cairo for an answer from Hamet Karamanli and Master Commandant Isaac Hull waited in Alexandria for news from Eaton. For Hull, the waiting was especially difficult. Although he had orders to transport Eaton to Egypt and bring Hamet to Syracuse, he did not have an infinite amount of time in which to accomplish both. Eaton had led him to believe he would be in touch with Hamet relatively quickly, and Hull expected to accomplish his entire operation in ten days.[20] Eaton had overoptimistically told Hull that Hamet was to arrive with three hundred followers, all of whom would need weapons, food, and money. Eaton had already drawn a thousand dollars from Samuel Briggs, and now he said he needed another four to five thousand. The money, coupled with the uncertainty surrounding Hamet, was simply too much for Hull.

"You must be satisfied that it is my wish to do everything in my power before we return, but when I look at the situation we are sent here in, I lose all patience," Hull wrote to Eaton on Christmas Eve of 1804. "With a little Vessel, without friends, without authority to act, without a single friend except such as we have by our own good fortune procured—in short, without everything that is absolutely necessary to insure success to an enterprise—I say as I have said before, that I do not see that anything more than getting the man can be done." Hull spelled out to Eaton all of his misgivings concerning Hamet, starting with how to finance the campaign: "I have made arrangements for paying Messrs. Briggs the thousand dollars, which you inform me you had drawn for, but as for the four or five thousand you say you shall want—God knows how we are to obtain that, unless

you have the means at Cairo, for I know of none here. I am already penniless, and the disbursements of the brig amounts to more money at present
than our credit on Messrs Briggs, so that if we can avoid it we must not
enter into many engagements for cash under our present circumstances."

Hull had more concerns than money. "The plan you have formed of
taking Derne, I think rather a hazardous one, unless the Bashaw can bring
into the field from Eight hundred to one Thousand Men, particularly as
we are destitute of every article necessary for an expedition of the kind."
Although, Hull admitted, he believed "a very few men will take the palace,
and hold it," any force "must have the means, they must have and be sure
of supplies, which is out of our power to promise them." He advised Eaton
to lower his expectations somewhat and not make any rash promises; "I
think the most we can do, is to get the Bashaw, make as many friends in this
country as possible, and make the best of our way to Syracuse, get some little addition to our force, and make arrangements for our being supported,
when we have got possession, and set off anew for Derne or Benghazi as
may appear most proper."

Finally, Hull expressed his frustration at not even knowing where
Hamet was in Egypt and whether the "rightful bashaw" was willing to cast
his lot with the Americans. "I am anxious to hear whether you can get
any intelligence from our friend, and what our prospect is."[21] Three days
later Hull again wrote to Eaton, reiterating his Christmas Eve letter and
again asking Eaton for any information on Hamet and how the mission
was unfolding: "I expect to see your party with you, and I hope very soon."[22]
He sent a third letter on New Year's Eve, expressing his fears for Eaton
and Hamet: "I am becoming fixed in the suspicion that Hamet Bashaw
is under the restraint of the Mameluke Beys; though we have hitherto no
direct advice from him, this may retard our progress with him, but does
not threaten to defeat the object," Hull told Eaton. "I shall not leave this
'till after receiving your answer to mine above mentioned. The Mameluke
Army is approaching Cairo with imposing strides—let which party soever
be master it alters not our situation."[23]

William Eaton too was waiting. After his first meeting with the viceroy,
he realized he had maneuvered the "rightful bashaw" into a trap of sorts.

If the Turks found Hamet and offered him free passage, the Mamelukes would almost certainly accuse him of treachery and kill him. If Hamet refused the offer, the Turks would kill him. Eaton met with the viceroy on December 29, looking for a way out. Khoussref Pasha again promised to give Hamet safe passage to Cairo, but Eaton wanted to send his own emissary to keep Hamet out of the hands of the warring factions.[24] He found his man in one of the coffeehouses of Cairo.

On the twenty-ninth a muscular European "gentleman" approached the Americans in a café in the European quarter. Could Eaton use someone who spoke the language, knew the land, and could pass in and out of Turkish or Mameluke lines almost invisibly? That was exactly what Eaton needed. The man introduced himself as Jerome Eugene, although he was currently using the nom de guerre of "Leitensdorfer."[25] Born Gervaso Prodasio Santuari in October 1772 in the Tyrol region bordering Austria and Italy, Leitensdorfer could speak English, French, German, Italian, Turkish, Arabic, and the lingua franca of the region, or so he claimed. His parents wanted him to become a Catholic priest, but a celibate religious life didn't appeal to him. Lietensdorfer had quit the church, married, and enlisted in the Austrian army. The Hapsburgs in 1792 were embroiled in a war with France for the Veneto, the region of northern Italy that includes Venice and Tyrol. The ideals of the French Revolution appealed to him, and Leitensdorfer deserted from the Austrian army and joined the forces of revolutionary France. Using the name of "Carlo Hosondo," Leitensdorfer made his way to Switzerland, where French soldiers arrested him as an Austrian spy. When his story failed to convince his captors, he managed to obtain a small amount of opium, with which he drugged his guards, and escaped. He became a traveling watch salesman, making his way around Switzerland, France, and Spain. That lasted until Napoleon began recruiting an army for his Egyptian invasion. Leitensdorfer boldly reenlisted in the French army, but as soon as he touched Egyptian soil, he again deserted.

Leitensdorfer had made his way to Alexandria, where he apparently enlisted in the British army, although he also ran a coffee shop for British officers. He earned enough money to purchase a house and marry a Coptic woman, seemingly forgetting he had left a wife in Tyrol. As long as the

British remained in Alexandria, Leitensdorfer's life had been good. When the British left in 1801, however, it quickly fell apart. He deserted his wife and fled to Messina, where he entered a monastery as a Capuchin friar. He stayed there for only a short time before he sailed for Smyrna and Constantinople, earning a living as a wandering magician. He accidentally crossed paths with the French general who commanded the unit in which he had served, but before the Frenchman could recognize him, Leitensdorfer fled from Constantinople and joined the Turkish army.

He returned to Egypt with the Turks and once again deserted, joining a band of Bedouin. He turned up again in Constantinople in 1802, where, under the name of "Murat Aga," he converted to Islam, joined a band of dervishes, and circumcised himself with his own razor. He wandered along the Black Sea, selling quotations from the Koran until the pasha of Trebizond summoned him to cure his failing eyesight. The locals believed dervishes had the ability to heal, and Leitensdorfer had put on a great show, chanting incantations and whirling around the pasha before "treating" him with a solution of lime and milk. The pasha had paid Leitensdorfer handsomely before the healing session, after which the Tyrolean, telling the pasha his eyesight would be restored in the morning, fled from the palace and joined a caravan. He soon returned to Trebizond, when he received a letter telling him of the pasha's miraculous recovery. The old man heaped further riches on "Aga," who decided he had enough money to make the pilgrimage to Mecca. He made it as far as Jidda, a port city on the Red Sea coast of the Arabian Peninsula. There he met the Scottish explorer Lord Gordon. "Aga," apparently tired of both Islam and being a dervish, joined Gordon's expedition as an interpreter. He traveled with Gordon to Abyssinia, Nubia, and finally Cairo. On his return to Egypt, he changed his name to Leitensdorfer and headed for Alexandria. There he found his Coptic wife, who demanded a divorce, which he graciously granted.

Leitensdorfer knew that Eaton was also in Alexandria and headed for Cairo and ever in search of adventure, he decided to seek out the American. When the two met, Eaton sized up the man. Although something of a ne'er-do-well, Leitensdorfer was clearly ambitious, intelligent, brave, and, above all, he knew Egypt. His adventures likely fired Eaton's imagination and admiration, and his services came relatively cheap—Leitensdorfer offered to collect Hamet Karamanli for just fifty dollars. Eaton immediately enlisted him and advanced his fee. The Tyrolean, with just one servant, set off for Minyeh, where information from several sources placed Hamet, albeit trapped under siege with the Mamelukes.[26]

Meanwhile, the waiting was taking a mental toll on everyone in Eaton's party and threatened to tear the group apart before it even found Hamet. The Americans had little to do but sightsee, drink, play billiards, and visit brothels (which several of them did with gusto). Eaton tried to play the role of tourist, but unrest in Cairo and the presence of marauding Albanian soldiers and Arabs outside the city prevented him from seeing much, not that he cared. "Ruined temples, pyramids, and catacombs, monuments of the superstition, pride and folly of their founders, disgust my sight," he told Congressman Cotton Smith in a letter, "for with their magnificence I cannot but couple the idea of the slaves who must have groaned under the oppressive folly of their fabrication."[27] On December 29, Richard Farquhar, the Scotsman who represented Hamet on Malta, and Robert Goldsborough, the purser of the *Argus*, got into a fight while playing billiards. It was an ugly scene as the two men exchanged punches and wrestled one another to the floor. A group of Turkish officers cheered as Farquhar pummeled Goldsborough, threatening to "break his bones." No one intervened until Selim, Eaton's Janissary, pulled the two apart. Both men suffered black eyes, while Goldsborough also had a collection of bruises.

It was only the latest problem that Goldsborough, the son of the chief clerk of the Navy, had caused since he joined Eaton's party.[28] "It were to have been wished that Mr. Goldsborough's curiosity to see Grand Cairo had been restrained, he has behaved disgracefully, and very much to the injury of the reputation of the cloth [i.e., uniform] he wears," Eaton told Hull. "He is accused of swindling at-play at a gentleman's board, of offering indecencies to Turkish ladies in the public street, and what is somewhat more base, of bilking his courtesan in a brothel. I certainly should not mention these last two circumstances, were it not that formal complaint of them as an injury has been made to me, and a demand of redress, which I with difficulty silenced."[29]

Goldsborough had been the instigator of the fight with Farquhar, "his shameful exhibition [had] originated in a subject equally shameful, a bet of half a pint of Rose Olio," Eaton said in a report to Hull. "It is matter of great exultation to the Turks, and I confess I am mortified with regret that an incident so unfavorable to American character has happened at our first introduction to this capitol. . . . I do not know how the Gentlemen of his rank will reconcile their sensibility, and their respects to such a representative of their characters. . . . Good God! When will our young men learn the weight of respect which ought to attach itself to uniform and a sword."[30]

Farquhar was just as problematic. He too frequented the brothels and had a huge thirst for alcohol. Eaton decided that both men were or could become major embarrassments and decided to ship them both out of Cairo. He gave Goldsborough orders to return to the *Argus* via Rosetta on board a packet, ostensibly to carry dispatches but really to get the young man out of Eaton's hair. He told Farquhar to head back to Alexandria and commence recruiting Christian soldiers for Hamet's army, as well as to prepare quarters for the "rightful bashaw" and his followers. After dealing with the two problems he could easily fix, Eaton again settled in to wait.

Meanwhile, Leitensdorfer was as good as his word. He stealthily made his way south to Minyeh, avoiding marauders and brigands, as well as Turkish army patrols and Mameluke war parties. He never revealed how he did so, although his linguistic skills and chameleon-like ability to assume any persona that suited him probably played a major part. Minyeh is 120 miles south of Cairo, and Leitensdorfer covered the distance in just four days. He convinced the Mameluke sheik, Osman Bey Berdissi, to allow him into the city, where he soon found Hamet. Taking the elder Karamanli to a private room, Leitensdorfer introduced himself as an emissary from Eaton, who was waiting for him at Cairo, ready to support his bid to regain the throne. He suggested that Hamet quietly slip into the desert, where Leitensdorfer would meet him and take him to Eaton. Hamet took a moment to write Eaton, "We have received your letter and after having noted its contents, we rendered thanks unto God on learning that you are in perfect health. You must know that I am always the same as you have known me, being at Tunis, my steadfast friendship is the same. . . . On this date I am leaving."[31] It would take a week for Hamet's letter to reach Eaton. It would take even longer for the two men to reunite.

～⊰ ⊱～

President Thomas Jefferson knew he had made a mistake in relieving Edward Preble of command in the Mediterranean. It was clear by the new year that Samuel Barron, whatever his qualities, was not cut from the same cloth. He lacked the aggressive spirit of Preble, and he did not command the respect and loyalty of his junior officers the way Preble had. In fairness, Barron's illness had hampered him since he arrived on station, but even in gathering his squadron the new commodore had appeared to dawdle a bit. The news of Preble's relief had preceded him to the United States, and by the time the former commodore left the Mediterranean on January 6, 1805, on board the frigate *John Adams,* many in America openly wondered why the president had replaced the most effective commander to date in the war against Tripoli. Jefferson implicitly admitted his mistake by letting it slip that he was considering Preble as his next secretary of the Navy. He also asked Congress to award the commodore a special medal for his service, a request the Senate and House quickly granted.[32]

In one of the first cabinet meetings of 1805, Secretary of the Treasury Albert Gallatin and Secretary of the Navy Robert Smith presented a dismal financial outlook. Gallatin, ever eager to cut expenses, especially those of the military, told the president that even though the country was rapidly paying off its debt, the military's costs continued to run above projections. Augmenting the force in the Mediterranean, he added, would cost another $605,000. Jefferson, in fact, had already decided to increase the squadron with a small flotilla of gunboats and two bomb vessels then under construction in ports from Boston to Charleston. The prospect of increased military expenses worried the president. The expected spring campaign against the corsairs was his last hope. After the meeting, he wrote in his diary, "Not to give a dollar for peace. If the enterprise in the spring does not produce peace and delivery of the prisoners, ransom them."[33]

13

FEARS OF THE UNKNOWN

HAMET KARAMANLI had not survived nearly a decade of attempts on his life by his brother by trusting just anyone. When Eugene Leitensdorfer arrived at Minyeh Hamet agreed to go with him, but that didn't mean he was ready to entrust his safety completely to the Americans. Hamet had good reason to doubt Eaton, having waited two years for the former consul in Tunis. "You have delayed," he upbraided Eaton in a letter. "However, the delay must have had a good cause."[1]

The idea of entering the Turkish seat of power did not set well with Hamet either. Eaton wanted the "rightful bashaw" to meet him in Rosetta. Instead, Hamet told Eaton to meet him outside Cairo at the oasis of Rehera, where Hamet planned to stay with a local sheik he knew. The Arabs figured large in Hamet's plans, but they too were embroiled in the war between the Mamelukes and Turks. Both sides courted the Arabs, but Hamet could appeal to them as a fellow Arab.[2] Osman Bey Brendissi, the Mameluke leader in Minyeh where Hamet was then fighting the Turks, feared Hamet might either take all of the Bedouin with him or suddenly join forces with the besieging Turks. Brendissi allowed Hamet to leave, but no one else, locking up thirty sheiks who volunteered to fight with Hamet in Tripolitania.[3]

Deprived of his force of Bedouin, Hamet set out for Rehera on January 3, 1805, with Leitensdorfer and a small band of fellow Tripolitan exiles. He slowly made his way north, traveling on foot until a messenger arrived on January 15 with a small amount of money from Eaton. He was then able to purchase a few horses and camels, but that did little to speed his march. "If you ask for [are seeking] news of me we arrived in the village called Ohu'isa after 3 o'clock Saturday, in good health. I began immediately to make purchases and [attend to] our business with the money given me; we found the horses and camels very dear," he wrote to Eaton.[4] How small the sum Eaton had sent must have alarmed Hamet, who told him, "Friend, you must have courage; do not think about money because the occasion demands heavy expenditure. It is a matter of making war, and war calls for money and men."[5]

Hamet composed a second letter, this one to his Arab contact Mahmud. In it he confessed doubts about working with the Americans and expressed grave fears that Eaton would once more leave him, much as he had when the two were in Tunis. "The money that was given me [by] the general [was] very little and this displeased me [but] at the moment I could say nothing," he told Mahmud. "Know that he gave me 1500 pesos duros; this is not enough for the horses nor the camels nor for the horses for my men nor for the provisions. You know my situation very well, and that [the money that] I had [when I] was in Giza is all gone and we have no more, so tell the General that he must have much courage with respect to expenditures; make him understand that this [is] war, and whoever wishes to make war must spend without thought and take no account of the money."[6] Satisfied that he would soon benefit from American riches, Hamet decided to slow his march north to a crawl, waiting for the money and equipment he expected Eaton to have.

∽✦✦∾

William Eaton knew Hamet needed money. The problem was there were few sources of cash, and one of them was about to weigh anchor. Master Commandant Isaac Hull, commander of the *Argus*, was done waiting for Eaton and Hamet. He had no idea Hamet had replied to Eaton or that Eaton had sent Leitensdorfer south, nor did he have any idea of Eaton's arrangement to meet Hamet at Rosetta. All he knew was the *Argus* had been in Egyptian waters for nearly two months with nothing to show for it. On January 5 Hull told Eaton, "I am unhappy that appearances are so much against our getting information from the Bashaw, as we have been here so long, and not able to gain the least intelligence from him I fear that something stands in the way, that we are not acquainted with, and I expect we will find that to be the case."[7]

The upshot of the lack of intelligence, Hull said, was time had run out for Eaton. "It is time to determine on something, for it is impossible for us to remain here long, and have a sufficiency of provisions to carry us down," Hull told Eaton. "You well know if they were to be purchased here, we have not the means." Maybe Hull should take the *Argus* back to Syracuse while Eaton remained in Cairo and report to Barron that Eaton was in contact with Hamet. He could also give the commodore a briefing on "what your prospects of success are, etc. which will enable him to furnish you with everything proper for the expedition, and give us such assistance as he may think necessary."[8]

There was another problem. The *Argus*, Hull explained, was out of money, and he could provide nothing to help. Hull had to draw on British commercial agent Samuel Briggs for a thousand dollars just to feed his crew. He advised Eaton to hold off engaging any of the mercenaries Richard Farquhar was trying to recruit in Alexandria until they resolved the question of money. "I think it will be well not to do it at present, but to have them and as many more as can be found, in such a situation, that they can be collected in a short time, without making any further promise than to employ them, if you should leave this by land, as they will be only lumber on board of a ship."[9]

There was very little Eaton could do, Hull said. He could stay in Cairo and search for Hamet, in which case the *Argus* would "leave this as soon as possible, as it will certainly be improper for me to remain here while you make the experiment." Alternatively, he could return to Alexandria and reboard the *Argus*, in which case "we shall both be on the spot to act as we might think best." Either way, Hull wanted Eaton to make a decision. Otherwise, he was set to return to Syracuse.[10]

Eaton well understood Hull's frustration. He too could not understand why there was so little information about Hamet. The waiting was becoming more and more difficult for Eaton, and on January 3 he wrote

Hull that "if no intelligence comes from the Bashaw, am inclined to think it will be best to make an attempt to pass both armies, and seek an inter-view with him in person, it would at once do away all doubts on his part." With his usual bravado, Eaton told Hull that should he head south, "The undertaking will be hazardous, but this is a world of adventure, in which little is to be expected without enterprise and perseverance, and not a great deal to be realized with them."[11]

One of the problems Hull and Eaton had in communicating was that Eaton often wrote rolling letters over a series of days. He started the letter to Hull saying he would journey south to find Hamet on December 29 but did not finish it until the thirty-first. The gap in correspondence left Hull to guess what might be happening in Cairo. The arrival of Hamet's first letter on January 8 did little to correct the situation. Eaton immediately wrote Hull about it, but that letter would take nearly a week to reach the *Argus:* "I cannot but congratulate you and felicitate myself after so much apprehension doubt and solicitude, that we now calculate with certainty on the success of our expedition, we are sure of the Bashaw." Eaton also disclosed some disquieting intelligence he acquired in Cairo, that Yusuf Karamanli had reinforced Derne and Benghazi with "troops from Tripoli and a gun boat at each port." He said he suspected now-disgraced Maltese businessman Joseph Pulis "of treachery as he alone was my confidant at Malta, and as nobody else in the brig could have had any [communica-tion with Tripoli]." He told Hull he would move to Alexandria, where he planned to meet Hamet's secretary to give him Hamet's passport from the viceroy. He ended his letter with a hopeful, "Our voyage to Cairo has not been unproductive."[12]

⊰⊱

Tobias Lear would have been happy if Hull had scuttled the Hamet scheme. The consul general for the United States in North Africa had no appetite for the type of intrigue Eaton's plan involved, wanted nothing to do with replacing what he saw as the legitimate ruler of an Ottoman province with a man who had proven unable to govern, and he had a general dislike of the idea of the United States fomenting a civil war. He also had a job to do.

Ironically, Lear had the job of making sure that shipments of beef and lamb for the Royal Navy reached Malta from Tripoli. The Americans allowed Yusuf, although under blockade, to meet this contractual obligation, permitting neutral-flagged ships, usually either Tunisian or British, to carry food supplies to Malta (much to the chagrin of the French, who viewed the food shipments as U.S. aid to Britain). As starvation continued to grip Yusuf's city, the quality of those supplies depreciated greatly, as Lear reported to Barron after one ship pulled into Valetta Harbor: "The transport to which you had given a passport to go from hence [Malta] to Tripoli, for Bullocks, arrived here . . . with one hundred and nine bullocks and some sheep, all in a very miserable condition."[13]

Lear's main reason for being on Malta was to hold himself in readiness should Yusuf Karamanli decide to open serious negotiations. It also put him close to Barron, who remained bedridden in Syracuse. In fact, the commodore's health came to dominate Lear's thoughts. He told his wife Fanny after an overnight trip to Sicily, "I visited him immediately upon arrival, and found him very low indeed. He is not able to walk without help. He rejoiced much on seeing me and said he should soon be well."[14] In a letter to Barron, Lear admitted, "I am distressed to find, by the letter from Mr. [George] Dyson . . . that you was [sic] too ill to write; the latter part of his letter saying your complaint had taken a favorable turn the night before, relieved me a little from my anxiety; but I shall not be satisfied until I see you here or hear directly from you. . . . Mrs. Lear unites with me in most sincere prayers for the restoration of your health, and in Compliments and best wishes for all those with you."[15] To a fellow diplomat Lear confided, "The dangerous situation in which Commodore Barron has been, gave me great anxiety. . . . I pray God he may soon recover his health."[16]

With the commodore ill and Rodgers still in quarantine in Portugal, Lear saw diplomacy as the only viable method of dealing with Yusuf Karamanli, and according to information Lear had received, now could well be the time for talks. Lear's main source of information, however, was Captain William Bainbridge, who, on New Year's Day of 1805 had spent 428 days as a captive. Lear never questioned the veracity of anything Bainbridge wrote, not making allowance for the fact Bainbridge was desperate for any solution that would win his release. Bainbridge began writing more and more frequently to Lear—in lime juice, to keep his observations secret. Each letter had the same theme: Yusuf was unprepared for a new onslaught against his city. "I believe the Bashaw is desirous of peace, and was a negotiation attempted I think it probably would succeed, for the Bashaw apprehends a very severe attack; and the apprehension perhaps would have as great an effect as the attack itself," he told Lear in a letter January 28, 1805. "I hope when an attempt is made to negotiate it will be by a person coming on shore, and not carried on by letter as it was last summer. How happy I should be dear Col. to see you here on that embassy from your efforts— I should greatly calculate to have our fetters broken, and again breathe the air of [MS mutilated] liberty, and that compatible with our country's dignity."[17]

Bainbridge shared Lear's misgivings about Eaton's gambit, having even more reason for fearing what might happen if Hamet suddenly arrived: Yusuf had publicly announced that he would execute his prisoners if the Americans backed Hamet.[18] It was an empty threat, as Yusuf needed his hostages for their economic value. Torture, however, was another avenue. Yusuf had yet to subject Bainbridge and his officers to the horrors of his dungeons, but that could change if Eaton and Hamet seized Derne or Benghazi, and that had Bainbridge running scared. "The Bashaw is now very attentive upon your transactions with his brother in Alexandria. A camp is gone against Derne," he wrote to George Davis in Tunis. "The Bashaw's agent at Malta [Gaetano Andrea Schembri] endeavors to persuade the Bashaw that by hard treatment of the captive officers he might force his terms of peace. Hitherto Schembri has not entirely succeeded but he may. Give me leave to tell you that I find your plan with his brother very wasteful and that you sacrifice your prisoners here in case of success."[19]

Bainbridge's information reinforced Lear's opposition to the plan to put Hamet on the throne and his conviction that military action, however glorious, would not free Bainbridge and his crew. Taking advantage of his access to Barron, Lear repeated what he learned from Bainbridge and his diplomatic sources and also began to push his own views on the ailing commodore, to persuade Barron to let diplomacy, not intrigue, end the war.[20] Barron himself was inclined toward Lear's stance. Taking the diplomat into his confidence, he revealed doubts as to whether the Neapolitans would again lend or lease a flotilla of gun- and mortar boats to the Americans. The small ships were as "essential to our contemplated operations" against Tripoli for Barron as they had been for Preble the previous year. However, the Neapolitans, citing a renewed French threat, now refused to let any of their warships leave their control; Barron confessed, "My hopes from this quarter are very slender indeed."[21] The unspoken message was Barron had scant hope of subduing Tripoli without these small warships, a fact that only bolstered Lear's effort to get Barron to agree to a diplomatic solution. The ailing commodore even told Lear that recent positive communications from the Spanish consul in Tripoli could prove beneficial and expressed his confidence in the "perfect knowledge you [Lear] have of my sentiments on this subject; you will doubtless feel yourself fully prepared to answer."[22]

In a sign of Lear's growing influence and intimacy with the commodore, Barron admitted to the diplomat that "recovery from the painful sickness I have experienced is so slow and gradual and impeded by such frequent and debilitating relapses that I cannot calculate with any certainty on leaving this place at present." Barron, then, would remain in Syracuse, and Lear would continue gathering information and increasing his clout with the commodore.

The letter from Hamet Karamanli that William Eaton received on January 3 was welcome, but it did little to end the frustratingly long wait for the "rightful bashaw." Hamet was making his way north, but slowly, so Eaton remained in Cairo another ten days. Hearing only silence, Eaton, always impatient, decided to go to Rosetta, where he expected to meet Hamet. He left Cairo on January 13 and arrived at Rosetta two days later, reporting to Hull on his arrival that he planned to head next to Alexandria. Hamet, he told Hull, had "gotten as far on his march in lower Egypt as the province of Fiaune [Fayyum]. It appears he is accompanied by a host of Arabs, who are gathering round his standard, zealous to aid the measure of recovering their country. I am impatient to have an interview with you and him in order to arrange and decide on proper measures to be pursued."[23]

Eaton never divulged where or how he received the impression that Hamet had a "host of Arabs" following him, when in fact barely two dozen people (including Leitensdorfer) accompanied Hamet from Minyeh. Whatever excitement Hamet's letter generated slowly dissipated as again the days dragged on without further communication. Eaton duly went to Alexandria, where he found nothing had changed since he left the place more than a month before. He was ready to return to Cairo to mount his expedition to find Hamet when, finally, a letter, dated January 15, reached him. Eaton decided to set out and meet Hamet south of Cairo, admitting to Hull that the trip had its dangers: "We shall have three perils to encounter, danger of robbery and assassination by the wild Arabs; danger of falling into the hands of the Arnaut Turks [Albanians] and being murdered as enemies, and danger of being executed as spies by the Mameluke Beys." He made light of the dangers, telling Hull that if he failed, "Do us the justice to believe us marty[r]s to a cause in which we feel the honor and interest of our Country deeply involved—release of our prisoners without ransom, and peace without the disgraceful condition of tribute."[24] He certainly expected to meet Hamet at any moment and asked Hull to send him his "gilded trousers and long plain coat" so he could greet Hamet properly.[25]

Eaton left Alexandria on January 22 with Lieutenant Joshua Blake, Midshipman George Mann, and twenty-one followers, most of them Tripolitans whom he had found in Alexandria. Two days later he arrived in the Nile town of Damanhur. The center of Beheira Province, Damanhur was an example of what Egypt could be when the Turks, Mamelukes, Arabs, and everyone else worked together. The province was one of the richest agricultural areas in the country, and its location on the Nile between Cairo and Alexandria made it a center of trade—as well as of competing interests, which Eaton soon discovered. When Eaton was in Cairo, the French consul, a Piedmontese businessman named Drouetti, had accused the Americans of being British spies and claimed their true intention was to rally Mamelukes to aid a British takeover. The viceroy dismissed the accusations, but other Turkish officials were more open to them. It was, to Eaton, a strange turn of events. He was "totally at loss to account for this strange conduct of Mr. Drouette."[26] When Eaton and his party approached Damanhur, those same accusations returned, this time nearly derailing Eaton's entire project.

The viceroy had issued Hamet a passport that would allow him to enter and exit Turkish lands, but not all of his officials were in agreement. The admiral in charge of Alexandria was one of them. He refused to allow Hamet or any of his followers to enter the city, claiming Hamet had consorted with the Mamelukes against the sultan and now was likely consorting with the British.[27] Eaton left Alexandria because of the admiral's intransigence, and now he was stuck at Damanhur because of those same rumors. The local sheik had received word from Cairo that he should not trust the Americans. On January 24, as the Americans approached the town, the sheik met them with a force of five hundred Ottoman cavalry.

The sheik at first refused to allow them to pass. "No argument I could devise could at all mollify the severity of his first resolution, not to let me pass his lines, though in everything else he treated us with distinction and great hospitality," Eaton reported. "However mortifying the confession, I cannot but applaud the correct military conduct of this chief; for it was, in itself, a suspicious circumstance, that a body of armed, unknown foreigners, should be found shaping a course for his enemy's rendezvous, with no other pretext than to search for a *refugee Bashaw*."[28] Nevertheless, however properly the Turks treated the Americans, Eaton knew he was running out of time, and after waiting for nearly five days for the sheik to release him, he decided enough was enough.

"Our situation here was somewhat perplexing, and vastly unpleasant. I do not recollect ever having found myself on a ground more critical. To the natural jealousy of a Turk this general added a fierce and savage temper; of course proud and vain," Eaton reported. The rumors the French had spread had reached Damanhur, and "this suspicious circumstance was strengthened and aggravated by the insinuation gone out from the French Consul, that we came into this country with secret views hostile to the Turks." In typical fashion, Eaton chose a direct mode to break the stalemate. "Here was my point of approach," Eaton told Edward Preble: "I was determined to have an interview with him, in full confidence that he would aid a measure so purely humane, and so manifestly favorable to the Turkish interest in Egypt." Eaton disclosed the nature of his mission to the Turkish official and showed him the viceroy's letter of amnesty for Hamet. He then asked the Turk for any news of Hamet. The official called into the meeting a young Arab sheik, who absolutely gushed with enthusiasm: "He *knew everything!*" The sheik told Eaton where he could find Hamet and about his circumstances, boasting that "twenty thousand Barbary Arabs were ready to march with him from this border to recover their native country and inheritance." The young man "repeated that he *knew our plan;* and, now that he had seen me, he would pledge his head to the Turkish general to bring me Hamet Bashaw in ten days."[29]

The sheik's information won over the Turk. He agreed to let the young man go to Hamet while Eaton remained behind, with just Blake, Mann, and their servants. Eaton sent his escort back to Alexandria and settled down for yet another wait. Although the Turk had agreed to let the youth seek out Hamet, it was clear he remained suspicious of the Americans. Eaton moved into "lodgings in Turkish style" the official provided, where he found himself essentially a prisoner. "The next day after our entering the house where we quarter a markee [tent] was pitched upon the terrace of an adjoining house, and a Turkish guard mounted there under pretext of *fresh Air.* Armed Turks were sent into the house for the purpose of accompanying us as a *life guard* in our walks. And a sentinel was placed at our door in the lower court, to *prevent intruders.* Though these arrangements were vastly polite I should have been very willing to have dispensed with them."[30] There was little Eaton could do. The Turkish official, he told Preble, although fair to the Americans, was as ruthless as any petty despot to those he ruled. The Turk cut off "between fifty and sixty peasants' heads for no other crime but *poverty* and, just without the eastern gate of the village a gallows is now erecting to hang a child of twelve years, the only son of a chief of the village Rahonania, because his father cannot pay the contribution levied on him!" The time he spent in the Turkish camp only reinforced Eaton's disdain for the Turks and Arabs and his belief in the preeminence of the United States. "God! I thank thee that my children are *Americans*."[31]

Eaton remained in Damanhur for nearly two weeks, during which he attempted to assuage fears that he was an English spy or that Hamet was in fact marching to attack the Turks. He also had to deal with his own mounting frustration at the failure of Hamet to arrive and the lack of communication from him. On January 29, he finally received a new letter from Hamet, which told Eaton the "rightful bashaw" was still in Fayyum and had only just received the viceroy's passport. He pledged to meet Eaton wherever was convenient for the American, although neither man thought it prudent for Hamet to go to Alexandria;[32] there French intrigues had turned many against the Americans, including Isaac Hull and Richard Farquhar.

For Hull, the entire experience was one long, exasperating exercise in Egyptian politics. The French-spread rumors made the governor of Alexandria, who had originally greeted the Americans with warmth and friendship, cold and suspicious and openly hostile toward Farquhar, who was recruiting Christian mercenaries in the city. "I sent word to the governor that we had recruited a few men, since he gave permission, but as he received orders that they must not be recruited here, I should give orders for their being discharged," Hull informed Eaton on January 28, 1805. "He appeared perfectly satisfied, but said he had received information that we were recruiting, and that some of the Turkish soldiers were about to desert."

Hull said he went to the house where Farquhar had established his recruiting rendezvous and ordered the Scotsman to close down his operation and discharge any men he had managed to recruit. At that moment, "a guard of about twenty soldiers came in from the governor," Hull wrote. "I enquired what they wanted. They said they had orders to warn the Greeks against visiting that house. I suppose however their object, was to see if any Turks were there, and on informing the commanding officer, that I was there, for the purpose of discharging the few men that were engaged by the governor's permission, he went away apparently satisfied." Hull had Farquhar move on board the *Argus* for his safety and banned any further recruiting until Eaton returned.[33] Somewhat ominously, he warned Eaton not to expect a hero's welcome for Hamet: "You will see by what has happened, that they are very much afraid, both at Cairo and here, but without cause, but, God knows how far their fears may carry them."[34]

Eaton did his best to alleviate Hull's impatience and his worries. He explained to the master commandant that the French were behind the problems in Alexandria, adding, "Does that madman [Drouetti] reflect that his presumption in exposing us to an *infamous death* to gratify a cowardly resentment, will not pass unnoticed?"[35] He also approved of Hull's dismantling of the recruiting rendezvous. "You have certainly done wisely in discharging the men, and breaking up the rendezvous, but I will have the viceroy's permission to take those Christians out of his country if necessary," he told Hull. "It is to be recollected that every step we took in Alexandria was with the knowledge and approbation of the governor."[36]

Having received Hamet's letter of January 28, Eaton was full of optimism. He wrote to Hull, "There then is at length an end of our uncertitude, *we shall have the* Man." He asked Hull to keep track of the recruits at Alexandria and also suggested that "some small field pieces should be sought for and conditionally be stipulated for. The object before us seems so certain and the advantages so important, that it seems to me we need not hesitate a moment about some extraordinary preparations."[37] Eaton's optimism failed to dent Hull. The commander of the *Argus* was all too aware of how quickly allegiances and attitudes could change, and he urged Eaton to be cautious: "Should you find the Bashaw approaching you with a number of men about him, it will certainly be imprudent for him to come near, under the present circumstance, for fear of alarming the people more, it will therefore be necessary to send and meet him, and fix on some place if possible a distance to the westward to see him. In fact, take what steps you may. I fear the people's ignorance will prevent their seeing our object."[38]

It wasn't fear that drove Hull as much as prudence. The number of Hamet's followers seemed to grow with each tidbit of news coming from the Egyptian hinterlands. Eaton, on his arrival in Alexandria, told Hull to expect about a hundred men to accompany Hamet. That number soon ballooned to two hundred, then five hundred, while the young sheik who went in search of Hamet had said he expected the elder Karamanli to rally as many as 20,000 Arabs. A force of Arabs of any size marching under a banner other than Turkish, however, could easily spark a war with the Ottomans, and Hull and Eaton both had explicit orders to avoid irritating the local government. Plus, Hull had no way to transport more than a corporal's guard, so any followers, retainers, well-wishers, or actual fighters would have to march overland to Tripolitania. Eaton too knew there was scant chance of transporting Hamet and his "army" by sea, and the naval agent began to look at maps detailing the land route from Alexandria to Derne.[39]

After two weeks of waiting, near captivity, and nail-biting impatience, Hamet Karamanli emerged from the Egyptian desert on February 6 to meet William Eaton at Damanhur. Hamet arrived under an escort of honor the sheik had sent to meet him. Once in the village, he found pavilions and tents ready for the "rightful bashaw" and his entourage. After years of planning and months of waiting, Eaton was actually low-key in his description of his reunion with the thirty-nine-year-old Hamet, telling Hull simply, "Hamet Bashaw arrived here this afternoon."[40] Eugene Leitensdorfer was there as well, well worth the fifty-dollar investment Eaton had made in him. Eaton was so pleased with the former French, Austrian, and Turkish soldier that he made Leitensdorfer his chief of staff.[41] Eaton had also received a new letter from the viceroy, granting him permission to retain the Christian soldiers Farquhar had found in Alexandria. Eaton also had a stack of mail from Hull, all bearing the same message—the Turkish governor continued to refuse to allow Hamet or his followers to enter the city.[42] For a week, Eaton and Hamet hovered outside of Alexandria, discussing what they should do. Hamet had brought just twenty-one men with him out of Minyeh, and it appeared Hamet's army would have to walk to Derne. Eaton doesn't note who made the suggestion first—he had already broached the idea of a ground attack against Derne with Barron—but on February 16 he wrote in his journal that he and Hamet had "come to a resolution to march by land to Derne and Benghazi."[43]

Eaton apparently made a second, equally important decision. It was around this time that, as a means of overawing the Arabs whom he expected to join Hamet, Eaton began referring to himself—and asking others to refer to him—as "General." It was a heady promotion. Now, the captain-turned-general and the failed bashaw were planning to follow in the footsteps of Alexander the Great and march five hundred miles through the desert to strike at their shared enemy. All they had to do to succeed was raise an army, equip and pay for it, convince a skeptical, ailing American commodore to lend sea support and financial aid, and somehow manage to survive a lifeless, arid desert.

14

A FEW GOOD MEN

WILLIAM EATON had a relatively short wish list for his campaign to restore Hamet Karamanli to the throne of Tripoli. At the top, of course, was money—money he believed the Navy Department, State Department, or private lenders could easily provide.[1] The second was arms and equipment for Hamet's men, upward of a thousand muskets and bayonets, as well as light field artillery, all of which Eaton believed Barron could purchase from Naples.[2] Third was a request all but unheard of in 1805 and one for which Barron, even if he wanted to fill it, probably didn't have the authority. Eaton wanted Barron to provide him with "100 Marines to deliver a coup de main" on any target the forces of Hamet might attack.[3] What seemed like a militarily logical request to Eaton, however, was in fact, the most difficult of the three things he wanted Barron to provide—not because of the commodore's continuing skepticism about the entire affair but because of the very nature of the Marine Corps.

The Marines were something of an afterthought on the part of federal lawmakers who voted to create the U.S. Navy in 1794. It wasn't until hostilities broke out with France in 1797 that legislators realized they would have to authorize and pay for some sort of force of marines to serve on the expensive new warships then sliding down ways from Boston to Baltimore. Those ships needed guards, men who could fight with small arms and act as shipborne infantry, although neither the House nor Senate saw those "sea soldiers" as anything more than musket-toting sailors. The congressmen were not alone. Major General James Wilkinson, the ranking officer in the Army, agreed, telling then Secretary of the Treasury Alexander Hamilton, "The marines corps should perform all duties relative to the Navy."[4] Jefferson's secretary of the treasury, Albert Gallatin, saw no need at all for a separate marine corps, arguing any troops on board ship should enlist only for that purpose and disband once the need for their service ended.[5] Practices then in place helped opponents of a permanent Marine Corps. As the United States launched and bought warships to counter French privateering in the Caribbean, Navy captains recruited their own Marines and hand-selected their officers.[6] Naval officers also routinely used Marines as extra deckhands, sending them aloft to raise or lower sails or having them perform other duties of seamen.[7]

The Marine Corps remained little more than an idea for four years. In April 1798, soon after the creation of the Department of the Navy, lawmakers advanced a bill creating officially the U.S. Marine Corps, a force that would number five hundred men, and "annexing them to the existing Military Establishment."[8] Massachusetts representative Samuel Sewall, a member of the House Committee for the Protection of Commerce and Defense of the Country, pushed the legislation, assuring lawmakers that "much advantage and economy" would come from creating a corps with its own commander who would oversee recruiting and discipline the rank and file when they were not on ships.[9] Many congressmen still had misgivings about adding to the standing military establishment, although the opposition lessened somewhat as the United States mobilized to combat French piracy. Gallatin was the leader of the opposition, for economic reasons, not because of excesses of the British before and during the Revolutionary War.[10] It took a month, but Sewall and his Senate allies—Uriah Tracy of Connecticut, James Lloyd of Maryland, and William North of New York—persuaded a majority of both chambers of the need for Marines. On June 1, the House approved the measure, fifty-five to twenty-five.[11] The Senate approved the bill on July 6 in an eighteen-to-four vote.[12] On July 11, 1798, President Adams signed the bill into law, creating the U.S. Marine Corps.[13]

Soldier-turned-diplomat-turned-adventurer William Eaton, the
architect and leader of the daring attempt to overthrow Yusuf
Karamanli, the bashaw of Tripoli, and replace him with his brother,
Hamet. Brash and abrasive, Eaton led an army across the Libyan
desert and was on the cusp of victory when he had to abandon
his troops and his dream of ending Barbary piracy. He appears in
the uniform of a U.S. Army general in this portrait by Rembrandt
Peale, though in fact he never held a rank above captain.
Maryland State Archives

U.S. Navy captain Edward S. Preble commanded the third expedition against Tripoli, nearly battering Yusuf Karamanli into submission. Relieved of command in September 1804 but staying in the Mediterranean, Preble remained an enthusiastic supporter of the plot to use Hamet Karamanli to supplant his brother as bashaw of Tripoli. *Naval History and Heritage Command*

Tobias Lear, a confidant of President Thomas Jefferson, was consul general for the North African coast, although his only diplomatic experience was as an unpaid commercial legate on the island of Santo Domingo (present-day Haiti). Bitterly opposing the Eaton scheme to overthrow Yusuf Karamanli, Lear negotiated a much-maligned treaty that ended the First Barbary War and forced Eaton to abandon his campaign. *Art Collection, National Museum of the Marine Corps, Triangle, Virginia*

U.S. Marine Corps first lieutenant Presley O'Bannon, who acted as
Eaton's second in command and led a squad of seven enlisted men in
the effort to take Derne. O'Bannon would return to the United States
with a Mameluke sword, the weapon that would become the symbol
of the Corps. Portrait taken from a miniature by an unknown artist.
Art Collection, National Museum of the Marine Corps, Triangle, Virginia

William Eaton, right, and Hamet Karamanli lead their army across the desert toward Derne in this highly stylized woodcut from the 1820s. The image correctly depicts Eaton wearing his Army uniform and not Bedouin robes. *Naval History and Heritage Command*

A woodcut of the U.S. brig of war *Argus* off the coast of Tripoli. The *Argus* provided much-needed supplies, money, and tactical support during Eaton's assault on Derne. *Naval History and Heritage Command*

Lieutenant Colonel Franklin Wharton, second commandant of the Marine Corps, fought his own war at home to keep the Corps alive while Presley O'Bannon was battling to take Derne. Painting by Louis H. Gebhardt. *Art Collection, National Museum of the Marine Corps, Triangle, Virginia*

Commodore John Rodgers, who took over command of the
Mediterranean Squadron from Samuel Barron, was a staunch
opponent of Eaton's attempt to launch a coup d'etat in Tripoli.
Rodgers supported the campaign only grudgingly until diplomat
Tobias Lear offered a way to end the war and Eaton's mission.
Naval History and Heritage Command

Lieutenant Commandant John Dent viewed Eaton's campaign
as a chance for glory, but as commander of the schooner *Nautilus*,
which supported the attack on Derne, he had few opportunities
for close combat. *Naval History and Heritage Command*

The law that created the Marine Corps also established the office of the commandant. Five days after creating the Corps, Adams appointed William Ward Burrows to lead the new force, with the rank of major. It was a fortunate choice. Born in South Carolina on June 16, 1758, Burrows grew up in Charleston, where his family had close ties to the powerful Pinckney family. His father, a successful lawyer, sent William in 1772 to England to study at the Inns of Court. He returned three years later when war between the colonies and England broke out. Burrows served briefly in the South Carolina militia in 1780–81. In 1783 he married Mary Bond, daughter of future purveyor general of the United States, Thomas Bond, and moved to Philadelphia, where he became a prosperous businessman and a well-known member of society. His financial success allowed him to rub shoulders with many members of the federal government, which established itself in Philadelphia, and his Federalist sentiments won him many friends, including Robert Morris, John Adams, and Alexander Hamilton. By the 1790s, he was among the inner circle of Federalists, and when Adams, now president, created the Marines, he tapped Burrows as its commandant, calling him a "gentleman of accomplished mind and polished manners."[14]

Burrows' appointment placed a vocal advocate for the Marine Corps in Navy circles. Burrows spent much of his time in his first two years as commandant trying to fill recruiting quotas while defending the independence of the Corps against encroachment from the Army and Navy. His primary task, though, was building a force that was equally adept whether operating on land or at sea, a task for which he had no real guide. He started with his officers, all of whom were political appointees and few of whom, if any, had military experience. Although he had scant military experience himself, Burrows was a master organizer, and he embraced the responsibility of building a professional fighting force. Burrows envisioned the Marine Corps as an elite military branch, and his first goal was to get his officers to act the part. All of them were young—late teens to early twenties—and most came from well-to-do families. Burrows spent nearly as much time trying to weed out bad officers as he did trying to train those he wanted to keep. The commandant had to strike a delicate balance, as many of the officers had powerful political ties.

One such officer was First Lieutenant Simon W. Geddes, son of Henry Geddes, a rich merchant-ship owner who had strong connections to Congress. Geddes was appointed as a lieutenant in the Corps after his father pulled several strings, and he quickly made a nuisance of himself. Away from home for the first time in his life and put into a position that required responsibility and attention to detail, Geddes was an abject failure as both an officer and a gentleman.[15] Assigned to recruiting duty, Geddes was drunk so often that he never met his manpower quotas; after one bender in which he had a very public fight with an Army artillery officer, Burrows had him arrested and charged with "drunkenness and ungentlemanlike conduct."[16] Other officers who sought appointments were competent enough to perform their duties but found the day-to-day monotony of military life more than they could bear. Second Lieutenant Benjamin Strother wrote to Burrows that he found the service "in every way disgusting" and resigned.[17]

Burrows faced an even greater struggle in just keeping his Marines as Marines. A large number of naval officers, Captain Thomas Truxtun the most outspoken, questioned the need for Burrows' office and the Marine Corps in general. Ship captains were often cavalier in how they treated the Marines, swapping officers or snatching individual Marines from one ship to serve on another. Marine captain Daniel Carmick complained "every [Navy] captain that chooses to swap[s] and take[s] wherever they can catch them."[18] It was a nearly impossible situation for the Corps' officers, and yet the Marines managed to flourish during the Quasi-War. In that conflict they served with distinction on board American warships that fanned out in the Caribbean to stamp out French attacks on American merchant vessels. They earned praise from Stephen Decatur Sr., Alexander Murray, John Barry, and Truxtun for their steadiness in action. Their combat abilities, however, did not prevent Navy officers from continuing to use their Marines for duties such as tarring rigging or soapstoning decks, duties that were not part of a Marines' normal agenda and that ruined their uniforms.[19]

Nor did their combat abilities win over a still-skeptical Congress, which was always looking for ways to cut the military budget. Gallatin and his allies were able to wrangle a caveat that would allow the president or the new Secretary of the Navy to disband the Marines if either believed there was no need for them.[20] The law that created the Marines failed to clarify the chain of command under which the Marines fell—Army or Navy. Instead, Congress left the new service in a somewhat nebulous place, subject to Navy rules when serving at sea but the Articles of War, which governed the Army, when serving on shore. Many Army officers used that proviso to bolster their claims the Army should command the Marines on land, even if the senior Army officer present was junior to the Marine Corps officer.[21] Many Navy officers already operated under that belief, prompting several Marine officers to write biting complaints about midshipmen assigning Marines to tasks without informing the Marine chain of command.[22] It was a practice that infuriated Burrows, who believed the Corps should operate as an independent and equal arm of the military. The question of seniority would continue until 1834, when Congress finally made Marine Corps ranks equal to those of the Army and Navy.[23]

The fight to preserve the Marine Corps engulfed Burrows' time and energy, as did his effort to professionalize the force. Burrows needed officers who could sell the Corps to a skeptical Congress as well as a public eager and ready to embrace American-born heroes. First Lieutenant Presley O'Bannon was exactly the man Burrows—and his successor as commandant, Lieutenant Colonel Franklin Wharton—needed, not only to embody the Corps' professionalism but to capture the public's imagination at a time when its future hung in the balance.

⊸⟨ ⟩⊶

Presley O'Bannon was everything a Marine Corps commandant could want in an officer. He was born in Fauquier County, Virginia, in 1776, the son of William and Mary O'Bannon. Presley was a third-generation Irish-American whose family had carved out a prosperous life on what the locals, at least, still considered the frontier. The O'Bannon family became among the first to move west. At the time of his birth Presley already had a number of relatives in Kentucky. He attended a school the Rev. James Thomson ran in Leeds Parish, the same school future Supreme Court Chief Justice John Marshall attended. He learned to shoot, hunt, and fish and developed a self-reliance that characterized what Thomas Jefferson referred to as Virginia's "backwoodsmen."[24]

O'Bannon's family was military, one with close ties to Thomas Jefferson and George Mason. His grandfather, John, was a militia captain during the Revolutionary War, the longest serving officer in the county regiment; a cousin was an aide-de-camp to the Marquis de Lafayette and married the daughter of famed Virginia soldier Daniel Morgan.[25] O'Bannon's own early life is largely unknown, other than his schooling, his reputation as a good shot, and his knowledge of music. His prosperous family was able to get Mason to nominate Presley for an appointment to the new Marine Corps in late 1800.

While he waited for his commission, O'Bannon accepted an appointment from the high sheriff of Fauquier County, Joseph Blackwell, as a tax collector. It was not a successful endeavor for either man. On December 15, 1801, Blackwell asked the Virginia legislature for more time to pay the county's taxes as O'Bannon had failed to collect any money. Blackwell stated he had appointed O'Bannon as a tax collector for the years 1800 and 1801 and O'Bannon had promised to provide "bond with approved security for the collection and payment of the public taxes agreeable to law." However, O'Bannon provided only "from time to time, various excuses." Finally, "soon after the above transactions O'Bannon left the Commonwealth [to take up his Marine commission] without coming to any settlement with your petitioner, having left his books and papers with a friend to be delivered to your petitioner by which it appears he has collected very little if any part of the taxes."[26] The sheriff duly received extra time to collect the taxes. He apparently made no effort to contact O'Bannon, either through his family or the Marine Corps.[27]

Presley O'Bannon was twenty-five when, on January 18, 1801, he received his coveted appointment as a second lieutenant in the Marines. He reported to Burrows' headquarters in the still-new national capital, where the commandant was attempting to establish a school for both officers and recruits.[28] Burrows insisted his officers learn drill and other basics so they could not only command but lead their detachments. Burrows also made new officers such as O'Bannon learn the mounting and relief of guards, the layout of warships, their general duties on land and on sea, and especially, paperwork, which was new to many of them.[29]

O'Bannon spent six months in Washington before he went to New York to take command of the Marine detachment of the frigate *Adams*. The *Adams* was to sail to the Mediterranean as part of the squadron under Commodore Richard Morris, although her captain, Hugh G. Campbell, had all but condemned the vessel, demanding a near-complete rebuild. O'Bannon reported to Burrows, "The frigate *Adams* is undergoing a thorough repair, which makes it uncertain as to the time she will be ready for sea. It is found necessary to have her new coppered and she might require two new masts as the old ones are considerably damaged."[30] O'Bannon's first task as a detachment commander was simply to keep his command together. The Marines cooled their heels at their camp in Brooklyn, where boredom became O'Bannon's biggest enemy. O'Bannon drilled his men every day, and the Marines had guard duty at both the frigate and the navy yard, but it was not enough to keep them fully occupied. O'Bannon reported several desertions, as well as the measures he took to apprehend the men.[31]

From the start, O'Bannon appeared to be a bright, attentive officer with a big personality, and he unquestionably formed a close bond with Burrows. He never failed to include in his correspondence a personal message to the commandant and the commandant's family. Soon after he arrived in New York, in a report on his detachment O'Bannon included a personal note to the commandant, expressing his disappointment at having to miss a fellow officer's wedding: "I should have no objections to have made one of your party at Lieut. Rankin's wedding and not the smallest objection to have been one of the party at the punch-drinking."[32] He also earned a reputation for scrupulous honesty. When the local authorities threw a former Marine sergeant into jail for debt, the man immediately asked to reenlist, because at the time, the debts were forgiven of anyone who enlisted in the Marine Corps. O'Bannon advised Burrows to leave the man to his fate: "I did not say anything in the way of inducement as I am convinced that had it not proceeded from a desire to injure his creditors, he never would have suggested a wish to do so, and I feel reluctance in acting in any respect in opposition [to] the civil authority."[33]

Despite his early success as an officer, O'Bannon found himself caught up in the struggle for control of the Marine Corps between Burrows and the

Truxtun-led faction of the Navy. Campbell, the captain of the *Adams*, was one of the Navy officers who believed Marines were important but there was no need for a marine corps. O'Bannon was not Campbell's choice for a Marine-detachment commander and the navy captain made sure O'Bannon knew it. The young lieutenant wrote to Burrows several times that he was "sorry to have it in my power to tell you that Capt. Campbell has conducted himself in such a manner as to forfeit all the respect of the Officers on Board his own Ship and I believe it extends to all who know him."[34]

O'Bannon never detailed exactly what Campbell did to make the Marine officer so unhappy. According to letters from other officers, Campbell often gave orders directly to his Marine detachments, sidelining Marine officers.[35] The situation between O'Bannon and Campbell became so bad that O'Bannon wrote to Captain Daniel Carmick, the senior Marine Corps officer in the Mediterranean, asking to transfer off the *Adams* "at the first opportunity."[36] When Burrows received letters from both O'Bannon and Carmick, he lodged a formal complaint with Secretary of the Navy Robert Smith.[37]

O'Bannon, meanwhile, decided to act on a piece of advice from Burrows and confront Campbell. "I was one of those Capt. Campbell thought he could treat with disrespect (as I thought) therefore I decided it not amiss to mention it to you and treat it as it deserved here," he wrote Burrows. "This I did so in a manner which my station demanded, since which there has remained a perfect understanding and bids fair to remain so during this cruise—in a word, I now have command of the Marines, which was not the case, and which was the cause of the difference."[38] After winning control of his detachment and, apparently Campbell's respect, O'Bannon reported, "I am not a little pleased at having it in my power to inform you that Capt. Campbell's conduct toward me has been of a very different tune." He called the entire episode "truly unpleasant to me," but expected no further problems, as it was his "determination to cultivate and maintain the most perfect harmony, there remains very little doubt of a good understanding in the future.[39]

The tug-of-war was apparently over by the time the *Adams* reached Gibraltar. Campbell, in a letter to Burrows, described O'Bannon as "one of the happiest fellows living, he has just returned from spending the Evening with a brilliant circle of Spanish ladies and by way of consolation for the loss of their company, philosophy and the fiddle is called to his aid, on the latter he is now playing, Hogs in the Cornfield."[40]

Almost as important as mending the rift with Campbell was the prospect of action. The *Adams* was under orders to keep an eye on Morocco, where the emperor was threatening war over the American seizure of a Moroccan ship at Gibraltar. O'Bannon's thirty-two Marines could now see a reason for their daily drill as well as for O'Bannon's fight for control of his men. As Campbell told Burrows in a letter, the emperor's "whimsical conduct since my arrival here, with his long and late silence on a subject that the voice of majesty is required, leaves Room for Conjecture not the most favorable. Be assured sir, they are slippery Politicians, and require good looking after either in peace or war."[41]

The Moroccan crisis, however, soon ended, and it would be more than a year before O'Bannon got his first taste of combat. On June 1, 1803, the *Adams*, with the frigate *New York* and the schooner *Enterprise*, gave chase to a group of grain-carrying galleys trying to sneak past the blockade off Tripoli. The Arab sailors ran the galleys ashore and abandoned them, but a large group of cavalry gathered to keep watch over the vessels, making a great show of "riding full speed flourishing their guns over their heads." The display only emboldened the Americans, who planned a night raid to burn the galleys and the grain.[42]

At a little past 8 p.m., Lieutenant David Porter, the first lieutenant of the *New York*, pushed off from the frigate in the ship's gig. Over his shoulder he could see Marine lieutenant Enoch Lane and Midshipman Henry Wadsworth with another boatload of sailors and Marines from the *New York*. They rowed stealthily toward the *Adams*, which loomed several hundred feet away. As the two boats from the *New York* neared the *Adams*, two more boats, under Navy lieutenants James Lawrence and Jonathon Thorne, joined them from the *Enterprise*. As the group reached the side of the *Adams*, three boatloads of sailors and Marines under Navy lieutenant

Charles Ludlow, Midshipman Francis Wise, and O'Bannon, rowed to the group. Porter, in overall command, pointed at the shore, and the seven boats, filled with fifty men, headed toward the galleys. Sailors had crammed combustibles into two of the seven boats with which to destroy the enemy vessels. As the crews rowed toward shore, gunners on the *Enterprise* and *Adams* readied their cannon, removing tampions and ramming powder and shot down the barrels. The gun ports, however, remained closed to ensure a measure of secrecy.[43]

The moon, which was just rising, shone brightly, illuminating the shore. At a signal from the *New York*, gunners on the *Adams* and *Enterprise* ran out their cannon and opened fire, covering the assault force as it fought through the surf to hit the beach. The Tripolitans had established a strongpoint in a small stone house and had "formed a barricade of the boat sails and yards at the corner of the stone house." Both opened fire. Others joined the fusillade "from behind the rocks and little hillocks." Porter led five of the boats right at the enemy, and the sailors and Marines poured fire into the Tripolitans. "The fire boats went in among the small craft and set them on fire under cover of our musketry," reported Wadsworth.[44]

As a handful of Americans tried to torch the galleys, the landing party fought an increasingly difficult covering action. "There were many horsemen prancing about at a distance," Wadsworth wrote. "Some of the bold would take a circuit and come near, one in particular on a black steed, flourishing his carbine in defiance began his circuit full speed: when he came near several took aim at him: he plunged forward fell and bit the dust." The Tripolitans, however, began to find their mark as well. Porter went down with a pair of thigh wounds. His men moved him back to a boat and fought on. Three Marines were hit, along with a sailor from the *New York*. Porter, who remained in command despite his wounds, saw the flames starting to lick at the galleys and ordered the assault force back to their ships, which continued to cover the boats. "The shot from the ships brought down several horsemen and foot," Wadsworth reported.[45]

The action lasted about two hours. The Tripolitans were able to extinguish the flames on the galleys and save the cargo of wheat, although they continued to take casualties from the fire from the *Enterprise* and *Adams*.

The Americans suffered five wounded, the Tripolitans far more, although accounts differed as to how many Arabs engaged the Americans. Commodore Richard Morris believed the enemy numbered in the "thousands," with at least a thousand cavalry. Wadsworth estimated the enemy at about a thousand horse and foot.[46] Porter in his official report praised all of the officers, including O'Bannon, for their bravery.[47]

O'Bannon returned to the *Adams* unscathed. He was promoted to first lieutenant three months later as the squadron underwent a command change. Edward Preble relieved Morris and Campbell received orders to return to the United States with the *Adams*. Preble plucked O'Bannon off the *Adams* to serve on his flagship, the *Constitution*. Although he did not take part in the battles involving gunboats, O'Bannon led his Marines in their secondary duty as gunners. On August 28 and September 3, 1804, the *Constitution* engaged Tripolitan shore batteries as part of a general assault on the city. To augment his ship's firepower, Preble placed four long twenty-four-pounders on the quarterdeck of the frigate and tapped his Marines under O'Bannon to man them. The Marines, exposed to enemy cannon fire, poured shot into the Tripolitan defenders, earning the commodore's praise.[48] When Samuel Barron arrived to replace Preble, there was another shuffling of positions, and in October O'Bannon found himself, briefly, transferred to the *President,* where he served as the detachment vice commander under Captain Anthony Gale. By December O'Bannon was on the *Argus,* where he commanded a nineteen-man detachment.

When William Eaton boarded the *Argus* for the trip to Alexandria, the effect was electric on the Marine, who almost instantly fell under Eaton's spell. O'Bannon accompanied Eaton in the initial search for Hamet. He apparently brought back to the *Argus* a goodly number of tales of Egypt.[49] He spent most of January on the *Argus* in Alexandria before returning to Eaton's service in February, when Eaton returned from Damanhur.

※

Eaton's request to have a hundred Marines ready for an assault on Derne didn't mean he wanted them to march across the desert with him. Eaton probably did some simple math and counted bayonets. Barron's flotilla carried 308 Marines, three-fourths of the 423 enlisted men then in the Corps.[50]

Eaton expected at least part, if not a good portion, of the American squadron to provide naval support to his attack on Derne and likely believed any ships involved in the attack could easily spare their Marines. The two biggest contingents were on the *Constitution*, fifty-two Marines, and *President*, forty-nine.[51] In Eaton's mind, either of those frigates could lend her Marines to his mission, as could some of the smaller vessels, such as the *Argus*, with her nineteen Marines under O'Bannon's command.

It seemed simple, but there is no record of Barron ever seriously considering the idea. Even if he had, command of a small battalion of Marines on land legally belonged to the Army, which meant the Marines would operate outside of the Navy chain of command. It was a situation in which no naval officer would ever willingly become ensnared. Eaton would not get his hundred Marines. He would not get the full detachment from either of the frigates, or even from one of the smaller warships. All he got was a squad of seven enlisted men—whom O'Bannon chose from his own detachment. If the small number of Marines disappointed Eaton, he didn't show it. Eaton wanted Marines, and he got them, and the Marines he got would prove equal to any task.

It was particularly telling that Eaton asked specifically for Marines, not simply a landing force of sailors armed with cutlasses and muskets. Although the Corps had only existed for six and a half years, the measures Burrows and his successor, Franklin Wharton, had taken to ensure the Marines had men who fit their idea of "elite" were already paying off. Both commandants knew that it was the men themselves who would make or break the Corps, and both were determined to enlist only men committed to the Marines.

Private Bernard O'Brien, one of O'Bannon's seven-man squad, was typical of the Marines serving with the U.S. squadron in the Mediterranean. O'Brien enlisted in 1803 for three years' service on the *Argus*. His recruiting officer, First Lieutenant Newton Keene, entered his name on the muster roll on May 18, listing his occupation as "journeyman."[52] Presuming Keene followed his recruiting instructions to the letter, O'Brien was at least five feet, six inches tall;[53] (that restriction was lowered to five feet, four inches in 1804).[54] He was "healthy, robust, physically sound, and of a build to support the fatigues and acquire the honors of a soldier," and he was between the ages of eighteen and forty. He was also white: the Corps wanted "no mulattos, negroes or Indians."[55] O'Brien enlisted in Boston, the second-largest city in the United States in 1803 and a hub of commerce and immigration. The city teemed with people from England, Scotland, the German states, France, and, increasingly, Ireland, where a bloody revolt in 1798 had triggered a tide of emigration. Whether O'Brien was part of this Irish immigration, had come to the country prior to 1803, or was in fact born in the United States, are all unknown. These things would have mattered in 1800, when the Marines were looking for "a few good men," but in 1803 they simply needed bodies.

Burrows, in 1798, tried very hard to make the Marine Corps the most American part of the military establishment. The Navy had hundreds of British seamen serving on its warships, while the Army had hundreds of Irish, Scottish, and German soldiers. Burrows wanted the Marine Corps to be different. His first instructions to recruiting officers were to enlist not more than one foreigner for every three "native" Americans, and the foreigners had to have established reputations for "sobriety and fidelity."[56] In the following year, "no foreigner or vagrants" or "men disordered" could be enlisted. Finally, in 1800, when applicants were numerous due to the downsizing of the Army, a recruit had to be "a very smart young fellow," a "handsome young American," and "then only enlisted as a great favor."[57]

By 1803, however, the need for Marines was great. Every ship in the Navy was either at sea or getting ready to go to sea. Navy yards from Portsmouth, New Hampshire, to Norfolk, Virginia, needed guards, and Wharton had committed the Corps to stationing up to a hundred Marines in New Orleans. Recruiting officers began bending the rules as Wharton pressured them to meet manpower quotas. By 1804, Marines were accepting many newly arrived German, Scottish, English, and Irish immigrants, although the successive commandants continued to press their recruiters to find Americans.[58]

In addition to the type of men recruiting officers were supposed to enlist, Burrows and Wharton spelled out how the officers could and could not recruit new Marines. They prohibited officers from using indirect methods to inveigle men into the service, such as enlisting a drunken man or swearing in an applicant earlier than twenty-four hours after he signed his enlistment papers. Officers could induce new recruits with advances of two dollars on their monthly pay of eight dollars and tell potential Marines they "would have more rations than they could probably eat." The commandants made the recruiting officers responsible for everyone they signed up: if a recruit deserted or proved unfit for duty, the officer had to pay for that man's expenses out of his own pocket.[59]

The strategies worked. By 1805, the Marine Corps was certainly the most "American" of the U.S. military services and, thanks to the cadre of Marines stationed in Washington, D.C., one of most visible. Daily parades and weekly concerts of the burgeoning Marine Band put the Corps squarely in the public eye. All of this was not enough, however, to stop the seemingly endless wrangle in Congress over whether to continue to fund a quasi-independent branch of the military that was actually part of the Navy. The Marine Corps needed heroes, and William Eaton needed Marines. The seven Eaton received—O'Brien, Arthur Campbell, David Thomas, Edward Stewart, Joseph Fisher, Joseph Joiner, and John Milton—would give both Eaton and the Corps exactly what they needed.[60]

15

AN ARMY GROWS IN THE DESERT

ALEXANDRIA WAS the perfect place for Richard Farquhar to operate. The "long narrow streets, the houses with overhanging windows of latticed wood-work painted and gilt, small shops, in which the wrangling of oriental bargains was vociferously carried on by merchant and purchaser," as well as the cafes and brothels, made an ideal hunting ground for the Scotsman to find recruits to serve under William Eaton and Hamet Karamanli.[1] Alexandria teemed with people, not only residents but also those coming, going, or simply drifting. Greek and Albanian soldiers—cast-offs and deserters from Ottoman armies—mixed with French, Neapolitan, and Sicilian soldiers, cast-offs and deserters from Napoleon's armies. Eaton gave him $1,500 to buy recruits, and the Scotsman apparently dove into his task. a little too enthusiastically. Twice Master Commandant Isaac Hull had to rein in Farquhar when his recruiting activities alarmed Turkish authorities. Hull finally shut down Farquhar's operation until he received permission from the Egyptian viceroy to recruit Christians openly to serve Hamet.[2]

Most of Farquhar's life is shrouded in mystery. He arrived on Malta sometime around the start of the Tripoli war and aligned himself with Hamet. A trader of some sort, he styled himself Hamet's "consul" on the island. From his letters, his support of Hamet seems to have been sincere, although he was always asking for money for Hamet's "cause." He was no stranger to drinking or gambling, as his public beating of the *Argus'* purser,

Robert Goldsborough, showed, and yet he was clearly an intelligent man. Despite his somewhat shadowy background, Eaton entrusted a central part of his plan and a good part of his scant money supply to him and put him in charge of finding the specialty troops Eaton and Hamet would need to take Derne.[3]

Whatever Farquhar's talents, keeping accurate records was not one of them. He did not record how many men he engaged during his first two recruiting drives and failed to keep accurate financial records after Eaton gave him $1,500 and ordered him to reopen his rendezvous. Farquhar enlisted forty-nine men and began asking Eaton for still more money, though he could not account for the funds he had already received. At the same time Hamet too, who was outside of Alexandria with about forty followers, began to ask Eaton for money, saying he needed it simply to feed and properly equip his retinue. Hamet established his camo on February 6 about thirty miles outside of Alexandria while Eaton was still at Damanhur.[4] Eaton received both requests for money at the same time and decided Farquhar's was far more worrisome. He had originally planned to go directly to Hamet's camp but instead returned to Alexandria, arriving there on February 11, so he could check Farquhar's books and discover why the Scotsman needed more money. Eaton's findings made him irate. Farquhar could only account for $150 of the money advanced him. Eaton accused him of theft, and the two men got into a shouting match. Although there are no accounts of what exactly transpired, letters from Farquhar to Hull suggest Eaton flew into a rage and swore up and down. In his journal, Eaton simply noted, "We had been several days delayed by the delinquency of Richard Farquhar, to whom I had entrusted the commissary's and quartermaster's department, and to whom from time to time I advanced a sum of $1350, which he chiefly embezzled or misapplied. In consequence of which I discharged him."[5]

Farquhar denied Eaton's allegations and claimed Hamet would not join Eaton unless he was there. Farquhar told Hull he would not rejoin the expedition unless "Mr. Eaton shall be more reserve[d] in his manner of speaking, and that my account shall be paid up till today, and that at least one hundred and fifty men shall go from this to join the Bashaw, with three or four small guns, and an agreement stating the pay and time of service."[6] Since it was Farquhar's own job to recruit soldiers and find equipment, his stipulation regarding men and artillery would appear to confirm Eaton's suspicion that the Scotsman had used money for his own purpose and not for recruiting. Hull appeared to side with Eaton in the dispute, telling Farquhar, "I find it will be impossible for you to join the expedition by land as I am sure Mr. Eaton will never consult you about the number of Men, or Measures he is to take, as he is the only responsible person[.] You will settle matters with him and go by land, or come on board this day as best suits you."[7]

Eaton put Eugene Leitensdorfer in charge of the commissary and quartermaster departments, and the Tyrolese was able to restore some semblance of order. Farquhar had enlisted forty-nine men, most of them Greek, with a smattering of Sicilians and Neapolitans. Many still wore Ottoman army uniforms, while a handful were in the Republican blue of France.[8] So many privates went only by the names Dmitri, Spiro, Petro, and Giorgio that Farquhar assigned them numbers—"Dmitri 2nd," "Petro 3rd." He found a squad of Italian infantry under a Lieutenant Constanti Bart (with two Giorgios and two Petros) and a group of Greek artillerymen under officers named Johan Tedesh, Eugene, Romano, and Deboa. Many men claimed to be officers, but, as Farquhar noted in his ledger, only three of the gunners could serve as officers; the rest had to be privates. All told, twenty-five of the forty-nine men Farquhar enlisted claimed to be artillerymen.[9] Leitensdorfer enlisted another fourteen men, mostly Sicilians, lured by a twenty-dollar bounty and ten dollars a month in pay, giving Eaton a total of sixty-three Christian solders. The number grew to seventy on February 19, when Presley O'Bannon returned to Eaton with seven U.S. Marines.[10]

Hamet too was recruiting, promising money he believed Eaton would provide. He slowly began to attract Bedouin, reaching out to them as a fellow Arab. Although the Karamanli family could trace its roots to Turkey and its first members to arrive in Tripoli had certainly been Turkish, the family had become arabicized in the intervening 250 years. By 1805 the Karamanlis were the only Arab dynasty in charge of an Ottoman province outside of the Arabian Peninsula.[11] With such credentials, Hamet was able to gather two hundred Arab cavalry at his camp by March 3 and promised to rally even more.[12]

On February 14, Eaton sent Barron a long, detailed letter informing the commodore of his actions. He still wanted a hundred Marines for a "coup de main," but his primary need was cash. He had already "disbursed about ten thousand dollars, which we have taken upon credit of Messr. Briggs Brothers; for four thousand of which sum Captain Hull has drawn bills on London and Malta; the balance we have promised, shall be sent up in one of the small vessels. Ten thousand dollars more at least will be necessary to accomplish our views on Derne and Benghazi. The Bashaw assures me he will be able immediately to refund these sums when established in those provinces." Eaton knew that Barron, who was barely lukewarm to the Hamet plan, was even more concerned than he was himself about expenses. To alleviate those worries, Eaton revealed to the commodore one of the most incredible compacts in American history.[13]

After meeting with Hamet at his camp, Eaton drew up an agreement between Hamet and the U.S. government, of which Eaton considered himself an agent. It didn't matter to him that he had no authority to sign a treaty, had no way to enforce it either in Tripoli or the United States, and that several of its "articles" were likely illegal. To Eaton, the treaty was as necessary as money and weapons. Several parts of the treaty were straightforward, simply acknowledging what both already knew, albeit with slight twists. The treaty called for a "firm and perpetual peace, and free intercourse, between the government of the United States of America and his Highness, Hamet Caramanli [sic]," and pledged the United States "to reestablish the said Hamet Bashaw in the possession of his sovereignty of Tripoli." In return for American aid in regaining his throne, Hamet promised "to release to the commander in chief of the forces of the United States in the Mediterranean without ransom, all American prisoners."[14]

Eaton was on solid diplomatic and even legal ground with those articles, but later ones went far beyond his purview. First, he promised that Barron would fully support Hamet's campaign against his brother, by supplying "cash, ammunition and provisions; and, if necessity require, debarkations of troops also, to aid, and give effect to the operations of said Hamet

Bashaw, by land, against the common enemy." Barron had promised that support in September when he issued Hull his orders, and Eaton believed he was only reiterating what was already policy.[15] Still, his orders from the Navy Department did not empower him to commit the squadron to anything. The treaty also brought to life one of Eaton's dreams—Hamet made him "general in chief" of his army for the duration of the campaign against Yusuf.[16] Eaton was already using the title of "general," a pretense he aimed at the Arabs, who could be unruly and needed firm reminding of who was in command.[17]

Perhaps the most extraordinary article, however, addressed how Hamet planned to repay the United States for any and all expenses—that is, with tribute money from other states: "Hamet Bashaw transfers, and consigns, to the United States, the tribute, stipulated by the last treaties, of his Majesty the King of Denmark, his Majesty the King of Sweden, and the Batavian Republic, as the condition of peace with the Regency of Tripoli, until such time as said expense shall be reimbursed."[18] William Eaton, champion of peace without tribute, had pledged the United States to receiving the tribute of three other countries, two of which, Sweden and Denmark, had either worked with or were working with the United States to care for the American prisoners in Tripoli. Just how he thought Jefferson and Congress would react to taking the tribute money of other nations as payment for ending America's own tribute payments is a mystery. Eaton also concluded a secret article by which the U.S. squadron would, if possible, snatch Yusuf's family and hold it hostage in exchange for the American prisoners. This secret article would later cause a major row with Barron, who not only questioned the legality of the article but its morality.

The deal with Hamet, at least in Eaton's eyes, settled the questions over command and finance. Hamet could—and did—recruit more Arab tribes to his cause with the promise of Yankee gold waiting for them at Derne. Eaton contracted for supplies, pack animals, drivers, and a few more Christian mercenaries with the small amount of cash he had left and the promise of more to come. For Eaton, the only obstacle left was strategy, and he and Hamet had already discussed the basics of how to get from Alexandria to Derne. Hamet had decided upon a land march with his followers after Isaac Hull refused to transport more than a handful of Hamet's people by water. Eaton would go with him. As Hamet's general in chief, Eaton knew he had to lead the army to Derne and that his own troops would have to accompany him. He asked Barron to assign O'Bannon to him, along with Midshipman Paoli Peck. He sent his stepson, Eli Danielson, back to the *Argus*.[19]

Eaton had good reason to want O'Bannon. Throughout February and into March 1805, the French consul in Alexandria had continued to spread tales of Eaton's collusion with the British. He also claimed Eaton was recruiting Turkish soldiers to fight against the sultan. The Turkish governor in Alexandria decided to find out for himself and on February 28 sent an officer and a squad of soldiers to Hamet's camp to investigate the charges. O'Bannon and his seven Marines met the Turks and refused to allow them to enter the camp. The Turks blustered, but O'Bannon held firm. The next day, a company of soldiers arrived at the camp. O'Bannon and the Marines again refused to allow the Turks to enter and again stood their ground when the Turks threatened to attack. The Turkish soldiers again left. The day after, they returned in battalion strength. O'Bannon refused to budge. When the Turks threatened to attack, O'Bannon drew his sword and had his Marines fix bayonets. The icy resolve of the Americans forced the Turks to retreat once more. Eaton noted in his diary, "The stern and decided conduct of Mr. O'Bannon prevented their movement."[20]

The incident enraged Eaton, who hurried to the office of the city governor and berated the man with the firman and safe-conduct for Hamet the viceroy had issued. The governor blamed the French consul for instigating the rumors that Hamet was recruiting disaffected Turks. Another official had become involved as well, because he believed the Americans had overlooked him when they handed out their gifts to the governor. "We found the impediments raised to us were occasioned by the influence of the supervisor of the revenue, who had not yet been bought," Eaton noted in his diary. "The day was spent in accommodating the affair. The influence of the British Consul prevailed; and we obtained the order of the Governor and Captain Bey for free passage."[21]

After dealing with the officials, Eaton and Hamet were at last ready to begin their five-hundred-mile trek to Derne. All that was left was to get final U.S. approval on the changes Eaton had made to the plan to aid Hamet. Eaton knew that when Hamet's army arrived outside Derne, Tripolitania's second city, he would need supplies, money, and weapons. Eaton sent letters to Hull, Barron, and Secretary of the Navy Smith, setting the Gulf of Bomba, about thirty miles east of Derne, as the assembly point for Hamet's army and the U.S. squadron. He expected the march to take twenty days.[22]

⤬

Yusuf Karamanli had no idea how many men his brother had managed to recruit, but the reigning bashaw of Tripoli knew one thing—Hamet was coming. By the beginning of March, Yusuf faced the prospect of a war on two fronts, one that could quickly devolve into a civil war if his brother prosecuted his campaign with even a little bit of vigor. Yusuf, however, was counting on his brother to lack the stomach to attack and hoped Hamet's reluctance would buy enough time to get reinforcements and a commander he trusted in Derne.[23] He turned to one of his most-trusted advisors, Hassan Bey, to accomplish both.

Hassan Bey was a Mameluke. How he had come to be part of Yusuf's inner circle is a mystery. The Karamanli family, throughout their reign, made wide use of foreigners in positions of importance. Yusuf's chief admiral was a Scotsman, his chief financier Neapolitan. Bey probably fled the chaos of Egypt and found employment with Yusuf, who had a penchant for selecting able subordinates. Bey held the title of Aga, a cross between general and defense minister, and had led a bloody suppression of the tribes in the Fezzan. He was also Yusuf's brother-in-law. Now, Yusuf gave him the job of not only retaining Cyrenaica for the Karamanli dynasty but of destroying, once and for all, his older brother's pretensions to the throne.[24] Yusuf ordered the American prisoners to help Bey gather provisions and weapons for his expedition, and on March 4, Hassan set out for Derne.[25]

On the same day, a pair of American warships appeared off the harbor, a reminder to Yusuf of his two-front dilemma. The return of the Americans was a signal to many in Tripoli that the blockade, which had brought the city to its knees in 1804, was about to begin again. Over the winter the blockade had weakened and finally disappeared, allowing Yusuf to receive several much-needed grain shipments. The return of American warships, however, sent a shiver through many of the city's residents. Marine private William Ray, could see from his prison, "the inhabitants, expecting a siege, [as they] began to move their families and effects into the country."[26]

To dispel some of the fear his people clearly felt, Yusuf instituted a series of very public defensive upgrades. He had the American prisoners rebuild and reinforce the shore batteries that Preble's squadron had destroyed the previous summer. The effort was purely cosmetic. Both Ray and Cowdery noted that the guns, when fired, sank deep into the sand and became useless after two or three shots.[27] The bashaw turned to his prisoners for yet more labor when Gunner's Mate George Griffith claimed he could build a furnace to cast cannon shot, and shell. Yusuf gave Griffith masons and nine American prisoners to build the furnace, paid him a "gold doubloon" when he began work, and promised him a hundred dollars when he completed the job. Griffith went about his project, building his furnace—but never quite seeming to finish. Yusuf, "after lavishing more than five hundred dollars in making the experiment," finally realized the American had no intention of actually finishing the furnace and abandoned the project.[28]

Yusuf also began to look for a negotiated settlement to the conflict with the United States. In mid-March, he let it slip through the Spanish consul that he was ready to listen to serious offers to end the war.[29] He also attempted again to spread the rumor that Barron had died, hoping to cause confusion among American commanders not at Malta or Syracuse.[30] Yusuf, however, was still Yusuf. As Bey moved his force toward Derne, Yusuf rounded up the families of the officers in Bey's force and "invited" them to stay at Tripoli Castle, where they were "held as pledges of their loyalty, fearing they might attach themselves to his brother, the Ex-Bashaw." Others soon joined those families. Yusuf ordered several leaders of more restive tribes to send their sons to the city, where they too became hostages to ensure their fathers' loyalty. Finally, Yusuf dispatched his son-in-law Selim into the interior to raise soldiers to defend the city. He "returned with but a handful of men. The people had been oppressed by his exorbitant demands for money, and their women had been stripped of their rings, bracelets and jewels and they refused to fight for the Bashaw."[31]

Although he was now in danger of being caught between two advancing forces—the U.S. Navy and his brother's army—Yusuf had one bargaining chip: the three hundred prisoners from the *Philadelphia*. In a chilling reminder of how ruthless he could be, he told Spanish Consul Don Grerardo Jose de Souza, that if the Americans "drove him to extremities, or attacked his town, he would put every American prisoner to death." The threat quickly reached Syracuse, where the U.S. squadron was finally shrugging off its winter sluggishness and showing signs of resuming offensive operations.[32]

❧

There was very little Commodore Samuel Barron could do to make himself comfortable. The pain from his liver stretched throughout his body. He could not stand without help, could not lie down without pain, and could not sleep well. In early February, he decided to move from Syracuse, where doctors were unable to treat him properly, to Malta, where he hoped English doctors could.[33] When his liver failed to respond to treatment on Malta, Barron realized he would have to issue orders to his squadron so it could function without him.[34] He put Rodgers in operational command, yet hampered him by spreading the squadron across the Mediterranean to cover every contingency. Barron ordered his brother, James, to take the *Essex* to an area north of Tripoli, where he was to search for a pair of Tripolitan cruisers supposedly operating off Genoa. Hugh Campbell and the *Constellation*, John Smith in the *Vixen*, and George Cox in the *President* were to reestablish the blockade, subject to Rodgers' orders. Barron also wanted Campbell to "occasionally look into Tunis Bay," while the *President* was to remain off Tripoli only a few days before Barron wanted her on convoy duty, unless Rodgers decided differently. Stephen Decatur and the *Congress* received separate orders to head to Syracuse, where he was to procure "two to four guns, of caliber no more than 6 pounds" for Eaton. The *Argus* remained on special duty, while the *Nautilus* was to join the blockade.[35]

Barron was particularly concerned about the reports of the Tripolitan cruisers. "The information I have received of the Tripoline corsairs is that they were seen off Sardinia, apparently making for the Gulf of Genoa," he told Rodgers. "They are described as two ship Xebecs carrying each 6 guns and it is supposed about 50 Men." The ever-cautious commodore also warned the aggressive Rodgers against attempting a Preble-like attack on Tripoli: "It is my wish that you enjoin upon the different commanders, not to expose their vessels unnecessarily to the enemy's batteries . . . unless some adequate object should present itself to justify the risk."[36]

While ceding tactical command to Rodgers, Barron made it clear he remained in charge of the squadron. He would decide the ultimate destinations for the warships, although he granted Rodgers authority to adapt to the situation. "Should you have received any information with regard to the enemy's cruisers, or should any event occur that in your judgment may render an alteration in their instructions necessary, you will adopt such arrangements as are best calculated to promote the good of the service in which we are engaged."[37] He reinforced that instruction in a postscript, again enjoining Rodgers, "The foregoing instructions you will always view as subject to the changes that may result from the operation of circumstances which cannot be foreseen or calculated upon. As the senior officer on the station and having the fullest confidence in your judgement, I wish to give you the utmost latitude in adopting such dispositions as you may deem best adapted to accomplish the important objects confided to us."[38]

The commodore apologized to Rodgers for his ongoing illness and for a third time urged the Marylander to temper his natural aggression: "I therefore leave it to you Sir to act in the course of the cruise on which you are destined as well with regard to your own operations as those of the other Vessels of the Squadron, in such a mode as will approve itself to the service to our Country and to ourselves."

Barron had more problems than his liver. According to letters from Samuel Briggs in Alexandria, William Eaton was racking up debt and passing it on to the Navy, in direct violation of the orders he had received. On March 11, Briggs informed Barron that Eaton had already drawn $13,000 in credit on his firm and needed another $20,000. It would take, Briggs said, more work than usual to raise that amount of hard currency: "In a country of small resources like this where banking operations are totally unknown and specie is consequently the more valuable, you will easily conceive that it was not without considerable inconvenience, that at so short a notice we could collect, and dispose of this sum Mr. Eaton stated to us."[39] Before loaning that amount, moreover, Briggs wanted to be sure the U.S. Navy would guarantee repayment, "to provide against all contingencies. . . . Though we do not apprehend any disappointment yet[,] for the greater certainty, we deem it prudent to apprize you of the circumstance that every possible delay may be obviated."[40]

Although Briggs' note was addressed to Barron, Tobias Lear received it. Lear was on Malta with Barron and had almost immediately become in effect a private secretary and, in many ways, Barron's head of intelligence. As consul general, Lear saw all the dispatches that went from diplomat to diplomat in the Mediterranean, making him one of the best-informed people in the region.[41] He also was able to read the messages from Eaton, though they were addressed to Hull and Barron.[42] Plus, the diplomat continued to receive mail from William Bainbridge, whose messages conveyed a sense that the Americans' use of Hamet had frightened Yusuf enough to make him ready for talks. The Tripolitans, Bainbridge was sure, were now "sincerely desirous for peace." The blockade and the threat to Yusuf's throne had combined to "have the happy effect of making the Bashaw's subjects clamorous" for peace, and if Lear came up with a good offer, "they would then see that America had the disposition to make peace, and that the continuance of the war was owing to the Bashaw."[43]

Just as important, news from America pointed to a shift in thinking on the war. President Jefferson, with costs continuing to rise, was now looking for a way to end the war, quickly and for less money than it would take to support either Eaton or the Navy. In his annual address to Congress, Jefferson devoted just two sentences to the conflict with Tripoli, praising the tars and Marines for their successes but leaving out any mention of a completely military solution: "The activity and success of the small force employed in the Mediterranean in the early part of the present year, the reinforcements sent into that sea, and the energy of the officers having command in the several vessels will, I trust, by the sufferings of war, reduce the bashaw of Tripoli to the desire of peace on proper terms."[44]

Then the message from Samuel Briggs crossed Lear's desk. Although Eaton had sent several dispatches telling Barron he had found Hamet and was ready to begin the march to Derne, Lear kept that news to himself until March 22, when he handed Barron all of Eaton's messages as well as those of Bainbridge and Briggs. He made sure that Barron was aware not only of the diplomatic initiatives but that Eaton had far overstepped his authority in entering into a convention with Hamet and in incurring debts on the ledger of the U.S. Navy. He also made sure Barron knew that Lear's position on Eaton had not changed: "This is a business of which I have totally disapproved of the manner in which it has been conducted and I venture to pronounce that it will be the loss of much money to the U.S. and productive of great injury to our affairs without producing any good."[45]

It was all the commodore needed to know. He had come to depend on Lear, who was now telling him what he already believed, that any reliance on Eaton was folly. With Lear at his side, he wrote a new series of instructions to Eaton. First, he congratulated him for advancing his plan as far as he had. "I cannot but applaud the energy and perseverance that has characterized your progress through a series of perplexing and discouraging difficulties to the attainment of the object of your search," the commodore wrote.[46] Barron agreed to send the *Argus* to Bomba, along with a sloop carrying the weapons, food, water, and other supplies Eaton had requested. Surprisingly, Barron also agreed to send seven thousand dollars in specie, "which is likewise to be placed at your disposal."[47] Use of the supplies and money, however, was conditional. Barron did not want to distribute any cash or supplies unless he was absolutely sure that Hamet would see the campaign to its end. "Should you have encountered unexpected difficulties which place the chances of success upon more than precarious grounds, your own prudence will suggest the propriety of not committing these supplies and the money uncontrolledly to the power of the Bashaw. Indeed in the point of view in which I regard the measures already pursued as well as the subject of co-operation generally, I conceive you ought to tread with the utmost circumspection."[48]

Barron then tore into Eaton: "You must be sensible, Sir, that in giving their sanction to a cooperation with the exiled Bashaw, government did not contemplate the measure as leading necessarily and absolutely to a reinstatement of that Prince in his rights on the regency of Tripoli."[49] It was an odd criticism, as Barron had told Hull on September 15 that the *Argus* was to support Hamet in retaking the throne. Now the commodore was changing that order: "I fear by the convention you were about to enter into with Hamet and by the complexion of other measures that a wider range may have been taken than is consistent with the powers vested in me for that particular object."[50]

For Barron, then, whatever treaty Eaton had concluded with Hamet had no legal effect. He told Eaton, "I must withhold my sanction to any convention or agreement committing the United States or tending to impress upon Hamet Bashaw a conviction that we have bound ourselves to place him on the Throne. The consequences involved in such an engagement cannot but strike you forcibly and a general view of our situation in relation to the reigning Bashaw, and our unfortunate countrymen in Tripoli will be sufficient to mark its inexpediency."[51]

The "rightful bashaw" was, in the commodore's eyes, nothing more than a means of forcing his brother to make peace and release his captives. "I wish you to understand that no guarantee or engagements to the exiled prince, whose cause, I repeat it, we are only favoring as the instrument to an attainment and not in itself as an object, must be held to stand in the way of our acquiescence to any honorable and advantageous terms of accommodation which the present Bashaw may be induced to propose. Such terms being once offered and accepted by the representative of government appointed to treat of peace, our support to Hamet Bashaw must necessarily be withdrawn."[52]

The point was so important to Barron that he told Eaton twice. The squadron would essentially abandon Hamet to his fate should Yusuf agree to a peace. He also told Eaton that due to his own illness, Isaac Hull would be the final voice determining what if any support the Navy gave Hamet; he urged Eaton to work closely with the commander of the *Argus*. "The observations I here convey to you are far from being intended to cool your zeal or discourage your expectations, but they are what I conceive it necessary to make and drawn from me by the purest feelings of duty."[53] It would take Barron's letter a month to reach Eaton.

16

THE ROAD TO DERNE

MARCH 6, 1805, was an important day in the career of Sergeant Arthur Campbell of the U.S. Marine Corps. A member of the nineteen-man Marine detachment on the U.S. brig of war *Argus*, Campbell was one of the seven men his detachment commander, First Lieutenant Presley O'Bannon, selected to serve with William Eaton's "army" assembling to march on Derne. Campbell enlisted on August 22, 1803, in Boston, signing on for three years.[1] First Lieutenant Newton Keene administered Camp-bell his oath, after which he awaited assignment to either the *Argus* or the frigate *Constitution*. Both ships were fitting out in Boston for a cruise to the Medi-terranean as part of the squadron under Commodore Edward Preble. The *Argus* was ready to sail before the frigate, and Keene sent Campbell to serve on the brig.

Campbell was a Scotsman and may have had experience in the Royal Navy or Royal Marines.[2] He said his occupation was "mechanic" when he enlisted and also that he was an American citizen.[3] Whether Keene prompted him in his answers is unknown. Although Commandant William Burrows wanted to maintain a strict three-to-one ratio of Americans to foreigners in the Corps, it was nearly impossible for his recruiting officers to meet that goal.[4] Keene, as well as Navy lieutenants Joshua Blake and Joseph Tarbell, had no luck scouring for men, because, as Preble reported,

"Our fishermen are at present all abroad, and so many merchant vessels have lately been fitted out, as to make it difficult to procure men." Preble said it could take up to five months to get *Constitution* ready for sea, due to recruiting problems, a timetable Secretary of the Navy Robert Smith utterly rejected.[5] He ordered the recruiting parties to step up their efforts, but the low pay still failed to attract many Americans.[6]

Foreign-born recruits were a different story. Increased tensions between England and France meant war was looming, and many sailors were hesitant to board unarmed trading vessels and possibly fall into a privateer's clutches or face forced service in either the French or British navy. "The certainty of war increases our success in recruiting foreign seamen, as they dare not trust to the protection the Merchant Service affords them, and are sure of being safe from impressment with us," Preble reported.[7] British, Irish, French, Spanish, Scandinavian, German, and Italian mariners all bustled along Boston's docks. For those looking to remain at sea but avoid a sailor's duties, Keene's rendezvous provided a perfect escape. Even the commandant ultimately realized the abundance of foreign-born recruits was simply too much to ignore and told his recruiters, "You are not confined to nations, but will enlist every man qualified for a soldier."[8] Preble's recruiters signed up so many foreign-born sailors that the commodore groused, "I do not believe that I have twenty native American sailors on board."[9]

The muster roll for the Marine detachment on the *Argus* suggests Campbell wasn't alone as a foreign-born Marine. Such surnames as Duffy, O'Keefe, O'Brien, Stewart, and Owens pepper the list. Although Preble worried, and justifiably so, that many of his foreign crewmen would desert the moment the squadron reached Europe, it appears his junior officers did not share those fears. In the case of the *Argus*, neither Lieutenant Stephen Decatur, who commanded the brig briefly when she sailed to the Mediterranean, nor Lieutenant Isaac Hull, ever commented on the ethnic makeup of the vessel's crew or Marines, or mentioned fears their foreign-born men would bolt.[10]

Preble gave Hull the task of keeping watch on the western Mediterranean, and *Argus* spent six months cruising between Morocco and Tunis, making sure those powers remained at peace with the United States. The brig rejoined the squadron in April and played an important part in the summer campaign against Tripoli, and Private Arthur Campbell was there for all of it. Campbell volunteered to serve on *Gunboat No. 3,* one of the six vessels Preble borrowed from Naples. The crew of the *Argus,* under Lieutenant Joshua Blake, manned *No. 3* in the first assault on Tripoli on August 3, 1804, but due to contrary winds, poor construction of the craft, or, some officers whispered, cowardice, Blake never engaged closely with the Tripolitans. Although he was one of his favorites, Preble relieved Blake and put *Argus'* sailing master, Samuel Brooke, in command of the gunboat. Campbell was part of the attacks on August 7, August 28, and September 3, during which Brooke pushed *No. 3* into the thick of the action. The Neapolitan crews that came with the gunboats handled the vessels, while the Americans manned the twenty-four-pounder cannon at the bow, used muskets and pistols to sweep onto the decks of enemy ships, and wielded tomahawks and pikes in hand-to-hand combat with the corsairs.

After the attack of August 3, the Tripolitan gunboats remained moored in an anchorage under the guns of the bashaw's castle and several forts. The next three attacks saw the American gunboats try to lure out the Tripolitans and when that failed, the Americans turned their cannon on the city. *Gunboat No. 3* expended more than 250 rounds of ammunition in its three engagements and helped batter the bashaw's defenses.[11] Campbell, as a Marine, likely split time between serving the gun and attempting to hit close-in targets with musket fire. When the gunboat was not in action, Campbell (and other Marines) would have been the ship's guard.[12] Campbell returned to the *Argus* with Brooke and the others who came from the brig when Preble returned his borrowed gunboats. He performed well enough on the gunboat to earn promotion to corporal in November 1804.[13] He remained on the *Argus* until February, when O'Bannon took him and six privates to join Eaton's army.

On March 6, 1805, the army prepared to set out for Derne. The Marines and Christian mercenaries struck their tents, packed their rucksacks and haversacks, filled their canteens, and readied their weapons. When he woke up that morning, Arthur Campbell was still a corporal. At some point that day, O'Bannon made Campbell an acting sergeant (Hull would later confirm the promotion, dated March 6, 1805). Although O'Bannon still commanded the seven Marines, Campbell, as sergeant, took over the day-to-day routine of running the squad, while O'Bannon gave more time to commanding all the Christian soldiers.[14]

In the short time they had known each other, Eaton and O'Bannon formed a close bond. Eaton came to rely on the Marine officer, and O'Bannon boasted he would willingly follow "the general" anywhere.[15] Campbell and the other Marines also seemed to fall under Eaton's spell. There is no mention in any dispatch of the hardships of the campaign overwhelming the Marines. There was likely a lightness in Campbell's first steps toward Derne as the new sergeant not only had increased authority and responsibility but would now earn nine dollars a month.[16]

The force set out with Eaton, O'Bannon, and Midshipman Paoli Peck leading the procession on horseback. Marching right behind the officers was Sergeant Campbell and his six-man squad of Marines. The twenty-five mercenary artillerymen, under Selim Comb and Lieutenants Connant and Rocco, marched behind the Marines. Next came Hamet's men, who numbered about ninety, followed by the Bedouin cavalry that had joined. Behind the Bedouin came the 107 camels and mules that carried the army's provisions. They belonged to a cantankerous Arab sheik named Omar al-Tahib, who had agreed to rent the animals to Eaton for eleven dollars a head. Finally, a company of thirty-eight Christian soldiers, mostly Greeks, under the command of Captain Luca and Lieutenant Constantine Bari, brought up the rear.[17]

The combat troops covered forty miles the first day. Footsore, they arrived at a point twenty miles west of Alexandria called "Arab Tower." Eaton described it as "an immense ruin of regular fortification, of freestone, about three hundred feet square, the walls five feet thick and thirty two high, with bastions at the angles, and battlements on the curtains." The "tower," though, wasn't Arab but Greek, and it marked the start of the desert plain that stretched from the Egyptian border to Derne. The supply convoy, under al-Tahib, straggled badly and did not arrive until the next day.

Eaton spent March 8 reorganizing his force. He had the Greek infantry join the artillerymen at the front of the column, combining his Christian troops into a single company. The route that Eaton and Hamet chose paralleled the coast, traversing ground that was more rocky plateau than sandy desert. Travelers of the time described the region as: "Only hollows, low hills, and slopes occasionally intersect the wearisome plain, and when you have ascended one of these, another endless plain, with similar objects, comes to your view. The caravans, the flocks of sheep, and herds of camels, that now and then pass by, alone recall to mind the existence of men, or the barking of a dog announces the neighborhood of an encampment: the same may be said of the almost equally extensive tract from Agaba to Derna."[18] Although inhospitable, the area was not desolate. "The ground is throughout broken and irregular, and does not slope down into pastures as the woody and elevated nature of this country affords frequent and copious springs of clear and most delicious water, which may justly be considered by the traveler as a perfect blessing, so great is the thirst excited by moving about at this season under such a brilliant and scorching sun."[19]

Bedouin tribes populated the region, often preying on the caravans that traveled from Derne to Alexandria.[20] Eaton had to guard against those tribes while also allowing Hamet the chance to recruit them. Most had suffered at the hands of either the Ottomans in Cairo or Yusuf in Tripoli, and Hamet was optimistic he could convert at least some of them to his cause. The column moved out at 11 a.m. on March 8, covering fifteen miles before coming to a halt. The next day, Eaton had to deal with the first in a series of near mutinies fomented by Sheik al-Tahib. The Arab wanted more money for his drivers and demanded Eaton and Hamet pay his men in advance. Eaton knew better, noting in his journal, "It was not safe to do so." The drivers refused to break camp, gathered ominously around al-Tahib, and bedded down for the night. Throughout the evening al-Tahib spoke with his followers, warning them "if they performed their services before being paid, the Christians would be apt to defraud them." On the morning of March 10 the drivers again refused to move, demanding pay. It was the first real test of Hamet's leadership, and he looked unsure of himself, as his only source of money was Eaton. "The Bashaw seemed irresolute and despondent," Eaton noted. "Money, more money was the only stimulus which could give motion to the camp. The forenoon was consumed, and no appearances of a disposition to proceed ahead." The drivers, at the urging of al-Tahib, refused to move, and Hamet's followers remained on the sidelines. Hamet was unable to persuade the drivers to work.

Finally, Eaton had enough. "I ordered the Christians under arms and feinted a countermarch; threatening to abandon the expedition and their Bashaw, unless the march in advance proceeded immediately." Al-Tahib's followers were well aware that if Eaton left, there would be no hope of payment. Still disgruntled, the drivers agreed to return to work. "The mutiny was suppressed and we marched twelve miles," Eaton recorded.[21]

The column covered sixty-six miles over the next three days, marching from a countryside of "low sand valleys and rocky, desert plains," to one that had once flourished. Greek and Roman ruins abounded, as did signs the area had once been fertile and well populated.[22] At 2 p.m. on March 13, a courier arrived with news from Derne. According to the courier, the governor of Derne had heard of Hamet's approach and, struck with fear, had shut himself inside the city. The people, however, were ready to welcome Hamet as a liberator. The news—which Eaton would later learn to be false—made the Arabs break out in celebration. "Feats of horsemanship . . . were exhibited in front of the Bashaw, by his people." The cavalry began firing into the air and raising cries as they wheeled their horses in front of Hamet. The wild celebration in Hamet's camp completely surprised the footmen and drivers under Omar al-Tahib. "Our foot Arabs, who were in the rear with the baggage, hearing the firing, and apprehending that we were attacked by the wild Arabs of the desert, attempted to disarm and put to death the Christians who escorted the caravan," Eaton reported.[23] It was an alarming situation. Captain Luca and Lieutenant Constantine Bari led thirty-eight men, and al-Tahib had three times that many followers. As the Arabs moved toward the Greeks, one, an "Arab of some consequence among them," broke from the pack and demanded the others find out what was happening in the camp before they attacked a group of men who were supposed to be their allies. The drivers sent a runner to the camp; who returned with news of the celebration. The Arabs released the Christians, defusing the situation.[24]

That al-Tahib's followers had shown they would prefer to kill the Christians rather than fight off marauding Bedouin pointed to a major problem in Eaton's "army," which was split along religious and ethnic lines. Simply put, the Muslims and Christians loathed one another. The Muslims, spurred on by al-Tahib's tales, looked for any sign of European treachery. The Muslims had other reasons as well for their distrust. The history of Western interaction with the Muslim world and the Ottoman Empire was not especially good (from either side), and the Arabs saw European attempts to encroach on the sultan's domains as attacks on Islam.[25] The Christian mercenaries, especially those from Greece, had equal reason not to trust their Muslim allies. Although tolerated, Greek Christians were second-class citizens under the sultans and had to pay a special tax to practice their religion. They also seethed for independence.[26] Whenever Eaton's army stopped for the night, the Christian mercenaries pitched their tents next to O'Bannon's Marines, and the Arabs pitched theirs together, well away from the Christians. The guards each side set watched one another as much they watched for marauders.[27]

Another reason for the mistrust between the Christians and Muslims was money. The Christian mercenaries seemed to accept their payment terms with few if any reservations. The Muslim infantry and cavalry Hamet had recruited were much more troublesome. The "rightful bashaw", with his at times less-than-inspirational personality, did not at first command the loyalty of followers such as al-Tahib—he merely bought it. The Muslim mercenaries took every advantage of Hamet, which placed him in a difficult situation. Before he hired his Arab troops, Hamet had written to Commodore Barron to make sure Eaton had the authority to make promises of money and material and that Barron would honor those commitments. Barron had replied he would;[28] Hamet had told his followers his American friend would see to it they would all get paid. His dependence on a Christian for his finances, however, made him look weak. When his own troops demanded money and he could not provide it, Eaton noted, Hamet often appeared lost, torn between keeping faith with his followers and doing what was best for the mission.[29]

⌒≍⌒

Sergeant Arthur Campbell had no idea of the politics going on behind the army. Like the other Christian soldiers, Campbell probably felt unease, even distrust when he looked at the Arabs that followed Hamet, but he had his orders. Eaton asked the Marines to do just one thing—be Marines—and Campbell and his men responded. They marched each day right behind Eaton, O'Bannon, and Peck, who always led the way. They scouted the route ahead of the column, wary of ambushes. Most of all, if they grumbled, they grumbled to one another. To their superiors, the Marines always presented a solid, professional face.

Much of that spirit was probably due to First Lieutenant William Amory and Sergeant Edward Bancroft. Amory had commanded the *Argus'* Marines for nearly two years. Over that period, he had drilled his men constantly in accordance with Burrows' orders, paying particular attention to guard duty, which Burrows stressed. On board ship, his Marines turned out in full uniform, right down to powdered hair.[30] This attention to detail set the Marines apart and began to instill an esprit de corps. Bancroft, however, was the actual taskmaster for the *Argus*, Marines. Burrows had advised all of his officers to rely on their sergeants,[31] and it was Bancroft who trained the nineteen Marines each day, ensuring they knew musket and bayonet drill, their positions in battle, and how to mount guard. Now that he was a sergeant, the job of keeping the Marines sharp fell to Campbell, and acting on O'Bannon's instructions, at the end of each day's march he put his six men through a proper mounting of the guard.

For the Marines it was tiring work, especially after marching twenty to twenty-five miles in the late-winter sun and they quickly learned the most important lesson of desert warfare—water is king. One of Campbell's responsibilities would have been to ensure his squad had water and to replenish it at every opportunity. Midshipman Paoli Peck had a harsh lesson on why. After the march of nearly forty miles on March 6, the column arrived at a well only to find it dry. Peck had not

taken the precaution to procure a small skin of water to carry on my horse, [and] had it not been for a few oranges I had, I should hardly have been able to move next morning. I laid myself down on my bed to sleep, but I could not, being for the first time in my life almost dead with thirst. Had I possessed thousands I would have given them for a gill of water. About day light, a little water was found, worse, if possible than bilge water; but to me it was more delicious than the most precious cordial.[32]

Campbell, meanwhile, learned a lesson about his so-called Arab allies, one that would cause the Marines many sleepless nights. On March 15, after covering twenty-six miles, the column stopped for the night and set up camp in rocky terrain. It was cold and rainy, the rain making visibility difficult. Although the Marines were on guard, a few Arabs managed to sneak into their camp and steal a cartridge box, musket, and bayonet, as well as all of the cheese provision from the magazine tent. From that day on, the Marine guards and Arabs played a cat-and-mouse game as the Arabs continued to try to steal provisions and equipment from the Marines.[33]

The weather kept the army in camp for the next two days. Heavy rains on March 16 forced Eaton to move his camp to higher ground when a flash flood threatened to inundate the area where he had pitched his tents. The next day al-Tahib's followers again refused to march unless Eaton paid them in advance. He was able to placate them with "promises," and the column moved out, covering twelve miles before camping for the night in a ravine where the tired soldiers and drivers found "good rain water."[34] On March 18, the column covered fifteen miles, arriving at the ruins of a castle called "Masroscah." Vestiges of its former glory were plain. Eaton thought the land looked very fertile, although the locals grew only a little "badly cultivated wheat and barley." A local sheik had used material from some of the ruined buildings to build a hundred-foot-long battlement and house, while several families lived nearby in tents. The sheik made his living bartering goods from passing caravans. He kept "cattle, sheep, goats, [and] fowls" and offered "butter in skins, dates and milk" for sale at very high prices.[35]

While the men haggled for fresh food to augment their rations, Eaton took a moment to speak with Hamet about the drivers and their own supply caravan. Hamet looked nervous, and the caravan drivers appeared to be packing their gear and preparing the camels and mules for a march. Eaton demanded to know what was happening. "I now learned, for the first time, that our caravan was freighted by the Bashaw only to this place, and that the owners had received no part of their pay. No persuasion could prevail on them to proceed to Bomba, nor to wait our arrival thither for their pay," Eaton wrote in his journal. The drivers claimed that "they had fulfilled their engagement with the Bashaw, and would now return to their families in Behara, for whose safety they had serious apprehensions." The ever-troublesome Sheik al-Tahib "favored their pretensions." Only when Eaton "promised to procure the cash for their payment on condition that they would proceed two days further, where we expected to find Arab tribes and hire another caravan," did the drivers listen. To pay them Eaton took up a collection among the Christian officers, raising $140, and added nearly every dime of his own cash fund to give the Arabs $673. Hamet too had taken up a collection, and together they met the "claims of these chiefs of the caravan."[36]

It was a short-lived victory. When Eaton awoke the next morning, the drivers were gone, along with most of the supply animals. Only forty men and a few camels remained, and they steadfastly refused to proceed, even though Hamet had paid them. Eaton and Hamet were in a "perplexed and embarrassed situation." They had spent nearly all of their cash—Eaton was down to just "three Venetian sequins"—and without the pack animals there was no way to continue the advance. Hamet suggested leaving the baggage behind at the small Arab castle, but Eaton rejected the idea, as they had no money to purchase provisions on their march. The column remained idle throughout March 19 and 20 while Eaton and Hamet formulated a plan to transport their provisions and ammunition.

Eaton now uncovered the real reason why the drivers had bolted, and it centered once more on Omar al-Tahib. The ever-restive sheik had again spread rumors the Christians intended to abandon the Muslims and argued none of the Arabs should take another step until Eaton proved the U.S. Navy would be at Bomba with money and supplies. In addition, a pilgrim on his way to Mecca from Morocco reported "that a force consisting of eight hundred cavalry and numerous foot were on their march from Tripoli for the defense of Derne" and had already reached Benghazi. Eaton wanted

212 ~~~ CHAPTER SIXTEEN

to leave immediately, in case the rumor was true, but al-Tahib had stirred up the few drivers remaining, and they refused to listen to anyone else.[37]

As for the Bomba rumor—the suspicion that no U.S. force was there—Eaton at first believed Hamet was part of what he called a "complot" to frighten the Arabs. The various sheiks gathered in Hamet's tent for a private meeting, to which they denied Eaton entry. The "general" could hear "a great deal of noise and some counsel" among the Arabs. One thing was clear: Hamet was frightened. The sheiks agreed to send a scout to Bomba to see whether Eaton was telling the truth and the Navy was waiting for them. The column would remain in camp until the scout returned. Eaton exploded when Hamet told him about the decision: "I ordered their rations stopped, and resolved myself to take possession of the castle and fortify myself there." He threatened to abandon the entire enterprise and remain at the castle "until I could get intelligence to our naval detachment to come to our relief, when I would take off our Christians and leave them [the Arabs] to take measures for their own subsistence and safety." Eaton stormed back to his tent around midnight, leaving the sheiks, in his words, "confused and embarrassed."[38]

Once in his own tent, Eaton confided to his journal his impatience with and disgust for his Arab troops: "We have marched a distance of two hundred miles, through an inhospitable waste of world without seeing the habitation of an animated being, or the tracks of man, except where superstition has marked her lonely steps over burning sands and rocky mountains, whence the revelation of one of her most hypocritical fanatics trains her wretched victims a tedious pilgrimage to pay their devotion at his shrine."[39] Despite the nearly endless problems with al-Tahib and the drivers, Eaton kept his eyes firmly fixed on what he wanted the outcome of the expedition to be—"the liberation of three hundred Americans from the chains of barbarism, and a manly peace."[40]

⊂∞⟨ ⟩∞⊃

Eaton was wise to object to sending a scout to Bomba to see if the U.S. Navy was waiting in the bay. It wasn't. Master Commandant Isaac Hull was not off Bomba but Malta, where he had arrived on March 10. He reported to

Commodore Samuel Barron, taking with him Hamet's secretary, Mahmud, who presented Barron with another letter. In it "bashaw" again asked for money, weapons, and cooperation in his assault on Derne. Barron had already anticipated Hamet's needs and contracted a small sloop, which he had armed and named the *Hornet*. He put Lieutenant Samuel Evans in charge and loaded it and the *Argus* with food and ammunition.[41]

Although Barron had pilloried Eaton's treaty with Hamet and the expenses he had racked up on the credit of the United States, the letter from Hamet must have cheered the ailing commodore. Hamet reported that his march was already under way and that he and Eaton had a plan of attack. Despite the counsel he continued to receive from Tobias Lear, who wanted to suspend, if not cancel, Eaton's mission, Barron decided to continue backing Eaton. He ordered Hull to head first to Alexandria, where he was to pay off Briggs Brothers before sailing for Bomba. In his orders to Hull Barron enclosed the letters from Eaton and Hamet and his own to them. Hull was to make use of "the personal knowledge you possess of my sentiments and wishes" to "form a correct and to yourself satisfactory Idea of the service on which you are destined, with the United States Brig *Argus* and Sloop *Hornet* (Lieutenant Evans) under your command."[42]

Hull was not to commit to backing any land campaign until he had met with Eaton and formed a "just estimate of the chances of success, and thence, how far it is safe and expedient to pursue the object. Should it be determined to persevere, you are authorized to afford him every support and assistance, consistent with your means and situation." Barron also gave Hull full authority over the supplies he carried. He was to distribute them only if he believed there was a strong probability of success. The same was true for any naval support of an attack on Derne: "Its execution must necessarily depend so much on a variety of events and circumstances which may happen and it, is probable have happened to Mr. Eaton and his co-adventurers and which we are totally unable to foresee."[43] Barron gave Hull latitude to make his own decision on whether to support Eaton; he was to use his "own judgment and discretion, in which allow me to assure you I entertain the highest confidence, [and which] will frequently be your sole directors."[44]

Hull, never the most enthusiastic supporter of the attack on Derne, had an escape clause. If Eaton was unable to deliver on land, the Navy would do nothing by sea. Hull was ready to sail for Egypt on March 28 along with Evans and the *Hornet*. A gale delayed the *Argus* and *Hornet* until April 2. The transit to Bomba took just two days, but when Hull arrived, he saw no sign of Eaton. It would be another two weeks before he did.

17

MARCHES, MUTINIES, AND U.S. MARINES

DELAYS, DELAYS, and still more delays beset the army marching under "General" William Eaton, and all the delays had the same source: Sheik Omar al-Tahib. The Arab leader constantly caused trouble among the caravan drivers and the Bedouin tribes that followed Hamet Karamanli. Hamet was at least cordial with al-Tahib. Eaton loathed the man, and with each artificial delay, his impatience turned more to outright hostility.

The first delay came on March 19, when al-Tahib convinced the supply caravan drivers to abandon the army. For two days Eaton and, to a lesser extent, Hamet tried to convince the sheiks in charge of the supply caravan to resume the march. It took a mixture of threats and promises of money to induce fifty of the drivers to agree to rejoin the army for two days, when Hamet expected to replace them from allied Bedouin tribes. The column set out on March 21 at 11 a.m. and covered thirteen miles, camping on a "stony, barren plain." The next day, after a march of twelve and a half miles, the column arrived in a fertile coastal plain that was home to upward of four thousand Bedouin. They raised cattle, sheep, and horses, kept "vast herds of goats and goats," and had fresh produce they were more than willing to sell to hungry soldiers.[1]

Upon arrival, Eaton and the Marines became the center of attention as they were the "first Christians ever seen by these wild people," as Eaton reported. "We were viewed by them as curiosities. They laughed at the oddity of our dress; gazed at our polished arms with astonishment at the same time they observed the greatest deference towards such of us as bore any distinctive marks of office." The Bedouin were especially interested in the brass buttons adorning the officers' and Marines' uniforms. The Marines found the Bedouin thought the brass was gold and bartered them not only for food but "companionship," in the form of the Bedouin women.[2] The seven Marines took so many buttons off their uniforms that First Lieutenant Presley O'Bannon threatened to dock a month's pay of any man who turned out for muster without the requisite number of buttons on his uniform.[3]

The food the Arabs offered was perhaps an even more valuable commodity than the women. The army had already eaten all of its fresh provisions and was down to a small amount of beans and rice. It was out of corn for the horses. The Bedouin offered everything the soldiers could want, though at steep prices. Most of Eaton's men were broke, still waiting for promised payments or having surrendered their scant cash to pay the caravan drivers, and they traded their small amount of rice for the Bedouins' offerings. The rice enthralled the Arabs. One woman offered her teenage daughter for a small sack of rice, an offer even Eaton found difficult to refuse: "She was a well-proportioned, handsome brunette of about thirteen or fourteen years, with an expressive hazel eye, inclining to black, arched eye brows, perfect teeth, and lips formed for voluptuousness." Despite the girl's willingness to go along with any deal, "prudence forbid it."[4] The Bedouin also took an instant liking to the soldiers' biscuit, or hard bread, something else they had never seen. At first, the Arabs were not sure just what to make of the stuff: "They examined it carefully; and, breaking it with their shepherds club or hatchet, tasted it with symptoms of hesitation; finding it palatable they sought every means to obtain it from us."[5]

Although welcome, the camp diversions failed to conceal the fact that once more the army was not moving. After going into camp on March 22, the army remained idle for five days, which was more than enough time for Sheik al-Tahib to again stir up trouble. It was also enough time, however, for Hamet to fulfill one of his promises and recruit more men. On March 24, he signed on 80 more cavalrymen, and on March 25, 47

Arab families joined, bringing with them 150 infantrymen. Hamet and Eaton also managed to hire ninety camels, at eleven dollars a head, to organize a new supply train. On March 26, a courier arrived from Derne with news that Yusuf had sent a force of five hundred cavalry and a "huge number of Arabs," and it was three days away from Derne. The information immediately threw the camp into turmoil. Hamet appeared completely unmanned, unsure if he wanted to continue. The caravan drivers again fled into the desert. It was more than Eaton could take. He ordered O'Bannon and the Marines to secure the rations, allowed no Arab near the supply tents, and gave orders that no Arab was to receive food unless the drivers returned and Hamet's people agreed to continue their march.

al-Tahib refused. He once more demanded that Eaton send a scout to Bomba so he, al-Tahib, would have definitive knowledge of the backing of the U.S. Navy. Eaton nearly spat in the man's face. "I could not but reproach that chief with want of courage and fidelity. He had promised much and fulfilled nothing," Eaton wrote in his journal. The general told the sheik he "regretted having been made acquainted with him; and should be well satisfied if he would put his menace in execution of returning to Egypt, provided he would not interfere with the dispositions of other chiefs."[6] al-Tahib flew into a rage, vowing to ride back to Egypt and take all of his people with him, "swearing by all the force of his religion to join us no more." The potential loss of his main Arab ally made Hamet even more upset, and he begged Eaton to allow him to send an envoy to the sheik. Eaton at first refused. The day ended in a tense standoff between the Arabs and the Christians.

On March 27, al-Tahib inspired mutiny among nearly all the army's Arabs and convinced about half to join him in marching back to Egypt. Hamet again begged Eaton to send an envoy to make peace with al-Tahib. Eaton exploded. "No consideration whatever could prevail on me to ask as a favor what I claimed as a right. The services of that chief were due to us: we had paid for them; and he had pledged his faith to render them with fidelity. It did not belong to him, at this period, to make terms nor dictate measures: I should not debase myself to propose an accommodation." Hamet remained afraid that al-Tahib would "turn his influence and take a part against us." Eaton dismissed the argument, declaring, "Let him do it. I like an open enemy better than a treacherous friend. When he shall have taken this ground it will, perhaps, give me an opportunity to punish eventually what I would do summarily if the respect I had for his Excellency did not prevent it." He made sure all those who could hear him conveyed a challenge al-Tahib: "Carry the message to the chief [that] I had a rifle and a sabre true to their distance."[7]

Eaton's message utterly terrified Hamet and made al-Tahib "mad with rage." The sheik, who had never trusted Eaton and rightfully believed Eaton was manipulating Hamet, "swore vengeance against the Bashaw, and his Christian sovereigns, as he styled us." Eaton ignored al-Tahib's anger and ordered what was left of the column to prepare to march. At 7 a.m. the army set out without al-Tahib. Three hours later, a messenger rode up to inform Eaton that al-Tahib had broken camp and was preparing to march back to Egypt. Eaton dismissed the messenger with the reply, "Since he has taken that route, I have nothing further with him but to take steps for the recovery of the cash and property he has fraudulently drawn from me."[8] The column moved on. Two hours later, around noon, another messenger arrived. If Eaton would halt, al-Tahib would rejoin. After a brief conversation with Hamet, Eaton agreed, and the march stopped. Eaton realized there was little chance of making any further progress that day and ordered the army to camp. It had moved just five miles. Ninety minutes after stopping, al-Tahib rode up and made a beeline to Eaton's tent. Upon seeing the general, the sheik, "with visible chagrin in his countenance, said, 'You see the influence I have among these people!'" The bluster did not impress Eaton, who retorted, "Yes! and I see also the disgraceful use you make of it."[9]

Just why al-Tahib would rejoin a man he had vowed to eviscerate became clear on March 27, when none of the Arabs appeared willing to continue the march. The rumors Yusuf had sent reinforcements to Derne had frightened Hamet, and al-Tahib did his best to fan that fear. Hamet seized the horses he had given to O'Bannon, Peck, and some of the mercenary officers and gave them to his own foot soldiers. It was an ominous sign. Worse, al-Tahib was again spreading tales of Christian treachery and managed to coax the Bedouin who had just joined the expedition to desert. Eaton decided to show a firm hand and resume the march, order-ing the Marines and Christian soldiers to escort the baggage. He upbraided the "bashaw" for his weakness. "High words ensued." Eaton set out. Two hours later, Hamet rode up. He apologized for the misunderstanding and congratulated Eaton and the Christian soldiers on their "firmness." Hamet explained that "he was obliged to dissemble acquiescence in the wishes of his people to render them manageable."[10]

The column marched twelve miles and made camp. Eaton then dis-covered the new drivers had not come with Hamet. Instead, with al-Tahib at their head, they had again decided to abandon the expedition to return to their homes. Hamet dispatched one of his officers, Hamet Gurgies, to convince the drivers to rejoin. The army remained in camp on March 28, awaiting Gurgies. On the twenty-ninth he returned with the drivers in tow, and the following day Eaton set out at 6 a.m. with the Marines, Christian mercenaries, and baggage. He left Hamet, who was again having problems getting his followers to move, to catch up. Word quickly arrived of a new problem among the Arabs, and Eaton came to a halt. Once again, al-Tahib was the center of the dispute. Hamet had given him $1,500 to "equally dis-tribute" among the drivers. Al-Tahib, however, had pocketed some of the money, and when the other sheiks, particularly a Sheik Mohamet, found out they demanded immediate payment and refused to march with al-Tahib. Hamet Gurgies was again trying to make peace.[11]

Eaton had already covered fifteen miles. He debated whether to stop but had no real choice. Sheik Mohamet and the others wielded consid-erable influence among the tribes near Derne, and Hamet needed them to rouse the populace. Eaton not only stopped but reversed course and marched back three miles, camping by a cistern of water. Hamet went off with twelve others to negotiate with the drivers. The delay lasted four days. In his journal Eaton recorded what he thought of his allies: "They have no sense of patriotism, truth nor honor; and no attachment where they have no prospect of gain, except to their religion, to which they are enthusiasts. Poverty makes them thieves and practice renders them adroit in stealing. The instant the eye of vigilance is turned from an object on which they have fixed a desire, it is no more to be found. Arms, ammunition and provisions, most engage their furtive speculations; but sundry of our people have been robbed of their clothes and other articles."[12]

Before the column could again move out, Eaton faced yet another challenge from al-Tahib. Eaton expected to reach Bomba in fourteen days and had planned his rations accordingly. The many delays the column encountered had forced Eaton to stretch those rations, and now he could not stretch his food anymore. On April 1, as the army was preparing to set out, al-Tahib went to Eaton's tent and demanded full rations for him and his men. Eaton refused, and al-Tahib drew himself into a threatening pose. Eaton "reproached him as the cause of all our delays in the march and with a total failure of all his engagements with me[;] . . . he was on all occasions throwing obstacles in our way."[13]

Al-Tahib then unleashed a diatribe about Hamet and the other sheiks, to which Eaton replied he "thought the Bashaw and sheiks [whom] he accused [were] better men than himself and would not hear them calumniated." Al-Tahib accused Eaton of playing favorites. "I said to him, if he had experienced any evidence of my partiality it was in his favor until after his hypocrisy betrayed itself. It was true I now held him in no consideration, for I could place no reliance in anything he said or undertook."[14] The Arab didn't blink at Eaton's insults. In a somewhat subdued voice he "cautioned me against persisting in the resolution I had taken not to augment the ration; it would unavoidably produce an insurrection. The other sheiks and caravan would leave me. As for himself, he could not subsist on rice alone; he would have bread also." Eaton asked the sheik if he planned to back up his words. Al-Tahib replied "with a menacing tone, 'Remember you are in a desert, and a country not your own. I am a greater man here than either you or the Bashaw.'"[15] Eaton, enraged, stormed, "I have found you at the head of every commotion which has happened since we left Alexandria[!] You are the instigator of the present among the chiefs. Leave my tent but mark; if I find a mutiny in camp during the absence of the Bashaw, I will put you to instant death as the fomenter of it."[16]

Al-Tahib rode off with several of his followers. Hamet being still absent, Eaton turned to Hamet's treasurer to placate the remaining sheiks. The treasurer met with them at 10 a.m. Four hours later, al-Tahib returned. He first went to Midshipman Peck and George Farquhar (Richard's son, who had signed onto the expedition against his father's wishes), imploring both to use their influence with Eaton to bring a reconciliation. The sheik spent three hours with the officers, telling them he "regretted that he had lost my [Eaton's] confidence, [that he] apprehended that some secret enemy had insinuated unfavorable impressions against him: was devoted to [Eaton] and would even abandon the Bashaw to follow [him]." At 5 p.m. a very contrite al-Tahib finally went to see Eaton. He "professed eternal obligations and attachment would seek every occasion to give proofs of it; and hoped that an opportunity would offer to him at Derne to convince me that he was a man." Eaton somewhat curtly replied that he "required nothing of him by way of reconciliation but truth, fidelity to the Bashaw, pacific conduct among the other chiefs, uniformity and perseverance in this conduct." Al-Tahib "promised by an oath and offered me his hand."[17]

The meeting solved, at least temporarily, the problem with al-Tahib. Eaton faced a much larger issue, as Hamet had yet to return from his mission to retrieve the caravan drivers. Eaton began to fear that he had "suffered himself to fall into a snare of his brother." He decided to stay put one more night, a correct decision it turned out—Hamet finally rode into camp at the head of the drivers on April 2. Hamet rode nearly sixty miles to catch up to the drivers and, after convincing them to return, had retraced his steps. He suffered through cold rains and subsisted on milk and dates until he finally arrived at the encampment. That night, Eaton and the sheiks met in Hamet's tent. Some of them were afraid to continue because of the rumors of Yusuf's army. Others were unsure if their food would last and had doubts whether the American navy would in fact be in Bomba with supplies and money. Eaton attempted to raise their spirits. "I exhorted them, as on other instances of disagreement, to union and perseverance, as the only means of insuring success to the important enterprise in which they were engaged; to which they gave pledges of faith and honor."[18] Just as important were Hamet's actions. He had a reputation for weakness and vacillation, but he was disproving it the deeper the army moved into Cyrenaica.[19]

At 6 a.m. on April 3, the army moved out. As usual, Eaton, Peck, and O'Bannon led the way, with Sergeant Campbell and his squad of Marines marching behind them. Next came Selim Comb and his twenty-five European artillerymen. Hamet led his Arab cavalry, which now numbered more than five hundred. Sheik al-Tahib and the caravan were next, with the company of Greek infantry, marching with the baggage. Behind them was a vast array of Bedouin families that had attached themselves to Hamet's cause, and marching with the families was 150 Arab infantry. All told, the army numbered close to eight hundred fighting men, while the column, which stretched for miles, numbered nearly 1,200.[20] The force managed just ten miles.[21]

⌒⌒

Each day the army advanced it grew a little weaker, from not desertion but hunger. By April 6, Eaton's army was down to just a half-cup of uncooked rice per day, a meager 103 calories, while the men and animals had gone two days without water.[22] The army still advanced, each step a trial. Men and animals, already worn from the 250 miles they had marched, grew more and more fatigued. On April 8, the column stopped at the site of an ancient Roman fort, complete with a cistern Legionnaires had hewn through the rock. The water was a godsend, and there was enough low grass and scrub brush for the horses to forage. Nevertheless, the soldiers and, increasingly, the camp followers were slowly starving.[23]

The next day, following a march of eighteen miles, the army camped in a valley four miles from the coast. At six the following morning, Eaton walked to the shoreline to get his bearings, leaving orders for the army to prepare to set out upon his return. When he got back to camp, however, he found Hamet had made no preparations to leave. Hamet declared that the soldiers and camp followers all needed rest and "suggested" the army remain in camp for the day to recover. Although this had merit, Eaton soon discovered Hamet's real motive: He had no intention of moving another inch until he knew the U.S. Navy was waiting at Bomba. Eaton tried to persuade Hamet to march, pointing out the army was down to just six days' rations and was still some days out. They simply could not afford to use up rations and not move. Hamet refused to budge. "He said the Arab chiefs were resolved to proceed no further till the camp shall have recruited themselves [recouped their strength] by a little repose," Eaton confided in his journal. "I told him if they preferred famine to fatigue they might have the choice; and ordered their rations stopped."[24]

The camp remained in a state of tense stasis until late that night. Around 3 a.m., Hamet bowed to the pressure from his sheiks and began to pack up. His fortitude was gone. He was ready to march back to Egypt with the Bedouin. To do so they would need food, and they planned to take everything that was left, but Eaton heard of the plan and ordered the Marines and Christian mercenaries to arms. He stationed them outside the supply tent, where they drew up in two lines. Facing them, several hundred Arab cavalry and infantry also drew up. The two sides eyed one another for an hour while Hamet decided what to do. Eaton's resolve again restored Hamet's courage, somewhat, and he dismounted and convinced his followers to remain. He pitched his tent and sullenly called a council of his sheiks.[25]

Eaton, believing the standoff was at an end, decided to entertain the Bedouin by having Marines go through the manual of arms. It was a near-constant of camp life for the Marines, but they usually performed drill in the morning, while the camp was preparing to move out. Now they were to put on a show of discipline for the entire army.[26]

First Lieutenant Presley O'Bannon moved smartly to the front of his Marines. At a shouted command, Sergeant Arthur Campbell, Private Bernard O'Brien, and the five other Marines snapped smartly into position, their backs straight, muskets at left shoulder arms.[27] On the command "Right . . . face!" the seven Marines pivoted to the right on their right heels and left toes, their left feet coming parallel with the right, with a stamp. At the command of "Left . . . face!" they repeated the movements but with the opposite feet. Once more facing the Arabs, the Marines began to go through the manual of arms. Already at left shoulder arms, O'Bannon commanded "Support . . . *arms!*" Seven right hands moved as one, grasping the small of the musket stocks. The orders came quickly: Slope . . . *arms!* Trail . . . *arms!* Shoulder . . . *arms!* Present . . . *arms!* Shoulder . . . *arms!*[28] At each command the Marines moved smartly, almost effortlessly, despite their fatigue and hunger. O'Bannon then ordered "Fix . . . *bayonets!*," and the Arabs suddenly seemed concerned. At the command "Charge . . . *bayonets!*" the Arabs went wild.[29]

Crying out "The Christians are preparing to fire on us!," about two hundred of the Bedouin cavalry wheeled and rode at full charge at the Marines, who never flinched. Hamet threw himself in front of the horsemen, imploring them to stop. More cries rose from the Arab ranks, calling on their comrades to open fire on the Christians. "Some of the Bashaw's officers exclaimed, 'For God's sake do not fire! The Christians are our friends,'" Eaton recalled. "Mr. O'Bannon, Mr. Peck, and young Farquhar, stood firmly by me, Seleni Aga, (Capt. of Cannoneers,) his Lieutenants and the two Greek officers, remained steadfast at their posts," although much of the Greek infantry wilted and fled.[30] Farquhar nearly became the first casualty when an Arab rode up to him and "snapped a pistol at his breast. Happily it missed him: had it been otherwise the fire would most probably have become general and the result serious." In a show of courage that awed even O'Bannon, Eaton stepped forward and walked alone toward Hamet.[31]

"At once a column of muskets were aimed at my breast," Eaton said. "The Bashaw was distracted. A universal clamor drowned my voice." Eaton raised his hand to silence the Arabs, who ignored him and closed in. A group of Hamet's followers rode up and placed themselves between Eaton and the mutineers. Eaton called out to Hamet and "reproached the Bashaw for his rashness or rather weakness." Hamet's treasurer "asked him if he was in his senses"; Hamet "struck him with his naked sabre." Once more voices rose with calls to kill the Christians. Eaton "took the Bashaw by the arm; led him from the crowd, and asked him if he knew his own interests and his friends?" The question broke Hamet. He called Eaton "his friend and protector [and] said he was too soon heated." Hamet went with Eaton to Eaton's tent, "giving orders at the same time to his Arabs to disperse. After a moment's breath, he said if I would give orders to issue rice it would quiet everything." Eaton agreed, on condition Hamet promised to resume the march the next morning. "He promised, and provisions were issued. Confessions of obligation and professions of attachment were repeated as usual on the part of the Bashaw and his officers; and the camp again resumed its tranquility."[32]

Eaton praised O'Bannon, whose "firm and decided conduct . . . as on all other occasions, did much to deter the violence of the savages by whom we were surrounded, as well as to support our own dignity of character." O'Bannon's bravery also impressed Hamet, who "embraced him with an enthusiasm of respect, calling him *The Brave American*." O'Bannon, for his part, remained in awe of Eaton: "The general can do no wrong. He always knows what to do in any situation."[33] As for Eaton, the mutiny had created doubts about Hamet and as to whether he could hold the army together long enough actually to attack Derne. "We find it almost impossible to inspire these wild bigots with confidence in us, or to persuade them that, being Christians, we can be otherwise than enemies to Mussulmen. We have a difficult undertaking."[34]

The army roused itself at 5:30 a.m. on April 10 on the last leg of the route to Bomba. Everyone was exhausted. The lack of food, especially protein, made each step agony for those on foot. The column marched just ten miles. On the eleventh it managed another ten miles before coming to halt around noon. As the men rested, Eaton again had to bolster Hamet's spirits after a rumor started that the Americans only wanted peace with his brother and were just using Hamet to achieve it. (Eaton had no idea how true the rumor was.) Eaton assured Hamet he was behind the "rightful bashaw" for the long haul and returned to his tent. There, O'Bannon brought him word of a mutiny among what had been some of his steadiest troops—the mercenary artillerymen. The twenty-five Christians were starving and demanded a full ration of rice, or they would quit the army. Eaton told O'Bannon to talk very quietly to the mercenaries, explain the situation, and "to caution them on pain of death, not to appear in arms to make any remonstrances with me." The mercenaries soon came back into line.

Just when Eaton must have been wondering what could happen next, a courier Hamet had dispatched to Bomba on April 5 returned to camp. His news electrified everyone. He had seen the sails of the American flotilla. Almost at once thoughts of mutiny or abandonment of the mission vanished. Some of Eaton's exuberance lessened around 9 p.m., though, when he received word that Hamet had become violently ill. The army moved out at five o'clock the next morning but could make only five miles before it had to stop for Hamet, who remained gravely ill. Hamet remained sick the rest of the day, although by 6 p.m., Eaton noted, he began to feel better.[35]

Eaton now decided to make one last push for Bomba. On April 12 he pushed the column for twenty-five miles and handed out the last of the rice. From that point on, there would be nothing to eat except what the soldiers and camp followers could forage. Everyone went hungry that night. The next day the army marched slightly more than seven miles before fatigue and hunger forced a halt. The column spread over the countryside, looking for anything edible. Some found sorrels and fennel bulbs, but many went without food again that night. On the fourteenth Eaton pushed the exhausted army as hard as he could, coaxing it forward fifteen miles. The next day the army reached Bomba, but what Eaton expected to be a joyous arrival was anything but. The bay was empty.

Master Commandant Isaac Hull was a worried man. He had arrived off Bomba with the *Argus* and *Hornet* on April 2. Poor weather prevented him from approaching the coast until April 4, when he saw no sign of Eaton's force. Hull sailed along the coast as far as Derne before turning around and sailing back toward Bomba. On April 9, Hull sent a boat ashore. The landing party met an Arab who agreed to carry a message to Eaton: "I hope you will lose no time in informing me of your situation, and what time you will be at Bomba, that I may meet you, as I do not think the Bay safe to lay at Anchor in long, for fear of Gales Wind. I shall stand out to sea, and call in every two or three days, and see if you are there—when you arrive on the Coast, it will be well for you to make fires, or some signal that we may find you." Hull knew how important it was for Eaton to receive the supplies loaded on the *Hornet:* barrels of beef and pork, beans, bread, vegetables, corn, rice, and flour. She also carried powder and ball for muskets, ammunition for a pair of four-pounder howitzers, and other equipment. He sent word through the Arab messenger to "come to the bottom of the Bay of Bomba, and should the *Argus* not be there, to remain until she comes."[36] Hull remained in the bay, sailing along the coast, looking for any sign of Eaton.

Hull wasn't the only naval officer who felt like he was marching in place. Captain John Rodgers, the new tactical commander of the U.S. Mediterranean squadron, was at something of a loss as to how far his authority extended. Commodore Samuel Barron, who remained ill on Malta, continued to issue orders to the other ship commanders. Rodgers wanted to resume the blockade with full force, but Barron's orders prevented him from gathering the entire squadron off Tripoli. The rumored escape of a pair of Tripolitan corsair ships had the *Essex* hunting the seas off Sardinia, while the crew of the *Constellation* was dealing with an outbreak of smallpox. Her captain, Hugh Campbell, had asked Rodgers for permission to return to Syracuse to deal with the sick. Rodgers ordered Campbell to remain on station until another frigate arrived to replace him, but Barron, hearing of the outbreak, ordered Campbell to return to Syracuse and put the sick in the Navy hospital there. Rodgers kept an eye out for the *President,* which was supposed to be on the way, as well as the *Congress,* which, to Rodgers, seemed to have no orders. The *Vixen* was still on station, as was the *Syren.* "In regard to the term of your own cruise, I leave it, as well as the general dispositions on the station entirely to your discretion," Barron told Rodgers in an April 15 letter, "observing only that in consequence of some recent occurrences here, which Capt. Cox can explain, it will be advisable for you to remain outside of this harbor provided the weather be favorable."[37] Barron's fuzzy orders left Rodgers wondering what he was supposed to do; he had no idea that Cox was bringing a message that both the *Congress* and the *Nautilus* were off to support Eaton. Stephen Decatur had procured a pair of fieldpieces for the army, but the *Congress* drew too much water to enter Bomba. Instead, the *Nautilus* would carry the cannon to the coast, where she would join with *Argus* and *Hornet* in supporting the land attack on Derne.[38]

Rodgers, aggressive by nature, told Barron he intended to "preserve as minutely as the season of the year will admit, not only to prevent the enemy's cruisers getting out of port, which consequently must endanger our Commerce . . . but [also] to prevent their receiving such supplies as can in any way augment their force to the prejudice of our intended opera-tions." Rodgers wanted to keep at least two and preferably three ships off Tripoli at all times, in rotation. He counted in all five frigates, two brigs, and two schooners, but with many of them away on missions Barron had assigned, he actually had no idea what ships he could use for the block-ade.[39] "To maintain a blockade effectually[,] two if not three vessels, ought always to be stationed before the port to prevent, as far as circumstances of bad weather will admit, the possibility of vessels of every description get-ting either out or in."[40] Rodgers wanted to hit Tripoli and Yusuf Karamanli's fleet with the firepower he could bring to bear with the full squadron. Barron, however, cautioned Rodgers to wait.[41] It was a frustrating time for a captain who would be commodore.

The camp was in a state of complete confusion. Everyone except the small group of U.S. Marines and a handful of Christian mercenaries was pack-ing belongings and planning to abandon the expedition to return Hamet Karamanli to the throne of Tripoli. The starving army had force-marched to its present camp along the shores of the Gulf of Bomba in anticipation of finding the U.S. Navy there, waiting with provisions. The army was just sixty miles short of its objective of Derne and had covered nearly five hundred miles from Egypt, thanks mainly to the willpower of "General" William Eaton. But now, not even the strength of Eaton's personality was enough. "Nothing could prevail on our Arabs to believe that any [ship] had been there," Eaton recorded. "They abused us as imposters and infi-dels; and said we had drawn them into that situation with treacherous views. All began now to think of the means of individual safety; and the Arabs came to a resolution to separate from us the next morning." Hamet, for whom the army had already suffered so much, was ready again to quit and return to Egypt. It was the low point of Eaton's campaign, and the self-styled general was quite simply powerless. He had fully expected to find Isaac Hull and the *Argus* waiting for him.[42] Not knowing what else to do, out of food and running low on water, Eaton withdrew with the Marines and the Christian mercenaries to a hilltop, where they raised a large fire and settled in for the night.[43]

At sunup on April 16, the Arab forces under Hamet began loading their baggage and weapons on the remaining pack animals and prepared to begin the long walk back to Egypt. By 8 a.m., with Hamet at their head, the Arabs were ready to leave. Just as their column was about to move out, a cry came from the hilltop on which Eaton had camped. One of Hamet's aides who had remained loyal to the mission was shouting at the top of his voice—he could see a sail. "It was the *Argus*. Capt. Hull had seen our smokes, and stood in," Eaton said. "Language is too poor to paint the joy and exultation which this messenger of life excited in every breast."

The brig worked her way into the bay and at noon sent a boat ashore. Eaton had the camp move five miles to where he had found a source of water. He then went on board the *Argus* to discuss the next steps in the campaign. Hull had provisions sent ashore, which immediately cheered the army and the families following it. While on board the *Argus* Eaton finally received Barron's letter of March 22 in which the commodore condemned the treaty Eaton had signed with Hamet, told Eaton to rein in his expenses, and warned that he would help the mission only up to a certain point. Eaton fired back a reply in which he defended all of his actions: "The advantages calculated to result from the success of this measure have been heretofore stated: and thus far, the experiment has not disappointed those calculations."[44]

The *Hornet* arrived on April 17 and landed her precious cargo of food. Eaton marched on the eighteenth and nineteenth, then allowed three days' rest along the shore. On April 23, the column set out for the final push to Derne, marching ten miles into the mountains that marked the border of Cyrenaica and the beginning of the fertile plain that fed Tripoli.[45] On the twenty-fourth the column made fifteen miles before camping in a forest of cedars. The army was just five hours from Derne, but Eaton had to halt to quell new rumors. Word had come that the governor, a Yusuf loyalist, had barricaded himself in the city and Hassan Bey, leading Yusuf's reinforcement army, was just a days' forced march away and would arrive before Eaton. Complicating matters was the weather. A strong gale had blown up in the Gulf of Bomba, forcing Hull to take the *Argus* and *Hornet* to open water. The seeming loss of their support frightened the Arabs. The following morning the Arabs again mutinied, Sheik al-Tahib at their head. Eaton harangued the ringleaders, calling them cowards and miscreants, guilty of breaking their own promises. "After much persuasion, some reproach, and a promise of two thousand dollars to be shared among the chiefs, they were prevailed on to advance and at two o'clock, P.M. we camped on an eminence which overlooks Derne."[46]

Now, he had to take the city.

18

BATTLES FOR DERNE

YUSUF KARAMANLI had done all he could to prepare for the American onslaught. The information that reached Tripoli from outside was spotty at best and often wrong. One of Yusuf's most dependable sources of information, however, remained U.S. Navy captain William Bainbridge, who on April 15, 1805, was in his 532nd day of captivity in Tripoli. The former commander of the frigate *Philadelphia* continued to write to American diplomats and military officers, and it is almost certain that Yusuf's foreign minister, Mohammed Dghies, read every word that Bainbridge wrote.[1]

News that William Eaton had joined forces with his brother reached Tripoli sometime in April. However, there was confusion as to what the Americans planned to do with Hamet. On April 11 Bainbridge wrote to Tobias Lear, "This day the Bashaw has heard the news of the arrival of his Brother in Malta. [H]e is greatly enraged—and so is [*sic*] all his people."[2] Perhaps it was simply a show. Yusuf knew that Hamet had never gone to Malta and that in this case Bainbridge's information was wrong. News that correctly reported that Hamet was, with Eaton pushing him forward, actually headed to Derne had trickled out of Egypt in late March, prompting Yusuf to dispatch his Mameluke general, Hassan Bey, with reinforcements to that city.[3]

The bashaw's biggest problem in April 1805 was that he was at the nadir of his popularity. The war with the Americans had all but wrecked his economy, and revolts in the gold-producing region of the Fezzan had deprived him of a major revenue source. Yusuf levied harsher and harsher taxes on his people, took hostages to maintain their loyalty, and dug in his heels against the Yankees. Surgeon Jonathan Cowdery reported that Yusuf, after hearing about American attempts to borrow gunboats again from the king of Naples for a summer campaign, decided his "women and children should stay at the castle during the summer. They said that if they must be taken, they would rather fall into the hands of the Americans than the Arabs."[4] Yusuf interrogated Cowdery about American military power, wondering how big a force the Navy could put ashore in assaults on Derne and Tripoli. "He asked me how many marines the United States kept in pay. My answer, for good reasons, was, ten thousand! How many troops he asked. Eighty thousand, said I, are in readiness to march to defend the country, at any moment; and one million of militia are also ready to fight for the liberty and rights of their countrymen! At this, his highness assumed a very serious look, and I returned to my room."[5]

Starting in February, the bashaw embarked on a boatbuilding campaign. His Spanish shipwright built several galleys and a ketch, which reinforced his existing fleet of fifteen gunboats.[6] He used his American prisoners to build more fortifications and to strip the countryside of lumber and food. Slowly, reinforcements trickled into the city. Private Ray reported of a single day, "Several companies of Arabs passed through the town and paraded under the Bashaw's balcony, in the navy-yard. There were about three hundred horse and seven hundred foot, and both made but a despicable appearance."[7]

The bashaw was ready, and as the reinforcements proved, his people were slowly beginning to support his war effort. What Samuel Barron, William Eaton, and President Thomas Jefferson did not understand was that Yusuf, as a nascent Arab nationalist, was not pursuing just an economic policy or even a religious agenda. Yusuf was fighting for what he saw as his right to rule his country as he saw fit. Moreover, he was fighting for respect. America, like much of Europe, looked down on Tripoli as backward and certainly did not accord Yusuf the respect it gave to the rulers of Morocco or Algiers. Yusuf saw the U.S. backing of Hamet as the ultimate sign of disrespect. He was not about to allow an upstart country simply to cast him aside and replace him with his brother without a fight. Bainbridge, in a letter to Barron, transmitted a message from Dghies that made Yusuf's position clear: "The Bashaw has said, that as long as the war was a war between America and him, it was a war of interest, that easily might be brought to a conclusion by a lesser or greater sacrifice upon one side or the other, but now it was a war directed against his personal safety, the view of which was his dethronation."[8] There would be no talks, no hope of a settlement, as long as the Americans backed his brother.[9]

∽ ⁍

Derne sits on a low coastal plain, with the hills of Cape Bon Andrea on its west and hard, rocky mountains to the east. The eastern mountains turn into massive rock formations that extend into the bay, forming a natural, though dangerous, breakwater. The bay itself is rocky, shallow, and studded with shoals. The high ground on either side protects a broad, fertile landscape that a traveler enviously described as having "palm trees, whose rough and singular tops extend and spread over the softer forms of European trees, over the finest vines, pomegranate, olive, fig, apricot, and other fruit trees." Away from the city, cattle, sheep, and goats all prospered as did corn, barley, and wheat. In the city, gardens filled with orange and lemon trees gave Derne a green, verdant look.[10]

The city dated from the days of the Phoenicians and had been an important trading post during the Roman Empire. Unlike many other cities in North Africa, it retained its Roman grid layout. From a distance, the city looked inviting, clean. Up close, however, it was easy to see that the houses, "which are very low, small, and built of pebbles, cemented with clay, but full of chinks on every side, convey no other idea than that of perfect wretchedness." The city fortress rose at the center of town, "but though of considerable extent, it is not less wretched and dilapidated, than the dwellings of the inhabitants."[11] The city's governor, who remained loyal to Yusuf Karamanli, had erected a water battery of eight cannon in the northeast quadrant of the city and in the southeast several breastworks. The governor, who controlled only about a third of the city, had the inhabitants loyal to him knock loopholes in their garden walls.[12]

Derne looked imposing, though not impregnable. As William Eaton stared down on Derne on April 25, 1805, from atop a hill several miles to the east, the biggest problem he could see was that there was nothing in the bay. The U.S. Navy had not made it to Derne on time. Consternation was rife throughout the army. Hamet Karamanli, in whose name the army marched, voiced his fear that without American naval support he could never capture the city. Numerous sheiks and tribal leaders called at Hamet's tent to pay their respects and promise their loyalty, but rumors the large relief force his brother had dispatched to Derne was already there plagued the "rightful bashaw." Throughout the night Hamet met with his new allies but could not shake his fear. Eaton said Hamet "looked like he wanted to be back in Egypt."[13] The next morning, Eaton lit signal fires to attract the attention of any U.S. warships over the horizon, and at 2 p.m. the schooner *Nautilus* hove into sight. Her captain, the twenty-five-year-old Master Commandant John Dent, sent a message ashore asking Eaton to come aboard, which the "general" did at 6 p.m.

Dent informed Eaton that Isaac Hull with the *Argus* and *Hornet* had only moved offshore during the recent gale and should be back any day. Dent also had a pair of field guns for him. That news must have disappointed Eaton, who was expecting four cannon. Still, two guns would help, and Dent sent them ashore in a longboat. Unfortunately, the Americans had time to land only one of the cannon; Eaton wanted to launch his attack the next morning, and the guns had to be hauled up a twenty-foot escarpment. Eaton and Dent, meanwhile, discussed how the American warships would support the ground attack. Dent wanted to wait until Hull returned and urged Eaton to be patient. Eaton agreed to wait one more day for the Navy, setting the attack for April 27. Satisfied, the two men parted, with Eaton returning to camp around eleven o'clock that night.[14]

Once more, Eaton's optimism let him down. The *Argus* and *Hornet* only arrived off Derne the morning of the twenty-seventh, forcing another delay in his assault. Eaton went on board the *Argus* to discuss plans, while O'Bannon supervised the eager unloading of more supplies from the *Hornet*. Now that the army was at Derne, excitement was rife among the Americans. O'Bannon and Midshipman George Mann, who had rejoined Eaton when the *Argus* arrived, both requested permission to remain with Eaton for the attack on Derne. Neither officer seemed to have any doubt of its success. O'Bannon was "unwilling to abandon an expedition, this far conducted[;] I have to request your permission to continue with Mr. Eaton during his stay on land."[15] Mann was slightly more sanguine, writing his commander, "I am aware that objections may be made from sentiments generally entertained as to the issue of the expedition, but should I succeed to your approbation I shall feel no hesitation in risking the event."[16] Midshipman Paoli Peck and young George Farquhar also determined to take part in the assault.

The plan Eaton developed to attack the city was not elegant, but it was about all he could do with the forces at his disposal. The three warships would engage and destroy the shore battery and suppress any troop movements along the shore. Eaton would lead the Marines, Greek infantry, European artillerymen, and the Arab infantry in a frontal assault on the governor's fortress. Hamet would lead the Arab cavalry in a flank attack also aimed at the fortress. If all went well, the two prongs would meet in the city center. Satisfied with their preparations, Eaton returned to shore to give orders to Hamet and O'Bannon. The attack would go off the next morning, the twenty-eighth.[17]

⌖

Tobias Lear was ready to launch his own, albeit different offensive. Lear, who had always opposed the use of Hamet to force Yusuf Karamanli to release his hostages and end his attacks, spent as much time voicing his opposition as he did looking for diplomatic openings. The consul general was then on Malta, where he maintained his close bond with Commodore Samuel Barron and held himself ready to leave for Tripoli to hold talks at a moment's notice. Lear also had the ear of John Rodgers, the tactical commander of the U.S. Mediterranean squadron. Rodgers too opposed Eaton's mission, but for a much different reason: Rodgers simply did not want to share the glory of defeating Tripoli with anyone else.[18]

Lear had helped Barron write his long letter of March 22 to Eaton and made sure to include his own opinion of Hamet in that note. Hamet, as Lear saw him, was simply a means to an end—a tool to bring Yusuf to the table. "Such terms being once offered and accepted by the representative of Government appointed to treat of peace, our support to Hamet Bashaw must necessarily be withdrawn." Although the words were Barron's, the sentiment was Lear's, as was Barron's warning, "Should the Bashaw be found deficient in these essential qualities or that it appears that we have been deceived with regard to the disposition of the inhabitants, he must be held as an unfit subject for further support or co-operation."[19] Lear was also hard at work at influencing Rodgers, who on April 17 wrote Lear that he intended to use naval force to make Yusuf come to terms. "I do not believe he will accede to what *you* will consider equal terms, until he is more sensible of our Force, and demonstratively convinced of our capacity to use it."[20]

Rodgers' plan dovetailed perfectly with that of Lear, who told George Davis, "All our accounts from the same quarter state also the strong desire for peace which prevails at Tripoli, so that I have good hopes that by the time we are ready to commence our operations the Bashaw may be brought to such terms as we can with propriety agree to." He made a point of telling Davis that "the operations by Land[,] I have always been opposed to them in the way they have been undertaken, and believe that they will ultimately be productive of no good to our Cause." He revealed new instructions from Secretary of State James Madison, who made it clear that Lear was not to pay for a peace treaty, though he could pay a "fair price" to ransom the crew of the *Philadelphia*, provided Yusuf agreed to a prisoner exchange prior to any ransom deal.[21] It was a huge change in policy that could only have originated with President Thomas Jefferson, who wanted to bring the war to a quick and inexpensive close.

⊂◄ ►⊃

The morning of April 27 dawned sunny and clear. Sergeant Arthur Campbell and Marine Corps privates Bernard O'Brien, John Wilton, David Thomas, Edward Stewart, Joseph Fischer, and Joseph Joiner started the day as they had started every day since leaving Egypt. First the Marines practiced the manual of arms. Once they finished, they polished their muskets and bayonets, cleaned their red-trimmed blue uniforms as best as they could, and waited for orders. Alongside the Marines, the platoon of

Greek infantry also cleaned and prepared weapons, while the little band of European artillerymen gathered around the army's lone field gun, determining which of them would work the cannon and which would, temporarily at least, act as infantry.

Most Western armies called the units that led attacks on fortified positions "forlorn hopes." The soldiers in those units knew they would take the heaviest casualties and would likely not survive to see their comrades in other units take the objective. "All was deathly silent amongst those men, who perhaps could not help thinking that it might be their last undertaking: in fact, this is much the worst business a soldier can enter upon, as scarcely anything but death looks him in the face," recalled British rifleman William Lawrence, who would a decade later participate in the assaults on Ciudad Rodrigo and Badajoz during the Peninsular War. "There they were watching with intense anxiety for the[,] to many[,] fatal signal; and at length the order was given to advance."[22] No doubt Campbell, the Marines, and the European infantrymen all felt the same way the morning of the attack on Derne.

Like his Marines, William Eaton was ready. On April 26 he had sent a pro forma note to Mustafa Bey, the governor of Derne, asking him to surrender the city and join the revolt against Yusuf. "Let no differences of religion induce us to shed the blood of harmless men who think little and know nothing. If you are a man of liberal mind you will not balance on the propositions I offer. Hamet Bashaw pledges himself to me that you shall be established in his government. I shall see you tomorrow in a way of your choice." The governor had replied simply "My head or yours."[23]

The army too was ready. Before it could attack, however, Hull had to maneuver his little flotilla past the reefs to a point from which it could engage the shore battery. It took several hours. The *Hornet* anchored closest to the shore, just a hundred yards from the shore battery, where the sloop could engage the enemy gunners and cover Eaton's infantry. The *Nautilus* anchored a half mile to the west of the *Hornet*, where she could fire on both the governor's fortress and the shore battery. The *Argus*, the most powerful of the three Americans, anchored a mile west of the *Hornet*, in a position to engage the fortress and sweep the beach of any reinforcements.[24]

The infantry set out at 2 p.m., advancing in a column toward the shore battery. Eaton rode at the head of the column, with the Marines marching directly behind, followed by the artillerymen, the Greek infantry, and finally the Arab foot soldiers. The column numbered about two hundred men. Hamet rode at the head of the five hundred or so cavalry, which covered the flank of the infantry before breaking off to launch its own attack.[25] As the infantry moved in, the gunners on the *Hornet* opened up, the little sloop belching fire from her nine-pounder cannon. The *Hornet* was close enough to the enemy battery to use grape and canister, devastating antipersonnel munitions that sent hundreds of musketball- and melon-sized iron balls whizzing through the emplacement. *Nautilus* and *Argus* also opened fire, blasting the governor's fortress with long nine-pounder and eighteen- and twenty-four-pounder carronade shot.[26]

On shore, the Marine-led infantry had broken into a trot as the troops loyal to the governor opened fire. The range was long for muskets, which were accurate only to seventy or eighty yards, but the volume of fire made the Marines and others bend forward as they ran. The Marines broke into a sprint, and the distance shrank—fifty yards, then forty. The entire western side of the fortifications disappeared in smoke as Mustafa Bey's infantry and artillery opened fire. Eaton urged his foot soldiers forward through musket and cannon balls all around them. The Marines clustered near O'Bannon, and the Greek infantry and mercenary artillerymen closed in around the Americans. The *Hornet*'s gunners found their mark and battered the beach fort, mixing solid shot with the grape and canister. The *Nautilus* too turned her guns on the shore battery, each salvo smashing the breastwork behind which the defenders tried to shelter. The solid shot shredded the brick-and-sand fortifications, and antipersonnel rounds cut down anyone brave enough to stand. It was finally too much for the defenders, who broke and ran for the safety of the town and its fortified houses and gardens.[27]

O'Bannon led his Marines and the Greek infantry toward the fortress, while the European artillerymen turned the now-abandoned nine-pounder in the water battery onto the fleeing defenders, routing them from several fortified homes near the battery. Hamet meanwhile had seized an old castle in the southwest corner of the city and was pushing his horsemen into the plain, where they could strike at more of the defenders. Mustafa Bey's troops fled before Hamet but stubbornly held on in front of O'Bannon. "The fire of the enemy's musketry became too warm, and continually augmenting," Eaton reported. The Arab infantrymen "were thrown into confusion, and undisciplined as they were, it was impossible to reduce them to order[;] I perceived a charge—our dernier [last] and only resort[.] We rushed forward against a host of Savages, more than ten to our one." The Marines and Greeks led the charge, driving the defenders from their positions but failing to rout them. The governor's solders fell back in good order, "firing in retreat from every palm tree, and partition wall in their way."[28]

The attackers now began to take casualties. Private John Wilton fell with a shot to the heart that killed him instantly. Private Bernard O'Brien was shot in the leg but continued in the assault.[29] Eaton too was hit: "At this moment I received a ball through my left wrist, which deprived me of the use of the hand and of course of my rifle."[30] The Marines turned to the bayonet as they tried to force their way into the fortress, fighting at close quarters. The Americans and the Greeks bludgeoned through the Tripolitans, but their casualties mounted. Marine private David Thomas went down mortally wounded, followed by Private Edward Stewart. A musket ball cut down Captain Luca, one of the Greek officers, although it did not kill him. A dozen other Greek infantrymen suffered sword and knife wounds as the contest devolved into hand-to-hand combat. It was one-on-one, eye-to-eye combat, and it was personal. Lawrence, the British rifleman of 1812, was to recall killing a French soldier in the assault on Ciudad Rodrigo:

> I was at the time in the trenches when he came on the top and made a dart at me with his bayonet, having, like myself, exhausted his fire; and while in the act of thrusting he overbalanced himself and fell. I very soon pinioned him to the ground with my bayonet, and the poor fellow soon expired. I was sorry afterwards that I had not tried to take him prisoner instead of killing him, but at the time we were all busily engaged in the thickest of the fight, and there was not much time to think about things.[31]

The governor tried to rush reinforcements to the fortress along the beach, but combined fire from the *Argus* and *Nautilus* drove the force back in confusion.[32] The mercenary artillerymen joined the barrage on the fort, and the combined fire overwhelmed its defenders. O'Bannon and Midshipman George Mann urged their men forward, slashing at their fleeing foes with their swords. Eaton watched in near disbelief: "O'Bannon, although powder streaked, appeared to be in a festive mood, and when he saw me watching him, he raised his sword in salute. I immediately returned this gallant officer's salute."[33]

As O'Bannon's infantry bashed its way in the center of the city, the lone field gun supporting the Marines became the target of the defenders, who concentrated their fire on it. A round smashed the gun's carriage and another burst its barrel, putting the cannon out of action. Without artillery support, O'Bannon's small group faltered. Eaton ordered Selim and the Greek infantry, as well as a company of Arab footmen, to support the Marines. Reinforced, O'Bannon charged again, "sweeping aside like chaff, the defending force," Eaton reported.[34]

O'Bannon found himself as much in awe of Eaton as Eaton was of him. Despite his wound, the "general" continued to lead the attack, and O'Bannon reported seeing him lop the heads off several defenders with his sword; "The general's clothes were covered in blood," O'Bannon noted. Now Hamet's cavalry closed the pincers sweeping in, cutting down many of the fleeing defenders, and overrunning Mustafa Bey's palace, forcing the governor to seek refuge in a mosque.[35]

On board the *Argus*, Master Commandant Isaac Hull expertly guided the naval bombardment. With his spyglass he was able to watch the progress of the infantry attack, signaling his own gunners and those on the *Nautilus* when and where to concentrate their fire. As the infantry stormed the shore battery, the ships shifted their fire to other strongpoints, silencing every gun that fired on the infantry. When Hull saw O'Bannon and the Marines enter the shore battery, he ceased fire and watched breathlessly for the outcome. For several agonizing minutes Hull could see nothing but smoke. Then the scene cleared, and above the parapets rose a fifteen-star, fifteen-stripe flag. A massive cheer went up among the sailors and Marines on the *Argus,* in which the crews of the *Nautilus* and *Hornet* quickly joined.[36] Against all odds, the flag of the United States was floating over the ramparts of Derne, marking the first time ever that American forces had raised the national flag over foreign territory. The battle had lasted for slightly more than two hours. Eaton had done it.

Now that he had Derne, Eaton knew, he had to keep it. Hassan Bey, with an army numbering from five hundred to eight hundred soldiers, was somewhere close to the city. Eaton also knew he had to deal with Mustafa Bey, Yusuf's governor and brother-in-law. Mustafa was the third-highest official in Yusuf's court, and Eaton wanted him as a hostage, as "he may perhaps be used in exchange for Captain Bainbridge," he told Barron. The problem was that Eaton could not touch Mustafa, at least not then. The governor, after fleeing to a mosque, had taken refuge in a harem, "the most sacred of sanctuaries, among the Turks," as Eaton put it.[37] The harem belonged to a Sheik Mesreat, and while the old sheik professed his loyalty to Hamet, "neither persuasion, bribes nor menace, could prevail on this venerable aged chief to permit the hospitality of his house to be violated . . . and should he suffer himself to transgress that sacred principle, the vengeance of God and the odium of all mankind would justly fix on him and his posterity." The sheik was just as adamant that no Christians could enter the harem. It was a source of great irritation for Eaton to have his enemy so close and yet out of reach.[38]

The biggest surprise of the day, however, was Hamet Karamanli, who had once more proved himself an adept and brave combat commander and was now walking and talking like a true bashaw, not a pretender. Hamet's cavalry had performed well in the assault on Derne, and his force was slowly growing, as people came over to his side. He seemed eager to meet Hassan Bey and had lost his fear of facing his brother's army. Hamet, like Eaton, wanted to get Mustafa Bey out of his hiding spot, but not even Hamet could convince the sheik to surrender the governor.[39] The standoff lasted twelve frustrating days, during which Mustafa did his best to continue the fight. The governor sent messages throughout the city asking the people to rise against their Christian invaders; Eaton, "apprehending a counter-revolution through the intrigue of Mustapha Bey[,] . . . again demanded him of his host." Eaton tried every tactic he could think of to make Mustafa leave the harem, but nothing worked, and the old sheik continued to protect him.[40]

On May 12, Hassan Bey finally arrived, camping at the spot where Eaton had camped the night before he attacked Derne. Hassan's force looked large, but Eaton could not discern how many soldiers Yusuf's general had actually brought with him. In the city, many of the residents who had welcomed Hamet turned quiet, fearing retribution should Hassan defeat Eaton's army. Hassan's arrival emboldened Mustafa, who continued to foment a revolt in the city. Finally, Eaton again confronted Sheik Mesreat. Since Mustafa had been "endeavoring to corrupt and bring over the people of the town, the late Governor acting from his sanctuary must be considered as an active enemy, entitled to no privileges of hospitality." The sheik stood his ground. "I resolved to try an experiment of compelling him," Eaton reported. "I accordingly marched into the quarter near him at the head of 50 Christians with bayonets, and declared my intention to wrest the Bey from his sanctuary."[41]

The move backfired. "A general alarm spread through the department. 'The Christians no longer respect the customs of our fathers and our laws of hospitality!'" Eaton railed at Sheik Mesreat that Mustafa was "an outlaw; he had forfeited his title to protection . . . and was by all the laws of war my prisoner." By trying to subvert the residents of the city, Mustafa "had forfeited also the lenity due to a prisoner." Eaton ominously concluded, "I would therefore have him dead or alive."

The sheik again protested his fealty to Hamet but said he could nothing to violate the laws of his religion and people. His followers began to gather near the harem, ready to fight if Eaton decided to send in O'Bannon and the Christian soldiers. Seeing that Eaton might set off an insurrection, Hamet intervened. He begged Eaton not to remove Mustafa forcibly from the harem, and Eaton relented. Hamet then had a long talk with Sheik Mesreat, defusing the situation with a deftness that impressed Eaton.[42] That evening, Mustafa disappeared. Eaton believed the old sheik had aided the former governor in his escape, but Mesreat, his religious obligation fulfilled, now brought over all of his followers to Hamet.[43] They came just in time. On May 13, Hassan Bey was ready to launch his counterattack.

Hassan's force outnumbered those of Eaton, who was gratified that Yusuf's general had delayed his attack as long as he had, as it gave Eaton time to ready his defenses. He rebuilt the shore battery, turning its guns inland and building parapets to cover the other inland approaches; it was now Fort Enterprise.[44] Off shore, the Hull's force was down to two ships. The sloop *Hornet* had departed on May 2 and was on her way back to Malta. The little sloop could no longer fire her guns, having suffered structural damage in the attack on April 27. Hull had decided to send Evans back to Malta with dispatches and repairs rather than keep her with him.[45] The *Argus* and *Nautilus* moved as far inshore as they could, so their nine-pounder long guns could disrupt any land attacks. Eaton, as he watched Hassan prepare his attack, had asked Hull to land as many Marines and sailors as he could, "in order to intimidate the Arabs, who will be sure generally to attach themselves to the strongest side."[46]

Hull had no time to reply to the request before Hassan launched his attack. His total force numbered about 1,600 cavalry and infantry, but more than half were Bedouin whom he had recruited on his march to Derne. The Bedouin refused at first to fight, and when they did join the battle, it was only when it appeared Hassan might gain a victory. The Tripolitans struck early in the morning, targeting a redoubt Hamet held with about a hundred of his cavalry. Hamet fell back to the governor's palace following a brief but fierce struggle, Hassan's troops (joined by the now-emboldened Bedouin) close behind. At the palace Hamet's soldiers wheeled and made a stand, while other soldiers loyal to the "rightful bashaw" opened heavy fire from loopholes and garden forts, hitting Hassan's soldiers from three sides. Hassan's Tripolitan soldiers continued their attack, but the Bedouin recruits broke and ran. The *Argus* and *Nautilus* supported Hamet's position with fire from their long cannon. Smoke enveloped the city center as the fighting reached a crescendo.[47]

⌐⊲⊳⌐

Giorgio Carofalla still wore the uniform of a French artilleryman. Although the Americans liked to call him one of the "Greeks," Carofalla and many of the artillerymen were actually ethnic Italians, probably from the Piedmont region, which had provided a number of recruits for Napoleon's invasion of Egypt.[48] When that army fell apart due to disease and defeat, Carofalla and many others simply drifted away. Since 1801, when the last of the French in Egypt were defeated, deserters like Carofalla found themselves in great demand as civil war gripped the nation. Trained Christian soldiers fought for Mohammed Ali and his Albanian army, for the khedive, for the Mamelukes—for anyone with the money to pay them.[49] Now in the employ of William Eaton and the Americans, Carofalla and the other mercenaries had found a cause for which they could fight with a will. The Europeans were fighting not simply to restore Hamet but against Muslim tyranny. That was an enemy they knew from personal experience. In Eaton they had found a leader with fervor and daring they not only respected but on which they knew they could depend. All of the mercenaries vowed, "Yes! We swear that we shall follow you and that we shall fight unto death." They assured Eaton, "We offer our services in the campaign, to strictly carry out your orders, to exact respect for the honorable flag of the United States of America, and to encounter the enemy wherever he may be. Everything assures us of a complete victory under your command. We are only waiting for the moment to win this glory, and to fall on the enemy."[50]

Eaton knew he could depend on his Christian soldiers and held them back as a "flying column." He had the infantry fix bayonets and stationed them at Fort Enterprise, while the artillerymen opened a bombardment on the attacking enemy. O'Bannon wanted to lead the Marines and Christian infantry in an attack on the Tripolitans, but Eaton would not risk his best soldiers in an assault. The artillerymen, including Sergeant Carofalla, however, were free to strike at Hassan's forces. As Hamet's troops penned in the Tripolitans, concentrated artillery fire from the *Argus, Nautilus,* and the shore battery drove Hassan back. A shot from one of the nine-pounders landed among several Tripolitans ready to storm the palace, killing two and wounding several more. That took the heart out of the attack, and Hassan's forces fled to their hilltop camp. Hassan's force had lost thirty-seven dead and forty-five wounded, while Hamet had suffered fourteen dead and wounded.[51]

The victory, which belonged to Hamet, increased the standing of the "rightful bashaw" among the Bedouin. The night after the battle, several deserters from Hassan's camp came in with news that Hassan's Bedouin were refusing to take any further part in the campaign. Also, they would not allow the Tripolitans to use their camels as "moving breastworks" to cover an assault force (at the expense of the camels). The Arabs' refusal to fight or participate in any attack left Hassan with about four hundred troops, two hundred from Tripoli and two hundred more who had fled Derne when Hamet and Eaton captured it. "The Beys [Yusuf's generals] are embarrassed. They must make a desperate push, or a retrograde march," Eaton noted.[52]

The dissension in Hassan's camp made a perfect opportunity for Eaton to crush the only real force Yusuf could muster against any land attack on Benghazi or Tripoli. He made sure word leaked out that Hamet would reward any Bedouin tribes that left Hassan and joined him against Yusuf. The ploy backfired at first, as the Arabs Hamet already had clamored for their pay. Eaton and Hamet went on board the *Argus* to ask Hull for any cash he had. Hull had none, but he gave Eaton "prize goods" that O'Bannon was able to sell for nearly two thousand dollars. That quelled at least the loudest voices clamoring for money.[53] On May 16, a hundred Arabs deserted Hassan in a group and joined Hamet. Others trickled in by tens and fifteens. Hassan made a show each day of readying a new assault on the city, but it never came.[54]

While Hassan blustered, O'Bannon and Captain Constantine Bari urged Eaton to launch an attack on his camp. O'Bannon, in particular, urged Eaton to strike at Hassan—he was willing to lead the five remaining Marines and all the mercenaries in a rush—but Eaton denied him permission. Eaton wanted to hit Hassan at night, to cause maximum confusion, but the Arab soldiers refused to fight at night, and the opportunity slipped away.[55]

19

DUPLICITY AND DEALS

IT TOOK NEARLY three weeks for news that Hamet had captured Derne to reach Tripoli.[1] In those three weeks Yusuf had done all he could to stabilize the situation, sending his brother-in-law Hassan Bey to defeat Hamet or retake the city if it had fallen, but an old problem was again plaguing him—starvation. Rodgers reestablished the blockade, and the effects were immediate. George Davis, in Tunis, reported to Secretary of State James Madison, "Tripoli is much distressed for grain; everything is extravagantly high; the Bashaw's treasury, is nearly exhausted; his people are not in a Situation to make him advances; and there is not powder sufficient, to defend his forts four hours."[2]

On April 25, the *Constitution* fell in with a xebec (a small three-masted trading ship, often lateen rigged) flying Tunisian colors that was escorting two prizes into Tripoli Harbor. Rodgers stopped and boarded the xebec, much to its captain's chagrin. Although she flew the Tunisian flag, Rodgers believed the xebec was one of several small Tripolitan cruisers that had managed to slip out during the winter, when the American blockade had all but ceased. Her prizes were a pair of Neapolitan ships, both of which carried full loads of grain. Rodgers did not believe in coincidences. He sent all three ships to Malta, telling Commodore Samuel Barron, "My reasons for sending these vessels into port for examination are too obvious to require commentations of me."³ Yusuf needed that grain. Even his own family was down to just one meal a day, and the less fortunate sought food anywhere they could find it.⁴

Yusuf was also the victim of misinformation. He had sent a spy to Malta to get a precise idea of the size of the American force arrayed against him, and the numbers he received must have come as a tremendous shock. The spy reported that Rodgers had four frigates, three brigs, three schooners, twenty-four gunboats, and six bomb ketches, along with three transport ships that were to carry an allied force of Americans and Hamet-led Arabs along the coast, capturing each city and town until they reached Tripoli.⁵ It was precisely what Yusuf did not want to hear. He could see himself caught between an American anvil and his brother's hammer and knew he had to find a way to extricate himself. Until he got word from Derne, he decided, he would play to the one weakness he saw in the Yankees—their desire for peace. As much as Edward Preble had frightened him with his attacks and aggressiveness, Yusuf had sneered at the former commodore for his peace efforts.⁶ Yusuf sent out feelers through the Spanish consul, feelers that found fertile ground in Samuel Barron and Tobias Lear.⁷

Barron, still suffering from his liver ailment, was actually on the verge of resigning command of the squadron to Rodgers, who wanted to strike Tripoli by June 1. On April 17, Rodgers wrote to Lear, "If the attack is made within six weeks, under proper regulations; I will pledge all that's sacred and dear to me in this world! That we succeed in the most perfect, handsome and honorable manner." Barron saw flaws in the idea. The commodore was all too aware of how spread out the squadron was and believed it would take much more than six weeks to assemble all of the warships off Tripoli.⁸ Lear, still with Barron, believed no amount of direct action would work, that the mere threat was actually much better. He, like Barron, saw no hope of a June 1 attack, writing Rodgers on May 1, "I see no prospect of all our force being concentrated and ready to act against Tripoli sooner than the beginning or middle of June; so that I must regret that you will not have your just and sanguine wishes accomplished of seeing us ready to make an attack before that time."⁹

Lear had been cultivating his relationship with Barron, staying by the ailing commodore's side and feeding him information. Eaton would later openly accuse Lear of "poisoning" Barron toward him. There is little doubt Lear made every effort to turn Barron against the Hamet plan, but there is no record as to how much he tried to get Barron to abandon a military solution in favor of a diplomatic one. It is telling that it was Lear who wrote to Rodgers about a June 1 assault, not Barron, raising the unanswerable question of how much under Lear's control Barron was. Again, Eaton would later argue that Lear used an officer's extreme illness to gain ascendancy in policy. At the time, however, when Derne fell, there was simply no way to know how much the commodore was still driving the force's tactics and making decisions and how much Lear was influencing both.

One thing that is certain is Lear's commitment to negotiating with Yusuf. He continued to operate under the authorization Madison had sent him on June 6, 1804, allowing him not only to ransom the crew of the *Philadelphia* but to restore to the status quo by paying for a peace treaty and to ensure future peace through modest annual tribute.[10] He had received those instructions when Barron arrived, and they had shaped his every move, including his decision to remain close to Barron. His antipathy toward Eaton and the attempt to overthrow Yusuf were well known, and they likewise colored his decisions. He told Rodgers he believed he could readily negotiate a treaty if the United States would drop both the Hamet scheme and its desire to bash Yusuf into a peace: "I am perfectly convinced that they wish a peace, and nothing but the example it would set to other Nations tributary to them, prevents their coming forward with terms which we could admit."[11]

To bring Yusuf to the bargaining table, however, Lear would have to do something about Eaton and his scheme. Lear knew Yusuf would never agree to any deal so long as the United States remained involved with Hamet. "This is a business which I have totally disapproved of in the manner in which it has been conducted," Lear wrote in his journal, "and I venture to pronounce that it will be the loss of much money to the U. States and productive of great injury to our affairs, without producing any good."[12]

Both Eaton and Hamet, then, would have to stand down if Lear was to have any success in ending the war, but since Barron (with Lear's help) had made it clear in his letter of March 22 that Hamet was an expendable pawn, Lear had no qualms about sacrificing the "rightful bashaw" if it would bring peace.

As though to buoy Lear's position, Richard Farquhar, Eaton's former recruiter and quartermaster, had turned up on Malta, looking for revenge on his former employer. Farquhar alleged to any American official he could find, "Mr. E. is a madman—that he has quarreled with the Ex-Bashaw etc., etc.," Lear reported. Although he took Farquhar's rantings with a large grain of salt, Lear had low expectations of any success from Eaton. "We are in daily expectation of more authentic accounts from that quarter; but I make no calculation in our favor from that source."[13]

Yusuf's first peace feeler reached Lear on Malta. The reigning bashaw opened the negotiations by proposing a man-for-man prisoner swap and a $200,000 ransom for the remaining crew of the *Philadelphia*. Lear dismissed the demand as "totally inadmissible" but also noted, "This is the first direct overture which has been officially made. . . . The Spanish Consul observes that these propositions are mentioned merely to begin a negotiation."[14] In the meantime, he had another task, and that was to keep Barron in command long enough to negotiate.

As the summer campaign season approached, the commodore knew he could not remain both in bed and in overall command of the squadron.[15] He had given Rodgers tactical command of the blockade, but Barron had retained the final say over squadron strategy, as well as the disposition and mission of each ship. The pressure on Barron was tremendous. A prize that Hugh Campbell had taken had caused a breach in relations with the Russians, and George Davis reported that Bey Hamouda of Tunis was livid over the seizure of the xebec.[16] Barron also had to deal with convoy requests, questions and correspondence from the Navy Department and diplomats around the Mediterranean, supplies for his squadron, and, most of all, with events outside of his control in Derne. The combined stress was draining the commodore of what little energy his liver ailment didn't rob him.[17]

Barron was just thirty-nine years old—he would not turn forty until September—but his illness made him look and feel much older. Barron wanted to cede command to Rodgers so he could seek full-time hospital care, but both Tobias Lear and Barron's younger brother, James, albeit for different reasons, urged the commodore to remain in command. Lear wanted Barron to keep his command because he believed the commodore was more amenable to opening talks with Yusuf Karamanli than was the warlike and aggressive John Rodgers.[18] James Barron wanted his brother to keep command mostly to deny Rodgers the satisfaction of commanding the squadron. James Barron and Rodgers detested one another, and the last thing James wanted was for Rodgers to vault to glory with his brother's squadron.[19]

For three weeks, Lear and James Barron cajoled, soothed, buoyed, and bolstered Samuel Barron. On May 1, the commodore sent an optimistic note to Rodgers: "My health I am happy to say has greatly improved within a few days. My strength begins to return and I have sanguine hopes that I shall be able to appear personally before Tripoli as soon as the season is sufficiently advanced for entering upon offensive operation."[20] It was unfounded optimism. Within days, Barron was again bedridden and weighing whether to resign his command. The news that Yusuf was apparently willing to talk made Barron's decision even more difficult, as he did not want to cede command if there was a chance he could end the war. The commodore spent days debating his next move. All the while, Eaton waited in Derne, Rodgers waited off Tripoli, and Yusuf looked for some way to keep his throne.

⌒⟩⟩

The distance from Derne to Tripoli across the Bay of Sirte is 482 nautical miles, a passage that would normally take three, perhaps four days. The land route, which follows the coastal plain, is nearly twice as long at 801 miles. Hassan Bey, commander of the Tripolitan forces trying to retake Derne, had no ships and he had to send his dispatches back to Tripoli by land. It took his messenger slightly more than three weeks to cover the distance from Derne to Tripoli, arriving at the bashaw's palace on May 21. The news he carried was not good. Hamet had taken Derne and had defeated an attempt to retake the city Each day, more and more people joined Hamet. The news stoked Yusuf's fears the insurgency could spread to Tripoli. Surgeon Cowdery reported that the reigning bashaw was showing signs of paranoia. On one excursion into the country outside Tripoli, Cowdery said, Yusuf had packed all his clothes onto a pair of mules, "through fear he might be served as he served his brother, the ex-bashaw, who was denied to return to the castle when the present bashaw usurped the throne."[21]

Somehow, Cowdery became privy to the news of the defeat at Derne, noting in his diary on May 22, "I was desired not to mention it, because it is a great secret, and the bashaw did not wish to let his people know it." More chilling, Yusuf had held a council of war during which his chief advisors "proposed to put all the Americans to death." Yusuf had overruled them and refused.[22] The next day, however, Yusuf renewed his threats against the hostages. He pulled Cowdery aside to tell him, "The war between him and our country was at first about money; but now it was whether he or his brother should be the Bashaw." Yusuf declared, "The Americans had bound themselves to his brother in such a manner that it was not in their power to make peace with him; and that his brother and the Americans were determined to take Tripoli and put him to death. He swore by the prophet of Mecca that if the Americans brought his brother against him he would burn to death every American prisoner."[23]

The threat hung over the Americans for two days. Yusuf took his anger out on a party of twenty-five American sailors he sent into the countryside for timber. He placed over them a particularly cruel guard who refused to allow the Americans to rest or drink. The sailors, working through a sandstorm, had to drag a heavy cart laden with wood back to the city, beaten all the while with a heavy club. "They returned toward night almost perished," Cowdery reported.[24]

It was the last time any of Yusuf's people abused the sailors of the *Philadelphia*. The bashaw had come to the realization that he had to find a way to make peace. "The bashaw was so much agitated at the news of the approach of his brother, that he declared, that if it was in his power now to make peace and give up the American prisoners, he would gladly do it, without the consideration of money," Cowdery noted. "His funds were so low, that his steward [had] run in debt for the supply of the kitchen. He gave his mamelukes and domestics, and myself, but one meal per day. The rich Turks in town took turns in supplying his few troops. He heartily repented for not accepting the terms of peace last offered by our country."[25] All Yusuf had to do now was to make—or receive—an offer neither side could refuse.

The same day the news of the fall of Derne arrived in Tripoli, Commodore Samuel Barron came to his own decision. He addressed himself first to Captain John Rodgers: "By this letter [I] communicate officially my resignation to you[,] on whom the command devolves by the law of seniority."[26] Barron's long, rambling letter offered numerous apologies for his ill health, and it also put into motion the final diplomatic showdown of the campaign. Barron was well aware that Rodgers wanted to attack Tripoli with the full squadron before Tobias Lear held any talks with Yusuf Karamanli. In what was essentially his last order as commodore, Barron flatly declared to Rodgers that he was to allow Lear to open immediate negotiations. "The Consul General has expressed his coincidence with the opinion which I officially communicated to him respecting the propriety and policy of meeting the recent overture of the Bashaw of Tripoli so far as to open a negotiation for which I am persuaded, that the present moment is eminently favorable."[27]

Although he had laid down his command, Barron had no intention of surrendering his influence. Through Tobias Lear he told Eaton that Barron, in his last act as commander of the U.S. Mediterranean squadron, had decided to abandon the mission to use Hamet to overthrow Yusuf. Three days before he ceded command, Barron and Lear had exchanged notes on both Eaton and the prospect of opening talks with the reigning bashaw of Tripoli. "The recent dispatches from Mr. Eaton have been communicated to you. From their tenor and the knowledge, I have within a short time obtained of certain features in the character of Sidi Hamet Bashaw, I must candidly own that I have no longer the same expectations which I once entertained of the result of the cooperation with him," Barron wrote to

Lear. The commodore listed what he saw as Hamet's deficiencies—"want of energy and military talents, his total deprivation of means and resources, the great expense already incurred" in aiding him. As commander of the U.S. squadron and the man with the final say on whether to continue the land campaign, Barron believed Hamet, "must be considered as no longer a fit subject for our support and cooperation."[28]

In his letter, Barron confided to Lear his doubts that Rodgers would be able to attack Tripoli with sufficient force due to the "complaining condition of some of the ships of our squadron[;] . . . three of the frigates are in such a state as in my opinion and in that of the commanders renders them unfit." If Rodgers could not attack and Hamet, despite the help of the squadron and the urging of Eaton (whom Barron at least thought "gallant" and valorous), would not attack, there was only one thing the commodore could do. "I am induced to state to you my earnest wish that you may deem it expedient to meet the overture lately made by His Excellency, through the Spanish Consul so far as to found on it the commencement of a negotiation."[29]

Barron sent his letter to Eaton on May 19. It was this letter more than any other that betrayed Barron's intention to undermine any effort other than his own. On May 19, Yusuf Karamanli had yet to make more than an initial request for talks, so Barron could not have known whether the reigning bashaw would even listen to peace offers. Since he had decided to resign his command, Barron, by all rights, should have left the decision to his successor. As Rodgers too opposed Eaton's mission, as the new commodore he in all likelihood would have withdrawn Navy support, although Rodgers had no idea of the fall of Derne until he received Barron's letter. He admitted that Eaton's capture of Derne "has had a powerful effect upon the reigning Bashaw," but he did not see its value in terms of "regime change." To the contrary, "It may be fairly presumed, that the gallant conduct of our friends in the affair at Derne, and the capture of that place will have its influence and dispose him to moderate his pretensions and to think seriously of peace."[30] Barron actually had no idea when he decided to make Lear—not Rodgers or Eaton—responsible for ending the war that the diplomat could actually accomplish the task.

By the time Barron decided to resign, events in Tripoli had already begun to move quickly. On May 19, George Davis told Tobias Lear, "All combine in the opinion that the Bashaw, would accede to a peace on very favorable terms; and which opinion is wholly confirmed, by the measures, which this government have taken, and to which, I beg your prompt, and early attention."[31] The dey of Algiers sent Yusuf a letter commending Lear as a man with whom Yusuf could work.[32] There was, as far as Lear was concerned, just one blot on his horizon, and that was the prospect of sharing credit with William Eaton. He bristled somewhat at Barron's assertion that Eaton's capture of Derne and the manifest support for Hamet had softened Yusuf: "And as, *in his opinion,* the operations at Derne would make an impression on the Bashaw of Tripoli; he thought it a proper moment to open negotiations for peace and ransom."[33]

Lear, however, knew that once news of Eaton's epic march and the role of the U.S. Marines in capturing Derne reached the United States, both would receive accolades. He was thus very careful not to let his personal disdain for Eaton or his mission color his remarks. He wrote to Barron, "I cannot, sir, agree with you in the opinion, that any impression favorable to us has been made on the mind of the Bashaw from our co-operation with his brother thus far." Lear believed Yusuf was far more afraid of what the U.S. Navy could do to him than of anything involving Hamet, "excepting what may arise from the undaunted bravery and perseverance of the few of our countrymen at Derne, which will be to him a further proof of what we can do alone against him." The ultimate goal, Lear said, was to end the war and "relieve our unfortunate countrymen out of his [Karamanli's] power," and it would be diplomacy's "small punctilios" that would accomplish it.[34]

Lear boarded the *Essex* at 2 p.m. on May 24 for the transit to Tripoli.[35] The trip took slightly more than thirty-six hours. Upon his arrival off the Tripolitan coast, Lear boarded the *Constitution,* gave Rodgers the letters from Barron, and briefed the new commodore on the diplomatic mission. Lear never recorded how Rodgers took the news that although he was now in overall command he would not have the chance to defeat Tripoli on his own. The log of the *Constitution* is equally silent, noting only that lookouts first spotted the *Essex* at 5:30 in the morning of May 26 and that at 8:30 Lear and James Barron boarded the frigate. At two that afternoon, all three men boarded the *Essex*, which drew less water than the *Constitution*, and set sail for Tripoli Harbor with the *Constitution* and *President* as escorts.[36]

The inhabitants of Tripoli could clearly see the masts of the American frigates.[37] The *Essex* led the way into the harbor, hoisted a white flag to the top of the mainmast, and stood by for a reply. Yusuf Karamanli saw the flag and called a council of his chief advisors, as well as several foreign consuls, including the Spanish and Algerian diplomats. All but one agreed that Yusuf had just one course of action, to open talks with the Americans. Only the Algerian chargé d'affaires urged the bashaw to keep fighting. Yusuf ignored the Algerine, who left the council chamber. At 11 a.m. Yusuf asked Don Joseph de Souza, the Spanish consul, to open formal negotiations with the Americans.[38]

On board the *Essex*, Lear, Rodgers, and James Barron waited anxiously for a signal from the Tripolitans. The fact the corsairs had not fired on the *Essex* was evidence of Yusuf's disposal toward peace, but no one could be sure. At 2 p.m., the Tripolitans answered with a white flag over the castle; soon after, de Souza was alongside the frigate, asking to come on board as the envoy of the bashaw. Rodgers consented and ushered the Spanish consul into the *Constitution*'s great room, where they sat down with Tobias Lear to discuss the terms of an accord.[39]

The two men talked for three hours. De Souza held fast to Yusuf's demand that the Americans pay both a sum for a peace treaty and a ransom for the crewmen of the *Philadelphia*. Lear adamantly refused. Although he was heartily opposed to Eaton's mission, the diplomat knew he was dealing from a position of strength as the Americans (and Hamet) held Derne, and a powerful squadron was gathering off Tripoli. "After much conversation with him," Lear wrote to this wife, Fanny, after the meeting, "and my absolutely rejecting the position made by the bashaw, it was determined he should go on shore and return on board again in the morning after communicating to the bashaw my absolute rejection of his terms."[40] De Souza returned to shore spreading "the joyful news of a prospect for peace," Doctor Cowdery reported. "There was a visible change, from gloominess to joy," throughout the city.[41]

The next day, May 27, dawned cloudy and blustery. The three American frigates were gone. A storm had blown in from the north, forcing the *Essex*, *Constitution*, and *President* well off shore to avoid being beached in the shallow harbor. As the *Essex* fought the storm, one of her sailors fell over-board and drowned. On shore, "the terraces and every eminence in town, were covered with people of all classes and ages, who were looking for the wished-for peace-maker." The American prisoners had gotten wind of the peace talks, and they too were enjoying a respite from the abuse they had suffered for nearly two years. "Our men were in paroxysms of joy, notwith-standing the issue was yet precarious," noted Private Ray.[42] The anxious watch for the American squadron went on throughout May 27 and into the twenty-eighth. The storm that had brought onshore winds had blown itself out, but now the three frigates had to battle foul winds out of the south (when there was wind at all) to return to Tripoli. The *Vixen* made a brief appearance on May 27, raising hopes briefly, but she sailed away. "A gloominess again appeared on every countenance," Cowdery reported. "The Turks began to think the frigates had gone to fetch the whole fleet, which they heard consisted of sixty sail of different types. They thought that the flag of truce was only a plan of the Americans to find out the force of Tripoli."

The anxiety dissipated around sunset on May 28, when the *Essex* led the *Constitution*, *President*, and *Vixen* into the harbor and hoisted the truce flag. The Tripolitans immediately replied in kind, and both sides settled in to wait for daylight to re-open the negotiations. At 9 a.m., de Souza and Leon Farfara, a Jewish merchant in Tripoli, boarded the *Constitution*, and the talks resumed. The bashaw continued to insist the Americans pay for both the release of their captives and a permanent treaty. Lear again refused. The American diplomat, however, readily agreed to another demand from Yusuf—the Americans were to remove all support from the elder Karamanli brother and abandon the effort to unseat Yusuf from his throne. Still, the talks again reached an impasse over the price the United States would pay

for peace. "I gave the Spanish consul in writing the following as my ultimatum," he told his wife, "If His Excellency the Bashaw will send within
two days of this time, on board the U.S. squadron now lying off Tripoli, all
the Americans now in his power, I engage on behalf of the United States
to give him $60,000, and cause to be delivered to him all the subjects of
Tripoli now in the possession of the U.S., and to make a treaty with him
beneficial to both nations."[43]

De Souza returned alone to the *Constitution* on May 30. He urged Lear
to go ashore for the talks, but Lear refused "until the Americans [i.e., hos-
tages] should be sent onboard agreeably to my demand." De Souza stalled
and asked for permission to go back ashore. Returning at 2 p.m., he again
urged Lear to go ashore, and Lear again refused unless Yusuf released the
American prisoners. "I gave him in writing a confirmation of my former
demand and allowed twenty-four hours more for the Americans to be sent
on board, and if they were not within that time, the white flag shall be
taken down and never more hoisted by us." De Souza protested that if
Lear would grant the bashaw a "small favor," Yusuf would be more likely
to accede to the terms—that if Yusuf had agreed to release his prisoners,
the *Essex* would answer a salute from the castle. De Souza also asked for an
American flag, which he would hoist over the former U.S. consul's house
if everything went well. Lear agreed, and the two set a meeting at noon
the next day.[44]

On May 31, there was no flag over the consular house and De Souza
was actually early for the negotiations, boarding the *Constitution* at 8 a.m.
For four hours, he tried to convince Lear that the bashaw simply could not
release the American prisoners without something in return. It would be a
disgraceful loss of face for Yusuf, de Souza said, if he allowed the Americans
to leave while the Americans kept his own people in prison. Yusuf agreed
to the $60,000 ransom, settling that codicil of the treaty, but de Souza con-
tinued to insist on a simultaneous prisoner exchange before the bashaw
would sign a treaty. The meeting broke up around five, with Lear again
threatening to break off talks unless Yusuf released his prisoners.[45]

It was the last time de Souza took part in the talks. Yusuf was unhappy
with how the Spaniard was representing him and equally upset that after

three days de Souza had been unable to work out a deal. He sacked the Spanish consul and asked Danish consul Nicholas Nissen to lead the negotiations.[46] Nissen was already friendly with the Americans and had provided Bainbridge with credit and a postal conduit to the outside world. Yusuf knew that; his choice of Nissen was a signal to Lear of how much the bashaw wanted to end the war. Nissen and the bashaw spent most of June 1 discussing what terms would be acceptable and what would not. Then, to convey unmistakably the clear softening of his stance, Yusuf sent a very special and extremely symbolic messenger: at 11 a.m. on June 1, for the first time in 578 days, Captain William Bainbridge stood, albeit only on parole for the day, on the deck of an American warship.[47]

It was a savvy, almost Machiavellian move. Yusuf knew from his letters that Bainbridge opposed aiding Hamet. The bashaw was also aware of how desperate Bainbridge had become and, conversely, that the sight of him would likely instill an even greater sense of urgency among the Americans to win the freedom of their countrymen and be done with Tripoli. His plan worked to perfection. Upon boarding the *Constitution*, Bainbridge, thin and haggard, conveyed to Lear once again Yusuf's desire to have a treaty in place prior to a prisoner exchange: "It would be cruel to let our country-men languish in captivity merely on the punctillio [sic] of negotiating the treaty before or after their delivery, as whatever related to them was already understood."[48] Those words, coming from the long-imprisoned American naval officer, had the desired effect. Lear agreed to draw up the articles of a draft treaty he would send ashore the next day.[49]

When Nissen boarded the *Constitution* on June 2, there was an air of expectancy now, as both sides could clearly see the end. Nissen read the treaty Lear had drafted and, somewhat wryly, commented, "There were some articles more favorable to us [i.e., the United States] than were to be found in any treaty which the Bashaw had with any other nation"— including Denmark, Nissen's own country. The Dane expressed some doubt as to whether Yusuf would agree, but he took the draft to the bashaw that afternoon. He returned around 4 p.m. with word the bashaw had agreed to all of the articles except those pertaining to his brother. Yusuf, through

Nissen, insisted on clauses in which the United States renounced its alliance with Hamet and guaranteed its withdrawal from Derne, demands Lear had no problem meeting. The American diplomat, however, not entirely without sympathy for Hamet, insisted Yusuf release his brother's wife and children; Yusuf was adamant he receive guarantees Hamet would swear fealty to himself and drop any claims to the throne before he released any of Hamet's family. Lear had no real objection, in principle, to those demands but wanted another day to decide on language. He and Nissen parted company at 5 p.m., promising to meet again the next day.[50]

On June 3 Nissen duly returned. Yusuf had agreed to every part of the treaty but one—the return of Hamet's wife and children. Yusuf continued to demand assurances that his brother would never again try to regain the throne, and he wanted a specified period of time to elapse before he freed Hamet's family. Lear held fast, but only for show. As Nissen rowed back to shore, Lear revealed his bluff to Rodgers and John Smith of the *Vixen*, who was also on board the *Constitution*. "I told [them] that if the Bashaw should persist in his opposition to that article, I would not suffer the business to be broken off, and leave our countrymen in slavery; but would, at all hazards, take a boat and go on shore, if the white flag should be hauled down, which Mr. Nissen said would be the signal if the Bashaw persisted in his determination."[51]

Lear did not have to wait for the signal. Nissen returned to the *Constitution* at 4 p.m. with the news that Yusuf still did not agree to the article relating to Hamet's family. This put Lear on the spot. He and Nissen huddled in the great room to reach an agreement. Finally, the two men shook hands. Yusuf wanted the delay in releasing his brother's family to give him time to assess his intentions, and Lear had consented.[52] It was done. The war between the United States and Tripoli was over. All that remained was to write up a final treaty both sides could sign. Lear boarded the *Vixen*, which was able to hug the shore. The schooner sailed almost to the main wharf, where her crew hauled down the truce flag and fired a cannon, the signal the two sides had reached a deal. The Tripolitans immediately answered the signal with a twenty-one-gun salute. Lear, Rodgers, and Smith now all went ashore, where they met Bainbridge and the other officers of the *Philadel-phia* and gave them the news they were going home.[53]

The enlisted men didn't need a visit from dignitaries to tell them they were free. A shipment of food from the American squadron, including a good deal of rum, was all Private Ray and the others needed to know their confinement was at an end. The men ate their first full meal in months and quickly became riotously drunk on the rum. Ray noted, somewhat dryly, "Lest our men might wreak vengeance on some of the Turks, and especially the keepers, for past cruelties, which would have inevitably involved us in difficulties and dangers, our men were kept locked in the prison."[54] On June 4, sober and dressed in new clothes that the squadron had provided, the 291 remaining officers and men of the *Philadelphia* marched to the wharf and began boarding gigs and cutters that ferried them to the ships of the Mediterranean flotilla. Six of the enlisted men had died, and five others had converted to Islam and wished to remain in Tripoli. For the others, after 582 days the ordeal was at an end.[55]

As the crewmen of the *Philadelphia* returned, Lear appeared before the bashaw in Yusuf's chambers at Tripoli Castle and presented the final draft of the treaty. It was one of the most favorable treaties any Christian country had ever negotiated with a Barbary State. The first article called for "a firm, inviolable and universal peace." There were to be no payments of tribute, and there was no treaty payment. The second article called for the exchange of prisoners and the payment of a $60,000 ransom. Article 3 would become a particular point of contention. In it, the United States agreed to stop supporting Hamet and, moreover, to "use all means in their power to persuade the Brother of the said Bashaw, who has co-operated with them at Derne &c, to withdraw from the Territory of the said Bashaw of Tripoli." For his part, "the Bashaw engages," once Hamet had left Tri-politania, "to deliver up to him, his Wife and Children now in his powers."[56]

It was something of a canard. When the Senate ratified the treaty the next year, in 1806, the legislators would all believe the bashaw had either released or was about to release Hamet's family. A year later, however, they would learn the bashaw still held Hamet's wife and children. When George Davis, who had become consul in Tripoli, went to Yusuf to demand their release, the bashaw produced "the Lear declaration." To overcome Yusuf's concerns, Lear and the bashaw had cut a secret deal by which Yusuf would have "the term of four years, from the conclusion of said treaty . . . for the execution of the engagement of the Bashaw to deliver to his brother, his wife and children; during which time the said brother is to give evident proofs of his peaceful disposition towards the Bashaw, and of his determination not to disturb the internal tranquility of his dominions."[57]

The secret article would come to haunt Lear, but on June 5, 1805, he harbored no thoughts of what might happen in the future. The diplomat, along with the rest of the squadron, was too busy celebrating the release of the crew of the *Philadelphia* and the end of the war. It was Tobias Lear's greatest professional triumph, one he believed would enshrine him as a hero and finally earn him the recognition he craved. That it might place a stain on the national honor was never even a consideration.

20

A SAD TRUTH

ON JUNE 1, 1805, William Eaton and Hamet Karamanli still controlled Derne. Although the expected torrent of popular support for Hamet had not materialized, small bands continued to join the elder Karamanli's cause. Eaton remained convinced that with enough money he could overthrow Yusuf. That changed, however, when he received new orders from Samuel Barron, which reflected not only the commodore's continuing disapproval of Eaton's mission but the increasing influence of diplomat Tobias Lear, who was a vocal opponent of Eaton's mission and had helped Barron draft the letter that Eaton now held.[1] The letter reflected Barron's and Lear's antagonism toward Eaton's mission, although it was two sentences that continued to hold Eaton's attention: "His Excellency must be explicitly informed that our supplies of money arms and provisions are at an end and that he must now depend upon his own resources and exertions. This determination will suggest to you and your comrades that line of conduct most prudent to be adopted in the present posture of affairs."[2]

Barron justified his decision by telling Eaton that Yusuf Karamanli had made overtures of peace and the commodore, seeing a way to end the war and free the American prisoners, had decided to pursue the diplomatic route. "From a variety of concurring circumstances the present period appears propitious to such a step, and I cannot help indulging sanguine hopes that a very short time will restore Captain Bainbridge and his unfortunate comrades to freedom and their Country."[3] Barron also pointed to the lukewarm reception Hamet had received so far from the Tripolitan people. The "rightful bashaw" was not, in the commodore's eyes, the man Eaton thought he was: "The business is now arrived at that point where if the Ex Bashaw, after being put in possession of Derne, his former government and the district in which his interest is said to be the most powerful, has not in himself energy and talent, and is so destitute of means and resources[,] . . . he must be held as unworthy of further support."[4]

It was the death knell of the mission, even though it was a decision based on outdated information. The last dispatches Barron had received were those of Eaton and Hull in early May, soon after they had captured the city. Hamet had proved to be a brave combat leader, and after nearly a month in control he was slowly but steadily building up his army. Eaton saw that Barron had no idea of what was actually happening in Derne, but there was little he could do other than protest.[5]

It was not just that Barron had decided to abandon Hamet, with whom Eaton had signed a contract. To Eaton, the decision smacked of treason, and he was sure Lear had far more to do with the decision than Barron. The commodore had almost admitted as much in his letter: "Being myself still too weak for the exertion of letter writing and my secretary writing with difficulty, owing to an inflammation in his eyes, it is impossible for me to enter into a lengthy reply."[6] That left just one person to have written the commodore's letter—Tobias Lear. "It was needless for him to add this; it was easily perceivable by the drift and composition of the communication, there is no vestige of Barron's manly soul to be traced in it," Eaton raged to Samuel Smith. "It is the work of a Machiavellian Commissioner into whose influence the Commodore had yielded his mind through the infirmity of bodily weakness[;] it is a well-known fact that at this period he had been nearly six months unable to remain on shipboard and so debilitated by a painful and wasting illness that he scarcely retained the remembrance of occurrences from day to day."[7]

Eaton handed the letter to Marine Corps first lieutenant Presley O'Bannon, who grew as angry as the "general." O'Bannon urged Eaton to launch an attack immediately, not only to regain the initiative around Derne but to force Lear's hand in any negotiations by moving closer to Tripoli. O'Bannon offered to lead the attack with his Marines and a company of Christian soldiers. If nothing else, he said, it would prove to the commodore that the army could fight.[8] Eaton had liked O'Bannon almost from the moment the two men had met. The Marine Corps officer was aggressive and a solid combat leader; most of all, he was completely devoted to Eaton.[9] The general congratulated O'Bannon for his spirit but refused to attack. His forces, he believed, were simply not ready to break out of Derne. The sloop *Hornet* had returned—carrying Barron's letter—and Hull had remained with the *Argus*. How long these ships stayed would determine the next phase, if any, of his campaign.[10]

Finally, Eaton showed the letter to Hamet, who was justifiably indignant at the idea the Americans would use him solely to force his brother to the bargaining table. Eaton told Barron, in a letter he began on June 1 but did not send until the eleventh, that any support Hamet was building was contingent on his regaining the throne in Tripoli, and Yusuf for his part would use any ploy, including asking for peace talks, simply to keep his brother at bay. "Certainly the enemy will propose any terms of peace with us the moment he entertains serious apprehensions from his brother. This may happen at any stage of the war most likely to rid him of so dangerous a rival, and not only Hamet Bashaw, but every one acting with him must inevitably fall victims to our economy."[11]

Barron's orders left Eaton's position somewhat nebulous. The commodore expected Eaton to return with the *Argus* and *Nautilus* to Syracuse but left the ultimate decision of whether to stay with Hamet up to Eaton.[12] The general chose to stay. "At all events I am deeply impressed with the opinion that the post we have secured here should not be abandoned, nor terms of peace precipitately embraced," he wrote to the commodore.[13] Eaton also clung to the faint chance that Secretary of the Navy Smith, who was a proponent of Eaton's gambit, would send Barron orders to continue supporting Hamet. "I cannot but still indulge the hope that additional instructions from government will arrive in season to enable you to furnish the means of prosecuting the cooperation to effect, of chastising the temerity of our enemy, and of preventing the melancholy and disagreeable events, which present appearances threaten."[14]

The general had O'Bannon and the Christian soldiers dig in and reinforce Fort Enterprise, while Hamet's force continued to grow as Bedouin deserted Hassan Bey's force. It was a rather odd standoff. Hassan could not attack for fear his own troops would mutiny and join Hamet; Eaton could not attack either, as he had specific orders not to press forward while negotiations in Tripoli took place. On June 5, an Arab chieftain named Abdul Selim defected to Hamet with 150 followers. Selim brought the news that the governor of Benghazi was ready to declare himself for Hamet and that many of Hassan Bey's Bedouin would desert to Hamet, provided he could "have assurances that the Americans will not abandon him, in which case Joseph Bashaw would devour his family and lands."[15]

The two armies stared at one another for five days, Hassan Bey making feints to see if he could draw out Hamet's army, Eaton calmly holding his ground. On June 9, Hadgi Ismain Bey, Hassan's cavalry commander and the vice commander of his army, deserted with several followers, heading for Upper Egypt. It was, Eaton believed, yet another signal that if the Americans would simply stand by Hamet, they could topple Yusuf militarily and not have to pay for a treaty or for the release of prisoners.[16] Before that could happen, though Hassan made his final move to retake Derne.

On June 10, the Mameluke general sent a mounted force through one of the coastal mountain passes to scout a route to Derne that the Americans could not sweep with their artillery. The Tripolitan horsemen found a pass that led onto a rocky, red-clay plain. Hamet had posted some of his own cavalry there. The Tripolitan horsemen attacked them but were driven back in some confusion. Hassan sent in reinforcements as did Hamet, and a meeting engagement grew out of the raid. Eventually a total of five thousand men battled outside of Derne. Hassan's cavalry charged Hamet's several times, but Hamet's men, Hamet leading from the front, not only repulsed every charge but broke through Hassan's line with a counterattack. The battle lasted nearly four hours; O'Bannon asked Eaton to allow the Christians to launch a bayonet attack on Hassan's flank, but Eaton kept them in reserve. Hamet finally forced Hassan's troops from the field and pursued them into the mountains, where many of the Tripolitans abandoned their horses so they could escape through the narrow passes. "This action, though fought in the Barbary manner, was conducted judiciously on the part of the Bashaw, and the victory was decidedly his," Eaton boasted to Barron. "If we could have furnished but two hundred bayonets to assist a charge and cut the pass of the mountain, not a horse should have escaped."[17]

It was the final combat of the campaign, and it occurred five days after the war officially ended. Both commanders had known talks were progressing. Deserters from Hassan's camp had brought information that a courier from Tripoli had arrived on June 5 announcing the peace talks. They also brought information that Hamet was gaining in popularity, that more and more people were ready to desert Hassan and join the elder Karamanli. Hamet's performance on June 10 was all the proof Eaton needed that he was backing the right man, but the information from both Barron and deserters made him hesitant to push his growing advantage. "I had doubts whether the measures lately adopted by our commissioner of peace would justify me in acting offensively any longer in this quarter. Had the aids come forward seasonably, which we hoped, to receive here, we might now have been at Cape Mensurat and in fifteen days more at Tripoli."

The victory did little to raise Hamet's spirits. Ever since he left Egypt a feeling had gnawed at him that his American allies would desert him should his brother decide to soften his position and negotiate. Now his fears were coming true. Although his general, William Eaton, had done everything possible to help him, Hamet could not help feeling bitter. When Eaton broke the news of the peace talks and the withdrawal of U.S. naval support, Hamet replied that "even with supplies, it would be fruitless . . . to attempt to prosecute the war with his brother. . . . He emphatically says that to abandon him here is not to have cooperated with him, but with his rival!" Eaton added, "He wishes us to take him off in case of a peace. I am extremely anxious to learn the issue of the negotiation."[18]

On June 11, the day Eaton finished the letter to Barron he had begun on the first, the frigate *Constellation* arrived off Derne. Hassan, fearing the American frigate was bringing in reinforcements, fled fifteen miles inland, leaving behind much of his baggage and supplies.[19] Eaton learned the reason for the frigate's arrival at 6 p.m., when a lieutenant came ashore bearing two letters, one from the new squadron commander, John Rodgers, the other from Tobias Lear.

Rodgers' letter, dated June 5, was brief: the war was over, and the new commodore wanted "no further hostilities by the forces of the United States [to] be committed against the said Joseph Bashaw, his subjects or dominions." Eaton was to "evacuate and withdraw our forces from Derne, or whatever part of his territory this may find you in, agreeable to the enclosed articles of stipulation between Tobias Lear Esqr., Consul General, for Algiers and Commissioner of Peace on the part of the United States and the said Joseph Bashaw of Tripoli."[20]

The letter from Lear was something Eaton would never forget—or forgive. In a superior, almost chiding tone, Lear confirmed one of Eaton's worst fears. He appeared to take credit for Eaton's mission by making it seem as though the coup attempt had always been just a tool to force Yusuf to the bargaining table, an assertion that completely devalued Eaton's accomplishments. "I found that the heroic bravery of our few Countrymen at Derne, and the idea that we had a large force and immense supplies at that place, had made a deep impression on the Bashaw," Lear cooed in his letter. Once Yusuf agreed to hold talks, Lear had had no choice but to agree "that on the conclusion of peace, we should withdraw all our forces and supplies from Derne and other parts of his dominions." As for Hamet, Lear had, he told Eaton, done the best he could: "The Bashaw engages, that if his brother withdraws himself quietly from his dominions, his wife and family shall be restored to him. This is all that could be done, and I have no doubt but the United States will, if deserving, place him in a situation as eligible as that in which he was found."[21]

Lear never mentioned the secret accord he and Yusuf had reached about Hamet, nor did he acknowledge that the treaty meant returning the elder Karamanli to a destitute exile in Egypt. It was simply too much for

Eaton. He saw the peace deal, especially the abrupt abandonment of Hamet, as nothing short of a stain on the national honor. Lear, he told Rodgers, had "thrown [Hamet and allies] from proud success and elated prospects into an abyss of hopeless wretchedness. Six hours ago the enemy were seeking safety from them by flight. This moment we drop them from ours into the hands of this enemy for no other crime but too much confidence in us! The man whose fortune we have accompanied thus far experiences a reverse as striking. He falls from the most flattering prospects of a kingdom to beggary!"[22] Had the $60,000 ransom gone to the general, "I firmly believe we should have entered Tripoli with as little trouble as we did Derne."[23]

Most of all, there was the great disappointment at seeing his campaign stopped just when it appeared on the cusp of total victory. "After having been more than six months on the barbarous shore of Africa, my friends may probably think I ought not to complain at having gotten my share of the war off my hands. I ought perhaps, to be *satisfied*," he wrote to a friend in Massachusetts. "Yet, I confess, novel, arduous and hazardous as the enterprise may have appeared, I hoped to have stood on to see the temerity of Joseph Bashaw chastised and his perfidy punished. The lesson would have been awful to Barbary. Perhaps another such occasion will never offer."

Eaton never recorded his feelings about having to tell Hamet the Americans were leaving. In his report to Rodgers, Eaton made sure to emphasize the sense of betrayal the Arabs felt toward the Americans. What Lear had clearly never understood, despite his two years in Algiers and North Africa, was the basic principle of Bedouin culture—loyalty. He and Barron could grouse about the seeming greed and ever shifting allegiances of the desert tribes, but all that was simply business as usual for the fiercely independent Bedouin, whose primary loyalty was to their own sheiks. When it suited them, they were loyal subjects of the sultan. At other times, the Porte was just some distant figure. While they could be mercenary, they were not mercenaries, often fighting for less money for causes in which they believed.[24] It was these nomadic people that Hamet had begun to win over, not with promises of money but with his courage and even prowess in combat.[25] Now, the Americans were forcing Hamet to abandon his people:

"He had no safety but in leaving the country with us; and even this would be impossible with him and hazardous to us if the project should transpire before carried into effect: despair would drive his adherents to revenge and we must fall victims to it."[26]

Eaton understood the Arabs far better than any other American of his time, and while there was much about them he did not like, he did not want simply to abandon them. He was also well aware the Bedouin might turn on the Christians if they had any inkling the Westerners planned to leave. Eaton therefore continued to act as though he believed Hassan was going to attack Derne once more. On June 12 he passed out extra ammunition and rations, had the Marines and Greek infantry practice bayonet drill (much to the delight of the Bedouin, who were fascinated with Western drill), and spread the tale that Hassan planned a major assault. At 8 p.m. he had O'Bannon and the Marines mount guard as usual but this time positioned the Americans between Hamet's people and the Christian-held central fort. It was a departure from the normal routine, but no one questioned their "general."[27]

With the Arabs' attention focused outside of the city, Eaton quietly began slipping his soldiers out of Derne. Campbell sent all of the *Constellation*'s boats ashore, and slightly after 8 p.m. Eaton ordered the European artillerymen to load their field guns and a ten-inch howitzer they had captured. The artillerymen were surprised at the order but executed it as quietly as possible. Next came the remaining Greek infantrymen, who likewise left in silence. As they rowed to the *Constellation,* Eaton sent a message to Hamet, requesting an interview. It was the signal for Hamet to leave. He gathered his "retinue," quietly entered Fort Enterprise, and made his way down to the wharf. Eaton left no record of how Hamet looked or if he said anything as he once more headed into exile, this time having had victory in his grasp. Next to go were O'Bannon and his Marines. None of the Americans wanted to leave. They believed the order to abandon the expedition was a mistake, one Eaton should ignore. However, they obeyed Eaton's commands and entered the boats.

Eaton was the last man to leave and had just pushed off from shore when the secrecy surrounding the withdrawal dissolved. "When all were securely off, I stepped into a small boat which I had retained for the purpose, and had just time to save my distance when the shore, our camp, and the battery, were crowded with the distracted soldiery and populace; some calling on the Bashaw; some on me; some uttering shrieks; some execrations!"[28] It was likely the lowest point of Eaton's life. "There were tears in General Eaton's eyes when he stepped into the gig," O'Bannon reportedly told a joint House and Senate committee. "But he did not look back at Derne."[29]

The *Constellation* raised sail around 6 a.m. on June 13 and set a course for Syracuse. Before departing, Campbell sent Yusuf Karamanli's emissary ashore, where he offered amnesty to all of Hamet's followers if they swore fealty to Yusuf. According to Eaton, none of those remaining believed the offer. By noon the wind had come up, and the *Constellation* slowly sailed away from Derne. Eaton, Hamet, and O'Bannon all stood on deck as the Tripolitan coastline slowly faded in the distance.

William Eaton went first to Malta, then headed for Syracuse. Most of the Christian soldiers remained at Malta before drifting east once more and disappearing into the Ottoman Empire. Eugene Leitensdorfer, who had served Eaton continuously since Egypt, remained with him and booked passage to the United States. Hamet went on to Syracuse, where he persuaded Rodgers to grant him a stipend of two hundred dollars. He remained there, expecting his wife and children to arrive in accordance with the known articles of the peace treaty. Eaton made several stops before Syracuse. There he boarded the brig *Franklin* on August 6, 1805, arriving at Hampton Roads in November. He never returned to the Mediterranean or held a federal commission again.

Nearly five thousand miles from Derne, Lieutenant Colonel Commandant Franklin Wharton was fighting his own battle for survival. Wharton had become commandant of the Marine Corps in March 1804, when William Burrows resigned the position due to his failing health, as well as to his protracted battle with Congress to keep the Corps alive. That fight more than any other had sapped Burrows' strength and he spent most of 1803 on leave. When Wharton assumed command, the Corps was under attack as an expensive luxury from the Jefferson administration and its allies in the House and Senate.[30] He also inherited the residue of the Burrows–Thomas Truxtun feud, though Secretary Smith had at least partially settled it when he ruled on the command structure of Marines, as it related to the Navy, while on ships.[31]

The political battle that Wharton faced had no easy solutions. Virginia representatives John Eppes, who was Thomas Jefferson's son-in-law, and John Randolph had twice introduced "Act For the Reduction of the Marine Corps." The first time, in 1803, the bill had easily passed the Democrat-controlled House before dying in the Senate. Undeterred, Eppes reintroduced the bill in February 1804 and made an impassioned push for its adoption. The bill called for the reduction of the Corps to one captain, twelve lieutenants, and enough enlisted men to man the ships currently in commission. All other officers, including the commandant, would be released from the service. When serving on land, the Marines would fall under the auspices of the Army; while at sea, they would be wholly at the command of the Navy. Essentially, the Marine Corps would cease to exist.[32]

The office of the commandant came under particularly intense scrutiny. Eppes used an audit of the Corps' books to claim the commandant spent between $60,000 and $70,000 in 1803 and that there were no records for nearly $13,000. The commandant himself had cost the country nearly $3,000, Eppes claimed, with little to show for the expense. "The extravagant sum, paid for the support of this officer, was a sufficient reason of itself for reducing that office," Eppes argued. His supporters in the House were just as vocal. Pennsylvania representative Michael Leib called the Marines "the most expensive military establishment in any country. It was so far beyond the expenses of the ordinary military, that . . . the committee ought not to hesitate in reducing it or incorporating it as part of the Army."[33] When Federalist members of the House defended the Corps, Eppes and other Democrats pointed to the $353,573 already spent on the Marines, with what Eppes said was little to show for it.[34] The bill easily passed in the House again but once more languished in the Senate, where the Democrats held a slimmer edge and support for the military ran somewhat stronger.[35]

The tabling of the Marine Corps reduction act did not end Wharton's political problems. In early 1805, Eppes and other Democrats, together with Secretary of the Treasury Albert Gallatin, seized on Thomas Jefferson's passion for gunboats and crafted the Naval Militia Act. Under the act, a volunteer militia would man, fight, and maintain the hundreds of gunboats that Jefferson wanted to build for coastal and port defense. The militia would drill once every two months, and the captain of each boat would have the responsibility for its upkeep. Because, it was supposed, fishermen and other experienced seamen would form the militia, maintenance costs would be minimal. The militia would draw its essential gear, such as spars, cannon, and ammunition, from Army arsenals, where they would also store the equipment.[36] The Naval Militia Act had critics in both parties, who pointed out there was still a need for larger warships. The gunboats also came under immediate criticism regarding their actual usefulness in combat.

For Wharton, the idea that the militia would be responsible for guarding the gunboats meant another threat to the continued existence of the Marine Corps. Wharton launched his own political campaign for the preservation of the Marine Corps, and he knew how to maneuver in that field. A scion of an elite Philadelphia family, Wharton had strong political connections to many Federalists, and now he worked those connections. His role as commandant gave him the opportunity to travel to New York, Boston, Baltimore, and Philadelphia on a near-constant basis as he oversaw the construction of barracks and recruiting rendezvous. In Washington, he intensified the steps Burrows had taken to ensure the Marine Corps would be an elite force. He did not allow any foreign-born Marines to serve in Washington and reemphasized the need for officers and Marines alike to master drill and movement. He had Marines from the Washington barracks mount guard every day at the Capitol, which was one of the federal buildings the Marines were responsible for protecting. The changing of the guard soon grew into a daily parade, one that Wharton made sure drew a crowd. He staged concerts by the Marine Band that became a staple of life in the federal district and quickly drew acclaim. The band became a major weapon in Wharton's campaign to preserve the Corps; he volunteered his musicians to play at every possible event. Whether it was the city's July 4 celebration, New Year's, the president's birthday, or a dinner for U.S. or foreign dignitaries, the band was there, as were Marine Corps officers and noncommissioned officers in their distinctive red-trimmed dress uniforms.[37]

Wharton's campaign was successful, but only partially. The Marines became a part of the daily life in the capital, but that was not enough to keep them out of the crosshairs of lawmakers determined to cut military spending. The Marine Corps remained a favorite target for them as it continued to grow despite the efforts to cut its strength. Jefferson's insistence on building a gunboat navy of upward of two hundred boats would create a need for eight hundred Marines, each gunboat requiring a corporal or sergeant and three privates. There was a demand for a hundred Marines in New Orleans, and there were two squadrons needing Marine detachments currently operating in the Mediterranean. All told, Wharton would need slightly more than 1,500 Marines.[38] Secretary Smith told Wharton to fill his quota despite congressional efforts to curtail the Corps' strength. To do that, Wharton needed something that would not only hold off the lawmakers' attempts to cut the Corps funding but would help him recruit new Marines. He needed a hero.

On October 9, 1805, Wharton got exactly what he needed. The *National Intelligencer and Daily Advertiser,* a Washington, D.C., newspaper, ran a letter from Midshipman Paoli Peck to his father, Colonel William Peck; it was the first published report of the capture of Derne and the role of First Lieutenant Presley O'Bannon and the Marines in Eaton's campaign. "Certainly it was one of the most extraordinary expeditions to ever set out on foot." Peck captured the public imagination with his lurid description of the arduous trek from Alexandria to Derne: "When I think on our situation in the desert, where no other Christian ever set his foot, and consider what thieves Arabs are, who would shoot a man for the buttons on his coat, and their religious prejudices, which would have been sufficient our deaths as Christians and enemies to their religion, I frequently wonder how it was possible for us to succeed."[39]

The *National Intelligencer* had already carried several briefs concerning the peace and Eaton's march to Derne. The *Washington Federalist* had printed extracts of Barron's letters to Eaton in which the commodore cast doubts on the mission and Hamet—raising questions of why anyone would stand in the way of "so gallant an expedition. Is it possible that this sad news is true?"[40] On September 25, 1805, the *National Intelligencer* printed a toast to O'Bannon that would make the rounds of the country: "Lieutenant O'Bannon and Midshipman Mann, the heroes who planted the American banner on the walls of Derne!"[41]

O'Bannon's feats fired the imagination of the American public, and illustrations imagining the storming of Derne and O'Bannon hoisting the flag proliferated around the country. Although the tug-of-war over rank between the Marine Corps, Army, and Navy would continue for another thirty years, talk of defunding the Corps stopped, at least for a time. It was an unlooked-for yet long-lasting by-product of Eaton's campaign. Without O'Bannon's headlong charge at Derne, the Marine Corps might very well have succumbed to the whims of an antimilitary, budget-cutting Congress and disappeared as an independent force.[42] Although opponents of the Corps made several more efforts to abolish the Marines, none would come as close as Eppes' 1804 effort, and none would gain as much traction.

EPILOGUE

THE TREATY with Tripoli did not end the Barbary Wars, nor did it end the practice of paying tribute to the North African states. It did mark the first time a tribute nation broke free of that onerous practice, but only in one instance. Throughout the Tripoli war, the United States made its treaty-required payments to Tunis, Algiers, and Morocco, and it continued to do so until the War of 1812. In fact, when Lear was not busy trying to convince Barron to pull his support from Eaton (and all evidence shows Lear engaged in a very active campaign to do that), the consul general was busy advising George Davis in Tunis and James Simpson in Tangiers, Morocco, on how to deal with the leaders of those states when American tribute payments were late.[1]

The Tripoli war marked a number of firsts for the United States. Aside from being the still-new nation's first overseas conflict, it marked the first time the United States established its own military base on foreign territory. Syracuse also became home to the first U.S. naval hospital overseas, which Barron established under Surgeon Edward Cutbush soon after he took command of the squadron in 1804. Barron rented a large, two-story stone building that could house up to twenty men. The hospital remained in use until 1806, when Commodore John Rodgers closed the U.S. base at Syracuse and the last ships of the squadron returned home.[2]

There were, of course, other firsts—the first raising of the Stars and Stripes over a conquered foreign city; the first land campaign in a foreign nation; the first test of a transatlantic supply line; and others. In what may be the most important first, it marked the first time the chief executive exercised his powers as commander in chief to fight a war without approval of Congress, creating a precedent that exists to this day. The war provided the Navy with the opportunity to build upon the lessons it had begun learning in the Quasi-War and to develop them much further. Thanks largely to Edward Preble, the Navy emerged from the war with a solid cadre of young, aggressive, well-trained officers who were the foundation for the Navy's successes in subsequent conflicts. It also helped cement the role of the Marine Corps within the Navy Department, although questions about rank and seniority would take years to settle.

The treaty with Tripoli met with a mixed reception, due more to William Eaton's one-man campaign against the deal than to anything else, although even Democrats railed against the secret article regarding Hamet's family once it became public. Eaton's march across the desert fired the public's imagination, and tales of his and O'Bannon's bravery filled national newspapers. Even the *Portsmouth Gazette*, Lear's hometown paper, questioned the decision to negotiate rather than commit fully to Eaton's campaign.[3] Eaton and others were able to portray the treaty as a betrayal of a loyal American ally and to heap the blame on Lear and Barron—but the real culprit was Jefferson. The president's failure to select one policy and see it through created the vacuum that allowed Barron, Eaton, and Lear to pursue campaigns that were at odds with one another as much as they were with Tripoli.

William Eaton received a raucous welcome when he stepped off the brig *Franklin* in Norfolk, Virginia, on November 10, 1805. In the deeply divided political climate of the times, Federalist newspapers embraced Eaton and pilloried the Jefferson administration for not seeing Eaton's campaign to its conclusion. The hubbub, however, soon subsided, and the country moved on. William Eaton would not and could not. He went to Washington, intent on making Samuel Barron and Tobias Lear the culprits for what he saw as nothing less than cowardice and treason. He was also intent on finally pressing his financial claims against the government, and he knew his current hero status would aid that effort. Wrote Eaton's close friend and confidant William Prentiss,

> Throughout the United States his name stood exalted. Never perhaps before did that of any individual rise so rapidly and to such an altitude. He was considered as having, by his prowess and enterprise, compelled the Bashaw of Tripoli to make peace: while the general sentiment entertained was, that, had not Lear thus hastily made a treaty, he must, if properly sustained by the naval force then in the Mediterranean, in a short time have been master of the kingdom of Tripoli, and have been enabled to make his own terms of peace, as well as to have settled our concerns on the Barbary coast, so as to prevent hereafter the necessity of tribute.[4]

Eaton pursued a relentless campaign extolling his accomplishments while vilifying Barron, Lear, and the Jefferson administration. He leaked letters to the papers, gave speeches, and took any and every opportunity to heap scorn on his opponents, reserving his harshest criticism for Lear and the treaty. In his report to Secretary of the Navy Robert Smith, Eaton attacked Barron's decision of May 19 to abandon Hamet, placing the blame on Barron's illness and Lear: "This letter [Barron's] labors ingeniously to find some pretext for deserting Hamet Bashaw at the very moment we profit of his operations and his influence to secure peace to ourselves. But the ingenuity of the piece is not sufficient to disguise the hypocrisy of the design."[5]

Eaton went to great lengths to disparage to Smith every paragraph of the letter Lear sent him on June 6: "Whatever may be considered, by capacities capable of judging correctly, the merit or demerit of my conduct, I beg you will entertain a more favorable opinion of my pride than to suppose I ever lived a moment when I should have thought it an honor to receive a military compliment from the provisional Colonel Lear." He even composed doggerel heckling the consul general: "A Colonel / Who never set a squadron in the field, / Nor the division of a battle knows / More than a spinster."[6]

Eaton returned home to Brimfield in December 1805, reuniting with his family for the first time in two years. The Massachusetts legislature on February 25, 1806, granted Eaton ten thousand acres of land in Maine, while in Washington the Senate Committee of Claims took up Eaton's finances. The associated bill touched off a contentious debate; the Senate tabled the measure twice. Finally, on February 9, 1807, the Senate agreed to pay Eaton $40,000 for his services. After deducting his official debts, Eaton netted slightly more than $12,000 for six years of service, an amount that did not come close to covering his personal debts, which had accrued while he was in Tripolitania and in maintaining his family's relatively high social standing.

Eaton's intense dislike of the Jefferson administration caught the attention of former vice president Aaron Burr, who was concocting a plan to wrest New Orleans and much of the new Louisiana Territory from the United States and establish an independent country. Burr brought Eaton into the conspiracy, offering him command of the army that would conquer Louisiana. Burr did not know that his plan disgusted Eaton, who kept copious notes on his meetings with him and, upon his arrest on February 17, 1807, became the principal witness against him. Burr's defense attorney, Martin Luther, portrayed Eaton as a paid informant of the government, seizing upon the settlement Eaton had reached on his debts. Luther's ability to discredit Eaton played a large role in Burr's acquittal.

At the same time, Eaton championed the cause of Hamet, who in 1805 had written to Congress seeking financial help. Eaton returned home for good in 1808, and his life quickly spun out of control. He served a term in the Massachusetts legislature, tried to return to the Army, and grieved deeply when his stepson Eli Danielsson died in a duel. His drinking quickly went from bad to alcoholic, and his health suffered accordingly. He squandered his wife's fortune, sold off his property in Maine for just fifty cents an acre, and spent most days drunk. By 1810, the general who had led an army across a desert was bedridden, the victim of disease or drink or both. A year later, in April 1811, it was clear even to Eaton that his death was near. He made arrangements for his own funeral and slowly sank into delirium. On May 31, Eaton's breathing became labored. He did not recognize friends or family who came to see him. He held on until 9:20 p.m. on June 1, 1811, when he breathed his last.[7]

∽∽∽

Commodore Samuel Barron returned to the United States on the frigate *President,* which also carried Captain William Bainbridge and many of the freed prisoners of the *Philadelphia.* Barron went home to his family estate in Hampton, Virginia, and accepted command of the Gosport Navy Yard. He launched a vigorous defense of his actions against the accusations of William Eaton. He wrote directly to Eaton on April 21, 1806, warning the "general" that "you have made some comments which cannot pass unnoticed as it seems to reflect on a character the breath of slander has never dared sully."[8] It took nearly a year for Eaton to reply, and when he did he actually tried to soothe the commodore. "I disavow any intention . . . to derogate from your reputation or outrage your feelings," Eaton wrote on February 14, 1807. "The bad management, which no sophistry can veil, and the reproach due the inglorious finishing of the war with Tripoli, I meant should fix on our commissioner of peace."[9] It was the last time they exchanged correspondence.

In June 1807, war with England seemed likely after the British frigate *Leopard* attacked the U.S. frigate *Chesapeake,* ostensibly to retrieve Royal Navy deserters. Samuel's brother James commanded the *Chesapeake* and faced court-martial in the wake of the affair. Samuel attended the trial and vehemently disagreed with the censure the court handed down. He remained in command at Gosport, although his health continued to fail. Samuel Barron died on November 10, 1810, at the age of forty-five.

∽∽∽

Tobias Lear returned to his post in Algiers, sure that in his peace deal with Tripoli he had served his country well. He told his wife, Fanny, "I have finished all our affairs, much to my satisfaction and the honor of our country."[10] A month passed before Lear wrote his report on the negotiations and treaty. In it, he was very careful to avoid mention of the secret article with Yusuf that allowed the bashaw to hold his brother's family hostage for up to four years. Instead, Lear told Secretary of State James Madison that he "insisted that, if his brother should leave his territory, he should have his wife and family restored." He said Yusuf finally consented to return Hamet's family, provided he had "time." Lear never let on how much time he gave Yusuf to release Hamet's family.[11] He made no mention of Eaton or the capture of Derne, telling Madison, "As I have always been opposed to the Egyptian and Derne expedition, I shall say nothing on that subject, especially as, I presume, there will be full communications respecting it from other quarters."[12]

News of Lear's treaty hit the papers in August, just as many newspapers were printing "excerpts" of Eaton's correspondence, and it was Eaton, not Lear, who received the accolades. The *New Hampshire Gazette*, published in Lear's hometown of Portsmouth, made the treaty secondary to Eaton's feats. After telling readers, "In this gazette will be found the interesting, highly gratifying intelligence of the emancipation of our late brethren captives from the chains of Tripoline slavery," the paper extolled Eaton's accomplishments. The treaty, the paper wrote, was the direct result of "the success of an expedition projected and executed by William Eaton, Esq.[;] . . . the events of the battle are not fully disclosed, though said to be in favor of the Christian General who had taken possession of Derne."[13]

The treaty arrived before the Senate on December 27, 1805, and almost immediately opponents attacked it. Federalist lawmakers, Timothy Pickering in particular, wanted a complete time line so they could see why Lear chose to enter negotiations when America apparently had a military advantage both on land and at sea. Senators also demanded to know whether Yusuf had released Hamet's family in accordance with the treaty before them, knowing nothing of the secret proviso.[14] The debate went on until April 12, 1806, when the Senate approved the treaty in a party-line vote of twenty to ten and sent a note to Jefferson asking him to inquire about Hamet's family.[15]

On December 27, 1806, George Davis, now consul in Tripoli, learned of the secret clause, which Lear had accompanied with a promise that the U.S. government would never push the matter of Hamet's family. The news touched off a firestorm in the United States; newspapers and politicians alike denounced Lear. The loudest voice was that of Eaton. Lear finally had enough and fired back his own reply, through Secretary Madison: "The base and false aspersions which have been cast upon my conduct in the Tripoli business, in some of our unworthy public prints, gave me some pain, but I was conscious that what I had done was for the honor and best interest of my country, and the effects thereof would be acknowledged, when the contemptable aspersions should be in merited oblivion."[16] He also took a direct shot at Eaton and those second-guessing his decision to negotiate with Yusuf: "The more I see of Barbary affairs, the more I am convinced that government has been grossly imposed upon, by representations made from prejudice, resentment, vanity, or ignorance; and I confess I feel a little mortified to see some caressed who deserve more than censure."[17]

Lear remained in Algiers for seven years, returning to the United States when the newest dey, Haji Ali ben Khralil, sided with England at the start of the War of 1812. Lear went to work in the War Department as an auditor. He remained there through the war and appeared content. At the end of the war with England, Commodore Stephen Decatur led an expedition to North Africa that would forever end the scourge of Barbary piracy. The new treaties, which Decatur famously dictated "at the mouth of our cannon," renewed the debate over Lear's treaty of 1805. It was too much for the former diplomat to bear. On October 11, 1816, Tobias Lear put a pistol to his head and pulled the trigger.

Hamet Karamanli spent the three years immediately after the war moving between Syracuse to Malta, waiting for Yusuf to release his family in accordance with the publicly known terms of the treaty. He maintained a regular correspondence with Eaton until his general's death, often telling Eaton about his own pitiable existence. Hamet never stopped trying to recover his wife and children; he, like everyone else at the time, knew nothing about the secret agreement between his brother and Tobias Lear. On September 1, 1805, broke and relying on his Navy stipend, Hamet wrote directly to

Congress for help. The treaty, he said, had, "no article in my favor, no provision for me and my family, and no remuneration for the advantages I had foregone in trusting to American honor."[18] It took six months for Hamet's claim to reach Congress and another year for the lawmakers to take up the petition. By then, condemnation of Lear's treaty was widespread.

In April 1807, Hamet asked George Davis for help. The request surprised Davis, who had learned late the year before of the secret article.[19] The new consul pressed Hamet's demands, and on May 12, 1807, he wrote Hamet that Yusuf had agreed to release his family. The family went to Syracuse, where they reunited with Hamet (except the oldest daughter, who had married Yusuf's oldest son and decided to remain in Tripoli).[20] The Senate eventually voted Hamet a one-time payment of $2,400 and a monthly stipend of two hundred dollars, small reward for a man who had proven so willing to act in American interests and so loyal to them.[21] For a brief time he regained his place as "bey" of Derne and Benghazi, but by 1810 his brother had again driven him—with his family this time— into exile.

After his ouster from Derne, Hamet returned to Egypt. He lived a squalid existence, abandoned by all, in Alexandria until his death sometime in the 1820s. In 1832, a man called at the U.S. consulate in Alexandria claiming to be Mohammed Karamanli, the eldest son of Hamet. He said the family was now destitute and living in Cairo and asked the official to aid the family of America's ally. There is no record the government ever did anything to help.[22]

First Lieutenant Presley O'Bannon returned to duty on board the *Argus*, along with Sergeant Arthur Campbell and Privates Bernard O'Brien, Joseph Fischer, and Joseph Joiner. O'Bannon boarded the *Argus* clutching a precious gift from Hamet, who had promised to remember the Virginian's courage always. The "rightful bashaw," seemingly broke and now bereft of his kingdom, had given O'Bannon one of his last precious possessions, an ivory-and-gold-hilted, jewel-encrusted Mameluke sword that he had used while fighting in Egypt.[23] Thirty-eight inches long with a graceful curved blade, the sword became a symbol of the Marines' first victory on foreign soil and quickly became a favorite among O'Bannon's fellow officers, both because of its exotic design and because of what O'Bannon's feats meant to the Marine Corps. By 1825, so many officers had ordered their own versions of the sword that Colonel Commandant Archibald Henderson adopted the pattern as the official sword for Marine Corps officers.[24]

O'Bannon remained in the Mediterranean until May 27, 1806, when the *Argus* set sail with several gunboats for Charleston, South Carolina. The little convoy arrived on July 12; the *Argus* continued north to Washington, where she went into ordinary on July 29. O'Bannon reported to Lieutenant Colonel Franklin Wharton at Marine Barracks Washington, where he spent the next eight months on staff duty. It was probably a major letdown for the still-young Virginian, who had spent the past two years at sea and had seen more combat than any other Marine officer. O'Bannon likely expected a promotion or at least a brevet for his service under Eaton, especially after the hero's welcome he received on his arrival in Washington. Instead, he had to deal with the tedium of the peacetime Marine Corps, and by early 1807 he had had enough. On March 6, 1807, O'Bannon resigned his commission.[25]

O'Bannon first went to his family home in Salem, now Marshall, Virginia, where he waited roughly two years for yet another recognition of his exploits, this one from his home state. On December 26, 1805, the Virginia legislature had voted unanimously to present O'Bannon with a sword commemorating his raising of the flag over Derne. It appointed John Clarke, superintendent of the Virginia Manufactury of Arms, to design and produce the sword. Clarke came up with an elaborate proposal featuring a turban-wearing sheik and the crescent moon of Islam on the hilt; the blade was to bear a depiction of O'Bannon leading the Marines in the attack on Derne and raising the flag over its ramparts. Three years passed, and nothing happened. The legislature fired Clarke and hired John M. Parke to complete the project. Parke redesigned the hilt, replacing the sheik with an eagle and making the blade a fully curved scimitar—unlike the sword Hamet had presented O'Bannon, whose blade was only slightly curved.

Parke finished the sword in 1811, although O'Bannon would not receive it until October 1812. There is no record of how O'Bannon reacted to a major gaffe on the blade: the legislature had botched O'Bannon's first name, engraving "Priestly" on the sword instead of "Presley."[26]

Meanwhile, O'Bannon married Matilda Heard, the granddaughter of Revolutionary War hero Daniel Morgan, and handled family business. He sold off the farm in Salem and moved with his new wife to Kentucky in 1809, settling in Russellville, in Logan County. He reportedly received an appointment in the U.S. Army as a lieutenant in the Regiment of Artillerists in 1807 and an appointment as a captain in the Regiment of Light Dragoons in 1808, but there are no records of his serving in either unit.[27] Matilda had inherited nearly ten thousand acres from her father, and O'Bannon netted several thousand dollars from the sale of his Virginia holdings. In 1812, O'Bannon won an appointment to the Kentucky House of Representatives, serving for nine years. In 1824 he ran for the state senate and served for two years.

Although he was prosperous, O'Bannon's home life was difficult. Various reports have Matilda bearing either one or two children, neither of which, if there were two, lived past five years. By the time he was elected to the state senate, Matilda was showing signs of dementia, and sometime before 1832 the two divorced. They remarried on May 23 of that year, after Matilda agreed to allow Presley to administer "all and every parcel of property, real, personal and mixed now owned by her or that she may inherit or that she may obtain in any way." By 1843, her condition had deteriorated, and a court, assessing her property as "a houselot in Russellville and five slaves," declared her a "person of unsound mind" and committed her to an asylum in Lexington.[28]

O'Bannon spent the next seven years in retirement, "surrounded by devoted friends and lingering memories of his role in the Barbary War." Friends described him as a "man of rare sweetness and dignity and very popular." Presley Neville O'Bannon, the first American military officer to raise the flag of the United States over conquered foreign territory, died on September 12, 1850. He was buried in a small family cemetery near Pleasureville in Hunt County, Kentucky. Seventy years later, the Daughters of the American Revolution received permission from O'Bannon's descendants to exhume his remains and rebury them on the State Monument grounds at the state capitol in Frankfort.

∽◁ ▷∽

Yusuf Karamanli—wily, intelligent, ruthless—remained in power in Tripoli long past the deaths of William Eaton and Tobias Lear. In many ways, Karamanli was the true winner of what the Americans called the "First Barbary War" and the Tripolitans the "Four Year War." As Yusuf adroitly pointed out to Lear during the negotiations that ended hostilities, the war had morphed from a conflict over money to one over who would rule Tripoli, and Yusuf emerged as the clear victor of that contest. Although the treaty the Americans forced on him included a clause safeguarding his rebellious brother, Yusuf knew the throne was safe, at least for a time.

The treaty was also the first with a Western nation that did not include peace payments. The peace was to be perpetual and, other than the usual consular gifts, would contribute nothing to the Tripolitan economy. Yusuf likely expected to make up that money by sending his cruisers after his favorite targets—the vessels of Denmark, Sweden, Naples, Ragusa, or any other "small" power. His more immediate concern, however, was restoring order in the wake of the American blockade and the uprising in Derne. He used the ransom money to pay his troops and pacified Derne through a series of reprisals and bribes.[29]

In 1806, an uprising in Fezzan threatened to derail Yusuf's plans for an economic recovery for Tripoli, as it cut off the lucrative trade routes to equatorial Africa and the Sudan. Once more the bashaw had to draw on his slender reserves of hard currency to organize an army, which he sent south under his third son, Ali. The uprising lasted for four years, until the Tripolitan force laid siege to the town of Ghedames, which was the center of the uprising, and finally forced the rebelling tribes to surrender. The tribes paid an indemnity of $20,000 in gold and promised annual payments of the same amount; Yusuf installed a governor in the region to ensure stability.[30]

The Napoleonic Wars raging across Europe had a direct impact on Tripoli. Trade all but ceased, as did tribute payments. When the war ended, the United States, followed by European powers, ended permanently the

practice of paying for peace, placing a huge stress on the Tripolitan economy.[31] As its economic structure teetered, Yusuf tightened his reins over
the country, exacting every bit of wealth he could from the populace.[32]
In 1816, Britain, acting on behalf of Yusuf's creditors, called in his debts,
and his finances collapsed. He called a special meeting of his divan, which
authorized an extraordinary set of taxes to pay off the debts. The taxes,
which hit everyone in the country especially hard, caused a fracture among
Yusuf's supporters. Factions soon sprang up around two of his sons, Mehmed and Ali, both of whom were in positions to challenge their father.
Mohammed, in 1817, used Derne and Benghazi to launch a rebellion; Yusuf
dispatched his second son, Ahmet, with an army to put down the revolt.
Mehmed fled to Egypt but for the next fifteen years continued to lead
uprisings.[33]

Yusuf's third son, Ali, took advantage of the confusion and began a
revolt that soon embroiled all of southern Tripolitania. Yusuf again turned
to Ahmet to quell the rebellion but was never able to snuff out the flames
of revolt completely. The years from 1817 to 1832 were a dizzying spiral
into chaos for Yusuf and all of Tripoli. Mehmed and Ali at various points
claimed to have supplanted their father as bashaw, but each time, Yusuf
was able to raise just enough force to reverse his ouster. By 1832, however,
Yusuf was completely broke and had few if any loyal backers. He decided
to abdicate, but instead of giving the throne to Ahmet, who had apparently always remained loyal, Yusuf abdicated in favor of Ali II, who united
two-thirds of the country and faced off against his older brother in the
other third.[34]

Ali, however, was insufficiently strong to defeat his brother and in 1835
turned to his nominal overlord, Sultan Mohammed II of the Ottoman
Empire, for help. The sultan sent a force of five thousand Turkish soldiers
to Tripoli, but their orders were not to back Ali but to oust all of the brothers. They took Ali prisoner and sent him to Constantinople. It brought
an end to the independent Tripoli that Yusuf had worked so hard—and
shed so much blood, much of it innocent—to maintain. The Turks allowed
Yusuf to remain in Tripoli, where he died in 1838.[35]

NOTES

CHAPTER 1. SHORES OF TRIPOLI

1. Thomas Jefferson, Proposal for War Powers against the Barbary States (1786), Papers of Thomas Jefferson, Series 1, General Correspondence, 1653–1827, Library of Congress [hereafter LOC], Manuscript Division.

2. See Chipp Reid, *Intrepid Sailors: The Legacy of Preble's Boys and the Tripoli Campaign* (Annapolis, Md.: Naval Institute Press, 2012).

3. Robert Lambert Playfair, *The Scourge of Europe* (London: Smith, Elder, 1885), 30–32.

4. Kola Folayan, *Tripoli during the Rule of Yusuf Pacha Qaramanli* [hereafter *Tripoli under Qaramanli*] (Ife, Nigeria: University of Ife Press, 1970), 35–39.

5. See Reid, *Intrepid Sailors*.

6. Glenn Tucker, *Dawn Like Thunder: The Barbary Wars and the Birth of the U.S. Navy* (Indianapolis: Bobbs-Merrill, 1963), 347.

7. Folayan, *Tripoli under Qaramanli*, 35–39.

8. Samuel Edwards, *Barbary General: The Life of William H. Eaton* (Englewood Cliffs, N.J.: Prentice Hall, 1968), 16.

9. The Marine Corps used "Tripoli" to refer to the nation now called Libya. At the time, Libya did not exist and Tripoli—or Tripolitania—was a province of the Ottoman Empire.

10. Playfair, *Scourge of Europe*, 36–45.

CHAPTER 2. THE GENERAL

1. Cornelius C. Pelton, *Life of William Eaton* (New York: Parker & Brothers, 1902), 3–4; Charles Prentiss, *The Life of the Late General Eaton* (Brookfield, Mass.: E. Mirriam , 1813) [hereafter Prentiss, *General Eaton*], 10.
2. Edwards, *Barbary General,* 16–17.
3. Ibid.
4. Compiled Service Records of Soldiers Who Served in the American Army During the Revolutionary War, National Archives and Records Association, Washington, D.C. [hereafter NARA], Record Group [RG] 93, microfilm M881, roll 167.
5. Ibid.
6. Ibid.
7. Edwards, *Barbary General,* 23; Pelton, *William Eaton,* 4; Prentiss, *General Eaton,* 11.
8. Henry P. Johnston, ed., *Record of Service of Connecticut Men in the War of the Revolution, War of 1812, Mexican War* (Hartford, Conn.: General Assembly, 1889), 567.
9. Pelton, *William Eaton,* 6; Prentiss, *General Eaton,* 13.
10. "Sketch of General William Eaton," *New Hampshire Patriot and State Gazette* Concord, N.H., September 21, 1835.
11. Ibid.
12. Ibid.
13. Ibid.
14. Ibid.
15. Ibid.
16. Pelton, *William Eaton,* 6.
17. LaFayette Wilburn, *Early History of Vermont* (Jericho, Vt.: Roscoe, 1899), 216–19.
18. *American State Papers: Military Affairs,* vol. 1, *1794–1825* (Washington, D.C.: Gales and Seaton, 1834), 1:41.
19. Francis B. Heitman, *Historical Register and Dictionary of the United States Army, from its Organization, Sept. 29, 1789, to March 2, 1903* (Washington, D.C.: Government Printing Office [hereafter GPO], 1903), 1:395.

20. Prentiss, *General Eaton,* 14; "Sketch of General William Eaton."

21. Prentiss, *General Eaton,* 15.

22. Ibid., 15–16.

23. Ibid., 17.

24. Prentiss, General Eaton, 19–20.

25. Ibid.

26. Ibid., 25.

27. Ibid., 27–35.

28. Ibid., 33.

29. Pelton, *William Eaton,* 14.

30. William Eaton to Eliza Eaton, undated, William Eaton Letters and Papers, Huntington Library, San Marino, Calif. [hereafter WEP].

31. William Eaton to Eliza Eaton, June 6, 1800, WEP.

32. Ibid.

33. Prentiss, *General Eaton,* 53–54.

34. Ibid.

35. Ibid.

36. William Eaton Journal, March 22, 1799, WEP.

37. William Eaton to Timothy Pickering, April 15, 1799, WEP.

38. William Eaton Journal, February 22, 1799, WEP.

39. William Eaton Journal, March 14, 1799, WEP.

40. Tucker, *Dawn Like Thunder,* 116.

41. William Eaton Journal, March 19, 1799, WEP.

42. Ibid.

43. William Eaton Journal, April 7, 1799, WEP.

44. Eaton to Pickering, April 15, 1799.

45. William Eaton Journal, April 7, 1799, WEP.

46. William Eaton Journal, April 6, 1799, WEP.

47. Ibid.

CHAPTER 3. BROTHERLY LOVE

1. Miss Tully, *Narrative of a Ten Years' Residence at Tripoli in Africa, from the Original Correspondence in the Possession of the Family of the Late Richard Tully, Esq., the British Consul* (London: Henry Colburn, 1819) [hereafter *Narrative*], 218.

2. Ettore Rossi, *Storia di Tripoli e de Tripolitania dalla Conquista Araba da 1911 Edizione Postuma a Cura di Maria Nullino* (Rome: Instituto per l'Oriente, 1968), 222–24.

3. Faraj Najem, *Tribe, Islam and State in Libya: Analytical Study of the Roots of Libyan Tribal Society and Interaction Up to the Qaramanli Rule* (Westminster, U.K.: University of Westminster, 2004) [hereafter *Tribes of Libya*], 97–110.

4. Geoffrey Goodwin, *The Janissaries* (London: Saqi Books, 2006), 23–28.

5. Najem, *Tribes of Libya*, 115.

6. Folayan, *Tripoli under Qaramanli* 3.

7. Tully, *Narrative*, 33.

8. Tully, *Narrative*; Folayan, *Tripoli under Qaramanli*, 5.

9. Folayan, *Tripoli under Qaramanli*, 5.

10. Rossi, *Storia di Tripoli*, 246.

11. Tully, *Narrative*, 45–47.

12. Folayan, *Tripoli under Qaramanli*, 5; Najem, *Tribes of Libya*, 117.

13. Folayan, *Tripoli under Qaramanli*, 6–7.

14. Ibid.

15. Folayan, *Tripoli under Qaramanli*, 8–9.

16. Tully, *Narrative*, 40.

17. Ibid., 34.

18. Ibid., 37

19. Ibid., 258.

20. Ibid., 259.

21. Ibid., 260.

22. Tully, *Narrative*, 212–14; Tully, *Letters Written during a Ten Years' Residence at the Court of Tripoli* (London: Henry Colburn, 1816) [hereafter *Letters*], 222.

23. Tully, *Narrative*, 220.

24. Ibid., 222.

25. Ibid., 225.

26. Ibid., 226.

27. Mohammed al-Tawil, *Tripoli and the West* (Tripoli, Libya, 1971), 94–96.

28. Rossi, *Storia di Tripoli*, 254; Folayan, *Tripoli under Qaramanli*, 10–11.

29. Tully, *Narrative*, 265.

30. Ibid., 266.

31. Folayan, *Tripoli under Qaramanli*, 13–15; Tully, *Narrative*, 267–71.

32. Tully, *Letters*, 330.

33. Rossi, *Storia di Tripoli*, 263; Folayan, *Tripoli under Qaramanli*, 12.

34. Folayan, *Tripoli under Qaramanli*, 12.

35. Ibid., 17.

36. Al-Tawil, *Tripoli and the West*, 94–96.

37. Ibid., 105; Folayan, *Tripoli under Qaramanli*, 19–20.

38. Rossi, *Storia di Tripoli*, 259–61; Folayan, *Tripoli under Qaramanli*, 20.

39. Rossi, *Storia di Tripoli*, 262.

40. Ibid.

41. Simon Lucas to William Grenville, June 26, 1795, Records of the Foreign Office, FO160 Foreign Office and predecessors; Consulate, Tripoli, Libya (formerly Ottoman Empire) [hereafter FO160]; General Correspondence and Letter Books.

42. Simon Lucas to Messrs. Turnbull, Forbes and Co., June 20, 1795, *FO161*, Correspondence, various.

43. Rossi, *Storia di Tripoli*, 262.

44. Ibid.

45. Al-Tawil, *Tripoli and the West*, 121.

46. Simon Lucas to William Cavendish Bentick, Duke of Portland, July 26, 1796, FO161, Correspondence, various.

47. Simon Lucas to William Cavendish Bentick, Duke of Portland, August 19, 1797, FO161.

48. James Leander Cathcart, *Tripoli: First War with the United States. Inner History. Letter Book by James Leander Cathcart* (LaPorte, Ind.: Herald, 1901) [hereafter Cathcart, *Letter Book*], 2–3.

49. James Leander Cathcart to Richard O'Brien, October 29, 1800, in ibid., 198.

50. Bashaw Yusuf Karamanli to Richard O'Brien, September 7, 1798, in Dudley Knox, ed., *Naval Documents Related to the War between the United States and the Barbary Powers* (Washington, D.C.: GPO, 1935) [hereafter NDBP], 1:255.

51. James Leander Cathcart to John Marshall, February 19, 1801, in Cathcart, *Letter Book*, 264.

52. James Leander Cathcart to John Marshall, February 25, 1801, in ibid., 277.

CHAPTER 4. "TO CHASTISE THE BASHAW"

1. Najem, *Tribes of Libya*, 14–24.

2. M. Shahid Alam, "Articulating Group Differences: A Variety of Autocentrisms," *Science and Society* (Summer 2013), 210; C. R. Pennell, *Morocco: The Empire to Independence* (London: Oneworld, 2003), 8–84.

3. Thomas Jefferson to Albert Gallatin, August 9, 1802, in Albert Gallatin, *The Papers of Albert Gallatin*, ed. Henry Adams (Philadelphia: J. B. Lippincott, 1870), 83–84.

4. See Reid, *Intrepid Sailors*.

5. Ronald Bruce St. John, *Libya and the United States: Two Centuries of Strife* (Philadelphia: University of Pennsylvania Press, 2002), 21.

6. Ibid., 20.

7. James Leander Cathcart to William Eaton and Richard O'Brien, February 23, 1801, in Cathcart, *Letter Book*. 278–79.

8. Ibid., 279.

9. See Reid, *Intrepid Sailors*.

10. Samuel Smith to Richard Dale, July 2, 1801, NDBP, 1:499.

11. For a complete account of the Tripoli War of 1801–1804, see Reid, *Intrepid Sailors*.

12. Henry Wadsworth journal, NDBP, 2:273–74.

13. Samuel Smith to Richard Morris, April 26, 1803, NDBP, 2:396.

14. Samuel Smith to Edward Preble, May 13, 1803, in Papers of Edward Preble, Library of Congress, Manuscript Division [hereafter EPP].

15. Charles Morris, *Autobiography of Commodore Charles Morris, U.S. Navy* (Annapolis, Md.: Naval Institute Press, 2002), 14.

16. Edward Preble to Mary Preble, June 16, 1803, EPP.

17. Ibid.

18. Edward Preble Diary, September 14, 1803, EPP.

19. Edward Preble to Robert Smith, September 18, 1803, EPP.

20. Edward Preble to William Bainbridge, September 16, 1803, EPP.

21. Edward Preble Diary, January 23, 1804, EPP.

22. Anthony Irvin, *Decatur* (New York: Charles Scribner's Sons, 1931), 112; A. B. C. Whipple, *To the Shores of Tripoli: The Birth of the U.S. Navy and Marines* (Annapolis, Md.: Naval Institute Press, 1991), 131.

23. Logbook of the USS *Constitution*, January 30, 1804, EPP.

24. Robert Smith to Thomas Jefferson, November 13, 1804, NDBP, 3:423–24.

25. See Reid, *Intrepid Sailors*, chaps. 10–11.

26. Ibid.

27. Edward Preble to Robert Smith, September 18, 1804, EPP.

28. Ibid.

29. Ibid.

30. Noadiah Morris to unnamed recipient, September 7, 1804, NDBP, 4:355.

31. Stephen Decatur to Keith Spence, January 9, 1804, NDBP, 4:346.

32. Bonaventure Beaussier to Edward Preble, August 4, 1804, EPP.

33. Preble to Smith, September 18, 1804, EPP.

34. Ibid.

35. Isaac Hull to Edward Preble, August 7, 1804, EPP.

36. James Fenimore Cooper, *History of the Navy of the United States* (New York: Lea and Blanchard, 1840), 1:394–95.

37. Preble to Smith, September 18, 1804, EPP; Cooper, *History of the Navy,* 1:395.

38. Jonathan Cowdery, *American Captives in Tripoli* (Boston: Belcher & Armstrong, 1806), 10.

39. Reports of gunboat commanders, August 28, 1804, EPP.

40. Darby Journal, August 28, 1804, NDBP, 4:475–76.

41. Beaussier to Preble, August 4, 1804.

42. Ibid.

43. Preble to Smith, September 18, 1804.

44. Cowdery, *American Captives,* 15.

45. Ibid.

CHAPTER 5. DUNGEONS AND DIPLOMACY

1. Thomas Harris, *The Life and Services of Commodore William Bainbridge* (Philadelphia: Carey Lea & Blanchard, 1837) [hereafter Harris, *William Bainbridge*], 18–21.
2. John Rea, *A Letter to William Bainbridge, Esq., formerly Commander of the United States Ship* George Washington (Philadelphia, 1802), 16.
3. Ibid.
4. William Bainbridge to George Davis, October 31, 1804, NDBP, 5:83.
5. Nicholas Nissen to George Davis, September 30, 1804, NDBP, 5:58.
6. James Renshaw to John Rodgers, October 15, 1804, NDBP, 5:87.
7. Bonaventure Beaussier to Edward Preble, August 6, 1804, NDBP, 4:382.
8. Bonaventure Beaussier to Edward Preble, August 29, 1804, NDBP, 4:482.
9. Folayan, *Tripoli under Qaramanli*, 38–41; Rossi, *Storia de Tripoli*, 211–14.
10. Beaussier to Preble, August 29, 1804.
11. William Eaton to Timothy Pickering, May 25, 1800, WEP.
12. William Eaton to John Marshall, June 28, 1801, WEP.
13. Eaton to Pickering, May 25, 1800.
14. William Eaton to Timothy Pickering, May 11, 1800, WEP.
15. William Eaton to John C. Smith, February 23, 1804; Prentiss, *General Eaton*, 247.
16. Eaton to Pickering, May 11, 1800.
17. William Eaton Journal, January, October 6,1801, WEP.
18. William Eaton to James Madison, August 23, 1802, WEP.
19. Ibid.
20. William Eaton to James Madison, October 22, 1802, WEP.
21. William Eaton to Eliza Eaton, August 15, 1800, WEP.
22. William Eaton to Timothy Pickering, July 21, 1800, Timothy Pickering Papers, vol. 26, Massachusetts Historical Society, Boston.
23. Ibid.
24. Eaton to Eliza Eaton, August 15, 1800.
25. Tucker, *Dawn Like Thunder*, 228–29; Folayan, *Tripoli under Qaramanli*, 38–39; Whipple, *To the Shores of Tripoli*, 180–81; Al-Tawil, *Tripoli and the West*, 133–34.
26. Tucker, *Dawn Like Thunder*, 229.

27. Treaty of Amity and Peace between the United States and Tripoli, in *American State Papers: Foreign Relations*, vol. 2, *1797–1807* (Washington, D.C.: Gales and Seaton, 1833), 697.

28. William Eaton to James Madison, August 19, 1802, WEP.

29. Ibid.

30. William Eaton to James Madison, September 5, 1801, WEP.

31. William Eaton to Samuel Barron or William Bainbridge, September 2, 1801, NDBP, 2:567.

32. William Eaton, Deposition to Congress, February 29, 1804, in *American State Papers: Claims*, vol. 1, *1789–1809*, Documents: Legislative and Executive of the Congress of the United States (Washington, D.C.: Gales and Seaton, 1834) [hereafter ASP Claims], 301.

33. Ibid.

34. Ibid., 1:302; William Eaton to Daniel McNeill, March 24, 1802, NDBP, 2:95.

35. William Eaton circular, March 23, 1802, NDBP, 2:97.

36. Alexander Murray to William Eaton, May 6, 1802, NDBP, 2:145.

37. William Eaton to James Madison, August 9, 1802, WEP.

38. Eaton to Madison, August 23, 1802.

39. William Eaton to James Madison, June 8, 1802, WEP.

40. Ibid.

41. William Eaton affidavit, November 27, 1805, ASP Claims, 1:324.

42. Ibid.

43. Report of the Committee of Claims on the Memorial of Daniel Cotton, February 19, 1807, ASP Claims, 1:337–38.

44. William Eaton affidavit, March 10, 1804, ASP Claims, 1:338

45. Affidavit of Richard V. Morris, Court Martial Proceedings of Richard Morris, RG 45, microfilm M87, NARA.

46. Ibid.

47. Ibid.

CHAPTER 6. GATHERING STORM

1. William Eaton to Robert Smith, August 12, 1804, NDBP, 5:35.

2. Charles Morris Journal, December 8, 1804, NDBP, 5:179.

3. William Eaton Journal, August 12, 1804, WEP; John Rodgers Journal, August 11, 1804, NDBP, 4:403.

4. William Eaton to Robert Smith, September 18, 1804, WEP.

5. Cooper, *History of the Navy*, 1:245.

6. Cowdery, *American Captives*, 15.

7. Ibid.

8. Tully, *Narrative*, 1:214.

9. Cowdery, *American Captives*, 16.

10. Ibid., 18.

11. William Ray, *Horrors of Slavery, or The American Tars in Tripoli* (Troy, N.Y.: Oliver Lyon, 1808), 142.

12. Cowdery, *American Captives*, 19–20.

13. Ibid., 20.

14. Ray, *Horrors of Slavery*, 142.

15. Christopher McKee, *Edward Preble: A Naval Biography* (Annapolis, Md.: Naval Institute Press, 1972), 308.

16. Edward Preble to Mary Preble, September 9, 1804, EPP.

17. Edward Preble to Samuel Barron, September 10, 1804, and Edward Preble to John Dent, September 7, 1804, EPP.

18. Samuel Barron to Edward Preble, September 10, 1804, EPP; Logbook of the USS *John Adams*, September 15, 1804, NDBP, 5.

19. Logbook of the USS *Constitution*, September 12, 1804, EPP.

20. Samuel Barron to Edward Preble, September 14, 1804, EPP.

21. Charles Oscar Paullin, *Commodore John Rodgers: Captain, Commodore and Senior Officer of the American Navy, 1773–1838* (Annapolis, Md.: Naval Institute Press, 1972), 18.

22. *Federal Gazette and Baltimore Daily Advertiser*, October 23, 1794; September 23, 1795; October 1, 1796.

23. Paullin, *Commodore John Rodgers*, 27.

24. *Federal Gazette and Baltimore Daily Advertiser*, September 5, 1796.

25. Benjamin Stoddert to John Adams, October 17, 1798, in Dudley W. Knox et al., eds., *Naval Documents Related to the Quasi-War between the United States and France* (Washington, D.C.: GPO, 1935) [hereafter NDQW], 1:542–43.

26. Thomas Truxtun to Simon Gross, August 30, 1797, NDQW, 1:13.
27. Benjamin Stoddert to Thomas Truxtun, December 18, 1798, NDQW, 2:93–94.
28. Thomas Truxtun to Samuel Barron, January 28, 1799, NDQW, 2:288.
29. Thomas Truxtun to Benjamin Stoddert, February 10, 1799, NDQW, 2:330.
30. Ibid.
31. John Rodgers to Benjamin Stoddert, February 15, 1799, NDQW, 2:336.
32. Ibid.
33. Truxtun to Stoddert, February 10, 1799; Andrew Sterrett to Charles Sterrett, February 14, 1799, NDQW, 2:335.
34. Andrew Sterrett to Charles Sterrett, February 14, 1799, NDQW, 2:337.
35. Benjamin Stoddert to John Rodgers, June 13, 1799, NDQW, 3:335.
36. Paullin, *Commodore John Rodgers*, 56–60.
37. John Rodgers to Benjamin Stoddert, September 20, 1800 (three separate reports of same date), NDQW, 6:364–67.
38. An Act providing for a Naval peace establishment and for other purposes, March 3, 1801, *Public Statutes at Large of the United States of America*, Richard Peters, ed. (Boston: Charles C. Little and James Brown, 1845), 2:110–111
39. Robert Smith to John Rodgers, October 22, 1801, NDQW, 7:292.
40. Ray Brighton, *The Checkered Career of Tobias Lear* (Portsmouth, N.H.: Portsmouth Marine Society, 1985), 62–66.
41. Paullin, *Commodore John Rodgers*, 79–80.
42. Robert Smith to Richard V. Morris, April 20, 1802, NDBP, 2:131.
43. Robert Smith to John Rodgers, August 25, 1802, NDBP, 2:250.
44. William Eaton to Hamet Karamanli, February 23, 1803, WEP.
45. Alexander Murray to William Eaton, May 6, 1802, NDBP, 2:145.
46. James Leander Cathcart Journal, February 26, 1803, in Cathcart, *Tripoli*.
47. Ibid.
48. Richard Farquhar to Thomas Jefferson, November 15, 1803, NDBP, 3:222.
49. Affidavit of Said Ahmed Gurgi, February 20, 1803, NDBP 2:363.
50. Salvatore Bufutil to Edward Preble, January 22, 1803, NDBP, 3:352.

51. Edward Preble to Robert Smith, January 22, 1804, EPP.
52. Logbook of the USS *Constitution*, September 15, 1804, EPP.
53. Farquhar to Jefferson, November 15, 1803.
54. Joseph Pulis to Edward Preble, November 26, 1803, NDBP 3:236.
55. Salvatore Bufutil to Edward Preble, January 4, 1804, NDBP, 3:314.

CHAPTER 7. PLANNING STAGE
1. Richard V. Morris to James Leander Cathcart, March 28, 1803, NDBP, 2:378.
2. William Eaton to U.S. House of Representatives, February 16, 1804, ASP Claims, 1:306.
3. Ibid., 1:302.
4. Ibid., 1:301–306.
5. William Eaton Journal, July 16, 1804, WEP.
6. Eaton to House of Representatives, February 16, 1804, 1:303–304.
7. Ibid.
8. Ibid., 1:304.
9. Ibid.
10. *American State Papers: Finance* (Washington, D.C.: Gales and Seaton, 1832) [hereafter ASP Finance], 8th Congress, 1st Session, 1:47–48.
11. Ibid., 1:50–51.
12. ASP Finance, 9th Congress, 1st Session, 2:158.
13. William Eaton to Thomas Dwight, July 22, 1804, WEP.
14. Ibid.
15. Eaton to House of Representatives, February 16, 1804, 1:303–304.
16. William Eaton Journal, March 30, 1804, WEP.
17. Eaton to Dwight, July 22, 1804.
18. Whipple, *To the Shores of Tripoli*, 123–24.
19. James Madison, Circular, April 12, 1804, in *The Papers of James Madison, Digital Edition*, ed. J. C. A. Skagg (Charlottesville: University of Virginia Press, 2010) [hereafter *Madison Papers*].
20. Eaton to Dwight, July 22, 1804.
21. James Madison to Cotton Smith, February 27, 1814; James Madison to Richard Harrison, January 10, 1804; Richard Harrison to James Madison, January 19, 1804; all *Madison Papers*.

22. Robert Smith to William Eaton, May 26, 1804, NDBP, 4:120.
23. Eaton to Dwight, July 22, 1804.
24. George Davis to Edward Preble, May 12, 1804, NDBP, 4:109; Tobias Lear to Edward Preble, June 8, 1804, NDBP, 4:164.
25. John Rodgers to Robert Smith, August 12, 1804, NDBP, 4:403.
26. George Davis to William Bainbridge, May 27, 1804, NDBP, 4:122.
27. Rodgers to Smith, August 12, 1804.
28. Robert Smith to Samuel Barron, June 7, 1804, NDBP, 4:136.
29. John Rodgers to Robert Smith, August 30, 1804, NDBP, 4:487.
30. Robert Smith to Isaac Chauncey, April 21, 1804, NDBP, 4:89; Edward Preble to Isaac Chauncey, August 5, 1804, EPP.
31. Samuel Barron to Edward Preble, September 10, 1804, EPP.
32. William Eaton Journal, August 21, 1804, WEP.
33. William Eaton to Robert Smith, September 18, 1804, WEP.
34. William Eaton to Robert Smith, September 6, 1804, WEP.
35. Eaton to Smith, September 18, 1804.
36. Samuel Barron to John Rodgers, September 23, 1804, NDBP, 5:46.
37. Edward Preble to Thomas Robinson, September 5, 1804; Edward Preble to Isaac Chauncey, September 5, 1804; Edward Preble to Stephen Decatur Jr., September 6, 1804; Edward Preble to Charles Stewart, September 6, 1804, all EPP. Robert Smith to Archibald Bullock, July 7, 1804, NDBP, 4:253; Barron to Rodgers, September 23, 1804.
38. Robert Smith to Samuel Barron, June 6, 1804, NDBP, 4:152–53.

CHAPTER 8. WASHINGTON INSIDER
1. Brighton, *Checkered Career*, 172.
2. Ibid., 17–30.
3. Ibid., 36–37.
4. Ibid.
5. Ibid., 48–50.
6. Ibid., 37.
7. Ibid., 37–40.
8. Ibid.
9. Ibid., 128.

10. Ibid., 105.

11. Ibid., 91–93, 11–113.

12. Ibid., 110; George Washington, *The Papers of George Washington*, ed. Donald Jackson et al. (Charlottesville: University of Virginia Press, 1976–78) [hereafter GWP], *Diaries*, August 18, 1789, 3:172.

13. Brighton, *Checkered Career*, 137.

14. Jeff Dickey, *Empire of Mud: The Secret History of Washington DC* (Guilford, Conn.: Globe Pequot, 2014), 4–8.

15. Agreement between James Greenleaf and Rocquiette, Elzevier, and Beeldemaker, August 15, 1794, in Charles E. Sigety Collection, New York.

16. Dickey, *Empire of Mud*.

17. GWP, 34:305.

18. George Washington to Tobias Lear, March 27, 1798, GWP, 3:237.

19. See Tobias Lear, *The Last Words of General Washington: A Circumstantial Account of the Illness and Death of George Washington* (Philadelphia, 1800), for a full account of Washington's death.

20. Thomas Jefferson to Filippo Mazzei, April 24, 1796, in Papers of Thomas Jefferson, LOC, Manuscript Division, Series 1, General Correspondence, 1629–1827 [hereafter TJP].

21. Ibid.

22. Thomas Jefferson to Joel Barlow, May 2, 1800, TJP.

23. Brighton, *Checkered Career*, 172–75.

24. Ibid.

25. Ibid.

26. Brighton, *Checkered Career*, 177.

27. Tobias Lear, Claim to Congress, ASP Claims, 7th Congress, 2nd Session, 274–76.

28. Brighton, *Checkered Career*, 182–87.

29. Lear, Claim to Congress, ASP Claims, 274–76.

30. Ibid., 190.

31. *American and Commercial Daily Advertiser*, March 4, 1802.

32. Brighton, *Checkered Career*, 192; Paullin, *Commodore John Rodgers*, 80.

33. Lear, Claim to Congress, ASP Claims, 274–76.

34. *Annals of Congress, Senate Journal,* 7th Congress, 2nd Session, 102.

35. Brighton, *Checkered Career,* 188.

36. Thomas Jefferson to Tobias Lear, June 14, 1802, TJP.

37. Brighton, *Checkered Career,* 196–200.

38. Ibid.

39. See Reid, *Intrepid Sailors,* chap. 7.

40. Tobias Lear to Edward Preble, March 23, 1804, NDBP, 3:517.

41. See Reid, *Intrepid Sailors,* chap. 15.

42. Lear to Preble, March 23, 1804.

43. See Reid, *Intrepid Sailors,* chap. 16.

44. James Leander Cathcart to Edward Preble, June 11, 1804, EPP.

45. Tobias Lear to William Bainbridge, August 24, 1804, NDBP, 4:321.

46. James Madison to Tobias Lear, June 6, 1804, NDBP, 4:155.

47. Ibid.

48. Tobias Lear to Samuel Barron, July 30, 1804, Barron Family Papers (I), Special Collections Division, Swem Library, College of William and Mary, Williamsburg, Va. [hereafter SBP(I)].

49. Tobias Lear to Edward Preble, July 30, 1804, EPP.

CHAPTER 9. BACKROOM POLITICS

1. Bruce Grant, *The Life and Fighting Times of Commodore Isaac Hull* (Chicago: Pellegrini and Cudahy, 1947) [hereafter Grant, *Isaac Hull*], 117.

2. John Frost, ed., *American Naval Biography, Comprising Lives of the Commodores and Other Commanders Distinguished in the History of the United States Navy* (Philadelphia: E. H. Butler, 1844), 232

3. Samuel Barron to Isaac Hull, September 13, 1804, NDBP, 5:19–20.

4. Samuel Barron to Isaac Hull, September 15, 1804, NDBP, 5:20.

5. Ibid.

6. Ibid.

7. Ibid.

8. There is no mention in any of Hull's personal papers of his mission with Eaton, in his published papers (*The Papers of Isaac Hull,* ed. Gardner W. Allen [Boston: Athenaeum, 1929]), or in his unpublished papers at the Massachusetts Historical Society.

9. Grant, *Isaac Hull*, 120–21.

10. Crew list of the *Philadelphia*, NDBP, 3:184–89.

11. Cowdery, *American Captives*, 16; Ray, *Horrors of Slavery*, 138.

12. Ray, *Horrors of Slavery*, 149.

13. Ibid., 150.

14. Ibid.

15. Harris, *William Bainbridge*, 116.

16. George Davis to William Bainbridge, September 9, 1804, NDBP, 5:13.

17. Tobias Lear to William Bainbridge, August 28, 1804, NDBP, 4:471–72.

18. Nicholas Nissen to George Davis, September 30, 1804, NDBP, 5:59.

19. Tobias Lear to William Bainbridge, September 15, 1804, NDBP, 5:23.

20. William Bainbridge to George Davis, October 14, 1804, NDBP, 5:83.

21. Ibid.

22. Ibid.

23. George Davis to James Madison, September 25, 1804, NDBP, 5:52.

24. Cowdery, *American Captives*, 18.

25. Ibid.

26. Samuel Barron to John Rodgers, September 23, 1804, SBP(I).

27. Tobias Lear to John Rodgers, October 16, 1804, NDBP, 5:88.

28. Edward Preble to Stephen Decatur, September 24, 1804, EPP.

29. Edward Preble to Samuel Barron, September 17, 1804; Samuel Barron to Edward Preble, September 17, 1804; both EPP.

30. Hugh Campbell to Samuel Barron, October 24, 1804, NDBP, 5:96.

31. Edward Preble Diary, October 28, 1804, EPP.

32. John Rodgers to Edward Preble, undated, Rodgers Family Papers, LOC, Manuscript Division.

33. John Rodgers to Robert Smith, November 6, 1804, NDBP, 5:124.

34. William Eaton to Robert Smith, September 27, 1804, WEP.

35. William Eaton to Robert Smith, September 6, 1804, WEP.

36. Ibid.

37. William Eaton to Thomas Dwight, September 20, 1804, WEP.

38. Alexander Ball to Edward Preble, September 20, 1804, EPP.

39. William Eaton Journal, September 30, 1804.

40. Morris, *Autobiography*, 37.

41. William Eaton Journal, October 1, 1804.
42. Edward Preble to Samuel Barron, October 8, 1804, EPP.
43. William Eaton Journal, October 3, 1804.
44. Ibid., October 27–November 10, 1804.

CHAPTER 10. PLANS IN MOTION

1. William Bainbridge to Tobias Lear, November 7, 1804, NDBP, 5:137.
2. William Eaton to James Leander Cathcart, September 7, 1804, WEP.
3. Richard Farquhar to Samuel Barron, October 15, 1804, NDBP, 5:85.
4. Ibid.
5. Richard Farquhar to Samuel Barron, October 21, 1804, NDBP, 5:94.
6. Salvatore Bufutil to Samuel Barron, October 21, 1804, NDBP, 5:95.
7. Ibid.
8. Ibid.
9. William Eaton Journal, November 3, 1804, WEP; Tobias Lear to Samuel Barron, December 6, 1804, SBP.
10. Tobias Lear to James Madison, November 5, 1804, NDBP, 5:116.
11. Samuel Barron to Tobias Lear, November 13, 1804, NDBP, 5:139.
12. Brighton, *Checkered Career*, 211–12.
13. Ibid., 221.
14. Samuel Barron to John Rodgers, November 12, 1804, NDBP, 5:139.
15. William Ward Burrows to Robert Smith, July 18, 1803, Records of the Office of the Commandant of the Marine Corps [hereafter MCR], Letters Sent, Series 1, vol. 2, RG 127, NARA.
16. John Hall to William Ward Burrows, November 1, 1804, MCR, Series 8.
17. William Eaton to Robert Smith, November 13, 1804, WEP.
18. Ibid.
19. Ibid.
20. Eugene Tognotti, "Lessons from the History of Quarantine, from Plague to Influenza A," *Emerging Infectious Diseases*, no. 2 (February 2013 (Atlanta, Ga.: Centers for Disease Control), 19.
21. Edward Preble to Alexander Ball, November 14, 1804, EPP. William Eaton to Alexander Ball, November 16, 1804, NDBP, 5:144–145; Alexander Ball to William Eaton, November 16, 1804; both NDBP, 5:145.

22. William Eaton to Samuel Barron, November 17, 1804, WEP.

23. Isaac Hull Journal, November 25, 1804, NDBP, 5:135.

24. Midshipman Charles Morris Journal, extracts in NDBP, 5:140–58.

25. Edward Preble, General Orders, August 3, 1804, EPP.

26. Numerous letters from Marine officers describe shipboard duty; see MCR, Series 8.

27. Court-martial of William Johnson, NDBP, 5:158–59.

28. William Amory to William Ward Burrows, July 8, 1804, MCR, Series 8.

29. Hezekiah Loomis, *Journal of Hezekiah Loomis, Steward on the U.S. Brig Vixen under Capt. John Smith USN during the War with Tripoli, 1804*, ed. Frank Middleton (Salem, Mass.: Essex Institute, 1928), 58.

30. Cowdery, *American Captives*, 19.

31. Rossi, *Storia de Tripoli*, 266.

32. Cowdery, *American Captives*, 19–20.

33. Ibid., 20.

34. James Renshaw to John Rodgers, November 6, 1804, NDBP, 5:124.

35. Ray, *Horrors of Slavery*, 142–43.

36. Bainbridge to Lear, November 7, 1804, 136.

37. Ibid., 136–37.

38. Ibid., 137.

39. Ibid.

40. Ibid.

CHAPTER 11. INTO EGYPT

1. Isaac Hull Journal, November 26–27, 1804, NDBP, 5:159.

2. William Eaton Journal, November 25–27, 1804, WEP.

3. Samuel Briggs to Isaac Hull, November 26, 1804, NDBP, 5:161.

4. William Eaton Journal, November 27, 1804, WEP.

5. William Eaton to Robert Smith, November 28, 1804, NDBP, 5:167.

6. William Eaton to Isaac Hull, December 2, 1804, WEP.

7. William Eaton to Robert Smith, December 8, 1804, WEP.

8. William Eaton Journal, December 2, 1804, WEP.

9. Eaton to Hull, December 2, 1804.

10. Eaton to Smith, December 8, 1804.

11. Eaton to Hull, December 2, 1804.

12. William Eaton to Hamet Karamanli, December 2, 1804, WEP.

13. Angelo S. Rappoport, *History of Egypt: From 330 B.C. to the Present Time* (London: Grolier Society, 1904), 3:82–90.

14. Ali Bey, *Travels of Ali Bey in Morocco, Tripoli, Cyprus, Egypt, Arabia, Syria and Turkey* (Philadelphia: James Maxwell, 1815), 1:333–34.

15. Ibid.

16. Afaf Lufti Al-Sayyid Marsot, *A Short History of Modern Egypt* (Cambridge: Cambridge University Press, 1985), 26–60.

17. Arthur E. P. Brome Weigall, *A History of Egypt from 1798 to 1914* (London: William Blackwood and Sons, 1915), 4–54; Marsot, *Modern Egypt*, 26–60.

18. Andrew A. Paton, *A History of the Egyptian Revolution: From the Mamelukes to Mohammed Ali; From Arab and European memoirs, oral tradition, and local research* (London: Trubner, 1870), 2:4–11.

19. Samuel Barron to John Rodgers, November 27, 1804, NDBP, 5:163–64.

20. Logbook of U.S. Schooner *Vixen*, November 30, 1804, NDBP, 5:170.

21. Ray, *Horrors of Slavery*, 150.

22. Ibid., 150–51.

23. Ibid., 151.

24. William Eaton to Robert Smith, December 15, 1804, WEP.

25. Ibid.

26. Ibid.

27. William Eaton Journal, December 7, 1804, WEP.

28. Eaton to Smith, December 15, 1804.

29. Ali Bey, *Travels*, 2:16.

30. Ibid., 2:17.

31. Eaton to Smith, December 15, 1804.

32. Ibid.

33. Paton, *Egyptian Revolution*, 2:14–33.

34. Ali Bey, *Travels*, 1:363–67; Paton, *Egyptian Revolution*, 2:14–33.

35. Eaton to Smith, December 15, 1804.

36. Ibid.

37. Ibid.

38. William Eaton to Edward Preble, January 5, 1805, WEP.

39. Eaton to Smith, December 15, 1805.

40. Ibid.

41. Ibid.

42. William Eaton to Hamet Karamanli, December 17, 1804, WEP.

43. Ibid.

44. William Eaton to Isaac Hull, December 17, 1804, NDBP, 5:197.

CHAPTER 12. WAITING GAME

1. John Rodgers to Robert Smith, December 30, 1804, NDBP, 5:226.

2. John Rodgers to William Jarvis, December 27, 1804, NDBP, 5:223.

3. John Rodgers to William Jarvis, January 1, 1805, NDBP, 5:245.

4. William Jarvis to John Rodgers, January 1, 1805, NDBP, 5:246.

5. Rodgers to Jarvis, January 1, 1805, 5:247.

6. William Jarvis to John Rodgers, January 3, 1805, NDBP, 5:250–51.

7. Ibid.

8. Ibid.

9. John Rodgers to William Jarvis, January 4, 1805, NDBP, 5:253.

10. Paullin, *Commodore John Rodgers,* 399–400.

11. See Reid, *Intrepid Sailors,* 18–21.

12. *Annals of Congress: The Debates and Proceedings of the Congress of the United States; With an Appendix, Containing Important State Papers and Public Documents with All the Laws of a Public Nature* (Washington, D.C.: Gales and Seaton, 1852), 8th Congress, 1st Session, 1011–12 [hereafter *Debates and Proceedings*].

13. Paullin, *Commodore John Rodgers,* 399–400.

14. William Jarvis to John Rodgers, January 7, 1805, NDBP, 5:263; John Rodgers to William Jarvis, January 7, 1805, NDBP, 5:264–65.

15. William Jarvis to John Rodgers, January 7, 1805.

16. George Davis to Tobias Lear, January 2, 1805, NDBP, 5:255.

17. Morris, *Autobiography,* 35.

18. Ibid., 34–35.

19. Ray, *Horrors of Slavery,* 152.

20. Isaac Hull to Edward Missett, December 24, 1804, NDBP, 5:215.

21. Isaac Hull to William Eaton, December 24, 1804, NDBP, 5:214–15.

22. Isaac Hull to William Eaton, December 27, 1804, NDBP, 5:222.

23. Isaac Hull to William Eaton, December 31, 1804, NDBP, 5:251–52.

24. William Eaton Journal, December 29, 1804, WEP.

25. Biographical sketch of Jerome Eugene Leitensdorfer, in Meade Min-nigerode, *Lives and Times: Four Informal American Biographies* (New York: G. P. Putnam and Sons, 1925), 75–77.

26. William Eaton to Edward Preble, January 25, 1805, WEP.

27. William Eaton to John Cotton Smith, December 26, 1804, WEP.

28. William Eaton to Isaac Hull, December 30, 1804, NDBP, 5:224.

29. Ibid.

30. Ibid.

31. Hamet Karamanli to William Eaton, January 3, 1805, WEP.

32. Resolution of the Congress of the United States Concerning the Attacks upon Tripoli, March 3, 1805, 8th Congress, 2nd Session, in *Journal of the Senate* (Washington, D.C.: Gales and Seaton, 1821), 3:471.

33. Thomas Jefferson, *The Works of Thomas Jefferson*, ed. Paul Leicester Ford (New York: G. P. Putnam and Sons, 1904), 1:383.

CHAPTER 13. FEARS OF THE UNKNOWN

1. Hamet Karamanli to William Eaton, January 3, 1805, WEP.

2. Najem, *Tribes of Libya*, 183–85.

3. Tucker, *Dawn Like Thunder*, 211.

4. Hamet Karamanli to William Eaton, January 15, 1805, WEP.

5. Ibid.

6. Hamet Karamanli to Signor Mahmud, January 15, 1805, WEP.

7. Isaac Hull to William Eaton, January 8, 1805, NDBP, 5:254.

8. Ibid.

9. Ibid.

10. Ibid.

11. William Eaton to Isaac Hull, December 29, 1804, WEP.

12. William Eaton to Isaac Hull, January 8, 1805, WEP.

13. Tobias Lear to Samuel Barron, December 27, 1804, NDBP, 5:220.
14. Brighton, *Checkered Career,* 240.
15. Lear to Barron, December 27, 1804.
16. Tobias Lear to George Dyson, December 27, 1804, NDBP, 5:221.
17. William Bainbridge to Tobias Lear, January 28, 1805, NDBP, 5:311–12.
18. Ibid.
19. William Bainbridge to George Davis, January 28, 1805, NDBP, 5:312.
20. Brighton, *Checkered Career,* 241–44.
21. Samuel Barron to Tobias Lear, January 15, 1805, NDBP, 5:277.
22. Ibid.
23. William Eaton to Isaac Hull, January 15, 1805, NDBP, 5:279.
24. William Eaton to Isaac Hull, January 9, 1805, NDBP, 5:268.
25. Ibid.
26. William Eaton to Edward Preble, January 25, 1805, WEP.
27. Ibid.
28. Ibid.
29. Ibid.
30. Ibid.
31. Ibid.
32. Hamet Karamanli to William Eaton, January 28, 1805, WEP.
33. Isaac Hull to William Eaton, January 28, 1805, NDBP, 5:317.
34. Ibid.
35. William Eaton to Isaac Hull, January 28, 1805, NDBP, 5:318.
36. William Eaton to Isaac Hull, January 29, 1805, NDBP, 5:319.
37. Ibid., 320–21.
38. Isaac Hull to William Eaton, January 30, 1805, NDBP, 5:322.
39. William Eaton Journal, January 31, 1805, WEP.
40. William Eaton to Isaac Hull, February 6, 1805, NDBP, 5:334.
41. Minnigerode, *Lives and Times,* 80.
42. Isaac Hull to William Eaton, February 6, February 9, February 12, 1805; Joshua Blake to William Eaton, February 13, 1805; Viceroy of Cairo to Hamet Karamanli, February 8, 1805; all NDBP, 5:334–41.
43. William Eaton Journal, February 16, 1805, WEP.

CHAPTER 14. A FEW GOOD MEN

1. William Eaton to Samuel Barron, February 14, 1805, SBP(I).
2. Ibid.
3. Ibid.
4. James Wilkinson to Alexander Hamilton, November 12, 1799, in Alexander Hamilton, *The Papers of Alexander Hamilton,* vol. 24, *November 1799 to June 1800,* ed. Harold C. Syrett (New York: Columbia University Press, 1976), 530–31.
5. *Annals of Congress: Debates and Proceedings,* 5th Congress, 2nd Session, May 28, 1798, 1835–36.
6. Ibid.
7. See multiple letters of William Ward Burrows to Marine Corps officers ordering them to fight the practice of naval commanders using Marines as common sailors, in RG 27, Correspondence of the Office of the Commandant, NARA [hereafter COC], Series 1, vol. 1.
8. President John Adams signed legislation creating the Navy Department on April 29, 1798.
9. *Annals of Congress: Debates and Proceedings,* May 28, 1798, 1835.
10. Ibid.
11. *Annals of Congress: Debates and Proceedings,* June 1, 1798, 1860.
12. *Journal of the Senate,* 5th Congress, 2nd Session, July 6, 1798, 352.
13. Ibid.
14. *Claypoole's American Daily Advertiser,* July 19, 1798.
15. William Ward Burrows to Simon Geddes, January 16, 1800, COC, Series 8.
16. William Ward Burrows to Simon Geddes, February 19, February 21, 1800; Burrows to Benjamin Stoddert, February 21, February 25, 1800; all COC, vol. 1, Series 3.
17. Benjamin Strother to William Ward Burrows, February 24, 1800, COC, Series 8.
18. Daniel Carmick to William Burrows, August 18, 1799, NDQW, 4:91.
19. Letters from Marine officers abound with complaints of Navy officers detailing Marines for duties the Marine officers believed were out of bounds. Daniel Carmick told Burrows in a letter dated May 21, 1799,

"I find it impossible to keep my men clean" due to the extra duties Alexander Murray, his commander, assigned them.

20. *Annals of Congress: Statutes at Large,* 5th Congress, 2nd Session, 595.

21. Wilkinson to Hamilton, November 12, 1799.

22. William Burrows to Henry Geddes, March 26, 1800, NDQW, 4:356.

23. *Annals of Congress: Statutes at Large,* 23rd Congress, 1st Session, June 30, 1834, 713.

24. Trudy J. Sundberg and John K. Gott, *Valiant Virginian: The Story of Presley Neville O'Bannon, 1776–1850, First Lieutenant, U.S. Marine Corps, 1801–1807* (Westminster, Md.: Heritage Books, 2007), 2–3.

25. Ibid., 14–19.

26. Petition of Joseph Blackwell, Legislative Petitions of the General Assembly, 1776–1865, Virginia State Archives, Accession no. 36121, box 72, folder 63.

27. Sundberg and Gott, *Valiant Virginian,* 41–42.

28. Franklin Wharton to Robert Smith, April 20, 1805, COC, Series 1, vol. 3.

29. Order Book of Franklin Wharton, August 31, 1804, Marine Corps Archives, Quantico, Va.

30. Presley O'Bannon to William Ward Burrows, January 4, 1802, COC, Series 8.

31. Presley O'Bannon to William Ward Burrows, January 22, 1802; February 10, 1802; both COC, Series 8.

32. O'Bannon to Burrows, January 4, 1802.

33. O'Bannon to Burrows, January 22, 1802.

34. Presley O'Bannon to William Ward Burrows, September 10, 1802, COC, Series 8.

35. Daniel Carmick to William Ward Burrows, August 10, 1802, COC, Series 8.

36. Ibid.

37. William Ward Burrows to Presley O'Bannon, October 2, 1802, COC, Series 1, vol. 2.

38. Presley O'Bannon to William Ward Burrows, December 15, 1802, COC, Series 8.

39. Ibid.

40. Hugh Campbell to William Ward Burrows, December 16, 1802, NDBP, 3:335.
41. Ibid.
42. Henry Wadsworth Journal, June 3, 1802, NDBP, 2:435.
43. Ibid., 2:436.
44. Ibid.
45. Ibid.
46. Ibid.
47. Court-Martial Proceedings of Richard V. Morris, NDBP, 2:530.
48. Edward Preble to Robert Smith, September 18, 1804, EPP.
49. Isaac Hull to William Eaton, December 16, 1804, NDBP, 5:196.
50. Franklin Wharton to Robert Smith, October 31, 1804, COC, Series 1, vol. 3.
51. Marine Corps Muster Rolls, USS *Constitution*, January 1, 1805, and USS *President*, January 1, 1805, RG 127, T1118, NARA.
52. Marine Corps Muster Roll, USS *Constitution*, May 30, 1803, ibid.
53. William Ward Burrows to James Weaver, September 27, 1798, COC, Series 1, vol. 1.
54. Franklin Wharton to Newton Keene, March 20, 1804, COC, Series 1, vol. 3.
55. Burrows to Weaver, September 27, 1798.
56. William Ward Burrows, Circular, August 20, 1798, COC, Series 1, vol. 1.
57. Commandant William Ward Burrows to Newtown Keene, March 5, 1800, COC, Series 1, vol. 2.
58. Franklin Wharton to Daniel Carmick, August 28, 1804, COC, Series 1, vol. 3.
59. Burrows, Circular, August 20, 1798.
60. Marine Pay Roll, USS *Argus*, RG 127, NARA.

CHAPTER 15. AN ARMY GROWS IN THE DESERT
1. James Laird Patterson, *Journal of a Tour in Egypt, Palestine, Syria and Greece* (London: C. Dolman, 1852), 32.
2. Isaac Hull to Richard Farquhar, February 13, 1805, NDBP, 5:352.
3. Tucker, *Dawn Like Thunder*, 308.

4. Patterson, *Tour in Egypt*, 35.
5. William Eaton Journal, March 3, 1805, WEP.
6. Richard Farquhar to Isaac Hull, February 12, 1805, NDBP, 5:352.
7. Hull to Farquhar, February 13, 1805.
8. Muster roll of men engaged for the Service of the United States under William Eaton, NDBP, 5:382.
9. Ibid.
10. William Eaton Journal, February 19, 1805, WEP.
11. Najem, *Tribes of Libya*, 131–32.
12. Eaton Journal, March 3, 1805.
13. William Eaton to Samuel Barron, February 14, 1805, SBP(I).
14. Convention between the United States and His Highness, Hamet Caramanli, Bashaw of Tripoli, WEP [hereafter Convention].
15. William Eaton to Samuel Barron, April 28, 1805, WEP.
16. Convention.
17. William Eaton Journal, March 10, 1805, WEP.
18. Convention.
19. Eaton to Barron, February 14, 1805.
20. William Eaton Journal, March 2, 1805, WEP.
21. Ibid.
22. Eaton to Barron, February 14, 1805.
23. Rossi, *Storia di Tripoli*, 265–66.
24. Cowdery, *American Captives*, 6, 7–8, 13–15; Najem, *Tribes of Libya*, 135.
25. Ray, *Horrors of Slavery*, 156.
26. Ibid.
27. Ray, *Horrors of Slavery*, 149–51; Cowdery, *American Captives*, 9–10.
28. Ray, *Horrors of Slavery*, 155.
29. Cowdery, *American Captives*, 10.
30. Folayan, *Tripoli under Qaramanli*, 35–36.
31. Ray, *Horrors of Slavery*, 156–57.
32. George Dyson to Edward Preble, March 20, 1805, EPP.
33. Tobias Lear to George Davis, March 6, 1805, NDBP, 5:393.
34. Samuel Barron to John Rodgers, February 28, 1805, SBP(I).
35. Samuel Barron, Instructions to Captains, February 28, 1805, SBP(I).

36. Samuel Barron to John Rodgers, February 28, 1805 (second letter of same date), SBP(I).
37. Ibid.
38. Ibid.
39. Briggs Brothers Co. to Samuel Barron, March 11, 1805, NDBP, 5:408.
40. Ibid.
41. See Tobias Lear to George Davis, William Jarvis, James Simpson, George Dyson, et al., NDBP, vols. 4 and 5.
42. Brighton, *Checkered Career*, 235–37.
43. William Bainbridge to Samuel Barron, March 16, 1805, NDBP, 5:419.
44. John Rodgers to William Bainbridge, March 1, 1805, NDBP, 5:380.
45. Brighton, *Checkered Career*, 242–43.
46. Samuel Barron to William Eaton, March 22, 1805, SBP(I).
47. Ibid.
48. Barron to Eaton, March 22, 1805.
49. Ibid.
50. Ibid.
51. Ibid.
52. Ibid.
53. Ibid.

CHAPTER 16. THE ROAD TO DERNE

1. Marine Corps Muster Roll, USS *Argus*.
2. Newton Keene to William Ward Burrows, May 10, 1803, COC, Letters Received. Keene never mentioned Campbell by name, but his recruiting returns indicate that many of the men he enlisted were Royal Navy or Royal Marine veterans.
3. Ibid.
4. Keene to Burrows, May 10, 1803; Joseph Tarbell to William Ward Burrows, May 8, 1803, COC, Letters Received.
5. Edward Preble to Robert Smith, June 26, 1803, EPP.
6. Robert Smith to Edward Preble, July 5, 1803, EPP.
7. Edward Preble to Robert Smith, July 5, 1803, EPP.
8. Franklin Wharton to Henry Caldwell, March 22, 1804, COC, Series 3, vol. 3.

9. Edward Preble to Robert Smith, July 16, 1805, EPP.
10. Marine Corps Muster Roll, USS *Argus*.
11. See Reid, *Intrepid Sailors*.
12. William Ward Burrows, Circular, July 15, 1798, COC, Series 3, vol. 1.
13. Marine Corps Muster Roll, USS *Argus*.
14. Sundberg and Gott, *Valiant Virginian*, 12–14.
15. Ibid.
16. Robert W. Goldsborough, Return of Goods Provided and Monies Paid to the U.S. Marines on the U.S. Brig of War *Argus*, RG 45, T1118, NARA.
17. William Eaton Journal, March 6, 1805, WEP.
18. Johan Martin Augustine Scholz, *Travels in the Countries Between Alexandria and Paratorium, the Lybian Desert, Siwa, Egypt and Syria, 1821* (London: Sire Richard Phillips, 1822), 18.
19. Paolo Della Cella, *Narrative of an Expedition from Tripoli in Barbary to the Western Frontier of Egypt in 1817 by the Bey of Tripoli* (London: John and Arthur Arch, Cornhill, 1822), 183.
20. Ibid., 185–86.
21. William Eaton Journal, March 9–10, 1805, WEP.
22. Scholz, *Travels*, 19–22; Cella, *Narrative*, 184; William Eaton Journal, March 13, 1805, WEP.
23. Eaton Journal, March 13, 1805.
24. Ibid.
25. Bruce Masters, *Christians and Jews in the Ottoman-Arab World: The Roots of Sectarianism* (Cambridge: Cambridge University Press, 2001), 18–23.
26. Ibid.
27. Tucker, *Dawn Like Thunder*, 274–376.
28. Hamet Karamanli to Samuel Barron, February 15, 1805, BFP; Barron to Hamet Karamanli, February 26, 1805, SBP(I).
29. William Eaton Journal, March 13, 1805.
30. William Ward Burrows to Simon W. Geddes, October 26, 1799, COC, Series 1, vol. 1.
31. William Ward Burrows to John Hall, September 27, 1798, COC, Series 1, vol. 1.
32. Paoli Peck to unknown recipient, July 4, 1805, NDBP, 5:362.

33. William Eaton Journal, March 14–17, 1805, WEP.

34. Ibid., March 17, 1805.

35. Ibid., March 18, 1805.

36. Ibid.

37. Ibid., March 19, 1805.

38. Ibid.

39. Ibid.

40. Ibid.

41. List of articles on board the *Argus* and *Hornet*, WEP.

42. Samuel Barron to Isaac Hull, March 23, 1805, SBP(I).

43. Ibid.

44. Ibid.

CHAPTER 17. MARCHES, MUTINIES, AND U.S. MARINES

1. William Eaton Journal, March 22, 1805, WEP.

2. Tucker, *Dawn Like Thunder*, 389–91.

3. Ibid.

4. William Eaton Journal, March 23, 1805, WEP.

5. Ibid., March 22, 1805.

6. Ibid.

7. Ibid., March 26, 1805.

8. Ibid.

9. Ibid.

10. Ibid., March 28, 1805.

11. Ibid., March 29, 1805.

12. Ibid.

13. Ibid., April 1, 1805.

14. Ibid.

15. Ibid.

16. Ibid.

17. Ibid.

18. Ibid.

19. Al-Tawil, *Tripoli and the West*, 103–105.

20. William Eaton Journal, April 3, 1805, WEP.

21. Ibid.

22. Ibid., April 2–8, 1805.

23. Ibid., April 8–16, 1805.

24. Ibid., April 8, 1805.

25. Ibid.

26. Ibid.

27. *Regulations for the Field Exercise, Manoeuvres, and Conduct of the Infantry of the United States; Drawn Up and Adapted to the Organization of the Militia and Regular Troops* (Philadelphia: Fry and Kammerer, 1812) [hereafter *Smyth's Manual*], 5. The cited manual, known as *Smyth's Manual*, was a later derivation of the infantry manual Commandant Franklin Wharton adopted for the Marines instead of the manual the Army used, which was a derivation of the manual of Baron Friedrich von Steuben

28. *Smyth's Manual*, 11–17.

29. Eaton Journal, April 8, 1805.

30. Ibid.

31. Ibid.

32. Ibid.

33. Sundberg and Gott, *Valiant Virginian*, 14. O'Bannon's statement appears in many places, but none cite a source.

34. Eaton Journal, April 8, 1805.

35. Ibid., April 10–12, 1805.

36. Isaac Hull to William Eaton, April 9, 1805, NDBP, 5:494.

37. James Barron to John Rodgers, April 15, 1805, NDBP, 5:504.

38. Samuel Barron to John Dent, April 15, 1805, NDBP, 5:506.

39. John Rodgers to Samuel Barron, March 26, 1805, BFP.

40. Ibid.

41. Barron to Rodgers, April 15, 1805.

42. William Eaton Journal, April 15, 1805, WEP.

43. Ibid.

44. William Eaton to Samuel Barron, April 15, 1805, WEP.

45. Giuseppe Haimann, *Cirenaica*, trans. Chipp Reid (Milan, Italy: Ulrico Hoepli, 1881), 96–99 (author's translation).

46. William Eaton Journal, April 25, 1805, WEP.

CHAPTER 18. BATTLES FOR DERNE

1. Nicholas Nissen to Edward Preble, September 6, 1804, EPP.
2. William Bainbridge to Tobias Lear, April 11, 1805, NDBP, 5:505.
3. Cowdery, *American Captives*, 22
4. Ibid.
5. Ibid.
6. William Bainbridge to Samuel Barron, March 22, 1805, NDBP, 5:484.
7. William Ray, *Horrors of Slavery*, 153.
8. William Bainbridge to Samuel Barron, April 11, 1805, NDBP, 5:506.
9. Ibid.
10. Cella, *Narrative*, 175.
11. Ibid., 175–76.
12. William Eaton Journal, April 25, 1805, WEP.
13. Ibid.
14. William Eaton Journal, April 26, 1805, WEP; John Dent to William Eaton, April 26, 1805, NDBP, 5:542.
15. Presley Neville O'Bannon to Isaac Hull, April 21, 1805, NDBP, 5:528.
16. George Mann to Isaac Hull, April 21, 1805, NDBP, 5:528.
17. William Eaton to Samuel Barron, April 28, 1805, BFP.
18. Tucker, *Dawn Like Thunder*, 378.
19. Samuel Barron to William Eaton, March 22, 1805, BFP; Brighton, *Checkered Career*, 244.
20. John Rodgers to Tobias Lear, April 17, 1805, NDBP, 5:518.
21. Tobias Lear to George Davis, April 24, 1805, NDBP, 5:536.
22. William Lawrence, *Autobiography of Sergeant William Lawrence, a Hero of the Peninsular and Waterloo Campaigns*, ed. George Nugent Banks (London: Sampson Low, Harston, Searle and Rivington, 1886), 108.
23. William Eaton Journal, April 26, 1805, WEP.
24. Isaac Hull to Samuel Barron, April 28, 1805, NDBP, 5:547.
25. Eaton to Barron, April 28, 1805.
26. Hull to Barron, April 28, 1805.
27. Ibid.
28. Eaton to Barron, April 28, 1805.
29. Hull to Barron, April 28, 1805.

30. Eaton to Barron, April 28, 1805.
31. Lawrence, *Autobiography*, 110.
32. Hull to Barron, April 28, 1805.
33. Eaton to Barron, April 28, 1805.
34. Ibid.
35. Eaton to Barron, April 28, 1805.
36. Hull to Barron, April 28, 1805.
37. Eaton to Barron, April 28, 1805.
38. William Eaton Journal, May 2, 1805, WEP.
39. William Eaton Journal, May 8–12, 1805, WEP.
40. Ibid., May 8, 1805.
41. Ibid., May 12, 1805.
42. Ibid.
43. Ibid., May 12–13, 1805.
44. Ibid., May 12, 1805.
45. Isaac Hull to Samuel Barron, April 29, 1805, BFP; Eaton Journal, May 2, 1805.
46. William Eaton to Isaac Hull, May 13, 1805, NDBP, 6:12.
47. William Eaton to Samuel Barron, May 13, 1805, WEP.
48. Virgilio Ilari, Bruno Pauvert, and Piero Crociani, *Il 31e Leggero: Storia di 31e Regiment d'Infantrie, 1799–1815*, trans. Chipp Reid (Milan, 2011), 3–7.
49. Weigall, *History of Egypt*, 50–54.
50. Officers of Artillery and Infantry to William Eaton, May 20, 1805, WEP.
51. William Eaton to Samuel Barron, May 15, 1805, WEP.
52. Eaton to Barron, May 15, 1805. (Eaton dated his letter May 15 but did not send it until May 17, having made several addenda.)
53. William Eaton to Isaac Hull, May 15, 1805, NDBP, 6:18.
54. Eaton to Barron, May 15, 1805.
55. Ibid.

CHAPTER 19. DUPLICITY AND DEALS
1. Cowdery, *American Captives*, 20.
2. George Davis to James Madison, November 19, 1804, *Madison Papers*.

3. USS *Constitution* Journal, April 24, 1805, NDBP, 5:538; John Rodgers to Samuel Barron, April 24, 1805, NDBP, 5:539.

4. Cowdery, *American Captives*, 21.

5. Ibid. The spy likely confused American and British naval vessels, as the Americans often flew the British flag to deceive potential spies or enemies. See Reid, *Intrepid Sailors*.

6. Bonaventure Beaussier to Edward Preble, August 28, 1804, EPP.

7. Samuel Barron to John Rodgers, May 22, 1805, BFP.

8. Barron to Rodgers, May 22, 1805.

9. Tobias Lear to John Rodgers, May 1, 1805, NDBP, 6:1.

10. James Madison to Tobias Lear, June 6, 1804, *Madison Papers*.

11. Lear to Rodgers, May 1, 1805.

12. Tobias Lear Journal, March 25, 1805, quoted in Brighton, *Checkered Career*, 243.

13. Lear to Rodgers, May 1, 1805.

14. Ibid.

15. Barron to Rodgers, May 22, 1805.

16. Samuel Barron to John Rodgers, May 3, 1805, BFP; George Davis to Samuel Barron, May 9, 1805, NDBP, 6:7.

17. Samuel Barron to William Eaton, May 22, 1805, BFP.

18. Brighton, *Checkered Career*, 248.

19. Paul Barron Watson, *The Tragic Career of Commodore James Barron, U.S. Navy* (New York: Coward-McCann, 1942), 19.

20. Samuel Barron to John Rodgers, May 1, 1805, BFP.

21. Ibid.

22. Ibid.

23. Ibid.

24. Ibid.

25. Ibid., 23.

26. Barron to Rodgers, May 22, 1805.

27. Ibid.

28. Samuel Barron to Tobias Lear, May 18, 1805, BFP

29. Ibid.

30. Ibid.

31. George Davis to Tobias Lear, May 19, 1805, NDBP, 6:26.
32. Mustafa Dey to Yusuf Karamanli, May 15, 1805, NDBP, 6:17–18.
33. Brighton, *Checkered Career*, 249.
34. Tobias Lear to Samuel Barron, May 19, 1805, NDBP, 6:24.
35. Brighton, *Checkered Career*, 251.
36. USS *Constitution* Journal, May 26, 1805, NDBP, 6:59.
37. Ibid.
38. Ibid.
39. Ibid.; Brighton, *Checkered Career*, 252.
40. Brighton, *Checkered Career*, 252.
41. Cowdery, *American Captives*, 22.
42. Ray, *Horrors of Slavery*, 160.
43. Brighton, *Checkered Career*, 253.
44. Ibid.
45. Tobias Lear to James Madison, July 5, 1805, NDBP, 6:161.
46. Ibid.
47. Ibid.
48. Ibid.
49. Ibid.
50. Ibid.
51. Ibid.
52. Ibid.
53. Ibid.; Harris, *William Bainbridge*, 124–25.
54. Ray, *Horrors of Slavery*, 163.
55. Ibid.
56. Hunter Miller, ed., *Treaties and Other International Acts of the United States of America* (Washington D.C.: GPO, 1931), 2:529.
57. Despatches from United States Consuls in Tripoli, 1795–1885, RG59, microfilm M466, NARA.

CHAPTER 20. A SAD TRUTH
1. Brighton, *Checkered Career*, 252.
2. Samuel Barron to William Eaton, May 19, 1805, BFP.
3. Ibid.
4. Ibid.

5. William Eaton to Robert Smith, August 6, 1805, WEP.

6. Ibid.

7. Ibid.

8. Whipple, *To the Shores of Tripoli*, 234–35.

9. Sundberg and Gott, *Valiant Virginian*, 23.

10. William Eaton Journal, June 1, 1805, WEP.

11. William Eaton to Samuel Barron, June 1, 1805, WEP (letter sent June 11, 1805).

12. Barron to Eaton, May 19, 1805.

13. Eaton to Barron, June 1, 1805.

14. Ibid.

15. Ibid. (written June 5, 1805).

16. Ibid. (written June 9, 1805).

17. Ibid. (written June 11, 1805).

18. Ibid.

19. William Eaton to Thomas Dwight, June 13, 1805, WEP.

20. John Rodgers to William Eaton, June 5, 1805, NDBP, 6:91.

21. Tobias Lear to William Eaton, June 6, 1805, WEP.

22. William Eaton to John Rodgers, June 13, 1805, WEP.

23. William Eaton to Thomas Dwight, June 6, 1805, WEP.

24. T. E. Lawrence, *Seven Pillars of Wisdom: A Triumph* (Garden City, N.Y.: Doubleday, Doran, 1935), 4:6–18.

25. Eaton to Barron, June 1, 1805.

26. Eaton to Rodgers, June 13, 1805.

27. Ibid.

28. Ibid.

29. Sundberg and Gott, *Valiant Virginian*, 37. A thorough search produced no record of O'Bannon's testifying at either the claims hearing for William Eaton or during any other proceeding involving Eaton.

30. Col. Gerald C. Thomas Jr., "Franklin Wharton," in *Commandants of the Marine Corps*, ed. Allan R. Millett and Jack Shulimson (Annapolis, Md.: Naval Institute Press, 2004), 40–41.

31. Allan R. Millett, *Semper Fidelis: The History of the United States Marine Corps* (New York: Macmillan, 1980), 37.

32. *Annals of Congress*, 8th Congress, 2nd Session, 987–88.

33. Ibid., 988.

34. Ibid., 989.

35. Ibid. The House voted 70–43 to "reduce" the Marine Corps. Also *Journal of the Senate*, 8th Congress, 2nd Session, 472.

36. Gallatin, *Papers of Albert Gallatin*, 272–74.

37. Edwin N. McClellan, *History of the Marine Corps* (Quantico, Va.: Marine Corps History Division, 1925), vol. 1, chap. XVI, 17–19.

38. Robert Smith to Franklin Wharton, July 21, 1804, COC, Series 8, box 6; Franklin Wharton to Daniel Carmick, August 21, 1804, COC, Series 1, vol. 3.

39. *National Intelligencer and Daily Advertiser*, October 9, 1805, 1–2.

40. *Washington Federalist*, September 16, 1805, 1.

41. *National Intelligencer and Daily Advertiser*, September 25, 1805, 4.

42. Millett, *Semper Fidelis*, 40–41.

EPILOGUE

1. See NDBP, 4–6, for numerous letters between diplomats relating to tribute payments.

2. Andre Sobocinski, "The Early Years of Navy Hospitals: From 1804 to Present," February 26, 2014, *Navy Medicine Live*, navymedicine.navy live.dodlive.mil/.

3. *New Hampshire Gazette*, September 3, 1805.

4. Prentiss, *General Eaton*, 406.

5. William Eaton to Samuel Smith, August 5, 1805, WEP.

6. Ibid.

7. Prentiss, *General Eaton*, 480–88.

8. Samuel Barron to William Eaton, April 21, 1806, SBP(I).

9. William Eaton to Samuel Barron, February 14, 1807, SBP(I).

10. Brighton, *Checkered Career*, 279.

11. Tobias Lear to James Madison, July 5, 1805, *American State Papers: Foreign Relations*, 2:716–18.

12. Ibid., 718.

13. *New Hampshire Gazette*, September 3, 1805.

14. *Senate Executive Journal*, December 27, 1805, 12.
15. Ibid., April 12, 1806, 32.
16. Tobias Lear to James Madison, March 15, 1807, NDBP, 6:512.
17. Ibid.
18. Hamet Karamanli to U.S. Congress, September 1, 1805, Hamet Claim, 719.
19. George Davis to Hamet Karamanli, April 23, 1807, NDBP, 6:517.
20. George Davis to Hamet Karamanli, May 12, 1807, NDBP, 6:522; Davis to Hamet, October 7, 1807, NDBP, 6:570.
21. Whipple, *To the Shores of Tripoli*, 270–71.
22. Ibid.
23. Multiple sources record the gift of the sword. However, there is no mention of it in the *Argus'* log, nor do any surviving papers of O'Bannon record the gift. Eaton too does not mention the gift in his journal.
24. Edwin N. McClellan, *Uniforms of the American Marines, 1775–1832* (Quantico, Va.: Marine Corps History Division, 1952), 87.
25. Franklin Wharton to Presley O'Bannon, March 6, 1807, COC, Series 1, vol. 3.
26. McClellan, *Uniforms of the American Marines*, 36.
27. Sundberg and Gott, *Valiant Virginian*, 41; William H. Powell, *List of Officers of the Army of the United States, 1779 to 1900* (New York: L. R. Hamersley, 1900), 42–45.
28. Sundberg and Gott, *Valiant Virginian*, 49.
29. Cella, *Narrative*, 15–17.
30. Folayan, *Tripoli under Qaramanli*, 48–50.
31. Ibid.
32. Ibid., 51–52.
33. Cella, *Narrative*, 6–10.
34. Rossi, *Storia di Tripoli*, 86–88.
35. Ibid.

BIBLIOGRAPHY

PRIMARY SOURCES

American State Papers: Claims. Vol. 1, *1789–1809.* Washington, D.C.: Gales and Seaton, 1834.

———. *Finance.* Vol. 1, *1789–1802,* and vol. 2, *1802–1815.* Washington, D.C.: Gales and Seaton, 1832.

———. *Foreign Relations.* Vol. 1, *1789–1797,* vol. 2, *1797–1807,* and vol. 3, *1807–1815.* Washington, D.C.: Gales and Seaton, 1833.

———. *Military Affairs.* Vol. 1, *1789–1819.* Washington, D.C.: Gales and Seaton, 1832.

———. *Naval Affairs.* Vol. 1, *1794–1825.* Washington, D.C.: Gales and Seaton, 1834.

Annals of Congress: House and Senate Journals. Washington, D.C.: Gales and Seaton, 1851.

———. *The Debates and Proceedings of the Congress of the United States; With an Appendix, Containing Important State Papers and Public Documents with All the Laws of a Public Nature.* Washington, D.C.: Gales and Seaton, 1852.

Barron, Samuel. Letters and Papers, Barron Family Papers. Swem Library, College of William and Mary, Williamsburg, Va.

Bey, Ali. *Travels of Ali Bey in Morocco, Tripoli, Cyprus, Egypt, Arabia, Syria and Turkey.* Philadelphia: James Maxwell, 1815.

Blyth, Stephen C. *History of the War between the United States and Tripoli and Other Barbary Powers.* Salem, Mass.: Salem Gazette, 1808.

Cathcart, James Leander. *Tripoli: First War with the United States. Inner History. Letter Book by James Leander Cathcart.* LaPorte, Ind.: Herald, 1901.

Compiled Service Records of Soldiers Who Served in the American Army during the Revolutionary War. National Archives and Records Administration, Washington, D.C. [hereafter NARA], Record Group [hereafter RG] 93, microfilm M881, roll 167.

Court Martial Proceedings of Richard V. Morris. NARA, RG 45, microfilm M87.

Cowdery, Jonathan. *American Captives in Tripoli.* Boston: Belcher & Armstrong, 1806.

deKrafft Cornelius Journal. NARA, RG 45.

Della Cella, Paolo. *Narrative of an Expedition from Tripoli in Barbary to the Western Frontier of Egypt in 1817 by the Bey of Tripoli.* London: John and Arthur Arch, Cornhill, 1822.

Eaton, William. *Interesting detail of the operations of the American fleet in the Mediterranean communicated in a letter from W.E., to his friend in the county of Hampshire.* Springfield, Mass.: Bliss & Brewer, 1805.

———. Letters and Papers. San Marino, Calif.: Huntington Library, Norris Collection.

Gallatin, Albert. *The Papers of Albert Gallatin.* Edited by Henry Adams. Philadelphia: J. B. Lippincott, 1870.

Hamilton, Alexander. *The Papers of Alexander Hamilton.* Vol. 24, *November 1799 to June 1800.* Edited by Harold C. Syrett. New York: Columbia University Press, 1976.

Heitman, Francis B. *Historical Register and Dictionary of the United States Army, from Its Organization, Sept. 29, 1789, to March 2, 1903.* Vol. 1. Washington, D.C.: Government Printing Office [hereafter GPO], 1903.

Henry Preble Letters to James Fenimore Cooper. New Haven: Yale University, Beineke Museum of Western Americana, Manuscripts Collection.

Hull, Isaac. *The Papers of Isaac Hull.* Edited by Gardner W. Allen. Boston: Athenaeum, 1929.

Jefferson, Thomas. *The Papers of Thomas Jefferson, Digital Edition*. Edited by Barbara B. Oberg and J. Jefferson Looney. Charlottesville: University of Virginia Press, 2008–15.

———. *The Works of Thomas Jefferson*. Edited by Paul Leicester Ford. 12 vols. New York: G. P. Putnam and Sons, 1904–1905.

John H. Dent Letter Book. Library of Congress, Washington, D.C. [hereafter LOC], Manuscript Division.

Johnston, Henry P., ed. *Record of Service of Connecticut Men in the War of the Revolution, War of 1812, Mexican War*. Hartford, Conn.: General Assembly, 1889.

Knox, Dudley, ed. *Naval Documents Related to the War between the United States and the Barbary Powers*. 6 vols. Washington, D.C.: GPO, 1935.

Knox, Dudley W., et al., eds. *Naval Documents Related to the Quasi-War between the United States and France*. Washington, D.C.: GPO, 1935.

Larpent, Seymour Francis. *The Private Journal of Seymour F. Larpent, during the Peninsular War, from 1812 to Its Close*. 2 vols. London: R. Bentley, 1853.

Lawrence, T. E. *Seven Pillars of Wisdom: A Triumph*. Garden City, N.Y.: Doubleday, Doran, 1935.

Lawrence, William. *Autobiography of Sergeant William Lawrence, a Hero of the Peninsular and Waterloo Campaigns*. Edited by George Nugent Banks. London: Sampson Low, Harston, Searle and Rivington, 1886.

Letters and Papers: Humphreys-Marvin-Olmstead Collection. New Haven, Conn.: Yale University, Sterling Library, Manuscript Division.

Logbook of the United States Brig *Argus*. NARA, RG 45.

Loomis, Hezekiah. *The Journal of Hezekiah Loomis, Steward on the U.S. Brig Vixen under Capt. John Smith USN during the War with Tripoli, 1804*. Salem, Mass: Essex Institute, 1928.

Madison, James. *The Papers of James Madison, Digital Edition*. Edited by J. C. A. Skagg. Charlottesville: University of Virginia Press, 2010.

Maxwell, W. H., ed. *Peninsular Sketches by Actors on the Scene*. 2 vols. London: Henry Colborn, 1832.

Morris, Charles. *Autobiography of Commodore Charles Morris, U.S. Navy*. Annapolis, Md.: Naval Institute Press, 2002.

Muster and Pay Rolls. NARA, RG 45:
>   USS *Argus*
>   USS *Constitution*
>   USS *Hornet*
>   USS *Nautilus.*
>   USS *Philadelphia*
>   USS *President*

O'Brien, Richard. *Message from the President of the United States, communicating the copy of a letter from Richard O'Brien, late Consul of the United States, at Algiers: Giving some detail of transactions before Tripoli.* Washington, D.C.: Duane & Sons, 1804.

Papers of Edward Preble. LOC, Manuscript Division.

Papers of Isaac Hull. Newton Historical Society, Newton, Mass.

Papers of James Madison. LOC, Manuscript Division.

Papers of Thomas Jefferson. LOC, Manuscript Division, Series I, General Correspondence, 1653–1827, 1999.

Public Records of the State of Connecticut. Vol. 3. Hartford, Conn.: Case, Lockwood and Brainard, 1922.

Public Statutes at Large of the United States of America, Richard Peters, ed. Boston: Charles C. Little and James Brown, 1845.

Ray, William. *Horrors of Slavery, or, The American Tars in Tripoli.* Troy, N.Y.: Oliver Lyon, 1808.

Rea, John. *A Letter to William Bainbridge, Esq., formerly Commander of the United States Ship* George Washington. Philadelphia, 1802.

Records of the United States Marine Corps. NARA, RG 127:

Records of the Office of the Commandant, Letters Sent, 1798–1801, 1804–1911, series 3, series 8, series 41; Letters Received, 1799–1903.

Rodgers, John. John Rodgers Letters and Papers. Rodgers Family Papers, 1740–1987, LOC, Manuscript Division.

"Sketch of General William Eaton." *New Hampshire Patriot and State Gazette,* Concord, September 21, 1835.

Stephen Decatur Jr. Letters and Papers. Philadelphia: Historical Society of Pennsylvania, Manuscript Division.

Timothy Pickering Papers. Massachusetts Historical Society, Boston.

Tully, Miss. *Letters Written during a Ten Years' Residence at the Court of Tripoli.* London: Henry Colburn, 1816.

————. *Narrative of a Ten Years' Residence at Tripoli in Africa, from the Original Correspondence in the Possession of the Family of the Late Richard Tully, Esq., the British Consul.* London: Henry Colburn, 1819.

Vane, Charles William. *Narrative of the Peninsular War, 1808–1813.* 2 vols. London: Henry Colburn, 1829.

Washington, George. *The Papers of George Washington.* Edited by Donald Jackson et al. Charlottesville: University of Virginia Press, 1976–78.

SECONDARY SOURCES

Alam, M. Shahid. "Articulating Group Differences: A Variety of Auto-centrisms." *Science and Society* (Summer 2013).

al-Tawil, Mohammed. *Tripoli and the West.* Tripoli, Libya, 1971.

Bartlett, Merrill L., and Jack Sweetman. *Leathernecks: An Illustrated History of the United States Marine Corps.* Annapolis, Md.: Naval Institute Press, 2008.

Brighton, Ray. *The Checkered Career of Tobias Lear.* Portsmouth, N.H.: Portsmouth Marine Society, 1985.

Chandler, David. *Napoleon.* New York: Saturday Review, 1973.

Cooper, James Fenimore. *History of the Navy of the United States.* 2 vols. Philadelphia: Lea and Blanchard, 1840.

————. *Lives of Distinguished American Naval Officers.* Philadelphia: Carey and Hart, 1846.

De Kay, James Tertius. *Rage for Glory: The Life of Commodore Stephen Decatur, USN.* New York: Free Press, 2004.

Dickey, Jeff. *Empire of Mud: The Secret History of Washington DC.* Guilford, Conn.: Globe Pequot, 2014.

Dictionary of American Fighting Ships. 2 vols. Washington, D.C.: GPO, 1963.

Edwards, Samuel. *Barbary General: The Life of William H. Eaton.* Englewood Cliffs, N.J.: Prentice Hall, 1968.

Ferguson, Eugene S. *Truxtun of the* Constellation: *The Life of Commodore Thomas Truxtun, U.S. Navy, 1755–1822.* Baltimore, Md.: Johns Hopkins University Press, 1956.

Folayan, Kola. *Tripoli during the Reign of Yusuf Pacha Qaramanli*. Ife, Nigeria: University of Ife Press, 1971.

Frost, John, ed., *American Naval Biography, Comprising Lives of the Commodores and Other Commanders Distinguished in the History of the United States Navy*. Philadelphia: E. H. Butler, 1844.

Glover, David. *The Napoleonic Wars: An Illustrated History, 1792–1815*. New York: Hippocrene Books, 1978.

Goldberg, Harvey E. *Jewish Life in Muslim Libya: Rivals and Relatives*. Chicago: University of Chicago Press, 1990.

Goodwin, Geoffrey. *The Janissaries*. London: Saqi Books, 2006.

Grant, Bruce. *The Life and Fighting Times of Commodore Isaac Hull*. Chicago: Pellegrini and Cudahy, 1947.

Haimann, Giuseppe. *Cirenaica (Tripolitania)*. Milan, Italy: Ulrico Hoepli, 1886.

Harris, Thomas. *The Life and Services of Commodore William Bainbridge*. Philadelphia: Carey Lea & Blanchard, 1837.

Hearn, Chester G. *An Illustrated History of the United States Marine Corps*. London: Salamander Books, 2002.

Hollis, Ira N. *The Frigate* Constitution. Boston: Houghton Mifflin, 1931.

Ilari, Virgilio, Bruno Pauvert, and Piero Crociani. *Il 31e Leggero: Storia di 31e Regiment d'Infantrie, 1799–1815*. Translated by Chipp Reid. Milan, 2011.

Irvin, Anthony. *Decatur*. New York: Charles Scribner's Sons, 1931.

Kimball, Horace. *American Naval Battles*. Boston: Charles Gaylord, 1837.

Lear, Tobias. *The Last Words of General Washington: A Circumstantial Account of the Illness and Death of George Washington*. Philadelphia, 1800.

Macdonough, Rodney. *The Life of Commodore Thomas Macdonough*. Boston: Fort Gill, Samuel Usher, 1909.

Maloney, Linda M. *The Captain from Connecticut: The Life and Naval Times of Isaac Hull*. Boston: Northeast University Press, 1986.

Marsot, Afaf Lutfi al-Sayyid. *A Short History of Modern Egypt*. Cambridge: Cambridge University Press, 1985.

Masters, Bruce. *Christians and Jews in the Ottoman-Arab World: The Roots of Sectarianism*. Cambridge: Cambridge University Press, 2001.

McClellan, Edwin N. *History of the United States Marine Corps*. Quantico, Va.: Marine Corps History Division, 1925.

———. *Uniforms of the American Marines, 1775–1832*. Quantico, Va.: Marine Corps History Division, 1952.

McKee, Christopher. *Edward Preble: A Naval Biography*. Annapolis, Md.: Naval Institute Press, 1972.

Miller, Hunter, ed. *Treaties and Other International Acts of the United States of America*. Washington, D.C.: GPO, 1931.

Millett, Allan R. *Semper Fidelis: The History of the United States Marine Corps*. New York: Macmillan, 1980.

———, and Jack Shulimson, eds. *Commandants of the Marine Corps*. Annapolis, Md.: Naval Institute Press, 2004.

Minnigerode, Meade. *Lives and Times: Four Informal American Biographies*. New York: G. P. Putnam and Sons, 1925.

Najem, Faraj. *Tribe, Islam and State in Libya: Analytical Study of the Roots of Libyan Tribal Society and Interaction Up to the Qaramanli Rule*. Westminster, U.K.: University of Westminster, 2004.

Palmer, Michael A. *Stoddert's War: Naval Operations during the Quasi-War with France, 1798–1801*. Columbia: University of South Carolina Press, 1987.

Paton, Andrew A. *A History of the Egyptian Revolution, from the Mamelukes to Mohammed Ali; From Arab and European memoirs, oral tradition, and local research*. 2 vols. London: Trübner, 1870.

Patterson, James Laird. *Journal of a Tour in Egypt, Palestine, Syria and Greece*. London: C. Dolman, 1852.

Paullin, Charles Oscar. *John Rodgers: Captain, Commodore and Senior Officer of the American Navy, 1773–1838*. Annapolis, Md.: Naval Institute Press, 1967.

Pelton, Cornelius C. *Life of William Eaton*. New York: Par-ker & Brothers, 1902.

Pennell, C. R. *Morocco: The Empire to Independence*. London: Oneworld, 2003.

Playfair, Robert Lambert. *The Scourge of Europe*. London: Smith, Elder, 1885.

Powell, William H. *List of Officers of the Army of the United States, 1779 to 1900*. New York: L. R. Hamersley, 1900.

Pratt, Fletcher. *Preble's Boys*. New York: William Sloane, 1950.

Prentiss, Charles. *The Life of the Late General Eaton*. Brookfield, Mass.: E. Mirriam, 1813.

Rappoport, Angelo S. *A History of Egypt: From 330 B.C. to the Present Time*. London: Grolier Society, 1904.

Reid, Chipp. *Intrepid Sailors: The Legacy of Preble's Boys and the Tripoli Campaign*. Annapolis, Md.: Naval Institute Press, 2012.

Rossi, Ettore. *La Cronaca Araba Tripolina di Ibn Galbun*. Bologna, Italy.: Licino Cappelli, 1923.

———. *Storia di Tripoli e de Tripolitania dalla Conquista Araba da 1911 Edizione Postuma a Cura di Maria Nullino*. Rome: Instituto per l'Oriente, 1968.

Rodd, Francis Rennell. *General William Eaton*. New York: Minton Balch, 1932.

Scholz, Johann Martin Augustin. *Travels in the Countries Between Alexandria and Paratorium, the Lybian Desert, Siwa, Egypt and Syria, 1821*. London: Sire Richard Phillips, 1822.

Sobocinski Andre. "The Early Years of Navy Hospitals: From 1804 to Present." February 26, 2014. *Navy Medicine Live*. navymedicine.navylive.dodlive.mil/.

St. John, Ronald Bruce. *Libya and the United States: Two Centuries of Strife*. Philadelphia: University of Pennsylvania Press, 2002.

Sundberg, Trudy J., and John K. Gott. *Valiant Virginian: Story of Presley Neville O'Bannon, 1776–1850, First Lieutenant, U.S. Marine Corps, 1801–1807*. Westminster, Md.: Heritage Books, 2007.

Tognotti, Eugene. "Lessons from the History of Quarantine, from Plague to Influenza A." *Emerging Infectious Diseases*. No. 2, February 2013. Atlanta, Ga.: Centers for Disease Control. https://www.ncbi.nlm.nih.gov/pmc/articles/PMC3559034/.

Tucker, Glenn. *Dawn Like Thunder: The Barbary Wars and the Birth of the U.S. Navy*. Indianapolis: Bobbs-Merrill, 1963.

Waldo, Loren P. *The Early History of Tolland County*. Hartford, Conn.: Case, Lockwood, 1861.

Watson, Paul Barron. *The Tragic Career of Commodore James Barron, U.S. Navy.* New York: Coward-McCann, 1942.

Weigall, Arthur E. P. Brome. *A History of Egypt from 1798 to 1914.* London: William Blackwood and Sons, 1915.

Whipple, A. B. C. *To the Shores of Tripoli: The Birth of the U.S. Navy and Marines.* Annapolis, Md.: Naval Institute Press, 1991.

Wilburn, LaFayette. *Early History of Vermont.* Jericho, Vt.: Roscoe, 1899.

Zacks, Richard. *Pirate Coast: Thomas Jefferson, the First Marines and the Secret Mission of 1805.* New York: Hyperion Books, 2005.

INDEX

Karamanli, Ahmed I, 20, 21
Karamanli, Ahmed II, 21, 22
Karamanli, Ahmet, 286
Karamanli, Ali I, 22–23, 25, 28, 31, 33, 34
Karamanli, Ali II, 285, 286
Karamanli, Hamet, 2, 3; after coup, 59–60; American support for, 87–88, 122–23, 263, 266; Arab soldiers/troops, 191–92, 193; as bashaw, 33; birth, 23; Cathcart and, 60; death of, 282; in Derne, 34, 81–82, 262–63, 282; Eaton's treaty with, 192–93; in Egypt, 54, 82, 94, 282; family of, 34, 270, 280–82; Jefferson, letter to, 81; in Malta, 62, 80–81, 281; Mameluke sword of, 282–84; negotiations with Eaton, 61, 81, 83; relationship with Hassan, 24–25; retreat from Tripoli, 32; search for, 110; in Syracuse, 270; in Tunis, 60, 62; U.S. stipend, 282; Y. Karamanli's early plots against, 29; Y. Karamanli's manipulation of, 24, 25–26
Karamanli, Hassan, 20, 23; assassination of, 25–28; Hamet and, 24–25; Y. Karamanli and, 24-25; popularity of, 24, 26, 28; training of, 33
Karamanli, Mehmed, 34, 286
Karamanli, Mustafa, 22–23
Karamanli, Yusuf, 1–2, 60; amnesty offer by, 270; assassination of Hassan, 25–28; attacks on Tripoli, 30–31; attempts on Hamet, 29–30; as bashaw, 33–34; as bey, 33; H. Bey and, 195; birth, 23; blockade and, 48–49, 52–53, 69,

82; Cathcart and, 107; death of, 286; declaration of war, 38; demands from U.S., 36; diplomatic negotiations with, 95, 106–7, 108, 255, 262, 266; early years, 20; family of, 285; jealousy of, 23–24; manipulations of brothers, 25, 80–81; marabout of, 69, 70; peace deal of, 48–49; peace talks and, 267–68; peace treaty, 285; plots of, 264; rebellions against, 286; and Selim III, 34, 53; siege of Tripoli, 32; taxation under, 54, 232; unrest against, 60, 196; U.S. tribute payments and, 40, 52; usurpation of throne by, 3, 80–81; Y. Karamanli's response to Eaton, 71. *See also* Cowdery, Jonathan
Karamanli family: Borghul and, 32; French influence with, 31; origins of, 20, 191–92; sultans attitude toward, 31; in Tripoli, 39; use of foreigners, 195. *See also specific members*

Lear, Tobias, 3, 102; in Algiers, 105–6, 279, 281; Bainbridge and, 107, 113; Barron and, 108, 262–63; death of, 281; decision-making of, 4; diplomatic negotiations, 95, 106–7; early life, 96–97; Eaton's criticism of, 276–77; ego of, 4; family of, 98–99, 105; financial issues, 105; in Haiti, 103–4; Hamet project and, 262–63; Jefferson and, 98, 99, 105; peace talks and, 267–68; politics of, 97–98, 99; Preble and, 106; real estate ventures, 99–101; Rodgers and, 79, 80, 104–5; treaty of 1805, 280–81; tribute payment advise,

ABOUT THE AUTHOR

CHIPP REID is a combat veteran, a licensed captain of traditionally rigged tall ships, an award-winning journalist, the author of the acclaimed *Intrepid Sailors: The Legacy of Preble's Boys and the Tripoli Campaign*, and the editor of Stanley Quick's *Lion in the Bay: The British Invasion of the Chesapeake, 1813–14*. This is his third book for the Naval Institute Press. Currently researching Captain James Lawrence for a future book, he continues to write about the formative years of the United States Navy and Marine Corps. He lives and works in the Washington, DC area.